CRESTLINE

ENCYCLOPEDIA OF AMERICAN POLICE CARS

Edwin J. Sanow

MBI Publishing Company

Dedication

To Cindy Jo, my wife and best friend
and inspiration for all that I do that is worthwhile.

First published in 1999 by MBI Publishing Company,
729 Prospect Avenue, PO Box 1, Osceola, WI 54020-0001 USA

MBI Publishing Company books are also available at discounts in bulk quantity for industrial or sales-promotional use. For details write to Special Sales Manager at Motorbooks International Wholesalers & Distributors, 729 Prospect Avenue, PO Box 1, Osceola, WI 54020-0001 USA.

Library of Congress Cataloging-in-Publication Data
Sanow, Edwin J.
    Encyclopedia of American police cars/Edwin J. Sanow.
       p. cm.—(Crestline)
    Includes index.
    ISBN 7603-0449-1 (hc: alk. paper)
    1. Police vehicles—United States—History Pictorial works.
I. Title. II. Series: Crestline series.
HV7936.V4S363   1999
629.2'088;3632—DC21   99-14539

On the front cover: The California Highway Patrol tested the mid-size 1975 Dodge Coronet and liked the results. In 1976 the CHP ordered 1,511 Coronets, like the one pictured, which was nearly half of all the 3,852 police Coronets sold that year. Because the CHP entering the mid-size market, the rest of the city, county, and state police agencies seriously considered the mid-size class. Two years later, the nation's largest sheriff's department (Los Angeles County) switched from mid-size to compact patrol cars, and the nation's largest highway patrol (CHP) switched from full-size to mid-size patrol cars. The CHP said the mid-size Coronet had a lower initial cost and a lower operating cost than the full-size Monaco. At the time, the CHP logged 110 million patrol miles per year.

On the back cover: A variety of many significant police cars of the 20th century, including a 1937 Ford Tudor sedan, 1955 Buick Special, 1975 Chevy Nova, 1963 Dodge 880, and 1998 Ford Crown Victoria.

Edited by Paul Johnson

Designed by Steve Hendrickson

Printed in the United States of America

Contents

Acknowledgements & Contributors

George Allen, Jr., Judy Ames, John Anderson, Glenn Anderson, John Antonelli, Claude Arnett, Dave Arnold, Sgt. Steve and Diane Arp, James E. Ashworth, III, Jack Attig, Jr., William Bagnole, James Baldwin, Ofcr. Greg Barbiera, Ofcr. Rick Barnes, Al Barnych, Dick Bartlett, Robert Bashor, Editor Jeff Bauer, Thomas J. Bautch, Lee Beach, Tpr. Scott Beard, Sgt. James Beaver, Lt. Barry Beck, Paul Beckett, Cpl. John Bellah, Robert Benedetti, Stand & Connie Benjamin, Tpr. Jim Benjaminson, Ofcr. David Bernecker, Bill Biesiada, Tpr. Charles Black, Michael Blackmer, Ofcr. Charlie Blazawski, Mark Boatwright, Tpr. Shelby J. Bodenhamer, Reginald "Bo" Bohanan, Deputy Mike Bondarenko, Bob Bondurant, Robert Booth, Sgt. Michael Borges, Ofcr. Susie Boring, Bryant Brambeck, Dawn Brinningstaull, Lt. Roy Brown, Off. III Tony Bruhn, Shane Bryant, John Bujosa, Deputy Chief Larry Bullington, James Burdette, Editor Dan Burger, Tpr. Bill Burkett, Dale Burkhardt, Ivan Burnett, Ofcr. Gerald Bush, Ofcr. Terry Buss, California Highway Patrol, Edit. Director Bruce Cameron, Ofcr. Vern Campbell, Matt Campbell, Editor Jim Campisano, Dan Canavan, Det. Omar Caraballo, Carl Caracciolo, Traf. Ofcr. George Caravas, John Carroll, Paul Casalese, Ofcr. Charles Casner, Prob. Ofcr. Joe Cella, Deputy Insp. John C. Cerar, Charles W. Chandler, Mike Charnota, Chevrolet Motor Division, John Christy, Chrysler Corporation, Sgt. Leo Clark, Sgt. Warren Clark, Robert Clope, Gene Coffing, Terry Cole, Lt. John Coleman, John Collier, Mike Collins, Ofcr. Billy Copeland, Don Cornelis, John Crawford, Traf. Ofcr. Paul Crescenti, Larry Crutchfield, Sgt. Taren Cummings, Billy & Joyce Ann Cusic, Leo D'Andrea, Sgt. Jay D'Angelo, W.W. Dalrymple, Bob Daschofsky, Kris Davis, Frank Davis, Bruce Davisson, Steve de Centro, Dennis Decker, Capt. (ret.) Ken T. DeFoor, Ofcr. Damon Dent, Ofcr. Ronald Derderian, Jim Dingell, Della DiPietro, Diversifleet Inc., James Donohoe, Ed Dooley, Ofcr. Dave Dotson, George Ducolumbier, Byran Duncan, Anne Dunn, Bill Eichhorn, Lt. Ken Elery, Rob Elliott, Sgt. John Evers, Ed Faxon, Joseph A. Fay, Harold Fay, Michael Fay, Curator Jerry Federspiel, Jack Fellenzer, Capt. James Ferrier, Greg Field, Chief Terry Fiene, Scott Filis, Rocky Finlayson, Ofcr. Bob Fitzer, Ford Motor Company, Mike Ford,

Wayne Fricke, Arnljot Fure, Gregory Gaetano, Steven Gallucci, Charles Gamber, Bob Gamber, Rick Garland, David Gasperetti, Earl Gautsche, Sgt. Joseph Gavula, Clarence Gibson, Tpr. Don Ginter, Ken Gipson, David Gittner, Thomas Glatch, Frank Goderre, Jon Goldin, Shirley Goodson, Sgt. Kevin Gordon, Walter Gourley, Galen Govier, Anthony Gratson, George Graves, Mark Grechniw, Lt. Donald Green, Dave Greenberg, Capt. Clarence Greeno, Editor John Gunnell, Walter Haase, Ofcr. Bill Hackley, Dave Hahn, Ofcr. Tony Halachoulis, Dennis Hale, Sgt. Florence Hall, Ric Hallett, Sgt. David Halliday, Don Hamilton, Lt. Lee Hamilton, Judy Hamilton, Sgt. Gary Hamilton, Sgt. Rick Hammer, Harry Hammond, Bruce Hampson, Lt. Douglas Hancock, R. Hankins, Commissioner Maury Hannigan, David Hansen, Bob Hapiak, Col. Clarence Harmon, Francis Harr, Bob Harrington, Tpr. Jean Harvey, Maj. John Hatfield, Bill Hattersley, Charles Havelka, Jerry Heaseley, Bill Hedgpeth, Ofcr. Clarence Heerdt, Commissioner Dwight Helmick, Sgt. Robert Helmick, Avery Henry, Mike Hensley, Ray Heron, Editor Gregg Herring, Maj. John Hershberger, Chief Larry Hertz, Jeff Hewlett, Bob Hickey, Ofcr. John P. Higgins, Joe Hill, Lee Hippensteel, Lt. J.G. Hippert, Allison Hodge, Beverly Hoeksema, Ronnie Hogg, Sgt. M.K. Holcomb, Bob Holley, Larry Hollingsworth, Tim Honchell, Patrick Howe, Thomas Hoxie, Victor Huff, Editor Alice Huffaker, Sheriff Rod Jackson, Brian Jackson, Larry & Connie Jacobson, Hank Jacoby, Sandra James, Ofcr. Rick Janich, Editor William Jeanes, Milt Jenks, Earl W. Jensen, Terry Jessee, Sgt. Rodger Jincks, Charles Johnson, Craig Johnson, Quay Johnson, Bob Johnson, Jr., Ronald Jones, G.M. Jones, Tpr. Jim Jordan, Marilou Joswick, Lt. Gary Kamm, NH Police Keene, Mike Keller, Editor Lee Kelly, Neal Kemp, Mike Kennedy, Cpl. Ken Kerrick, Mick "Barney" & Kathy Kieffer, Bob Kilgore, James King, Deputy J.L. Klaus, Marshal Bob Klaus, Chief Sid Klein, Robert Klimko, Ofcr. Karen Klobuchar, Sgt. Tom Knopp, Lanny Knutson, Charles Kobel, Det. Joe Kosala, Deputy Howard Kotarski, Mike Kottwitz, Dan Kranz, Bill Krejci, Ralph Krieger, Sgt. Don Krieger, Scott Kroetz, Ofcr. Eric Kurz, Jack LaBelle, Jon Lackman, Col. Harold LaGrande, Capt. Donald Lamb, Andy Lang,

Sgt. C.R. Larson, Deputy Joe Lawrence, Tpr. Jeff Leathley, Patrick LeBlanc, Bob Lees, Lt. Kirt Lenard, Rick Lenz, Larry Leonhardt, Ofcr. Clair Lindquist, Comm. Ofcr. Darryl Lindsay, Sgt. Dave Link, Brad Lisson, Ofc. Ken Little, Chief Robert Lockwood, Emil Loeffler, Ofc. Neil Loewe, Herb Losche, Ingrid Lotz, Rudiger Lotz, Tpr. Doug Lubahn, Lt. A.M. Lundy, Joseph Lutz, Rick Lybarger, Trp. Tom Lyon, Maj. Don Mack, Rhonda Madden, Chuck Madderom, Don Maddox, Editor Mike Magda, Lt. Greg Manuel, Dispatcher Greg Marsh, Bob Marshall, Mike Martin, John Martin, Ofcr. Ken Mason, Tpr. Louis Mavredes, Neil McAllister, Ofcr. Phil McArdle, Lt. Monty McCord, Bob McCreary, Sgt. Ed McCullar, Lt. E.G. McCutchen, Capt. Bruce McDonald, Agent Ed McDowell, Kirby McElhearn, Sgt. Bill McFall, Jack McGee, Jim McGuire, Master Tpr. Don McKinney, Tpr. Larry McKissick, Sgt. Richard McLaughlin, Kevin McMahon, Keith Mesey, Michigan State Police, Barbara Miksicek, Col. Sid Miles, Donald Miller, Ray & Pat Miller, Traf. Ofc. Kent R. Milton, Lt. Vincent Monticello, Sgt. Ed Moody, Dave Moon, Captain Terry Moore, Ofcr. Michael Morelli, Chris Morgan, Sgt. Dave Morrison, Deputy Philip Moser, Marty Mozille, Sgt. John Mull, Marvin Murphy, Ed Murrell, Ofcr. Robert Nelson, Andrew Nelson, Charles Neustaedter, Ofcr. Lin Newton, Mike Novatnak, Ofcr. Nick Noviello, Edward Nowicki, Cpl. Ernie Nybo, Ed O'Meara, William O'Neil, Rick Osbon, Rex Osborn, Editor Roland Osborne, Editor Robert Oskiera, Neil Painchaud, Jeff Papendik, John Pappas, Sgt. Jerry Parker, Thomas Parkinson, Tpr. Robert Parks, Richard Pearl, Arthur Peetz, Louis Pelletter, Ken Perkins, Sgt. Ronald Perron, Trp. Alex Petigng, Ofcr. Michael Piernicky, Curator John Podracky, Sgt. Jim Post, Sheriff B.L. "Butch" Pritchett, Lt. William L. Pritchett, Publications International, Darren Pupo, Tom Pyden, Clark Pyewell, Editor Greg Rager, Tpr. Mark Reaves, Mark Redelberger, Charles Reed, Sgt. Guy Reimche, Gary Reno, John Restall, Officer Greg Reynolds, Bob Rice, Ken B. Richmond, Sgt. Bob Ring, Lt. David Ritch, Lt. Gene Roberts, Cpl. A.W. Robinson, Melanie Robinson, Mario Rodriguez, Jim Rogaski, Editor Donna Rogers, Anthony Romano, Brandt Rosenbusch, Royal Canadian Mounted Police, LeRoy Rubinas, Marvin Ruffin, G.E.W. Rupprecht, Paul Russell, Ed Ruthinowski, Ronald Rysavy, Donald Sachs, Rex Sagle, Deputy Dennis Sanchez, Chief Annette Sandberg, Chris Sardo, Tpr. Jack Sareault, Greg Savernik, Bob Scheib, Traf. Ofc. Joe Schlelter, Leslie Schneider, Clifford Schneider, Bob Schreiber, Chuck Schroedel, Gil Schugart, Lt. David Schultheis, Agent Ned Schwartz, Tony Scotti, Tim Seaman, Matt Seaman, Lt. Robert Sedita, Mike Seebacher, Doug Serier, Thomas Seymour, John Shagath, Leo Shakker, Sgt. Chuck Shaw, Ofcr. Thomas Sheeny, Mark Shinost, Mike Shtogrin, Don Sierbert, Don Sierra, Grant Simmons, Phil Skinner, Ofc. Darryl Smith, Lee Smith, Mike Smith, Sgt. Mark Smith, D.J. Smith, Glenn Sokolofsky, Sgt. Manny Solano, Domenic Sorbello, Chief Brian Soucie, Ofcr. Bob Speed, Mary Spitery, Sgt. Denny Steendam, Glenn Steffen, Mark Steger, Bob Steger, Ofcr. Bob Stein, Thomas Stevens, Editor Robert Jay Stevens, Douglas Stiegelmaier, Deputy Melvin Stinnette, Sgt. Dave Storer, Sr., Richard L. Story, Larry Stout, Ofcr. Judd Strong, Agent George Stumph, Jennifer Sturgeon, Howard Sturgeon, Chuck Swift, Christopher Taylor, Ron Tekell, Jr. Thomas, Huge E., Lt. Robert Thomas, Pat Tode, Brian Tolen, Sgt. Fernando Tomicic, Greg Trego, Lt. Jerry Trent, Chief Michael Trevis, Kevin Trickey, Theresa Troutman, Tom Turner, Deputy James Turnin, P. Tuttle, Ofcr. Dan Tyrpak, Tom Utech, Ofcr. Gary Valencia, F/Lt. Curt VanDenBerg, Tpr. Greg Vandenberg, C. Vassallo, Bernard Veile, John Vetter, Manual Villalobos, Lt. Vincent, George Virgines, Al Wagner, Stanley Walker, Ken Walsh, Editor Tricia Walsh-McGlone, Chris Watson, Deputy Butch Weaver, Dave Weaver, Paul Weber, Sr., Tom Weglary, Jay Weinstein, Tpr. David Wells, Rich & Sonja Wells, Joe Wicks, Bruce Wiley, Robert Williams, Jack Williams, Richard Williams LTC, LTC, Rod Williams, Floyd Williams, Troy Williamson, Tom Wilson, Tpr. Rick Wilson, Ofcr. Mark Wilson, Ofcr. Joseph Winchell, Carl Woehrle, Tim Wolff, Trp. Tim Wood, Steve Wren, Tpr. Gordie Wright, Tom Yates, Traf. Ofc. John Yeaw, Corr. Ofc. Scott Zane, and Cpl. Dave Zuhlke

Foreword

Law enforcement officers have a strong interest in the vehicles they drive, be it a Ford, Chevrolet, Volvo, or Saab. After all, automobiles are a big factor in an officer's safety and well-being, as most officers spend a good part of their on-duty time behind a steering wheel. Many officers, including those who are retired, also have a keen interest in the vehicles their predecessors drove.

Until recently, however, people outside of law enforcement have shown little apparent interest in police vehicles. Police vehicles were occasionally acknowledged by vehicle enthusiasts but did not claim the same adulation as many other categories of vehicles, such as fire engines or "muscle" cars. But times have changed. Police car buffs, collectors, and hobbyists abound, not only in the United States but around the world. Model car manufacturers produce entire lines of scale police cars that collectors vie for. Photographs of old and new police vehicles are passionately sought and exchanged by individuals. Clubs have been organized specifically for the activity. Associations of car restorers have grown sharply and their exhibitions have proliferated as promotions have generated public interest.

Allied with all this activity, there are now some very good books available that detail the progression of vehicles adapted for law enforcement use. Ed Sanow is the dominant author in this field, having produced five books covering specific vehicle makes and time periods. This book, *Encyclopedia of American Police Cars*, a compilation of his extensive research, however, will be long recognized as the definitive work covering police vehicles.

In developing this work, Sanow had to dredge the outer limits of the historical preserves of law enforcement to gain the knowledge presented in the text. Much of this information, which was previously reserved for law enforcement, is available to the public for the first time.

This is a unique history book, for the facts, instead of being presented in long blocks of type, are illustrated by photographs. Many of the photographs, which document the inevitable rusting and disappearing artifacts of this topic, are gleaned from the dusty historical files of law enforcement agencies.

This book presents the most complete pictorial assembly of historical facts on the history of the vehicles used in law enforcement. It starts at the very beginning of motorized police vehicles, bicycles with motors, and progresses to the latest and newest vehicles used by police, the Sport Utility Vehicle.

Exhaustingly researched, the details are so finitely introduced in the captions that only a scholar of the subject might possibly pose a question that is not answered. If you want to know the horsepower of the 1925 Ford Model T used by early police departments (20 horsepower) or what year the California Highway Patrol used Nash Ambassador cars for patrol vehicles (1949), that kind of information is there.

Anyone interested in motorized vehicles will find this book more than adequately fills what has been a void in the industry. Finally, the history of police vehicles is presented in its entirety.

—*Bruce W. Cameron*
Editorial Director
Law and Order Magazine

In 1925, Fords were powered by a 20-horsepower, flathead four-cylinder. Chevrolets had a 26-horsepower, overhead-valve four-cylinder. A county traffic officer in California used this 1925 Chrysler with a 68-horsepower, 201-ci flathead six. This 1925 Chrysler was a great choice. It was far more powerful than the Fords and Chevrolets, and it had four-wheel hydraulic brakes.

Pictured is a restored 1949 Nash Ambassador black-and-white four-door cruiser. The California Highway Patrol used these cars as one of its 1949 Enforcement-class vehicles.

Introduction

As we look back over a century of police cars, a few of the cruisers, patrollers, pursuits, and interceptors stand out from the rest. These are the cars that defined the state-of-the-art or significantly influenced future police cars.

The first is the 1932 V-8 Ford. Before this car arrived, police officers did not have a true preference among any of the dozens of lower-priced makes. The power of the 1932 flathead V-8 changed all that. This became the beginning of a long Ford dominance in the police market. In fact, Ford would remain the best-selling police car from 1932 through 1968!

The second landmark police vehicle was the 1950 Ford. This was the first factory-produced "police-package" sedan. Prior to 1950, all cars used by the police were simply retail cars, frequently without any heavy-duty components at all. By 1957, all the makes had a formal, engineered police package. However, Ford had the first true police car, and that makes the 1950 model year very special.

The most prominent car of the 1960s is the 1966 Dodge Polara powered by the legendary 440 cubic inch (ci) big-block V-8. This was the engine that unseated Ford from the King of the Hill by the late 1960s. The 440-ci Polara defined the police car of the 1960s, and everyone expected all police cars to be powered by a big-block V-8. In fact, most police cars have been powered by a six or a small-block V-8.

One of the most significant police cars from the early 1970s was not made by Ford, Chrysler, or General Motors, although it did use a Chrysler transmission. The car, of course, was the 1972 401-ci AMC Matador. This was a whip-quick mid-size car that, while made famous in Los Angeles, was used from coast to coast. It was the most successful of the lesser-known makes of police car.

The 1975 Chevrolet Nova was another landmark police vehicle. Brought on by the early-1970s energy crisis and heavily promoted by *Motor Trend* magazine and the Los Angeles County Sheriff, the 350-ci Nova changed the way cops thought about mid-size cars. It had the best acceleration, braking, handling, and fuel economy of any police car in that era. Although the 1975 Nova wasn't Chevrolet's best police vehicle, it was its most significant.

Three police cars mark the end of an era of awesome performance. These are the 1976 Chevrolet Impala 454, the 1977 Dodge Royal Monaco 440 ci, and the 1978 Ford LTD 460 ci. These were the last of the big-block V-8, long-wheelbase, four-door sedans that literally defined the police pursuit cars at the time. After this time, police cars with engines over 360 ci and wheelbases longer than 119 inches were only a fond memory.

The 1982 Ford Mustang may just be the most significant police car ever made. Actually, this was a special-service-package car. Technically, it was a "severe" service-package car. The Mustang was the fastest American-made automobile of 1982; it was even faster than the Corvette. The short wheelbase, small-block V-8-powered Mustang totally changed the way cops thought about pursuit cars, and that was enough to secure its place in history. In addition, it bolstered the image of all police cars during a period of extremely low-performing police sedans. The Mustang was the darling of America's police fleets for all of the 1980s. Every traffic officer and road deputy wanted one.

The 1984 Dodge Diplomat defined police sedans in the 1980s. All the four-door sedans from Ford, Dodge, Chevrolet, and Plymouth were boxy with a 112.7- to 116-inch wheelbase, 318- to 360-ci small-block V-8, and sluggish performance. These cars ran a 19-second quarter mile and had top speeds under 120 miles per hour.

Honorable mention goes to the 1984 and 1985 Ford LTD, which was essentially a stretched Mustang. The mid-size car was affectionately called the Baby LTD to distinguish it from the full-size LTD Crown Victoria. With the Mustang's 302-ci HO fuel-injected engine, the Baby LTD performed like a roomier, four-door sedan version of the Mustang, and that is exactly what it was. The LTD was the only sedan of the 1980s with truly outstanding performance.

A reserved honorable mention goes to the 1991 Ford Taurus. It was not the first front-wheel-drive, mid-size police car. (In fact, it was the third, behind the 1982 Chrysler K-cars and the 1984 Chevrolet Celebrity.) It was, however, the first heavy-duty, police-package, front-drive car, and the first front-drive V-6 police car to perform like a full-size, rear-drive, V-8 police car. The Taurus was a paradox of being both successful and unpopular as well as fast but not durable. Cops, in general, do not like front-drive police cars, but there's a new model on the way. Only time will tell if the 2000 Chevrolet Impala will be accepted in the police community.

Since the release of the police package in the 1950s, each decade has been unique. In the 1950s, the V-8 engine came of age with overhead valves, multiple carburetors, and considerably more horsepower than the brakes and suspension could handle. In the 1960s, much more attention was given to overall and balanced performance. Mid-size police cars were introduced.

The 1970s will always be remembered as the decade of very-low-compression police engines, choked by restrictive emission controls. By the 1980s, the big-block cars were gone, and low-compression, small-block engines remained. The result was an entire decade of poor performance until the advent of fuel-injected police engines.

The 1990s brought a return to very well-performing, well-balanced police cars but also resulted in a great diversity of police cars, including front-drive mid-size cars and a wide variety of 4x4 sport/utilities.

Nearly all cruisers served well, with a good balance of power, reliability, and roominess. Some of the better all-around patrol cars were the 1969 383-ci Plymouth Belvedere, 1979 360-ci Dodge St. Regis, 1954 256-ci Ford Customline, 1984 318-ci Dodge Diplomat, and 1965 390-ci Ford Custom.

Of all police cars, only one can be considered the best. That one car is the LT-1-powered Chevrolet Caprice made from 1994 to 1996.

The LT-1 Caprice runs a road-racing course as fast as the 5.0-liter Mustang with the same acceleration, higher top speed, much better brakes, and much more room. In fact, the 350-ci LT-1 Caprice made the pony car–style traffic enforcement vehicle obsolete. These were the last of the V-8-powered, full-size, rear-drive Chevrolets. More than nostalgia drives us to the conclusion that these cars were the best. The 350-ci Caprice won the Michigan State Police "most bang for the buck" patrol vehicle tests 10 years in a row.

Ford was the first automaker with a police-package car in 1950, followed by Chevrolet in 1955, Dodge in 1956, and Plymouth in 1957. Of great significance, that is the same order they exited the full-size police market. Chrysler Corporation became a V-6 front-drive car company and dropped the V-8 rear-drive Dodge and Plymouth after 1989. Chevrolet experienced declining retail sales of its rear-drive Caprice, in spite of the popular Impala SS, and wanted to convert its factory lines from building cars to building the more profitable Chevy trucks. Therefore, Chevrolet discontinued the Caprice after 1996. This left Ford as the only manufacturer of a full-size, V-8-powered rear-drive, four-door sedan. To their credit, since 1996, Ford had dramatically improved its Crown Victoria. And it's a good thing. As we enter the new millennium, cops find themselves right back where they started in 1932: Ford standing alone with no real competition.

—*Cpl. Ed Sanow*

Chapter One

1900-1939

The first police patrol "vehicle" was certainly a horse. It seems fitting that mounted patrols exist to this day, still filling a vital enforcement role. Horses were also used to pull wooden patrol wagons; yes, paddy wagons, were used to transport prisoners.

Around the turn of the century, the bicycle came into widespread use, especially in the larger city departments. In 1897, the Detroit Police formed a bicycle patrol, and its job was to apprehend speeding bicyclists! Again, the bicycle remains in police use and is, in fact, enjoying a renewed popularity.

The bicycle led directly to the motorized bicycle. Circa 1903, Bill Harley and Arthur Davidson produced their first motorcycle, and the same year, the Connecticut State Police became the nation's first statewide law enforcement organization. The Pennsylvania State Police followed in 1905 and the Nevada State Police, not Highway Patrol, was established in 1908.

By 1909, the motorcycle began to be accepted as an enforcement vehicle, and the Pittsburgh, PA, Omaha, NE, and Houston, TX, police were among the first to use motorcycles for patrol. Harley-Davidson, Indian, and Henderson motorcycles would become legendary. Most early state police departments, in fact, issued motorcycles, not cars. From the New York City Police to the California Highway Patrol, today's traffic officer in a police car can trace his or her roots back to yesterday's motorcycle officer.

While law enforcement is conservative by its very nature, the horseless carriage was just too good of an idea to ignore for long. No, cops did not rush out to buy the 1896 Duryea, America's first production passenger car. However, by 1910, the police in most of America's larger cities used the car for certain kinds of official enforcement duties.

Many makes survived the first 100 years of the automobile, and would at some time be used as a police vehicle. Oldsmobile was founded in 1897. Henry Ford produced his first vehicle in 1903. By 1904, Buick was up and running, and that same year William Durant purchased Buick. In 1908, Durant formed a holding company under the name General Motors. The first true Chevrolet appeared in 1912, while the first Dodge hit the streets in 1914. In 1908, Durant purchased Oakland, which became Pontiac in 1926. Plymouth was a big name in the police car business but a latecomer to the auto business in 1928. Mercury, of course, is the youngest make of former police cars, appearing in 1939.

For the 1909 model year, Ford introduced its Model T, arguably the most significant motor car ever built. The economical Model T caught on with police departments, just like it did with the motoring public. In 1917, the New York State Police became the fourth statewide enforcement agency. The Michigan

State Police and the West Virginia State Police were both organized in 1919. By 1920, American law enforcement from coast to coast had become fully motorized, utilizing a wide variety of motorcycles, passenger cars, and light-duty trucks.

In 1921, the Detroit Police fitted a radio receiver to a Ford Model T, creating the country's first radio patrol car. In 1928, the Detroit Police organized the first police broadcasting system, which used the call letters, "KOP." Prior to that, some police departments installed conventional radios in their patrol cars and interrupted regular programming to give out police calls!

Nearly all of the cars used by the police in the 1920s were powered by a four-cylinder engine. This all changed with the overhead-valve six introduced by Chevrolet in 1929. This, in turn, prompted Henry Ford's famous retort, "If it's cylinders they want, we'll give them cylinders," and the result was the famous Ford flathead V-8 in 1932. Ford instantly recognized the appeal of its new V-8 engine to law enforcement. In 1932, it marketed an open Phaeton (four-door convertible) with a V-8 engine as its

For as long as there have been Fords, there have been Ford police cars. The Ford Model T was greatly restyled for 1917 with a new grille, new hood, new crowned and curved front fenders, and a new cylinder head. The engine remained the same 20-horsepower, 177-ci flathead four used since 1913. This engine had been around since the 1909 introduction of the Model T. In June 1917, Ford produced its 2 millionth Model T. The Model T still remains in the top five of the all-time best-selling cars in the world. During the 19-year production run, which ended in May 1927, Ford produced just over 15 million Model Ts. The New York City Police owned this 1917 Model T. In the early years, police cars were seldom marked in any way. This car has no emergency lights, no warning siren, and no door shields. In fact, the only marking on this patroller is the "P.D." on the doors.

The West Virginia State Police (WVSP) used this 1922 Ford Model T. The WVSP formed in 1919 to enforce criminal laws, which are misdemeanors and felonies. The WVSP did not become involved in traffic enforcement until 1929. Most traffic violations are infractions and fall under traffic codes rather than criminal codes. These two WVSP troopers were after "real" criminals, judging by the firearm hanging off the right side A-pillar. They used Thompson submachine guns! The 1922 Model T was a carryover from previous years with one exception. The engine block on all 1922 models was produced by Ford's huge new iron foundry, called the River Rouge plant. Operational in November 1921, River Rouge would become the most famous manufacturing facility in the world.

"Police Special." In spite of the marketing strategy, this was still a retail car and not really "special" in any way.

The police used a wide variety of passenger cars as patrol vehicles in the 1930s, including Buick, Cadillac, Chrysler, DeSoto, Dodge, Graham-Paige, Hudson, Lincoln, Mercury, Nash, Oldsmobile, Packard, Pontiac, and Studebaker. However, with some exceptions, American cops in the 1930s drove one of the Low-Priced Three: Ford, Chevrolet, and Plymouth. Of these three, the Ford with its powerfuxl V-8 clearly dominated the police market. The actual performance gap between the Ford V-8 and the Chevrolet six and Plymouth six would almost com-

pletely disappear by the early 1950s, but it would not matter. The Ford dominance during the formative years of many police departments secured Ford's reputation as THE police car well into the 1960s.

Cops have used cars almost as long as cars have existed. However, until the 1950s, these were simply retail cars used by the police, not "police" cars. Police cars, or more accurately, "police-package" cars did not exist until 1950 (Ford), 1955 (Chevrolet), 1956 (Dodge, Studebaker) and 1957 (Plymouth). It takes more than the police driving a car to make that vehicle a "police car."

In 1925, Fords were powered by a 20-horsepower, flathead four-cylinder. Chevrolets had a 26-horsepower, overhead-valve four-cylinder. A county traffic officer in California used this 1925 Chrysler with a 68-horsepower, 201-ci flathead six. The first official traffic officer in the state was M.F. "Mike" Brown, commissioned in 1911, who patrolled San Mateo County. Other counties soon followed with traffic officers of their own. These officers carried badges that read either "Traffic Officer," "Deputy Sheriff," or "Town Constable." They were expected to write enough tickets to pay for their salary! In 1929, these "county squad traffic officers" formed one department, the California Highway Patrol. Until then, the county traffic officers bought their own cars. This 1925 Chrysler was a great choice. It was far more powerful than the Fords and Chevrolets, and it had four-wheel hydraulic brakes.

This 1928 Ford Phaeton has been restored as a Dallas (Texas), police cruiser. The Model A was introduced in 1928 amidst incredible fanfare. It was a more complex car, with 6,800 components compared to 5,000 in the Model T. Yet it was still powered by a flathead, four-cylinder engine. Henry Ford would not consider a six-cylinder engine, for fear of being considered a "follower" rather than a leader. The Model A engine was bigger than the Model T (201-ci two-barrel versus 177-ci one-barrel) producing twice the power (40 horsepower versus 20 horsepower). The Model A was capable of "jackrabbit starts" and top speeds of 65 miles per hour, a 20 mile per hour increase. The new car used a three-speed sliding gear transmission, rather than the planetary gear set. It also had four-wheel mechanical brakes. This Dallas Police unit has a white door shield, the word "POLICE" in white letters on the hood, and a red light mounted in front of the grille.

The Baltimore (Maryland) Police restored this 1929 Ford Model A Tudor Sedan. Photographs from their archives were used to assure an accurate and authentic replica. The patroller is jet-black with twin cowl-mounted red lights. Note the "B.P.D. 01" license plate. This type of license plate was a common police marking in the 1920s and 1930s. The door markings include Baltimore's Battle Monument and the words, "Baltimore Police," all in gold. The Battle Monument was used as the door shield on BPD cruisers from 1926 to 1940. These vehicles were used by police officers with the rank of sergeant and above. However, several were also used by the Detective Division.

The Michigan State Police (MSP) was organized in 1919. This 1931 Ford Model A and 1936 Ford Model 68 belonged to the department. Both cars are black. The 1931 MSP cruiser has a simple white door shield. The 1936 version has an ornate gold shield and a gold "V" stripe that comes to a point at the hood ornament, which were painted by hand. The 1931 models were the last of the Model A Fords, all powered by the 40-horse-power, 201-ci four. The 1936 Ford was powered by the 85-horsepower, 221-ci V-8. The 1931 Ford rode on a 103.5-inch wheelbase, while the 1936 Ford used a 112-inch platform.

Interestingly, this 1930 Ford Model A has been restored as a California Highway Patrol (CHP) cruiser. The CHP was organized in 1929 with 80 cars and 225 motorcycles. The CHP was originally only authorized to enforce traffic laws on state and county highways and to serve related warrants. However, many traffic officers were also empowered by local sheriffs to enforce all state laws. Traffic officers were issued motorcycles. Automobiles were issued to captains and inspectors. The cars were painted white with black roofs for easy identification. This Model A is fitted with a bumper-mounted red light. Other CHP vehicles during this period had nonflashing red lights mounted to the cowl and very high on the A-pillar.

"If it's cylinders they want, we'll give them cylinders," was the famous rally cry of Henry Ford in response to the 1929 introduction of the Chevrolet six-cylinder engine. The result was the 65-horsepower, 221-ci flathead V-8, found in this California Highway Patrol 1932 Ford Model 18, a.k.a. Ford V-8. At last, Ford could respond to Chevrolet with a V-8 for the price of a six. With 4.33 rear gears, these V-8 Fords had the fastest acceleration of the Low-Priced Three, with a top speed of 85 miles per hour. It was also the only V-8 engine of the Low-Priced Three. This made Ford the police car of choice from the early 1930s through the late 1960s. Note the "V-8" hubcaps on this 1932 Tudor with the early model year louvers.

The Missouri State Highway Patrol used this 1933 Chevrolet Master Eagle. The two-door cruisers sported a bumper-mounted red light and door shields. The license plate read "STATE PATROL." The 1933 Chevrolet used a 110-inch wheelbase, 2 inches shorter than the 112-inch Ford. For 1933, the 194-ci overhead-valve six in the Chevrolet produced 65 horsepower. Ford had bumped its 221-ci flathead V-8 to 75 horsepower. For urban patrol speeds, the Chevrolet six was as fast as the Ford V-8. At speeds over 60 miles per hour, especially for extended periods of time, the Ford V-8 was more reliable, since the Chevrolet had lubrication problems at higher speeds.

This black and silver 1935 Ford has been accurately restored as a Colorado State Highway Courtesy Patrol unit. This was the first year of the Patrol, which shortened its name to Colorado State Patrol (CSP) in 1945. The black door lettering was used until 1945. With the name change, the CSP adopted an ornate, seven-point star. The Ford was restyled for 1935. It had a longer hood, fully skirted fenders, full bullet headlights, and a door that now hinged in the front. The wheelbase remained at 112 inches, but the 1935 Ford was 6.5 inches longer than the previous year. The mechanical brakes were now self-adjusting.

In 1934, the Nevada Highway Patrol used this two-door Pontiac as their primary cruiser. The Nevada State Police was organized in 1908, making it one of the first statewide police agencies. Later, the Nevada State Police changed their name to the Nevada Highway Patrol. In 1908, Oakland automobiles joined General Motors and became Pontiac in 1926. The Pontiac was more expensive than cars from the low-priced three (Ford, Chevrolet, Plymouth), and the Pontiac engine was less powerful than the Ford V-8. Pontiac would not get a V-8 until 1955. As a result, Pontiac was seldom selected by the police, especially as a state police or highway patrol car, until the Pontiac Enforcers of the 1960s and 1970s.

This 1938 Plymouth was used by the Maryland State Police. The emergency equipment used on this four-door sedan was very progressive for the era. The brown-over-black sedan has a fender-mounted combination red light and electro-mechanical siren. The cruiser also has twin red grille lights. The markings were very low key. The words "Maryland State Police" appear on the doors in black letters. One license plate reads "EMER-GENCY," while the other reads "Maryland State Police." Prior to the development of the police package in the 1950s, the city, county, and state police used whatever make and model of retail they could afford as a police cruiser. Most police departments, however, used the Low-Priced Three: Ford, Chevrolet, and Plymouth.

The California Highway Patrol used this pair of 1936 Chrysler Airflows. Note that the front car does not have the rear fender skirts while the rear does. The Airflow was basically an Airstream with a "humpback" luggage compartment. The Airflow was built on a 123-inch wheelbase and weighed 4,102 pounds! The four-door sedan was powered by a 115-horsepower, 324-ci in-line, flathead eight-cylinder engine. A higher-compression, 120-horsepower version was available. That was a lot of horsepower at the time, considering that the Ford flathead V-8 produced 85 horsepower. However, at 2,786 pounds, the Ford actually had a better power-to-weight ratio. The Ford accelerated as well or better, but the longer-wheelbase Chrysler had better high-speed stability. The Chrysler also had hydraulic brakes.

The 1936 Dodge four-door sedan sold for $760, which was more expensive than a comparable Ford at $650. However, the Dodge had a number of enforcement advantages over the Ford. First, at 116 inches, the wheelbase was longer, giving better high-speed stability. Second, the Dodge had four-wheel hydraulic brakes, which had been perfected since their 1928 debut. Third, the Dodge offered an over-drive transmission a dozen years ahead of Ford. The Dodge used an 87-horsepower, 218-ci flathead six, which produced more torque than the Ford 85-horsepower, 221-ci flathead V-8. The Dodge was indeed more of a police car than the Ford. However, since the department could buy seven Fords for the price of six Dodges, the Dodges weren't the economical choice of the day.

The door shield on this 1936 Ford Tudor owned by the Montreal (Quebec) Police notes the biggest police advancement of the 1930s: the radio! By 1936, the largest city, county, and state police departments such as the Montreal Police patrolled in radio-equipped cars. In the late 1990s, the New York City Police still referred to its patrol cars as RMPs, an acronym for Radio Motor Patrol. Prior to the police radio, officers from all jurisdictions had to stop every hour and call by phone into headquarters. As they passed from town to town, officers would watch at a particular business for a raised flag, which meant they should call headquarters.

In the 1930s, the California Highway Patrol purchased a wide variety of makes and models in search of the ideal Enforcement-class cruiser. Shown here are a 1938 Buick Century and a 1937 Chrysler Imperial. Other CHP E-class cars used during the 1930s were the 1931 Dodge, 1933 Graham, 1934 Chrysler Airflow, 1936 Ford, 1936 Buick, 1937 Pontiac, 1937 Buick, 1937 Studebaker, 1937 DeSoto, and 1939 Ford. All of the 1930s CHP cruisers had the same color scheme: black hoods, roofs, trunks, and fenders with white doors and side panels. All were slick-top with at least one red spotlight. Some also had red grille lights. This 1937 Imperial had a 115-horsepower, 274-ci straight-8 on a 121-inch platform and tipped the scales at 3,544 pounds.

In 1937, the Chicago Police, like nearly every other police department across the country, used the Ford V-8. The standard 85-horsepower Ford was the Model 78. The Ford with the smaller 60-horsepower V-8, weighing 200 pounds less than the more powerful model, was the Model 74. The 60-horsepower V-8 was introduced to give customers, including the police, a choice of a more economical engine. This Chicago patroller is jet-black with white door lettering. It has a spotlight but no visible emergency lights or siren.

In 1937, the Washington State Patrol (WSP) used this Ford panel truck as its primary patrol vehicle. This half-ton panel truck was powered by the 85-horsepower 221-ci flathead V-8. This was the last year the WSP used the truck-based vehicle. In 1938, Evergreen State troopers drove passenger-car sedans, which were introduced in 1932. This particular panel truck exhibits an array of typical cop gear for the 1930s. On the roof is a combination red light and mechanical siren along with a flashing red light. The grille and bumper area has spotlights, which could be fog lights. The overall color scheme is black over white. The hood has a black "V" coming to a point just behind the radiator cap.

Pictured is a 1938 Chrysler Imperial with a California Highway Patrol Traffic Officer standing at attention nearby. The Imperial was selected for its powerful 122-horsepower, 299-ci straight-8 engine and its long, 125-inch wheelbase. In the 1930s and 1940s, powerful engines and long wheelbase chassis were only available in upscale, luxury cars. Even at 3,560 pounds, the Imperial had a better power-to-weight ratio than the Ford V-8. The long wheelbase gave the Imperial unequaled high-speed stability. The chrome chevrons on the front fenders were one of the few ways to recognize an Imperial from the otherwise identical, but six-cylinder-powered, Chrysler Royal.

This 1938 Ford Deluxe Fordor sedan has been restored as a Huntington County (Indiana) Sheriff's unit. While the 1938 Standard models used much the same front-end sheet metal as the 1937 Standard models, the 1938 Deluxe models, like this HCSD patroller, were significantly restyled. A curved grille outline and separate side louvers distinguished the upscale Deluxe models. This Hoosier sheriff's unit is "two-tone, county brown" as it would be for at least the next 60 years. The hood, roof, trunk, and fenders were brown, while the rest of the body was tan. This four-door sedan is equipped with twin, bumper-mounted red lights. The siren is under the hood along with the 85-horsepower, 221-ci V-8.

Among the Enforcement-class vehicles used by the California Highway Patrol was the 1938 Buick Century. In 1936, Buick combined its smallest and lightest body with the big straight-8 from its upscale Roadmaster. The result was a car with a top speed of 100 miles per hour, hence the name Century. Ford with its V-8 and Chevrolet with its big six had top speeds in the 80- to 85-mile-per-hour range. The Roadmaster-powered Buick Century could keep up with any car on the road at the time, and was considerably faster than most. The seven-point star shield showed up on doors beginning in late 1947.

In 1938, the Indiana State Police selected the Chevrolet Master as its primary patrol vehicle. The Chevy cruiser was powered by an 85-horsepower, overhead-valve, 216-ci six. That was as much power as the big Ford V-8! The Chevrolet six actually produced more torque than the Ford engine. The Chevrolet was also built on a 112.25-inch wheelbase, a quarter-inch longer than the Ford. One area where Chevrolet had a clear advantage over Ford was the brakes. Chevrolet adopted four-wheel hydraulic brakes in 1936, three years ahead of Ford. This two-door sedan, parked at the state prison in Michigan City, Indiana, is black with a blue door shield and a gold body stripe. The ISP returned to this same color scheme in 1998.

It's interesting to note that this Sacramento, California, 1939 Dodge Special was part of the Accident Investigation Unit. It is loaded with cop gear including twin A-pillar spotlights, twin fender-mounted red lights, and a large, fender-mounted electro-mechanical siren. In accordance with California traffic law, the forward-facing red lights burn continuously, as opposed to flashing or alternating. This 117-inch wheelbase Dodge has a black hood and black door lettering. Sacramento marked its police cars with a unit number inside a seven-point star well into the 1950s. The 1939 Dodge was powered by an 87-horsepower, 218-ci six and stopped by hydraulic brakes, used since 1928.

Pictured is a restored 1939 Ford Standard Tudor. This base-trim 1939 Standard model (pictured) looked like the previous year's Deluxe model. The biggest technical advancement for 1939 was the use of Lockheed four-wheel hydraulic brakes. Ford was the last of the major auto manufacturers to use hydraulic brakes. Don't be confused by the license plate. This is a generically marked two-door, not a replica of a New York State Police cruiser, which were marked "STATE POLICE," along with a state seal.

This 1939 Chevrolet Master served with the Jersey City (New Jersey) Police, one of America's toughest jurisdictions. The jet-black two-door had gold lettering on the hood and doors. Chevrolet Masters were powered by the legendary "Stovebolt Six," officially known as the Blue Flame Six or Blue Streak Six. The "Stovebolt Six" was eternally reliable as long as the engine speeds were kept low. The Blue Flame Six did not get a fully pressurized lubrication system until 1953!

The Indiana State Police used the Chevrolet Master Deluxe in 1939. Both the Chevrolet Master and Master Deluxe were powered by the 85-horsepower, 216-ci overhead-valve six. While the Master used 3.23 to 1 rear gears, the Master Deluxe used 4.22 to 1 gears. Due to the torque from the big six and the numerically high rear gear ratio, the Master Deluxe was said to be the fastest-accelerating American passenger car of 1939! Faster than the V-8-powered Ford! Faster than the straight-8-powered Buick! This all-black, ISP two-door has a blue door shield and a gold body stripe that runs from the rear fender to the tip of the hood.

Chapter Two

1940-1949

A Washington State Patrol trooper stands next to this 1940 Ford Deluxe sedan delivery. Even though the vehicle has black fenders, it has a different black and white color scheme than regular WSP patrol vehicles. This sedan delivery has a bumper-mounted siren and roof-mounted red light. A regular-size WSP shield appears on the door, but note the tiny WSP shield on the leading edge of the hood! This sedan was based on the upscale Deluxe line rather than the standard line; hence the huge chrome trim rings around the headlights. Weighing 2,638 pounds, it was powered by the 85-horsepower, 221-ci flathead V-8.

The 1940s opened just like the 1930s closed. The hot ticket was the Ford Standard Tudor powered by the 85-horsepower, 221-ci flathead V-8. In 1939, Ford joined the rest of the motoring world in its use of hydraulic brakes. The other members of the Low-Priced Three got hydraulic brakes in 1928 (Plymouth) and 1936 (Chevrolet). The Ford V-8 would grow to 96 horsepower by 1942 and be bored out to 239 ci with 100 horsepower for 1946. It would remain at 100 horsepower through 1951.

For all of the 1940s, Ford remained the clear choice of law enforcement. Occasional exceptions to the rule were some state police and highway patrols that insisted on powerful, long-wheel-base cruisers like the Buick and Mercury. In 1949, Oldsmobile drew attention among luxury class police cars with its introduction

A Florida Highway Patrol trooper stands "at ease" next to a meticulously restored 1940 Ford Deluxe Tudor. The black-over-cream color scheme would last into the 1990s. This two-door cruiser has an orange and green shield on the door and trunk. The orange letters, "STATE HIGHWAY PATROL," appear on the leading and trailing edge of the roof. This 112-inch wheel-base cruiser was powered by an 85-horsepower, 221-ci flat-head V-8. A 60-horsepower, 135-ci flathead V-8 was also available as an economical engine to compete with Chevrolet. This was the second year of Lockheed hydraulic brakes for Ford. Chevrolet introduced hydraulic brakes in 1936, while Plymouth was the first to use them in 1928.

Note the door shield, which simply reads "Chief of Police" on this restored 1941 Ford Super Deluxe. This Tudor, sporting twin red lights on the bumper, is owned by Police Chief Terry Fiene of River Oaks, Texas. In 1941, the wheelbase was extended from 112 inches to 114 inches. The 1941 Ford car line consisted of the base-trim level Special, available only with a six, the mid-priced Deluxe, and the high-end Super Deluxe. The Super Deluxe was identified by the chromework along the fenders and the left fender script. The power on the 221-ci flathead V-8 was bumped to 90 horsepower for 1941. Oddly enough, the 226-ci flathead six also had a 90-horsepower rating!

The North Carolina Highway Patrol used this 1941 Ford Deluxe coupe. The NCHP was formed in 1929. This two-door cruiser has a black hood and a silver body. The door shield is blue, white, and gold. Emergency lights include an A-pillar-mounted red spotlight and twin red lights mounted in the grille. The Deluxe was the mid-priced Ford in 1941. The low-end special was not available with a V-8, while the Deluxe and Super Deluxe were available with either powerplant. The 226-ci flathead six was new for 1941. The six produced the same 90 horsepower as the 221-ci flathead V-8. The long-stroke six actually produced more torque than the venerable V-8. Regardless of horsepower parity, cops went for the V-8.

of the "Rocket V-8." This was the first overhead-valve V-8 in a car anywhere near to being economically justified by a police department. All of the other V-8s at the time had the valve-in-block, flathead design. Buick's hot Roadmaster engine was an overhead-valve straight-8.

For all of the 1940s, Chevrolet passenger cars were powered by the much-maligned Blue Flame Six. Introduced in 1929, this 216.5-ci in-line six was called the Stovebolt Special, Cast Iron Wonder, and Shaker Six, but mostly, the Stovebolt Six. The real name was either Blue Flame Six or Blue Streak Six. In the 1940s, it was rated between 85 horsepower and 90 horsepower. The Chevrolet six always produced just about the same performance as the Ford V-8. In fact, in 1939, the Chevrolet Master Deluxe was said to be the fastest-accelerating American passenger car. The big Chevy six actually had more torque than the Ford V-8. In 1952, the Chevrolet six had a 0- to 60-mile-per-hour time of 20.46 seconds compared to 20.47 seconds for the Ford V-8.

This actual performance mattered little to most cops. Like the rest of the motoring public, they wanted "An Eight for the Price of a Six." Throughout the 1940s, the Ford V-8 produced a higher top speed than the Chevrolet six. More important, the Ford flathead V-8, despite its overheating faults, was more reliable at higher speeds than the Chevrolet six. Incredibly enough, the Chevrolet six did not get a fully pressurized lubrication system until 1953! Reliable at low speeds, the Chevrolet six made a great urban police engine. Reliable at high speeds, the Ford V-8 made a great highway patrol engine.

In the 1940s, Plymouth was a nonplayer in the police market. The Plymouth was powered by a perfectly acceptable, 201-ci six, which was bored-out to 218 ci in 1942. With a 95-horsepower rating and a 117-inch wheelbase, the Plymouth was certainly a worthy competitor. Even as a member of the highly visible Low-Priced Three, the Plymouth was largely overlooked for the entire decade. Turn around is fair play. From the late 1960s and to the late 1970s, the largest-selling police car in America would be Plymouth.

In the 1940s, the most popular option to Ford and Chevrolet was not Plymouth. It was Buick. Of all the big-engine, long-wheelbase luxury cars used by the police, the car to beat was Buick. The 1946 Buick Special, for example, was built on a 121-inch wheelbase and powered by a 110-horsepower, 248-ci overhead-valve straight-8. It would be 1950 before a Ford police engine produced 110 horsepower, and 1969 before a Ford police car had a 121-inch wheelbase. At the time, a longer wheelbase was believed to produce better high-speed stability. Of course, for really serious traffic apprehension duties, the choice was the Buick Roadmaster. Powered by a 320-ci overhead-valve straight-8 with up to 150 horsepower, the Buick Roadmaster, built on a 126-inch platform, was simply the "ticket" to traffic enforcement.

Police cars from the 1940s did not have many mechanical advancements. Instead, the 1940s are best remembered as the era when the cop gear used in police cars evolved. Specifically, a large number of the nation's patrol cars were fitted with two-way police radios. The Ohio State Highway Patrol (1941), the Missouri State Highway Patrol (1942), the Washington State Patrol (1943), and the Kansas Highway Patrol (1945) were among those police departments to join the modern age of two-way radio communications. Also in 1948, Federal Sign and Signal introduced the "Beacon-Ray," the first widely accepted revolving emergency light.

Of course, the 1940s are best remembered for World War II. All of the nation's auto factories were shut down and converted to produce wartime material. Ford Motor Company, General Motors, Chrysler Corporation, and all of the smaller automakers halted production in February, 1942.

With the war over in 1945, it was a race to get converted back to passenger-car production, to meet a three-year pent-up demand for cars, and to introduce new models. The first postwar Fords and Chevrolets were built in October 1945. The first Plymouth was not introduced until February 1946, followed by Dodge in March 1946. As a rule, all of the 1946 to 1948 models were simply re-releases of the 1942 models. This made the 1949 model year the most exciting year of the decade in terms of automotive news.

The Missouri State Highway Patrol (MSHP) drove the Chevrolet Special Deluxe in 1942. This all-black two-door cruiser represented many firsts for the MSHP. It was the first patrol car to have "STATE PATROL" painted on the doors in bold white lettering. The car number was also painted on the roof for the first time. In 1942, two-way, FM-band police radios were installed in all MSHP cruisers after a late-1941 trial run with 10 MSHP cruisers. This permitted two-way communication up to 60 miles from the base station. This 1942 Chevrolet is powered by the 90-horsepower, 216-ci six.

The 1941 Plymouth Deluxe of the Nassau County (New York) Police Department is an attractive two-door cruiser with a fender-mounted red light. At the time, white cars were used by the Highway Patrol Bureau, called "ghost patrol," while the precinct cars were black. In 1941, the 117-inch wheelbase Plymouth was powered by one of three engines. These were the 82-horsepower, 87-horsepower, and 92-horsepower versions of the same 201-ci valve-in-block, in-line six. The driveline included a three-speed stick with 4.10 to 1 rear gears. This was the first year for the one-piece, "alligator"-opening hood and the first year for an under-hood battery. The battery used to be under the driver's seat.

The Ohio State Highway Patrol (OSHP) used this 1942 Ford Deluxe Tudor. Cops have been using two-door police cars as long as two-door passenger cars have existed, long before the police package was developed. This cruiser bears the famous "winged tire" on the door, which was used since the Patrol first organized in 1933 and is still in use today in the late 1990s. For 1942, Ford pumped power back into its 221-ci flathead V-8 to give it an advantage over its 226-ci six. The V-8 was now rated at 96 horsepower versus 90 horsepower for the pesky six. Yet the six still had 15 percent more torque than the V-8. Most cops, however, remained loyal to the V-8.

Right — A California Highway Patrol traffic officer stands next to his 1942 Chrysler New Yorker. The five chrome bars on the front fender wrap around the front of the big Chrysler to form the grille. The New Yorker script appears on the front fender below the red-lens spotlight. In 1942, Chrysler produced vehicles with two wheelbases. The short-wheelbase Royal and Windsor had a 121.5-inch chassis, quite long for police cars in the 1940s and 1950s. The long-wheelbase Saratoga and New Yorker rode on a 127.5-inch platform! This CHP New Yorker is powered by the 140-horsepower, 323-ci in-line flathead V-8. This was a lot of power for the early 1940s, but this massive Chrysler tipped the scales at 3,873 pounds.

From 1931 to 1947, the California Highway Patrol was under the California Department of Motor Vehicles. In 1947, the CHP became a separate department. A CHP traffic officer stands near this 1942 Mercury with a long, 118-inch wheelbase. It was powered by the 239-ci flathead V-8 with 100 horsepower. That was lot of horsepower for the time! This is the same basic flathead engine that would power Ford police cars after World War II. The 1942 Mercury had a very distinctive upper and lower grille. This four-door Town Sedan weighed 3,263 pounds. Note the clear-lens right-side spotlight and the red-lens left-side spot. Mercury began producing vehicles in 1939.

Pictured is a 1946 Chevrolet Fleetline bearing the markings of the Framingham (Massachusetts) Police. Conversion of the production plants from wartime use to civilian use started in July 1945. In late 1945, GM was hit by a labor strike. This allowed Ford to produce three times as many cars as Chevrolet, making 1946 Chevrolets rare. For 1946, the Stylemaster was the base trim level car while Fleetmaster and Fleetline were the more upscale models. The chrome "triple speedline moldings" on the front fender were a sign of the top-of-the-line Fleetline. The drivetrain was a 90-horsepower, 216-ci overhead-valve six, a three-speed stick, and 4.11 to 1 rear gears.

The Los Angeles Police drove Fords in 1946, as did the vast majority of city, county, and state police forces across the United States. After World War II, Ford restarted production quickly, while Chevrolet was held back by the GM strike during 1945. As a result, more Fords were available to civilians and cops alike. Ford had two series of cars in 1946: the base-line Deluxe and the upscale Super Deluxe. The chrome around the windows and the chrome body and fender strips identify this LAPD restoration as a Super Deluxe. This cruiser has an A-pillar-mounted spotlight with a California-spec red lens. The original LAPD patroller had black wheels instead of the white on this four-door.

The Oakland Police used this all-original 1946 Ford Super Deluxe Tudor from 1946 until 1951. The cop gear includes a red spotlight, a clear spotlight, and an underhood siren. All of the 1946 Fords were restyled 1942 models with redesigned grilles. The six was a carryover from 1942 while the V-8 was bored-out to 239 ci. This police car was sold off in 1951 and put into storage until 1989. Once out of storage, it was simply tuned-up and started. No other work was done! The powertrain is the original 239-ci flathead V-8 and three-speed stick.

In 1946, the California Highway Patrol selected the Mercury two-door as its Enforcement-class vehicle. The 1946 Mercury can be distinguished from the nearly identical 1947 Mercury by the chrome strip on the hood. This two-door Mercury was powered by the 100-horsepower, 239-ci V-8. At 3,240 pounds, it was about 80 pounds heavier than a similar-body-style Ford. While the Mercury had a 4-inch-longer wheelbase, which added to high-speed stability, the Ford with the same engine was as fast, or even faster, than the Mercury. The Lincoln-Mercury Division was formed in 1945, but it wasn't until 1949 that the upscale Ford took on an image all its own.

Restored as a Pleasant Hill (California) Police unit, this 1946 Ford Super Deluxe gray two-door sedan should have twin forward-facing reds instead of a red rotator. The roof rotator was not invented until 1948 and not popularized until the 1950s! Packing a 100-horsepower, 239-ci flathead V-8, this San Francisco Bay-area patroller weighs 3,190 pounds. The two-door, V-8-powered Super Deluxe was by far the most popular version of all the 1946 Fords. Ford was given permission by the War Department to resume auto production in July 1945. Warmed-over prewar models were introduced in October 1945. All but the high-priority buyers were placed on long waiting lists for new cars.

This meticulously restored 1947 Chevrolet bears the vintage markings of the Manteca (California) Police. Since new cars were in such demand, Chevrolet followed the practice of all other auto manufacturers by only slightly revising its cars. The 116-inch wheelbase and the 90-horsepower, 216-ci six were retained. The Stylemaster, Fleetmaster, and Fleetline trim levels were also carryovers from 1946. In fact, the only significant change was to the grille and hood ornament. This black-and-white Fleetmaster has twin bumper-mounted amber lights and a combination red light and siren mounted on the right front fender. Note that the whitewall tires are not official police issue, but they sure make this car look great.

It's interesting to note the oversize door shield from the Charleston (South Carolina) Police on this 1947 Chevrolet Fleetmaster, typical of many police cars from the 1940s. Two-door police cars were common, the all-black color was the rule, and the most frequent placement of red lights was on the front bumper. Most cars included a single clear-lens spotlight. Slick-top cars were the obvious trend. In the 1950s, the large door shields became smaller and red bumper lights gave way to a single rotating light on the roof. For 1947, the Stylemaster was the base trim level, while the Fleetmaster and Fleetline were more upscale. Chevrolet would keep its 116-inch wheelbase until the major restyling for 1949.

The 1947 Mercury models are different from the postwar 1946 models because of the Mercury script on the side of the hood. Underneath the Mercury name on the grille is the word "EIGHT" in a vertical stack of letters. From the very first Mercury in 1933, the models have been powered by a V-8. The 239-ci flathead V-8, a bored-out version of the 221-ci V-8, was restricted to the Mercury marque until 1946. Even then, the "EIGHT" emblem was there as a constant reminder. The 1947 engine was also the 239-ci V-8, rated at 100 horsepower. Of special interest is the roof-mounted red light. It has the word "POLICE" across the front of the red lens in black letters.

The Idaho State Police drove the Chevrolet Fleetline in 1948. This 1948 Chevrolet really had 1942 styling. The 1948 Fleetline continued with the triple, stacked stainless-steel "speed line" side moldings. This Gem State two-door has twin white stripes that form a "V" on the hood. The ISP was organized in 1939. They drove all-black cars with twin white stripes from the late 1940s until the early 1960s when light-blue cars with white doors were used. The ISP went back to the white over black color scheme in 1978. This 1948 Chevrolet has a spotlight, fender-mounted siren, and twin red lights mounted on the bumper. The letters "STATE POLICE" appear in white on the door along with the outline of the state of Idaho.

The Georgia State Patrol (GSP) used this 1947 Ford Deluxe. Notice the eye-catching black-and-white color scheme. The symbol on the door is the Georgia state seal. The border around the seal reads, "State of Georgia, Department of Public Safety." In the late 1940s, the GSP cruisers had black fenders, a black trunk, and a V-shaped portion of the hood in black. The cars would continue to have the V-shaped black graphics even when the hoods blended smoothly into the fenders. The hood on this 1947 Ford, however, has clear, V-shaped sheet metal breaks making this black-and-white color scheme a natural.

The California Highway Patrol used this 1947 Buick Roadmaster as one of its Enforcement-class vehicles. The longer and larger straight-8 engine used in the Roadmaster required a longer wheelbase, fenders, and hood than the Buick Special and Buick Super. The Roadmaster had a 129-inch wheelbase! The powertrain was an overhead-valve, 144-horsepower, 320-ci in-line eight-cylinder with a two-barrel carburetor teamed with a three-speed stick. This two-door Buick tipped the scales at a hefty 4,095 pounds. During 1947 the CHP became a separate department from the Department of Motor Vehicles. This was the first year the gold seven-point star appeared on the door shield.

The Iowa Highway Patrol drove this Ford Super Deluxe in 1948. The all-black, two-door sedan has a black-on-yellow door shield. This slick-top cruiser has only a red spotlight as a warning light. As with all the Fords driven by the various state police and highway patrols, this 114-inch-wheelbase Super Deluxe was powered by the 110-horsepower, 239-ci two-barrel flathead V-8. This V-8 made Ford the clear choice among cops since 1932. Ford would retain this reputation well after the other members of the Low-Priced Three produced overhead-valve V-8s. The Iowa Highway Patrol changed its name to the Iowa State Patrol in 1973.

The Los Angeles Police used this 1948 Ford Super Deluxe. The 1948 Fords continued with the same basic platform dating back to 1942. The 1948 model can be identified by the round parking lights located under the headlights. The upscale Super Deluxe could be identified by the chrome strips on the fenders. This LAPD unit is fitted with a forward-facing, continuously glowing red light mounted on the roof over the driver. The 114-inch four-door sedan is powered by the 100-horsepower, 239-ci flathead V-8. The venerable flathead V-8, introduced in 1932, would continue to power police cars through 1953. However, in 1954, the overhead-valve V-8 would replace it.

The Indiana State Police used this 1949 Chevrolet Special Styleline. The two-door sedans were black with a painted yellow body stripe and a blue door shield. The cruiser has a combination red light and mechanical siren mounted to the roof and a fender-mounted spotlight. Chevrolets were completely restyled in 1949, the first freshening since 1940. Although the cars looked longer, the overall length was actually .75-inch shorter and the wheelbase was reduced from 116 inches to 115 inches for 1949. In spite of a new body and chassis, the powertrain was a carryover. The 216-ci overhead-valve six was still rated at the same 90 horsepower it had produced since 1941.

The California Highway Patrol used this 1949 Chevrolet Special station wagon to tow a Safety Education Unit. In 1949, Chevrolet made two very different kinds of station wagons. The year started out with a wood-bodied unit. The body used a steel frame, shell, and top but an all-wood tailgate and other panels. General Motors intended for Chevrolet, Pontiac, and Oldsmobile to share an all-steel "Body by Fisher" but not enough bodies were available by the product launch. By midyear, the all-steel bodies were in full production. This CHP unit is an all-steel, late-1949 version. The wagon sports the black-and-white color scheme of the era including the black-lettered, seven-point gold star.

Sheriff's deputies used this 1949 Ford Custom to patrol Los Angeles County. The 1949 Ford used the same 114-inch wheelbase but sported an entirely new suspension. The chassis was a wishbone-type. Longitudinal rear springs replaced the old transverse rear springs. A three-speed stick with synchronizers for second and third gears was standard. A synchronizer for first gear would not come until 1963. A three-speed with overdrive was optional. This all-white four-door has a six-point star, twin forward-facing red lights, twin clear-lens spotlights, and a roof-mounted, electro-mechanical siren. The siren has a wire mesh over the front, not a red light. This cruiser also has twin amber lamps mounted on the front bumper and an amber flasher in the rear package tray. This was an incredible amount of warning gear for the time.

The Indiana State Police drove a mix of makes in 1949 including both the Chevrolet Special and this Ford Custom. The Ford Custom was the top trim level and could quickly be identified by the chrome strip along the lower half of the body. The ISP used all-black, two-door sedans, marking them with a yellow stripe and a blue door shield. The torpedo-style roof light is a combination red light and mechanical siren. The restyled 1949 Ford was lower and shorter than previous years, but it still used the same 114-inch wheelbase. This wheelbase was 1 inch shorter than the one used by rival Chevrolet. Plymouth used a 118.5-inch platform. The Ford would ride on a new, 115-inch wheelbase in 1952.

Left — The California Highway Patrol owned this 1949 Oldsmobile 88. The gold, seven-point star door shield with black lettering was new for late 1947 and continued for this model year. Emergency lights on this 119.5-inch-wheelbase Olds include a continuously burning, forward-facing red and a flashing, rear-facing amber, both mounted on the roof. The 1949 Olds 88 was the logical combination of the all-new Rocket V-8 engine from the Olds 98 dropped into the lightweight Futuramic 76 chassis. This Olds 88 was powered by the 135-horsepower, 303-ci overhead-valve V-8, which was Oldsmobile's first V-8. The Olds 88 came standard with the Hydra-Matic automatic transmission introduced in 1940. Oldsmobile's Hydra-Matic was not the first automatic transmission but, at its introduction, it was the best. The Hydra-Matic was soon offered on Cadillacs.

The all-black two-door 1949 Ford Custom of the Milwaukee, Wisconsin, police is equipped with a combination red light and siren, and clear-lens spotlight. The door markings simply read "POLICE" in white letters. The 1949 Fords were available in the base trim level Ford-series and the upscale Custom-series. The new Ford had the "slab-side" look, meaning the rear fender bulge was totally eliminated and the hood was wide enough to blend smoothly into the front fenders. The totally new styling was referred to as the "Can't tell the back from the front" look. Approval for the new car came from Henry Ford II. This marked his first major decision since taking control of Ford Motor Company.

It's interesting to note the amp-soaking electrical gear on this 1949 Ford from the Grizzly Bear State. Pictured from the top are twin red roof lamps; an electro-mechanical siren; twin clear-lens spotlights; and twin bumper-mounted amber lights. Some police agencies also wired the headlamps to come on any time the red overheads did. Out the back was an amber flasher on the driver's side of the package tray. This was the first year for the now-famous "bullet" spinner in the grille. This grille bullet would appear in one form or another through 1954. In the center of the bullet was either a "6" or an "8," indicating the engine. This hot California cruiser packed a 100-horsepower, 239-ci V-8.

In 1949, the Michigan State Police drove the jet-black Ford Custom with a gold body stripe that formed a "V" on the hood. The door shield was also gold. By 1949, Ford had started to develop the heavy-duty and extra-heavy-duty components for police use. The exact year of the first Ford police package is unknown even to Ford Fleet officials. The best information indicates individual heavy-duty parts for police use were available in 1949. The very first "police" component was oversize brakes available in 1949. By 1950, Ford engineers assembled various individual, heavy-duty components together in one commonly ordered package: the police package. This was a Ford first.

The 1949 Plymouths, like this standard-wheelbase Deluxe, were the first all-new models since World War II. Plymouth released two totally different versions: the 111-inch, short-wheelbase P-17 and the 118.5-inch, standard-wheelbase P-18. This beautifully restored cruiser, a four-door black-and-white, has a fender-mounted, public address system speaker on one fender and an electro-mechanical siren on the other fender. Bolted behind the siren is a red-lens "pull-over" light with the word STOP. A red, bumper-mounted light and an A-pillar-mounted spotlight completes the gear. The engine is a 218-ci flathead six producing 97 horsepower.

Pictured is a restored 1949 Nash Ambassador black-and-white four-door cruiser. The California Highway Patrol used these cars as one of its 1949 Enforcement-class vehicles. The Nash Ambassador had a 121-inch wheelbase. It had a one-piece windshield years before Chevrolet, Ford and Plymouth. In 1949, Nash became the first mass produced car in the world to use a unitized, single-unit construction. The Airflyte or "bathtub" Nash was one of the first cars successfully styled with aerodynamics in mind. The Nash powertrain was based around a 112-horsepower, 235-ci overhead-valve six with a three-speed Overdrive as an option.

Chapter Three
1950-1954

This Indiana State Police trooper seems quite at ease, leaning on his 1950 Chevrolet Styleline. The jet-black cruiser has a yellow body stripe and blue door shield. Note the huge roof visor bolted to both the A-pillars and the windshield, a look characteristic of the 1950s, but not of police cars! In 1950, both the 216-ci and 235-ci six-cylinder engines were rated at 90 horsepower. That would change for 1951.

In 1950, Ford set a precedent for police car technology, releasing a formal "police package" for its Deluxe and Custom series sedans. The blue oval became the first automaker to put together a number of commonly ordered, heavy-duty components into one ordering package—the police package. The resulting police package had heavy-duty brakes, heavy-duty shocks and springs, heavy-duty cooling systems, and a heavy-duty interior. Prior to this time, the retail cars used by the police may have had special-order or oversize brakes; they might have been ordered with larger radiators or other heavy-duty components developed for towing, export use, or various forms of racing. Of all the beefed-up parts, the heavy-duty brakes were the first components commonly referred to as "police" items.

Ford's police package was specifically designed to improve the drivetrain and suspension durability and reliability. To a lesser degree, the police package improved braking power, cornering ability, and high-speed stability. The police package did NOT make the car faster; instead, the package made the car more durable with whatever engine it had. In addition, the package

didn't increase horsepower, torque, acceleration, or top speed. The police package was available with the most sluggish, fuel-miserly, taxi-class six-cylinder engine and with the most powerful, multiple-carbureted, big-block V-8s.

The second development in police car technology for the 1950 model year was the Ford Law Enforcement V-8. Interestingly, the new Ford Law Enforcement V-8 was not a Ford engine. It was a Mercury engine introduced in 1949 and was never available in any retail Ford car. The police-only engine was a 255-ci flathead V-8, a stroked version of the Ford 239-ci V-8, and rated at 110 horsepower.

The use of a Mercury-marque engine in a Ford police car emphasizes the fact that police cars are an entirely different breed than consumer production cars. The powertrains were frequently different, and this trend has continued to this day, which can be quite confusing for people familiar with retail powertrains for the same model and year.

In 1950, Chevrolet unveiled the first automatic transmission offered by one of the Low-Priced Three—the two-speed Powerglide.

28

Chevrolet squad cars such as this 1950 LaHabra (California) police car came from the mid-trim level Deluxe series. Most police cars used the lowest trim level, which in 1950 was the Special series. Note the twin spotlights and the unusual roof-mounted red light. This jet-black cruiser was powered by a 90-horsepower, overhead-valve, 216-ci six. Being in the Deluxe series, this squad car could have had the brand-new two-speed Powerglide automatic transmission, but almost every police department used the three-speed stick.

The Indiana State Police used this 1950 Chevrolet Styleline Special. This all-black cruiser has a yellow body stripe and a blue door shield. The only emergency light on this Hoosier State patroller is a red spotlight, which was typical for state police and highway patrols during this era. The Stovebolt Six, which powered this Styleline, was not a performance engine but provided acceptable service. It had 0- to 60-mile-per-hour times of 20.5 seconds and top speeds around 81 miles per hour. The ISP used both two-door sedans and four-door sedans.

To make up for some of the fluid power losses in the new automatic transmission, Chevrolet revised the 235-ci six from its truck line for use in passenger cars. A bored-and-stroked version of the 216-ci six, the 235-ci mill produced 105 horsepower.

In 1951, Ford followed Chevrolet's lead by offering its first automatic transmission, the two-speed Fordomatic. The automatic could be ordered with either the 226-ci six or the 239-ci V-8, but these engines didn't increase in horsepower when teamed with the automatic. However, cars fitted with automatics had a larger radiator and different fan. By 1951, 36 percent of the retail Chevrolets were equipped with the Powerglide, and police cars in service made up less than 1 percent of that figure. It took some time before the automatic transmission became prevalent among the law enforcement agencies across the country. The Los Angeles Police was the first of the major police departments to use the automatic in the early 1950s. And it was not until the 1957 release of the Mopar three-speed TorqueFlite that the automatic gained respect in law enforcement. Nonetheless, it was well into the 1960s before more police cars came with an automatic than a manual shift.

Law enforcement continued to be creative with grille lights during 1951. The single and double grille spinners, or bullets, were the latest styling rage. Fleet managers simply removed the chrome spinner and inserted a red light. The 1951 Ford gave them the chance to run twin red lights in the grille. From 1949 to 1955, if the grille styling permitted it, the popular trend was to put red lights in place of spinners.

Ford released its first overhead-valve engine, the 215-ci six in 1952. Compared to the older 226-ci six, the new engine had a much larger bore and a much shorter stroke. The Ford six got overhead valves two years before the Ford V-8. The 101-horsepower six produced a quicker 0- to 60-mile-per-hour time, a

quicker quarter-mile time, and the same top speed as the Flathead V-8 rated at 110 horsepower. The Flathead got better gas mileage at low speeds, but the new overhead-valve six got better gas mileage at high speeds. For this particular year, the hot ticket remained the Mercury-based Law Enforcement 255-ci V-8, now rated at 125 horsepower. It was far more powerful than anything from Chevrolet, Plymouth, Dodge, or Pontiac, and it was even slightly more powerful than the Buick Special at 120 horsepower. It took an Oldsmobile Rocket V-8, a Buick Roadmaster straight-8, or the new DeSoto Firedome "Hemi" V-8 to outpower the Ford Interceptor.

It was Chevrolet, not Ford, that made big headlines in police news for 1953 with its totally redesigned six-cylinder engine. Although the new engine used the same bore and stroke as the old engine, it was the first time in Chevy history that aluminum pistons were used instead of cast iron. In addition, the new 235-ci six had a fully pressurized lubrication system, which was another first for Chevy. Along with Chevy, Buick made police news with the Buick Super and the awesome Buick Roadmaster, fitted with the new 322-ci overhead-valve V-8. The new engine produced 164 horsepower in two-barrel form and 188 horsepower with a four-barrel. A Buick Super cost 50 percent more than a comparable Ford Mainline but had 30 percent more horsepower than Ford's strongest engine.

In 1953 Dodge offered the 241-ci Hemi V-8, but only in the top-of-the-line Coronet. The Dodge police package was released in 1956 and this Hemi was one of the available police engines. However, the second generation and legendary 426-ci Hemi that hit the streets in 1966 never became a police engine. Ford made a huge impact in the police vehicle market when the overhead-valve, Y-block V-8 was introduced in 1954. It was a huge step forward for Ford, and the biggest law enforcement advance since the

1932 introduction of the flathead V-8. All else equal, the overhead-valve V-8 had an 18-percent horsepower advantage over the flathead design.

Ford had redesigned the chassis to accommodate the new engine. It was the first use of a ball-joint front suspension, replacing the kingpin and spindle design. In addition, it was also the first full year that power steering and power brakes were options on the Ford. In a year of firsts for Ford, this was the first year for a four-barrel carburetor on any Ford police car, available on the Mercury Law Enforcement engine used in Ford police cars.

From the late 1940s to the mid-1950s, police cars experienced a period of basic engine design changes. After the mid-1950s, the engine designs got bigger, but they used the same basic designs. Of the various makes of cars used by police, the overhead-valve V-8 engine was the pinnacle of development in that era. Oldsmobile was the first to use the engine configuration in 1949. Studebaker and the Chrysler Hemi were next in 1951. The DeSoto got its overhead-valve Hemi in 1952, followed by the Dodge Hemi in 1953. Buick offered overhead-valve straight 8s and V-8s in 1953. Buick dropped the straight-8 in favor of the V-8. Ford and Mercury adopted the new V-8 valvetrain in 1954. By 1955, Chevrolet, Pontiac, Plymouth, Hudson, Packard, and Nash were up to speed.

Bearing the markings of the Susanville (California) Police, this 1950 Dodge Meadowbrook has it all. Features include a fender-mounted growler siren; an A-pillar-mounted spotlight; twin forward-facing, continuous-burning, roof-mounted red lights; and a rear-facing, trunk-mounted, amber flasher. Notice the red, roof-mounted rotating light. This had just been introduced by Federal Signal in 1948. This white-over-black four-door sedan is exceptionally well restored. The 1950 Dodges were powered by a 103-horsepower, 230-ci flathead six. Dodges were extremely rare in police work before the release of the formal police package in 1956.

Note the markings of the Los Angeles Police Department on this 1950 Ford Deluxe. This was the first confirmed year for the Ford police package. The 1950 Ford was similar to the 1949 models, but Ford boasted "50 improvements for '50." The Deluxe was the base trim level while the Custom Deluxe series was the top trim level. Red lights on both the grille and roof along with a roof-mounted mechanical siren were common cop gear in the 1950s. Fords were clearly the top choice of city, county, and state police departments. The LAPD has used cruisers with all the doors white since the 1930s. By 1960 a white roof was added to the color scheme.

The Nebraska Safety Patrol drove this black-with-white 1950 Ford. The name of the agency was changed to Nebraska State Patrol in 1967. Note that the white paint on this two-door cruiser did not follow a particular body panel or crease line. This was a NSP trademark. Also note the red, fender-mounted "STOP" light. This was a common feature in the 1950s. Where is the red emergency light? Check out the center of the grille! The NSP removed a center chrome piece and installed a red light, a grille light in the truest sense.

These officers took time out from fighting crime to pose with their patrol cars. The two cars on the left are 1950 Fords while the right one is a 1949 Chevrolet. All three patrollers have a red "pull-over" light mounted on the passenger front fender. The Fords have a forward-facing red light bolted to the windshield center brace, while the Chevrolet red light is roof-mounted. The Chevrolet also has a bumper-mounted red light, while the Fords have A-pillar-mounted spotlights. The Fords used a 95-horsepower, 226-ci mill while the Chevrolet used a 90-horsepower, 216-ci engine. As long as the police agency did not have a need for the power of Ford's flathead V-8, which most did not, Ford and Chevrolet were considered equals in this era. However, if horsepower, torque, and high-speed driving were major deciding factors, Ford was the only real choice.

This nicely restored, properly marked, and correctly equipped 1950 Ford Deluxe belongs to the Oroville (California) Police. The red roof rotator, fender-mounted siren, and red spotlight were correct for the period. In 1950, Ford became the first auto manufacturer to develop a police package. Heavy-duty components had already been developed for towing, for export use, and for various forms of racing. Ford was the first to put all these heavy-duty suspension, brake, driveline, cooling, and interior components together into one ordering package. It made sense for Ford to have been the first. Cops had expressed a definite preference for Fords ever since the 1932 release of the flathead V-8.

This 1950 Ford Custom Deluxe was used to chase gangsters in the Windy City. During this era, Chicago police cars were all-black with white door lettering and a red roof rotator. CPD added a white roof to the black car in 1956. The department would make the transition to blue emergency lights in 1960. A formal police package was available in 1950 for both the Fordor (four-door) and Tudor (two-door). This new package included a 13-leaf rear suspension, heavy-duty "aircraft-type" shocks, and special 24-hour-duty seat frames with nonsag seat springs and heavy-duty vinyl upholstery. The police package also included a 60-amp generator and 130-amp alternator to handle the new, two-way police radios.

Restored as a Rio Vista (California) Police unit, this 1950 Dodge Coronet is shown on the grounds of the CHP Academy near Sacramento. A sharp restoration, the twin red roof lights and the external, trunk-mounted, amber flasher are straight from the California vehicle code. The red roof rotator certainly could have been used, but its use early in the 1950s would have been deemed very progressive for a tiny, northern California town. The fender-mounted electro-mechanical siren completes the required cop gear. The 123.5-inch-wheelbase 1950 Dodge was available as a base trim level Meadowbrook and the top-of-the-line Coronet. The engine was a 103-horsepower, 230-ci flathead six.

Two New York State Police troopers wearing old and new uniforms pose in front of this restored 1951 Ford Custom Deluxe. The all-gray Ford looks great, but this 1951 Ford has body-color headlight bezels from 1952 instead of the chromed ones from 1951. Also, in 1951, the NYSP car doors read only "State Police," not "New York State Police," and the letters were twice as tall. Yet the red lens in both A-pillar spotlights and in both grille spinners is feasible. It just shows how tough it can be to do an accurate restoration, even for a major police department. The huge whip antenna is absolutely correct.

This 1951 Ford Custom Deluxe belongs to the Colma (California) Police. The Bay-area sedan is all-black with a gold and blue seven-point star on the door. Many stars used by California police departments are of the seven-point design following the lead of the California Highway Patrol. This four-door sedan is powered by the 239-ci two-barrel flathead V-8 rated at 100 horsepower. This was the last year for the 114-inch wheelbase. The chrome strip along the lower body panels identifies this as from the upscale Custom Deluxe series.

Standing at "parade rest" are these Iowa Highway Patrol officers with their 1951 Fords. The IHP used a variety of different colored cruisers including white, tan, and black. A large amber flasher is mounted in the package tray to project a rear warning signal. The traffic safety message on the back of these Hawkeye State cruisers is clear: "To Date 385 Killed." Those letters were actually painted on the trunks! The artistic style of the lettering is questionable, but the message is not: Drive Safely.

Notice the two A-pillar spotlights on this 1951 Colorado State Patrol Ford Deluxe. The passenger side has a red lens while the driver's side has a clear lens. Of particular interest are the red light on the roof and the massive, fender-mounted mechanical siren. Note the missing right front turn signal.

Pictured is a 1951 Ford Custom Deluxe with the New Jersey State Police. This cruiser is loaded with red lights. The twin grille spinners have been replaced with red lights. The A-pillar spotlight on the driver's side has a red lens. The passenger-side spotlight has a clear lens. The roof-mounted red light is combined with a mechanical siren and a rear-facing red light. This white-over-black four-door sedan has white "State Police" lettering on the hood and trunk.

Note the gold door shield of the Belmont (California) Police on this all-black 1951 Ford Custom Deluxe. For 1951, the large center spinner on the grille was replaced with twin spinners. The single chrome spinner would return in 1952. Ford started using split windshields on its vehicles in 1937. This practice continued through 1951. Starting in 1952, Fords used a one-piece curved windshield. This advancement was one year ahead of Chevrolet.

The Colorado State Patrol used this all-white 1951 Ford Deluxe. The seven-point star is gold and includes the state seal. This star was used from 1945 to 1961. After that time, the CSP adopted a winged-tire door shield. This 1951 Ford is powered by the 112-horsepower, 255-ci Law Enforcement V-8. This was actually a Mercury engine, the result of stroking a 239-ci V-8. In 1951, the two-speed Fordomatic automatic transmission became an option, but nearly all Ford police cars had the three-speed stick. Some Ford police cars, however, had the three-speed with Overdrive. The Colorado State Highway Courtesy Patrol was formed in 1935. The name was changed to Colorado State Patrol in 1945.

The New Jersey State Police (NJSP) operated this 1951 Ford Custom Deluxe. The black-and-white unit was on a special patrol assignment. The door shield reads "New Jersey Turnpike Authority." The regular NJSP cruisers had triangular door shields that read "State Police N.J." It was common practice in New Jersey, as well as many other states, for some state police cars and officers to be permanently assigned to special traffic-enforcement duties. Note the different style of roof light and the roof lettering.

These 1951 and 1950 Fords belong to the San Francisco Police Department (SFPD) The roof gear includes a continuously burning red light, a mechanical siren, and a public address speaker. Mounted on the rear fender, just behind the C-pillar, is a rear-facing amber flasher. The front 1951 black-and-white has the standard SFPD door shield with gold letters on a blue seven-point star. The other two cruisers have the circular door shield of the Bay-area Accident Investigation Bureau, a special unit within the SFPD. These Fords are all packing a V-8.

This 1951 Ford Custom Tudor has been beautifully restored. The gloss-black, Lee County (Florida) Sheriff's unit has the gold five-point star on both doors and the trunk. Florida sheriffs' cars would continue to use this same basic design, but with different body panel colors, for the next 50 years. In 1951, Ford introduced the two-speed Fordomatic transmission in response to Chevrolet's 1950 introduction of its two-speed Powerglide. Even though it was quite popular among motorists, very few police cars were ordered with the Fordomatic.

The Missouri State Highway Patrol drove the Ford Custom Deluxe Tudor in 1951. This jet-black two-door was powered by the 112-horse-power, 255-ci two-barrel Law Enforcement V-8 bolted to a three-speed stick. The rear-axle ratio was either a 3.73 or 4.10 to 1. These MSHP cruisers packed a lot of firepower. The rifle is a .351 Winchester semiautomatic, while the pump shotgun is a 12-gauge Winchester Model 12. Flares and a first aid kit complete the gear carried in the trunk. This police car has an A-pillar-mounted spotlight and a roof-mounted mechanical siren with front- and rear-facing red lenses.

It's interesting to note the typical police graphics for the era on this 1951 Ford Custom Deluxe with the Fair Oaks (Illinois) Police. It has twin clear-lens spotlights and a gold door shield. The can-style roof light has front-facing and rear-facing red lenses. The rear deck has an amber flasher. The 1951 model year was the last for chrome headlight bezels. Chrome bezels have been a fixture on Fords for almost as long as Fords have existed. Starting in 1952, Fords were outfitted with body-color headlight bezels. This practice continued at least through 1960. Even still, chrome would no longer play as prominent a role as it once did. This Fair Oaks cruiser, like nearly all 1951 police Fords, was powered by a V-8. No other member of the Low-Priced Three offered a V-8 at the time.

The Washington State Patrol operated this 1951 Ford Deluxe. This particular cruiser was powered by the 95-horsepower, 226-ci six. Note the lack of a V-8 emblem behind the Deluxe emblem on the front fender. Most 1951 WSP Fords were powered by the much more powerful and more torque-laden 112-horsepower, 255-ci V-8. These six-cylinder-powered two-door sedans were simply an experiment for the WSP. The WSP had used V-8-powered vehicles since the patrol's first panel trucks in 1933. The six-cylinder Fords were reported to be reliable, but not fast. The experiment was short-lived. For 1952, the WSP returned to V-8-powered Fords.

Notice the unique color scheme of the Washington State Patrol's 1951 Ford Deluxe. The black portion of the black-and-white color scheme includes more than just the trunk lid, extending all the way to the top of the fenders. The WSP was among the first agencies to try the new 1951 two-speed automatic, but not until 1952. The Fordomatic was a torque-converter-based transmission with a three-speed planetary geartrain and a single-stage, three-element hydraulic torque converter. The Fordomatic was considered a two-speed because the automatic intermediate gear was used only for starting. The rear gear used with the Fordomatic transmission was the 3.31 to 1 instead of the 3.73 ratio.

This 1951 Plymouth Cambridge is a fully restored replica of the first official police car used by the St. Louis County (Missouri) Police. In 1955, the St. Louis County Police was formed after a change in the St. Louis County charter. In July 1955, the County Police assumed all law enforcement duties and responsibilities from the St. Louis County Sheriff. Prior to 1955, all sheriffs' deputies purchased their own cars and equipment. Once the change was made, all cars received the new door shield. During the first year of the department, formerly deputy-owned cars were marked with a county police door shield. This "Best Restored Police Car" trophy winner is cream in color, and sports twin A-pillar spotlights and a red rotating roof light. The door shield is a blue triangle with a red border and white letters.

The Michigan State Police owned this jet-black 1951 Chevrolet Styleline Special. The two-door sedan has a gold door shield and a gold V-shaped stripe that runs from the rear tire gravel guard up the door and across the hood to the hood ornament. Other gold lettering included the term "State Police" on the leading edge of the roof and on the trunk lid. Special cop gear included the roof-mounted combination red light and mechanical siren and the twin A-pillar, clear-lens spotlights. On the hood is the trademark of the Michigan State Police, the stop sign that is still used almost 50 years later. By the early 1950s, Chevrolet's 92-horsepower, 216-ci overhead-valve six gave almost the same performance as Ford's 100-horsepower, 239-ci flathead V-8.

Pictured is a black-and-white 1951 Plymouth Cambridge. This generically marked four-door sedan has a red roof rotator and fender-mounted combination red light and mechanical siren. Plymouth was one of the Low-Priced Three, which also included Ford and Chevrolet. The Plymouth drivetrain was a 97-horsepower, 218-ci one-barrel flathead six. Plymouth would not offer an overhead-valve engine until the V-8 in 1955. The six would not get overhead valves until 1960. The 1951 Plymouth had a 118.5-inch wheelbase and the four-door sedan tipped the scales at 3,104 pounds.

The 1951 Chevrolet Deluxe pictured is a replica of the first police car used by the Haysville (Kansas) Police. The original 1951 HPD Chevrolet was owned by the police chief and was later purchased by the city. The Deluxe was the top trim level for 1951 while the Special was the base trim level. The four-door Deluxe sedan weighed 3,150 pounds. This was quite a bit of weight for a six-cylinder to push, even if the six had overhead valves. This Chevrolet is bright green with a fender-mounted combination red light and mechanical siren.

This 1952 Pontiac Chieftain served the citizens of Nassau County, New York. This particular patrol car was used by the 5th Precinct. Nassau County Police cruisers at the time were deep blue with orange wheels. The car number and the lettering on the roof and doors are orange. The roof-mounted light is a red, four-way flasher that does not rotate. This 120-inch wheelbase Pontiac was powered by a 118-horsepower, 268-ci flathead eight-cylinder engine. Pontiac police cars did not have over-head-valve V-8 engines until 1955.

Notice all the chrome on the front end of this 1952 Macomb County (Michigan) Sheriff Chevrolet Deluxe. Added to this mas-sive chrome bumper is an additional twin chrome pusher bar with a cross-link that runs from bumper tip to bumper tip. In the 1950s, it was extremely common to bolt emergency lights, such as these two red flashers, to the front bumper. On the topic of bright work, it's interesting to note the trim that came with the upscale Deluxe option. It included gravel guards on the front fender and oversize gravel guards on the rear fenders. Very fancy!

Restored as a Macomb County (Michigan) Sheriff's cruiser, this 1952 Chevrolet Deluxe won "Best Restored Chevrolet Police Car". Macomb County lies just north and east of Detroit. The cruiser is jet-black with a red roof rotator and red, bumper-mounted flashers. A period-correct mechanical siren is bolted to the front fender. Gold lettering appears on the doors and the leading edge of the roof. A dri-ver-side spotlight and a whip antenna complete the external cop gear. The 1952 Chevrolet ran on a 115-inch wheelbase. Note the "teeth" in the grille!

This 1952 Chevrolet Styleline Special bears the markings of the San Ramon (California) Police. San Ramon is east of Oakland near Mount Diablo. By 1952, the Chevrolet 92-horsepower, 216-ci overhead-valve six had almost closed the performance gap with the Ford 110-horsepower, 239-ci flathead V-8. The six-cylinder Chevrolet reached 60 miles per hour in 20.5 seconds, matching the V-8-powered Ford! The Chevrolet had a top speed of 81 miles per hour, which was insultingly close to the Ford top speed of 86 miles per hour. Of course, the Mercury-based 255-ci "Law Enforcement" V-8 used in many Ford police cars had better performance. Nonetheless, the Chevrolet six made for a credible, urban police cruiser.

The Los Angeles Police Department operated this 1952 Ford Mainline. Note the pair of LAPD's famous "soup-can" or "tunnel" lights on the roof. These were continuous-burning red to the front and flashing amber to the rear. Also note the electro-mechanical, roof-mounted siren. For half a century, LAPD cruisers were marked on the door with a city seal, the word "Police," and a unit number. Note the "octagonal E" license plate indicating the car is exempt from taxes because it is owned by a city or county. The state-owned cars have the "E" inside a diamond. The Mainline LAPD squad car is powered by either the 255-ci Law Enforcement V-8 or a 239-ci V-8, which was now rated at 110 horsepower.

Parked in front of City Hall is a 1952 Los Angeles Police Ford Mainline. This four-door sedan has all the doors painted white, but the roof is still black. By 1960, the roof would be painted white. This LAPD cruiser was based on a 115-inch wheelbase, a 1-inch increase from 1951. In 1952, Ford released its new overhead-valve six-cylinder engine rated at 101 horsepower. To keep pace, the 239-ci flathead V-8, which powered this LAPD unit, was upped from 100 to 110 horsepower. This extra horsepower came from an increase in compression. Even then, the old flathead V-8 had completely lost its competitive edge over the six-cylinder engines of Chevy and Plymouth.

The Chicago Park District Police used this 1952 Ford Ranch Wagon. The Ranch Wagon was based on the two-door Mainline. The Park District Police merged with the city police in 1959. This police wagon is all-black with a red rotating roof light and a gold-on-black six-point star. The lettering inside the star outline reads, "Police, Chicago Park District." Wagons generally had the highest numeric axle ratios and the largest tires. The 1952 model year offered a one-piece windshield on a Ford for the first time. This was one year ahead of Chevrolet and Plymouth.

This fully restored and modernized 1952 Ford Crestline marked as a Fontana (California) Police unit, was one of the vehicles used during the *Dragnet* T.V. series in the 1950s. The original series, starring Jack Webb as LAPD sergeant Joe Friday, aired from January 1952 through September 1959. *Dragnet* was one of the most successful police dramas in television history. *Dragnet* actually began on the radio in 1949 and made a return to television in January 1967. The revival, known alternatively as *Dragnet, Dragnet '67*, and *Badge 714* ran through September 1970. *Badge 714* used by Webb on the *Dragnet* series is now on display at the LAPD Academy.

Restored with the markings of the Fontana (California) Police, this 1952 Ford Crestline four-door sedan has two white doors against a gloss-black body. Notice the "Exempt" license plate used on city and county police cars, which was characteristic of the time. In 1952, Ford released its very first overhead-valve engine, the 215-ci six rated at 101 horsepower. This replaced the 95-horsepower, 226-ci flathead six. The Ford six had overhead valves two years before the Ford V-8. The new six had a larger bore and shorter stroke than the old six. This cruiser, however, has the 239-ci flathead V-8 teamed with a three-speed stick.

The Washington State Patrol operated this 1952 Ford Mainline. This was the first year for the black-over-white color scheme with the scallop-trimmed front fenders. New for 1952, the wheelbase on the full-size Ford was bumped from 114 inches to 115 inches. It would remain at 115 inches just through 1954 and increase to 115.5 inches for 1955 and 1956. This WSP Mainline was powered by the 125-horsepower, 255-ci V-8.

The look on this Indiana State Police trooper's face, and the pose he has struck beside his 1952 Pontiac Chieftain, indicate an imminent altercation. The Pontiac Chieftain in 1952 was built on a 120-inch wheelbase. This was quite long for the time, considering the Ford and the Chevrolet used a 115-inch wheelbase and the Plymouth was built on a 118.5-inch chassis. Pontiac used two engines in 1952, with two different horsepower ratings each. One was the 100-horsepower, 239-ci flathead six, which was rated at 102 horsepower when teamed with a Hydra-Matic transmission. The other was the 118-horsepower, 268-ci flathead in-line eight, rated at 122 horsepower when teamed with an automatic.

This 1953 Chevrolet One Fifty was on-duty with the Indianapolis (Indiana) Police. The black cruiser has a wide white stripe, which wraps around the front of the hood and goes all the way back around the trunk. It's an unusual twist on the old black-and-white theme. This squad car has red flashers and a roof-mounted mechanical siren. The door shield has a medium-blue background. Like all other Chevrolet police cars in 1953, this city unit is powered by the 235-ci overhead-valve six, producing 108 horsepower. The 216-ci six was discontinued. New for 1953 Chevrolets was a curved, one-piece windshield.

The Georgia State Patrol owned this 1953 Ford Mainline. Note the bold orange letters "Georgia State Patrol" two places on the door. A combination red light and mechanical siren top this black, two-door sedan. The fender emblem reads "V-8," which always meant, on a state police or highway patrol cruiser, that it was the 255-ci V-8. For 1953, the 255-ci Interceptor was once again rated at 125 horsepower. This Mercury engine was also known as a "Law Enforcement" V-8 but never as a Mercury V-8. The Georgia State Patrol was founded in 1937.

Pictured is a 1953 Ford Mainline, a replica of the cars used by the Nevada Highway Patrol. Despite the need to stay competitive with Chevrolet in 1954, nearly all changes at Ford were placed on hold in order to devote time to the totally new overhead-valve V-8. This NHP four-door sedan sports a black hood, roof, and trunk over a cream body with a gold and blue seven-point star door shield. Emergency lights include a red driver-side spotlight and red "tunnel" light on the roof. The NHP also used two-door Fords. The engine emblem on the fender indicates a V-8 drivetrain.

Note the trunk-mounted star and lettering in the rear-quarter view of this 1953 Nevada Highway Patrol Ford Mainline. The 1953 Fords, like the 1952s, were built on a 115-inch platform. Ford police-package cars were as long as 121 inches from 1969 to 1978. Mercury police-package cruisers would hit 124 inches. Notice the roof-mounted emergency light. It produces a red signal to both the front and rear. This four-door cruiser has dual-side, A-pillar spotlights. One has a red lens, while the other is clear. Also note the whip antenna.

This 1953 Ford Mainline Nevada Highway Patrol four-door sedan does not have package tray lights, but the roof-mounted red flasher is more than obvious. The trunk has the same gold and blue seven-point star as appears on the doors. The trunk lid clearly identifies the police department. It also clearly indicates what transmission was used. In 1953, Fords were available with a three-speed stick, three-speed Overdrive or two-speed Fordomatic. This cruiser has the Overdrive, which means the rear gears were either 3.90 or 4.10 to 1. Teamed with a powerful V-8, the Overdrive was the hot ticket.

This 1953 Ford replica police car is built around the upscale Customline option. The base trim level was the Mainline. Both versions were available with Ford's police package. This four-door cruiser is marked as a Los Altos (California) Police unit. Since it does not have a fender emblem, this Ford is probably powered by the 101-horsepower, 215-ci overhead-valve six. With a three-speed Overdrive and 3.90 to 1 rear gears, this 3,370-pound Ford reached 60 miles per hour in 19.5 seconds. That was 1 full second quicker than the Ford powered by the 110-horsepower, 239-ci flathead V-8 using the same transmission and rear-axle ratio. The top speed on the overhead-valve six-powered Ford was 86.3 miles per hour. That was within a half mile per hour of the top end of the V-8-powered Ford.

This generically marked 1953 Ford Mainline was originally used by the New Hampshire State Police. Oddly, this two-door cruiser is powered by the 101-horsepower, 215-ci overhead-valve six. Yes, this engine was as fast as the 110-horsepower, 239-ci flathead V-8, but most state police and highway patrols ran the 125-horsepower, 255-ci flathead V-8. Drivetrains in 1953 included the three-speed stick with 3.90 or 4.10 rear gears, the three-speed Overdrive with 3.90 or 4.10 gears, and the two-speed Fordomatic with 3.31 or 3.54 rear gears. This was the last year for the flathead V-8 in either displacement. Introduced in 1932, the 229-ci engine had grown to 255 ci and the horsepower had almost doubled from its 65-horsepower starting point.

This all-black, two-door 1953 Chevrolet One Fifty was used by the Milwaukee (Wisconsin) Police. The markings are simply the word, "Police," on each door. Emergency gear includes an A-pillar spotlight and a combination red light and mechanical siren mounted on the roof. For 1953, Chevrolet dropped the names Styleline and Fleetline. The new series was the Special 150, which everyone called simply One Fifty, and the Deluxe 210, called again just Two Ten. For 1953, the name Bel Air would be used with the top of the line trim level. Cops would eventually drive Bel Air police cars as this nameplate was used with lower trim levels in the future. The Bel Air name would be used through 1975.

The 1953 Chevrolets could be identified by three "teeth" in the grille instead of five found on the 1952 and 1954 models. This 1953 Two Ten was the midprice trim level between the One Fifty and the Bel Air. The Missouri State Highway Patrol was known for using fancier cars and upscale trim levels. This was the first year for a one-piece curved windshield on the Chevrolet. Fords received a one-piece windshield in 1952 while Plymouth had a curved windshield in 1953.

This 1953 Chevrolet Two Ten is on display at the Missouri State Highway Patrol Museum on the Academy grounds in Jefferson City. The Missouri State Highway Patrol was formed in 1931. The Two Ten is identified by the body-long midlevel chrome strips, chrome rocker panel strips, and chrome rear-fender gravel guards. The One Ten had none of this brightwork. A large gold, blue, and gray door shield identifies this MSHP Two Ten. These shields were first used in 1948. The same basic shield is still used in the late 1990s, except that it is smaller in size. Note the combination red light and mechanical siren. This combination unit has a red light facing both forward and rearward.

The Iowa Highway Patrol used this 1953 Chevrolet Two Ten. The tan, slick-top two-door had a red-lens spotlight and a rear-facing amber flasher mounted on the package tray. The 1953 Chevrolet was built on a 115-inch wheelbase. This basic platform was used from 1949 through 1957. Options in 1953 included a radio, heater/defroster, whitewall tires, turn signals, backup lights, and sun visors. This was the first year Chevrolet offered power steering. Ford also offered power steering in 1953 but so late in the model year that no police car came equipped with the option. However, power steering would not become popular among cops until the 1960s. In fact, the Los Angeles Police did not adopt power steering until 1976.

A Wyoming Highway Patrol trooper stands proudly with his 1953 Chevrolet Two Ten. This two-door cruiser is white with a black roof and a black "V" down the hood. This same basic door shield with a bison was used through the 1970s. This cruiser has a red roof light. In 1953, Chevrolet released a brand-new Blue Flame Six. For the first time, aluminum pistons were used instead of cast iron. In addition, the six had a fully pressurized lubrication system instead of "splash" lubrication. The compression ratio was bumped from 6.7 to 1 to 7.1 to 1 for three-speed stick engines, and to 7.5 to 1 for two-speed Powerglide engines. The 235-ci six produced 108 horsepower and 115 horsepower respectively.

At a Missouri zone office and weigh station, this sergeant with Troop D of the Missouri State Highway Patrol posed with his 1953 Chevrolet Two Ten. The jet-black cruiser has a gold, blue, and gray door shield. Powered by the 108-horsepower, 235-ci overhead-valve six, this Chevrolet was the fastest vehicle purchased by the MSHP up until that time. It had a top speed of nearly 100 miles per hour. The 216-ci six was no longer available for 1953. The larger 235-ci six was used with both three-speed stick and two-speed Powerglide transmissions. This was the first year for aluminum pistons on the Blue Flame Six.

The trunk graphics on this 1953 Ford Mainline with the Iowa Highway Patrol are very unique. The Iowa Highway Patrol started a campaign to promote safe driving to Hawkeye State motorists. This cruiser reminded all those who viewed it: "To Date, 373 Killed!" These graphics were hand-painted by this IHP trooper under the careful, perhaps critical, eye of his sergeant. Note the large amber flasher mounted on the driver's side of the package tray. Research found that amber was more visible at greater distances than either red or blue.

A combination of the traditional 1950s black-and-white color scheme along with graphics from Chevrolet's 1990s police test vehicles adorn this 1954 Chevrolet One Fifty two-door. The door shield reads, "Chevrolet Police Vehicles." Note the hood-mounted "pull-over" sign. On the roof, this car has a modern siren but a vintage red rotator. In 1954, the power of the Blue Flame Six used with the Powerglide was boosted to 125 horsepower thanks to a high-lift cam. The six used with the three-speed stick was increased to 115 horsepower, thanks to higher compression.

The Grant's Pass Police used this 1954 Ford Customline. Grant's Pass is in the southwest part of Oregon on Interstate 5 near Medford. This black-and-white four-door sedan sports a fender-mounted combination red light and mechanical siren to go with the roof-mounted red rotator. The rear window-mounted, rear-facing traffic radar antenna is an especially nice addition to this restoration. Ford released two new overhead-valve engines for 1954. One was a Ford-marque 239-ci overhead-valve V-8. The other was a Mercury-marque 256-ci overhead-valve V-8. The Mercury engine was once again available in the Ford police car. With the Customline model, the V-8 emblem was on the front fender while the model script was on the rear fender.

The Sacramento, California, Police used this 1954 Ford Main-line. This outstanding restoration is accurate and complete right down to the "octagonal E" license plate. The lack of an engine emblem on the front fender means this four-door sedan was powered by the 223-ci six, which was new for 1954. The old 215-ci six was bored and stroked to displace 223 ci. The power was boosted from 101 horsepower to 115 horsepower. The new 115-horsepower Ford six produced less power than the 125-horsepower Chevy six used with the two-speed Powerglide, but it matched the power of the Chevy six used with the three-speed stick. And it was more powerful than the 100-horsepower six used by Plymouth.

The Tennessee Highway Patrol operated this 1954 Ford. The black-over-cream two-door sedan has a red roof rotator. The typical look of most police cars from the mid-1950s through the late 1960s included a single roof rotator, an under-hood siren, two-tone paint, and a door shield. New on 1954 Fords were the "double-drop" frame, ball-joint front suspension, variable rate rear leaf springs, and dual servo brakes. This was the first use of a ball-joint front suspension by Ford. The change allowed the engine to sit lower in the chassis, resulting in better handling. On the hills and hollows of the Volunteer State, better handling was much more important than more horsepower!

The life of a police cruiser can be rough. This 1954 Louisiana State Police Ford Mainline is missing a headlight bezel and has a dented fender. New for 1954, the Fords received a longer 115.5-inch platform based on the new double-drop frame. The police package was available on the Mainline and Customline models. The two-speed Fordomatic transmission was available with the police package. However, most cops preferred the three-speed stick. The three-speed stick was less expensive to purchase and maintain than the automatic.

The Chicago Police used this 1954 Ford Mainline. All-black cars with white letters were used through 1955. In 1956, the roof color changed from black to white. However, the door lettering remained unchanged and stayed that way through 1959. In 1960, CPD adopted white-over-light-blue squad cars and phased in the use of blue emergency lights. Previously, up through 1959, The Windy City cops used red emergency lights. This CPD two-door sedan is powered by one of the two new overhead-valve V-8s. The V-8 emblem and model emblem were both on the front fender behind the wheelwell on the Mainline model. The V-8 emblem on the Customline was in front of the wheelwell, while the script was on the rear fender.

The South Carolina Highway Patrol operated this 1954 Ford Mainline. The two-door cruiser is marked with a winged South Carolina state seal as the door shield. This same shield was still used nearly 40 years later! Note the lettering on the hood. The SCHP put the words "Hi-way Patrol" on its cars using the slang spelling, which was very unusual. With the exception of the flat-head V-8 in 1932 and the special-service-package Mustang in 1982, the release of the overhead-valve V-8 was the biggest news in Ford police car history.

The California Highway Patrol drove the V-8-powered Ford Mainline in 1954, just like every other police department. The two-door cruiser is black with white doors. The CHP continued to paint the front door white even when four-door sedans were used. The black roof, however, became white by 1961. This CHP car has the all-gold seven-point star but no door lettering. Door lettering was not used until 1959. This cruiser has a red-lens spotlight and an amber flashing light. The powertrain is a 160-horsepower, 256-ci Mercury-marque V-8. The overhead-valve V-8 was originally developed for the 1952 Lincoln. The 256-ci engine was the first Ford police V-8 to use a four-barrel carburetor.

This beautifully restored 1954 Ford Customline bears the clear markings of the Lisle (Illinois) Police. This white-over-black four-door sedan has a red rotator and twin red A-pillar spotlights. In 1954, the police packages were based on the 115.5-inch wheel-base Mainline and upscale Customline. Police powertrains included the 115-horsepower, 223-ci one-barrel six; the 130-horsepower, 239-ci two-barrel V-8; and the 160-horsepower, 256-ci four-barrel V-8. The overhead-valve 130-horsepower, 239-ci V-8 teamed with the three-speed stick pushed the police Ford from 0 to 60 miles per hour in 16 seconds and had a top speed of 96 miles per hour.

Note the gold, five-point star on this restored 1954 Ford Mainline bearing the markings of the Dade County (Florida) Sheriff's Department. The four-door cruiser is copper-brown and white. Notice that just part of the rear door and part of the rear fender are painted white, as is the trunk lid. The white wheels make an attractive contrast to the brown body color. Ford's new 239-ci overhead-valve V-8 had the same displacement as the old 239-ci flathead V-8. However, the new engine had a much larger diameter bore and a much shorter piston stroke. The old flathead V-8 lost 30 percent of its theoretical power to friction. The new overhead-valve V-8 lost just 18 percent.

The Washington State Patrol used this 1954 Ford Mainline. The drivetrain was a 256-ci "Interceptor" Mercury V-8 teamed with a three-speed stick. The old 255-ci flathead V-8 produced 125 horsepower in its final year. The new 256-ci overhead-valve V-8 produced 160 horsepower. One central Washington trooper was reported as saying, "That car would go faster than I wanted to drive it." A red spotlight and an underhood siren were the only warning equipment used on these WSP Fords. The black-over-white color scheme with the scallop-trimmed front fenders was used from 1952 to 1954. WSP troopers referred to these cars as Holsteins. Nonetheless, they were fast.

Indiana State Police troopers stand next to their 1954 Ford Mainlines during inspection. The ISP cruiser was jet-black with a long, gold stripe running from the headlight bezel to the rear fender gravel shield. The 256-ci overhead-valve V-8 powered these cruisers. The overhead-valve engine was easier to cast than the flathead engine, requiring only 14 sand cores compared to 29 sand cores for the flathead V-8. While the flathead V-8 had more power than the competition, it also had serious design problems. The flathead had two water pumps, two thermostats, and four main radiator hoses. If any one of these failed, the engine overheated. The new 1954 V-8 had a much more reliable cooling system.

With some apparent fanfare, this sergeant with the Missouri State Highway Patrol is shown handing over the keys to this 1954 Ford Customline. The MSHP Ford has a bi-directional red light and mechanical siren mounted on the roof. The cruiser is powered by the 160-horsepower, 256-ci four-barrel Y-block V-8. This was Ford's first police engine with a four-barrel carburetor. The new overhead-valve engine had a larger bore and shorter stroke than the old flathead. A larger bore allowed larger intake and larger exhaust valves. The overhead-valve head was also stiffer. The flathead head required 24 bolts to secure it to the block, while the overhead-valve head needed only 10 head bolts.

The Kaiser automobile was produced in the United States from 1947 through 1955. This 1954 Kaiser Manhattan was used by the Ohio State Highway Patrol. Since all Manhattans in 1954 and 1955 were supercharged, it can be assumed that this two-door cruiser was used on the Ohio Turnpike. The 1954 Kaiser had a 226-ci flathead six engine. The naturally aspirated version produced 118 horsepower, while the supercharged version pumped out 140 horsepower. The supercharged version was more exotic than truly powerful, since the 256-ci overhead-valve Mercury V-8 used in the Ford produced 160 horsepower. Kaiser cars were produced at the Willys plant in Toledo, Ohio.

This striking 1954 Packard Cavalier is decorated as the chief's car with Sparks (Nevada) Fire. The two-door hardtop is, of course, red with a red roof rotator. Also note the twin red lenses, which replaced the spinners in the grille. This Cavalier and the Patrician were built on a 127-inch wheelbase, while the Clipper and Packard 8 used a 122-inch wheelbase. The Cavalier was the lowest-priced true member of the Packard line. Yet it used the five-bearing, 327-ci flathead eight from the Clipper line. This four-barrel 327-ci engine was rated at 185 horsepower. The 359-ci Packard-line engine had nine main bearings and 212 horsepower.

Pictured is the famous 1954 1/2 Hudson Hornet. The 124-inch-wheelbase four-door sedan is a former sheriff's car, and it has a much easier life than beat patrol, namely Hollywood! The Hudson Special in LAPD trim is on the set of the made-for-T.V. movie, *Fallen Angels*. A midyear model, the Hornet Special used the Hornet engine and exterior trim but the lower trim level interior from the Super Wasp. The engine was a 160-horsepower, 308-ci flathead six. In late 1953, Hudson merged with Nash and production of the vehicles moved from Detroit to Kenosha, Wisconsin. The Hornet Special was the last Detroit-built Hudson.

The South Bend (Indiana) Police used this 1954 Studebaker Champion. Studebakers were made in South Bend, Los Angeles, and Ontario, Canada. The entry-level Champion series had three trim versions: Custom, Deluxe, and Regal. All used a 116.5-inch wheelbase in sedan form. This SBPD four-door sedan is black with a gold-outlined shield and gold lettering and numbers. The Champion engine was an 85-horsepower, 170-ci flathead six. Note the bumper-mounted red lights. In 1954, Studebaker merged with Packard to become Studebaker-Packard Corp.

Chapter Four

1955-1959

The 1955 model year was the year of the Chevrolet small-block V-8. Automotive historians still write about the Chevy small block. In 1996, when technical writers for *Ward's Auto World*, *Automotive Industries*, *AutoWeek*, and *Automotive News* looked back over the 100 years of the automobile, the powerplants identified as significant were the Ford flathead V-8, the Oldsmobile overhead-valve Rocket V-8, and the Chevy small-block V-8.

The Chevy small block was eventually bored and stroked into 11 different engines—262, 265 (original), 265 (L99), 267, 283, 302, 305, 307, 327, 350, and 400. The 1955 small-block V-8 was the first Chevrolet engine to use a four-barrel carburetor. Chevy offered the "plus power package," better known as the "power pack," with an imposing 180 horsepower. While this power pack is well known among Chevy enthusiasts, it is less well known than the "plus power package," which was originally released as a police-car-only option.

During the year, Chevrolet also released its first police package for the two-door and four-door One Fifty. The police

package required a long lead time and was considered a special order, but it was a real police package. A year later, in 1956, Chevy introduced its Bowtie police package, which required a standard car-production lead time. Meanwhile, totally unnoticed, Ford introduced its 272-ci Ford Y-block and 292-ci Mercury Y-block engines. These engines produced as much as 188 horsepower. Late in the model year, the company released a new High Output (HO) version producing 205 horsepower and ever since has used the "HO" term for its hottest engines. Dodge Division entered the police-car business with a formal police package for its Coronet in 1956. Studebaker Motors followed suit with its Champion police package.

The Dodge Coronet with police package had a wide variety of engine options. The early choice of most police departments was the "230" Pursuit engine, a 315-ci polysphere-head V-8 with a single four-barrel carburetor producing 230 horsepower. The hot choice was the 315-ci Hemi-head "D-500" V-8, a single four-barrel, and a rating of 260 horsepower. Dodge had a longer wheelbase

This 1955 Chevrolet Bel Air is a Best-Of-Show winner at a national police-car convention. While it bears the gold five-point star of a generic sheriff's department, it was carefully restored to be period-correct. In the mid-1950s, it was common for the smaller city police and county sheriffs' departments to drive an all-black cruiser with simply a red rotator, minimal door markings, and an under-hood siren. For 1955, the Chevrolet was totally redesigned. Many car buffs judge how unique any one model year is, based on the number of new parts from the previous year. The 1955 Chevrolet was made up of roughly 4,500 different parts. Of these, 3,825 were new for 1955 and different from 1954.

Ziv Television Productions made every effort to be technically correct with the props used during the filming of *Highway Patrol*. The 21-50 call sign on the trunk lid and hood of this 1955 Buick Special was actually the ID number of then-CHP Commissioner Bernard Caldwell. The cap badges on the traditional soft cap were authentic CHP pieces. And for the first two years of filming, the uniforms were authentic right down to the shoulder patch. The Roadmaster 322-ci, four-barrel V-8 rated at 236 horsepower, powered these 1955 Buick Specials, which ruled the highways with the highest level of performance available on a police budget.

(120 inches) than Ford (115.5 inches) and Chevrolet (115 inches), which gave it better stability at high speeds, at least theoretically.

Of the three available true police cars, Dodge attained instant success. It was fabled as the beginning of the line of enforcement vehicles that absolutely defined the police pursuit car. Ford would continue to be popular with city and county police departments, and even with some state patrols. However, when it came to unbridled performance, Dodge was the definitive choice. After the release of the Dodge police package and the D-500 engine, Buick was simply not heard of again! For 1957, Chevrolet pulled the covers off of the 283-ci V-8 small block, which was a bored-out 265-ci V-8. The 283-ci police engine was available with up to 220 horsepower. In 1957 Chevrolet also introduced its Turboglide, and the variable ratio transmission. Unfortunately, the Turboglide was complex, prone to fail, and hard to repair, and the problematic Hill Retarder selector gave the Turboglide a reputation as a two-speed; thus, it was dropped by 1961.

Ford was in the middle of a horsepower race with Chevrolet during the 1957 model year, and its 312-ci Y-block V-8 led the charge, fitted with dual four-barrel carbs and rated at 270 horsepower. It was the first, and last, Ford police engine to use dual quads. Dodge, for 1957, simply cranked out more of the horsepower for which it was legendary. Its 325-ci "Super D-500" Hemi-head V-8 with dual Carter four-barrel carbs and dual exhausts produced 310 horsepower. The swept-wing, 1957 Dodge Pursuits won the horsepower race. The Super D-500 was the most powerful engine available on any police car. The introduction of a formal police package for the Plymouth Savoy was, perhaps, the most significant development of 1957. Plymouth used its experience in the rough and tumble taxicab business to build a dependable and durable police car. While Dodge emphasized its performance image to market the Coronet to cops, Ply-

mouth capitalized on its fleet image. Dodge and Plymouth incorporated a revolutionary torsion bar front suspension system and the world's most reliable automatic transmission, the three-speed TorqueFlite. Unlike the other awkward automatic transmissions developed in the 1950s, the TorqueFlite was excellent to the point of being legendary. Interestingly, the TorqueFlite used push-button gear selectors from 1957 through 1964.

By 1958, every company that wanted to enter the police-car market had developed a specially engineered police package. All the automakers had huge new engines to brag about for their police cars. Ford had its new FE-series big-block V-8s and a new three-speed Cruise-O-Matic automatic transmission. Available in 332-ci, 352-ci, and 361-ci displacements, the FE (Ford-Edsel) series of engines would eventually include the 390-ci, 427-ci, and 428-ci police engines.

Meanwhile, Chevrolet introduced its W-block 348-ci V-8, which featured the wedge for combustion chambers that were built into the block instead of the heads. The 348-ci engine was available with both four-barrel and three two-barrel carburetion systems. The even-more-famous 409-ci V-8, of Super Stock fame, was a W-block engine. For the record, the fuel-injected, 283-ci V-8 was an officially listed police engine in 1958, which produced the same 250 horsepower as the four-barrel-equipped 348-ci V-8.

Dodge and Plymouth had as much big-block enthusiasm as Ford and Chevrolet. The 350-ci B-engine for Plymouth and a 361-ci size for Dodge were new for 1958. As a bit of an embarrassment, the dual-quad 350-ci Plymouth was considerably faster than the more prestigious, dual-quad 361-ci Dodge.

The 1958 model year was the year of 300 horsepower. All of the serious players in the police-car market hit this level. At the time, achieving 300 horsepower was so significant that Chrysler

The Chief of the Manteca (California) Police is shown receiving the keys to a brand-new 1955 Ford Mainline. This black four-door sedan has white front doors and a gold seven-point star. The roof has twin red lights and a public address system speaker. The Mainline was the base trim level in 1955. For the first time, the name "Crown Victoria" was used to describe an upscale option within the Fairlane series. The circular engine emblem in front of the wheelwell indicates that this Manteca cruiser is powered by a six instead of a V-8. The only six-cylinder engine was the 120 horsepower, 223-ci one-barrel six.

The 1955 model year was as big for Chevrolet as the 1954 model year had been for Ford. For Chevy-loving cops it was even bigger. Ford had had a V-8 since 1932, while Chevrolet had not had one since 1919. In 1955, Chevrolet introduced its famous 265-ci, overhead-valve, small-block V-8. This was the first Chevrolet V-8 since the ill-fated and poorly-received 288-ci overhead-valve V-8, circa 1917. The new Chevy small-block V-8, in one form or another, would power Chevrolet police or special-service-package cars through at least 1999. During that time, small-block V-8s would be available in 11 different engine sizes. This 1955 One Fifty is marked as a Western Springs (Illinois) Police unit.

named an entire series of cars to flaunt the fact: the 1955 Chrysler 300. Dodge hit 310 horsepower with its 325-ci eight-barrel V-8 in 1957. Buick, Mercury, Oldsmobile, and Pontiac also achieved 300 horsepower in 1957. Chevrolet extracted 315 horsepower from its 348-ci six-barrel V-8, Ford cranked out 303 horsepower with its 361-ci four-barrel V-8, and Plymouth used its 350-ci eight-barrel V-8 to reach 305 horsepower.

In 1959, Ford maintained clear control of the police market and was the choice of over 35 state police and highway patrol departments. Among city police and county sheriff's departments, Ford enjoyed a 70-percent market share. The horsepower race that fueled larger engines and multiple carburetors was over. Ford introduced a longer wheelbase for the Custom 300 and Fairlane, and it was now 118 inches at a time where every inch closer to 122 inches made a big difference.

At the same time, Chevrolet had a longer 119-inch wheelbase for its Biscayne and Bel Air. Chevrolet joined its GM stablemates, Pontiac, Buick, and Oldsmobile, in the corporation-wide use of the now-famous B-body. This same B-body platform underwent a few changes to the now "big car" wheelbase, up to 121.5 inches in 1971 and down to 116 inches in 1977, but it would be used until Chevrolet withdrew from the police market after 1996. Meanwhile, in 1959, the Dodge Coronet Pursuit vehicle was available with the brand-new, 383-ci B-engine V-8, and it lasted until 1971 with a production that ran over 30 million engines. Dodge had discontinued what is now called the first generation "Hemi," which was a 315-ci V-8 in 1956 Dodge police cars and a 325-ci V-8 in 1957 and 1958. Interestingly, the first-generation Hemi was never available in Plymouth police cars.

Note the large amount of warning gear this generically marked 1955 Chevrolet Bel Air sports. The gear on this four-door black-and-white includes bumper-mounted red lights; a fender-mounted siren; twin A-pillar spotlights (the driver's side should actually have the red lens); a red, roof-mounted rotator; twin package tray lights; and a fender-mounted whip antenna. All of the cop gear on this Bel Air is legitimate for the period except for the siren, which appears to be electronic rather than electro-mechanical. Chevrolets received one-piece windshields in 1953, a year behind Ford. For 1955, Chevrolet got its first "wrap-around" windshields, the same year as Ford.

The 1955 Chevrolet, like this Two Ten, was as much of a hot rod among the cops as it was among the kids. The 265-ci two-barrel V-8 produced 162 horsepower. Even bigger news was the "plus power package," originally released as a police-only option. This was not available as a regular production option until the spring of 1955. Also known as the "power pack," it included a four-barrel carburetor, an intake manifold with larger ports, and dual exhaust. This boosted the output to 180 horsepower. The three-speed Overdrive was also new for 1955.

An especially well-restored police car, this 1955 Chevrolet Two Ten displays simply a red rotator, a driver-side spotlight, and a bumper-mounted whip antenna. This 1955 Bowtie is powered by the 123-horsepower, 235-ci six. While the transmission is the three-speed stick, this black-and-white has the 4.11 to 1 rear gears from the three-speed Overdrive for a bit more punch. In 1955, the Chevrolet trim levels were the low-priced One Fifty, the midpriced Two Ten, and the high-priced Bel Air. Chevrolet's first police package was based on the One Fifty and available on the Two Ten in both two-door and four-door versions.

The right door shield on this restored 1955 Chevrolet Two Ten says: "Protect and Preserve 55-56-57." While the 1955 Chevrolet kept the 115-inch wheelbase, the frame and suspension were greatly improved. In fact, the frame was 50 percent more rigid but 18 percent lighter. The chassis had a new ball-joint front suspension and lengthened rear leaf springs. The geometry of the coil-spring front suspension was changed to reduce nose-dives during hard braking. Chevrolet claimed the anti-dive A-arm geometry was an industry first. The Chevrolet used 11-inch drum brakes. *Motor Trend* magazine called the 1955 Chevrolet one of the year's best-handling vehicles.

The Idaho State Police drove the Chevrolet One Fifty in 1955. This was the first year for Chevrolet's official police package. It was based on the One Fifty in both two-door and four-door versions. The police package, however, was a long lead-time option. In 1956, the police package would be available with standard lead times. The 162 horsepower, 265-ci two-barrel V-8 pushed the police One Fifty to 60 miles per hour in 12.5 seconds. The 180-horsepower, 265-ci four-barrel V-8 reduced that to just 9.6 seconds. The 180-horsepower Chevrolet set quarter-mile and flying-mile acceleration records easily, beating the best from Ford and Plymouth.

This 1955 Ford Customline with the Lansing (Illinois) Police wins a trophy every time it is taken to a car show. The car is perfect from the red-and-clear rotator with a clear globe right down to the red-trim hubcaps and bias tires. The 1955 model year is the only year red-centered hubcaps were used. Like most Ford police cars, this four-door sedan is packing a 188-horsepower, 292-ci, four-barrel V-8. The 292-ci V-8 was a bored-and-stroked version of the 1954 vintage 256-ci V-8. Late in the 1955 model year, Ford released its first High Output (HO) engine. This was a 205-horsepower version of the 292-ci V-8. Ford has used the "HO" term ever since.

The New York City Transit Authority Police used this solid-black 1955 Ford Mainliner. This four-door police sedan has white door lettering and a clear-lens spotlight, and that's it! A six-cylinder engine powers this cruiser, like it did most police cars in the Big Apple. This Mainliner had a 120-horsepower, 223-ci one-barrel six teamed with a three-speed stick. The six got a slight compression boost for 1955, which was good for 5 horsepower. The 120-horsepower rating might have been impressive in 1953. But by 1955, Ford started the horsepower race, which would end with dual quad engines that produced almost 1 horsepower per cubic inch!

These New York State Police troopers were lucky enough to have operated this 1955 Ford Mainline, which packed a 188-horsepower, 292-ci four-barrel V-8, Ford's most powerful police V-8. Actually, the Ford V-8 still held a horsepower advantage even though both Chevrolet and Plymouth had released overhead-valve, four-barrel V-8s. This NYSP cruiser has a black hood and roof over a white body. The words "State Police" appeared in white letters on the hood and in black letters on the trunk. The roof gear is a combination red light and mechanical siren. The markings include black letters and a state seal.

The Omaha (Nebraska) Shrine Provost Corps unit operated this 1955 Ford Customline. The cruiser has the traditional white-over-black color scheme with a red roof rotator. The Ford 272-ci two-barrel V-8 exactly matched the 162 horsepower produced by Chevrolet's much heralded 265-ci two-barrel V-8. The 188 horsepower from the Ford 292-ci four-barrel "Interceptor" V-8 had a higher rating than Chevrolet's 265-ci four-barrel "Power Pack" V-8 with 180 horsepower. Ford upped the ante late in the model year with a 205-horsepower, 292-ci High Output V-8. Ford police engines were advertised as having "trigger torque performance."

Pictured is a 1955 Ford Mainline restored as an Auburn (California) Police cruiser. Missing from the package are the emergency lights, the roof lights, and the red spotlight. There's also no amber package tray flasher. The red lights could be behind the grille, but that was simply not the "California" way. This cruiser does, however, show one of Ford's big advances for 1955, which was a wraparound windshield. Fords went to a one-piece, slightly curved, windshield in 1952. For 1955, the windshield wrapped around the body so far that the A-pillars were nearly vertical. This APD cruiser is powered by one of the new Ford V-8s.

The Iowa Highway Patrol drove the Ford Customline in 1955. The Ford police package was available for the Mainline and Customline in both two-door and four-door versions. The two-door Ranch Wagon and four-door Country Sedan station wagons were also available with the official police gear. This Hawkeye State cruiser is black with a black-on-yellow door shield. The powerplant is a 188-horsepower, 292-ci four-barrel V-8. This was a powerful engine for the era, but just a start. Horsepower ratings would increase every year through 1958. The less powerful 162-horsepower, 272-ci V-8 pushed the Ford through the quarter mile in 19.4 seconds at 74 miles per hour.

Notice the accurate restoration of the 1956 Dodge Coronet used by the California Highway Patrol. It is correct right down to the upscale and ultracollectible Dodge Lancer wheel covers. Some of the 260-horsepower CHP Coronets did use these exotic wheel covers. Note the clear-lens spotlight on the passenger's side and red-lens spot for the driver. This two-door cruiser is powered by the 260-horsepower, 315-ci four-barrel Hemi V-8. The Dodge Hemi was released in 1953. Displacing 241 ci and fitted with a two-barrel carburetor, the first Dodge Hemi produced 140 horsepower. The last of the first generation of Dodge Hemi engines in police cars was the 265-horsepower, 325-ci four-barrel V-8. This was a police-only option in 1958.

Calling in to headquarters, this CHP traffic officer operated this 1956 Dodge Coronet. Part of the first Dodges purchased in 1956, this two-door cruiser is powered by the 230-horsepower, 315-ci polysphere V-8. The 230-horsepower engine pushed the big Dodge to 79.6 miles per hour in the standing start mile. The 260-horsepower Hemi engine got the Dodge through the one-mile mark at an incredible 108 miles per hour! When released with the 230-horsepower engine, Dodge declared it had "the most powerful police car on the American road today." All of the Bonneville Salt Flats speed and endurance records were set with the 230-horsepower, polysphere-head V-8. Of course, these records were promptly broken by the 260-horsepower Hemi when it was released after the start of the model year.

This 1955 Buick Century has been carefully and accurately restored as a California Highway Patrol Enforcement-class vehicle. In 1954, Buick revived one of its old hot rod nameplates, the Century. In 1936, Buick had combined its smallest and lightest body with a Roadmaster engine. The result was one of the few production cars to be able to reach 100 miles per hour, thus the name Century. For 1954, Buick released the Century nameplate on the new, larger, 122-inch-wheelbase GM C-body used by the Buick Special. For 1954, the Century used the 195-horsepower, 322-ci Roadmaster engine. For 1955, now sporting four side "ventiports" for the first time, the Century had the 236-horsepower, 322-ci Roadmaster engine.

Notice this beautifully restored 1955 Oldsmobile 88 bearing the markings of the Morgan Hill (California) Police. This jet-black Olds has a gold, seven-point star and gold door lettering. The emergency lights include a red spotlight and a rear-facing, flashing amber light mounted on the package tray. With the legendary "Rocket V-8," this big Olds would have no problem with traffic enforcement duties. The standard engine was a 185-horsepower, 325-ci two-barrel V-8 while a 202-horsepower, four-barrel version of this engine was available. This four-door Olds 88 was built on a 122-inch wheelbase and tipped the scales at 3,865 pounds, quite a bit for a police car.

The Indiana State Police used this 1956 Dodge Coronet. Notice the twin public address system speakers on the roof. Those are not sirens. This ISP commission was powered by the 230-horsepower, 315-ci four-barrel V-8 bolted to a two-speed PowerFlite automatic with pushbutton controls. This was the first year for pushbutton transmission controls. These would be used through 1964. The 315-ci engine had semi-canted, "polysphere" overhead valves, hydraulic lifters, and a dual exhaust. Dodge called this vehicle the "230" Pursuit Car after the amazing 230 horsepower produced by the "Super Power Super Red Ram V-8."

This rear-quarter view of the 1956 CHP Dodge Coronet has three features that stand out. First, on the rear deck is a red flashing light mounted next to the amber flasher. Second, the crossed checkered flags on the trunk lid means that the D-500 260-horsepower 315-ci four-barrel Hemi powered this big, bad Dodge. Finally, notice the exotic Dodge Lancer full-dress wheel covers on this vintage Dodge. The police package was based on the 120-inch platform with a specially reinforced frame. The rest of the police package included heavy-duty engine, suspension, brake, and interior components. All police cars received the 12x2-1/2-inch drum brakes from the larger Chryslers.

The Cambrous Police Service in Alberta, Canada, used this 1956 Dodge Regent. In 1956 the police-package Dodge was available with three engines "recommended" for police use. These were the 230-horsepower, 315-ci four-barrel polysphere V-8; the 189-horsepower, 270-ci two-barrel V-8; and the 131-horsepower, 230-ci two-barrel flathead six. All of the V-8s had overhead valves. Two other engines were available if requested in police-package cars. These were the 218-horsepower, 315-ci two-barrel polysphere V-8 and the incredible 260-horsepower, 315-ci four-barrel Hemi D-500. Transmissions included the three-speed stick, three-speed Overdrive, and two-speed PowerFlite.

"They don't get away when you've got a Chevrolet" read the ads for the 1956 Chevrolet police car in *Law and Order* magazine. This sharp-looking, 1956 Chevrolet Two Ten was marked as an Ione (California) Police unit. The black-over-white color scheme following the Two Ten rear fender chrome strip is an especially attractive variation on the black-and-white theme. This cruiser also has the package tray rear flashers, true to California statute. For 1956, the Blue Flame Six was renamed the Blue Flame 140. The compression had been bumped from 7.5 to 8.0 to 1 and this increased the output to 140 horsepower. The same 235-ci six was used on both the two-speed Powerglide and three-speed stick for the first time.

A Royal Canadian Mounted Police constable stands at ease with his 1956 Chevrolet One Fifty. This two-door cruiser is black with white doors and a red roof rotator. On the roof is also a moveable spotlight. The crest of the RCMP is on the doors. Note the right front fender with a red "pull-over" light facing the driver being overtaken. As in 1955, the V-8-powered Chevrolets had a chrome "V" under the Chevrolet crest on the hood. This RCMP unit is powered by the 140-horsepower, 235-ci six.

This 1956 Ford Mainline is an extremely well-done replica of the first car used by the Harwood Heights (Illinois) Police. This northwest Chicago suburb was incorporated in 1947, but did not have a police department until 1956. This four-door cruiser was put together to commemorate the 50th anniversary of the village. This cruiser has twin clear-lens, fender-mounted spotlights and a red, roof-mounted rotating light. The color of the original HHPD car, incredibly enough, was light green with black letters. True to form, this HHPD replica is also light green. The cruiser is powered by the 173-horsepower, 272-ci two-barrel V-8 bolted to a three-speed stick.

For 1956, the Chevrolet police package was once again based on the low trim level One Fifty two-door and four-door sedans with a standard lead time. However, Chevrolet made it clear its police package was also available on the midlevel Two Ten sedans, like this Crazy Horse (South Dakota) Police unit. The delivery time was simply longer. This Crazy Horse Two Ten was powered by the 265-ci two-barrel V-8. A 162-horsepower version was used with the three-speed stick, while two-speed Powerglide cars received the 170 horsepower version. Power brakes were optional but only on the Two Ten and Bel Air. Late in the model year, the dual quad, 225-horsepower, 265-ci V-8 from the Corvette became available in police cars.

The Washington State Patrol used this 1956 Chevrolet One Fifty. In 1956, the WSP bought a mix of Fords and Chevrolets. Most of the Chevrolets had the three-speed stick, but a few came with the three-speed Overdrive. These cruisers were all powered by the 205-horsepower, 265-ci four-barrel V-8. The four-barrel small block was up 25 horsepower from 1955 and was very fast for its day. The three-speed car with 3.70 rear gears hit 60 miles per hour in just 8.5 seconds. That was faster than the 260-horsepower, Hemi-powered Dodges! The top speed of this sizzling Bowtie was 111 miles per hour. This WSP Chevrolet had an especially attractive blue paint scheme with a white accent that followed the chrome strip.

In 1956, the Missouri State Highway Patrol chose the Ford Customline. A sign in the MSHP Academy museum reads, "This 1956 Ford Interceptor was very popular with members of the Highway Patrol. It was stylish looking for the day and had a powerful engine. Not too many speeders outran troopers driving this vehicle." The 292-ci four-barrel V-8 rated at either 200 horsepower for the stick or 202 horsepower for the Fordomatic powered this two-door sedan. In 1956, over 70 percent of the state police and highway patrols drove police cars made by Ford. This cruiser is white with a combination red light and mechanical siren and twin fender-mounted spotlights.

The restoration on this 1956 Ford Fairlane marked as a Chaptico (Maryland) Sheriff's unit was beautifully done. In 1956, Ford had three trim levels: the low-level Mainline, the midrange Customline, and the high-priced Fairlane. The police package was typically based on the lowest trim level, regardless of year, make or model. However, the middle and top trim lines were often available if requested with the police package. These upscale trim lines were typically used on the cars of the chief, sheriff, chief deputy, superintendent, or commissioner. The red engine emblem on the front fenders means this cruiser is powered by one of the 312-ci "Thunderbird Special" V-8s.

This 1956 Ford Fairlane is marked as a Reno (Nevada) Police cruiser. The white roof and white doors over a black body are period-correct. So are the red roof rotator and the gold fender and trunk lettering. However, this 1950s sedan is wearing a 1990s door shield. This shield is a multicolored gold and blue seven-point star. The original was a black on gold seven-point star with the word "Police" extending all the way across the star. This cruiser is nicely restored; however, Reno PD did not run with full-dress wheel covers, and no self-respecting police department used whitewall tires. This is the upscale Fairlane model but without all of the Fairlane chrome trim.

This 1956 Ford Mainline has the exact look of a California cop car from the 1950s. This Campbell (California) Police cruiser has a black body with a white door. It has twin forward-facing, nonflashing red roof lights. The fender-mounted spotlight has a clear lens. The gold door shield is a true shield. It has the shape of the badge worn by Campbell officers. The 200-horsepower, 292-ci four-barrel V-8, bolted to a three-speed stick, powers this cruiser. This award-winning 1956 Ford Mainline is one of the Bay-Area's best-restored police cars, right down to the octago-nal-E exempt license plates.

This striking 1956 Ford Mainline is a true-to-form replica of what was driven by the Indiana State Police. This jet-black two-door has a roof-mounted combination red light and mechanical siren. The yellow, body-long stripe earned these cars the nickname "stripe." The yellow stripe would change to a gold "V" in 1959. In 1956, Ford upgraded from a 6-volt electrical system to 12 volts. One problem: many police departments had to buy all new electrical gear. For this reason, Ford made the 6-volt system optional at extra cost. That gave the departments one more year to use their 6-volt emergency gear and use up their inventory of 6-volt replacement parts.

The Chicago Police Department owned this 1956 Ford Mainline. This cruiser is significant for two reasons. First, it is the first CPD police car to sport a white roof. Up until this time, the CPD police car had been solid black. The white roof over black body lasted through 1959. Second, this CPD cruiser had a V-8! This was most unusual for the time. Nearly all of the Windy City patrollers used the taxi-class, 137-horsepower, 223-ci six. This four-door Ford has either a 173-horsepower, 272-ci Y-8 or a 200-horsepower, 292-ci Y-8. Clearly and simply, the use of a V-8 meant this police car was used for traffic enforcement instead of routine patrol.

Bearing the markings of the New Jersey State Police, this 1956 Ford Customline is an extremely well-restored piece of history. This four-door sedan is powered by the 210-horsepower, 312-ci Y-8. This was a bored-and-stroked version of the 292-ci Y-block V-8. The Y-block name comes from the twin banks of cylinders sitting on top of a deeply skirted engine block. The 312-ci "Interceptor Y-8" was exactly the same engine as the 312-ci "Thunderbird Special" V-8. Late in the model year, in time for the Daytona Speed Week in February, Ford released a 225-horsepower version of this 312-ci engine. However, this new High Output (HO) engine was restricted to the two-speed Fordomatic.

This 1956 Ford Mainline was used by the Middleburg Heights (Ohio) Police. Middleburg Heights is one of Cleveland's southern suburbs. This police car is significant in terms of police history. It shows that well into the 1950s, the police cars of many of the smaller city and county departments were sparsely equipped and only semimarked. This four-door sedan only has twin spotlights, and in Ohio, they would both have clear lenses. It didn't have any visible rotating light, but red lights mounted behind the grille are possible. It didn't have any package tray lights or hood or trunk lettering. Semimarked cruisers were very common in the 1950s and are again the latest trend in the 1990s.

In 1956, the St. Louis (Missouri) Police drove the Chevrolet One Fifty. The Chevrolet was based on a 115-inch wheelbase and weighed 3,186 pounds. Many state police and highway patrols at the time began to favor the heavier and longer-wheelbase cars. These were deemed to have better high-speed stability. For most city and county police, high-speed stability was not an issue. Thus the heavier Dodges would start to take a good share of the state police business, while Chevrolet, Ford, and Plymouth would battle it out, as they always had, for the rest of the police market. This all-white St. Louis unit has a roof-mounted combination red light and mechanical siren. The powertrain is the 140-horsepower, 235-ci six with three-speed stick.

This all-black 1956 Ford Fairlane bears the gold, seven-point star of the Santa Clara County (California) Sheriff's Department. As a correctly equipped California law enforcement vehicle, this four-door sedan has twin, forward-facing red lights on the roof and a rear-facing amber flasher, mounted on the package tray. Absent a "V" under the Ford crest on the hood, this SCCSD unit should be powered by the 137-horsepower, 223-ci overhead-valve six. The 1956 four-door Fairlane with a six-cylinder engine had a weight of 3,147 pounds. The four-door Fairlane was by far the most popular of the various versions and trim levels of the 1956 Ford.

Yes, it snows in California. This unfortunate California Highway Patrol traffic officer appears to be stuck in his 1956 Pontiac Chieftain. It was two more years before a Safe-T-Track limited-slip differential was an option. In 1956, a 316-ci overhead-valve V-8 powered the Pontiac Chieftain. When teamed with a three-speed Synchro-Mesh, the compression ratio was 7.9 to 1, resulting in 192 horsepower. The same V-8 bolted to the Hydra-Matic automatic had 8.9 to 1 compression and 205 horsepower. The Star Chief version of this same powerplant produced 216 horsepower and 227 horsepower, respectively. The CHP specified three-speed manual transmissions for its E-class cruisers.

The orange door letters stand out on this jet-black 1956 Ford Customline, which has been restored as a Georgia State Patrol unit. The state seal reading "State of Georgia" and "Department of Public Safety" completes the official markings. This 1956 GSP Ford is powered by the 210-horsepower, 312-ci Police Interceptor Y-8, as noted by the interceptor engine emblem on the front fender. The GSP transitioned from a bold, black-and-white color scheme to all-black vehicles in the early 1950s. This Peach State cruiser has a red spotlight for an emergency signal. Other GSP cars during this era had the combination red light and siren mounted on either the roof or fender.

Notice that this 1957 Chevrolet Bel Air is an exact replica of a Metropolitan Toronto Police vehicle. In fact, the work was done under the watchful eye of a Metro Toronto police sergeant. All features are correct, including the roof-mounted red light and siren, roof-mounted, rear-facing red flasher, and fender-mounted red light, which says "Police" when illuminated. The color of the 1957 Chevrolet is Chrome Yellow. Toronto area police cars have been painted this color of yellow since 1952. The letters "Accident Squad" form an arc across the trunk lid. In 1957, thirteen separate police forces were amalgamated to form the Metropolitan Toronto Police. This new force patrolled an area of 243 square miles.

With the exact markings of the St. Paul (Minnesota) Police, this 1957 Chevrolet has been restored precisely. It's interesting to note that it was restored by retired SPPD police officer Dennis Hale, who started on the force in 1956. Note the fender-mounted mechanical siren. It would take the mechanical siren the distance of an entire city block to "wind up" when activated. A black and white door shield with red scrolls accents the white-roof-over-jet-black cruiser with a red "gumball." This is car number 317, which identifies the patrol district and was the squad call number. Note the full-dress wheel covers.

Notice this great-looking 1957 Chevrolet One Fifty with Military Police trim. The car is so accurately restored that it is frequently displayed at the U.S. Military Academy at West Point. The four-door sedan is olive drab with a red roof rotator. Note the 12-gauge shotgun mounted to the dash. There are no spotlights, no grille lights, and no deck lights. However, a great deal of time was spent on the lettering and wraparound body stripe. With the exception of the radial tires, which are a smart idea for any cruiser that is actually driven, this car is exactly as it appeared in the European Theater in the late 1950s.

This 1957 Chevrolet One Fifty has been restored as a Chicago Police cruiser. While the CPD also used Fords in 1957, the Wabash District, on the South Side of Chicago, used Chevrolets. This CPD unit has a white roof over a black body with white door letters and numbers. This nicely restored cruiser combines two of the most exciting areas of car collecting: police cars and classic Chevrolets. This CPD cruiser is a great "crowd pleaser" at Midwest police and enthusiast car shows.

In the late 1950s, fins were one of the most popular features on cars. In fact, car buffs continued to want fins on every make and model through 1961. Chevrolet made a minor suspension change on 1957 cars, like this Chicago Police One Fifty, that affected both ride height and rear-axle gearing. The 15-inch wheels used earlier in the decade became 14-inch wheels for 1957. The police package included 7.50x14-inch tires on "safety-contoured" rim flange wheels. The flange prevented air loss during high-speed cornering. Four-ply tires were standard, while six-ply tires were optional. Blackwalls were standard, while whitewalls were optional. However, only the fire departments would order the gaudy whitewalls.

The White Settlement (Texas) Police, just west of Fort Worth, used this sharp-looking 1957 Chevrolet Bel Air. This black-and-white four-door has a red roof rotator and red spotlight lens. This WSPD Bel Air is powered by the 220-horsepower, 283-ci four-barrel V-8 teamed with the two-speed Powerglide and 3.36 rear gears. This new V-8 was billed as "The Hot Car For Police Duty." The 283-ci small block was a bored-out version of the 265-ci V-8. The stroke remained the same. In fact, the 265-ci engine had been bored out to 283-ci by racing enthusiasts since its introduction in 1955! The 283-ci engine would be a police engine for 11 years, while this would be the last year for the 265-ci V-8.

White Settlement (Texas) Police Officer Ken Mason stands with his 1957 Chevrolet Bel Air. It is powered by a 220-horsepower, 283-ci four-barrel V-8. This four-door cop car uses a two-speed Powerglide. New for 1957 was the Turboglide automatic transmission. This ill-fated, variable-ratio transmission was similar to the Buick Dynaflow. The Turboglide had a torque converter with three turbines: one for take-off, another for cruising, and a third for passing. This transmission had a single Drive range but also a Hill Retarder selection. The Turboglide was complex, prone to failure, and hard to repair. It was discontinued after 1961.

This 1957 Chevrolet Bel Air bears the markings of the Forest Hill (Texas) Police. This cruiser is powered by the 220-horsepower, 283-ci four-barrel V-8, which was brand new for 1957. The 185-horsepower, 283-ci two-barrel V-8 was also available. The dual-quad carburetor and the fuel-injected 283-ci V-8s were not listed as official police-package engines. However, these engines were offered in any Chevrolet from the One Fifty Utility to the Corvette. The twin four-barrel version produced 225 horsepower. The fuel-injected version produced 283 horsepower, making it only the second American production car engine to produce one horsepower per cubic inch. The first was the 1956 Chrysler 300-B with the 355-horsepower, 354-ci V-8.

Of particular interest is this 1957 Chevrolet One Fifty with the Washington State Patrol. Chevrolet's most nostalgic, most collectible, and most recognizable car ever made was available with a genuine police package on both two-door and four-door sedans. This WSP cruiser is blue with a white lightning bolt. The WSP used both 1957 Chevrolets and 1957 Fords. The Chevrolets were powered by the 220-horsepower, 283-ci four-barrel V-8, and the WSP specified an automatic transmission. While the Turboglide was new for 1957, the WSP wisely selected the two-speed Powerglide. The only emergency light on this WSP cruiser is a red-lens spotlight.

In 1957, Dodge strengthened its grip on the high-end, police-pursuit market. With engines up to the 310-horsepower, 325-ci dual-quad Hemi V-8, and nothing less powerful than the 245-horsepower, 325-ci two-barrel Hemi V-8, Dodge positioned itself for state police and highway patrol use. The least powerful Dodge police engine had 20 horsepower more than Chevrolet's most powerful police engine. Dodge had a single four-barrel engine more powerful than Ford's twin four-barrel engine. In the horsepower race, among police cars, Dodge was the clear and easy winner. The 310-horsepower, 325-ci "Super D-500" was the most powerful engine available on any police package regardless of make or model.

Bearing the markings of the Houston (Texas) Police, this 1957 Plymouth Savoy cruiser is white over black with white markings. The 1957 model year was a significant one for Plymouth. This was the first year for its formal police package. Ford released its police package in 1950. Chevrolet followed suit in 1955. Most cops expected Plymouth, the third member of the Low-Priced Three, to enter the police market next. Actually, in 1956, Plymouth focused on the taxicab business while Dodge went after the state police contracts with its Hemi-powered police package. For 1957, Plymouth used the knowledge gained with taxicabs to develop a police package.

Chevrolets were not the only cars with huge, vertical fins in 1957. Notice this Houston (Texas) Police Plymouth Savoy. The Plymouth police package was based on the low trim level Plaza and the midpriced Savoy. Both were built on a 118-inch wheelbase. The police engines included the 132-horsepower, 230-ci six; the 197-horsepower, 277-ci V-8; the 215-horsepower, 301-ci two-barrel V-8; the 235-horsepower, 301-ci four-barrel V-8; and the awesome 290-horsepower, 318-ci V-8 with twin 4-four-barrel carburetors. The 318-ci big block was the engine for ultra acceleration and absolute top-speed requirements. The 197 horsepower 277-ci "Hy-Fire" two-barrel V-8 powers this Houston unit.

Marked as a Las Vegas (Nevada) Police unit, this award-win-ning 1957 Ford Custom is powered by a 245-horsepower, 312-ci four-barrel V-8. The dual-quad, eight-barrel carburetors, responsible for 270 horsepower, are on a shelf in the garage. The four-barrel setup is better-mannered for police parades! The 270-horsepower Ford Interceptor 312 Super V-8 was the first, last, and only Ford police engine to use dual four-barrel carburetors. The 9.7 to 1 compression ratio used on all 312-ci engines was the highest ratio to date on a police engine. For the first time, all engines were available with all transmissions in 1957. This police Custom has a white roof and trunk over a black body. The emergency gear includes a red roof rotator, twin red grille lights, and a mechanical, fender-mounted siren.

Notice the white trunk on this 1957 Las Vegas (Nevada) Police Ford Custom. The large fender siren is of particular note. Also note the vintage traffic radar unit mounted to the passenger-side window. On a 1957 police Ford, dual exhausts meant one thing: a 312-ci V-8. The 190-horsepower, 272-ci V-8 and the 212-horse-power, 292-ci V-8, which were also police engines in 1957, both had two-barrel carburetors and a single exhaust. As legendary as the Ford 312-ci engine has become, some enthusiasts may be surprised to learn it was only used in 1956 and 1957! For 1958, it would be replaced by one of the FE-block V-8s.

A state-of-the-art California law enforcement vehicle for the time, this 1957 Ford Custom with Santa Cruz (California) Sher-iff markings has a black-on-gold, seven-point star. The all-black, four-door sedan also has a roof-mounted, moveable spotlight. The emergency lights are in clear compliance with California statutes for the time. The forward-facing red lights were simply fixed-position spotlights with red lenses. The rear-facing lights are amber-lens spotlights that flash, or more specifically, alter-nate back and forth like wig-wag headlights of the 1990s. In 1957, the Ford police package was based on the 116-inch wheelbase Custom and the upscale Custom 300.

Notice the twin amber roof lights on this 1957 Santa Cruz (Cal-ifornia) Police Ford Custom. California law required a rear-fac-ing amber flashing light for all vehicles that might pose a road-side hazard. This included a police car that had pulled over a traffic violator or was assisting a disabled vehicle. This Santa Cruz unit is also showing the correct license plate for a city-owned or county-owned vehicle. This cruiser has a door shield but no other markings on the hood, roof, or trunk. This was typ-ical for the 1950s. Transmissions for 1957 included the three-speed stick, three-speed Overdrive, and two-speed Fordomatic. Axle ratios varied from 3.10 to 4.11 to 1.

The Highway Patrol Bureau of the New York City Police operated this 1957 Ford Custom. This Radio Motor Patrol is fitted with a unique traffic safety device, a giant, roof-mounted speedometer. This cruiser was actually going 35 miles per hour, as displayed on the massive roof-top speedometer. The word "Police" appears in green letters on the white roof, while "Police N.Y." appears on the white trunk. The body of this cruiser is green except for the black front fenders. The easiest way to identify a Highway Patrol unit is the twin red, roof-mounted lollipop flashers. Unlike the regular NYPD cars powered by a six, this Highway car has a V-8, perhaps even the 245-horsepower, 312-ci V-8.

This 1957 two-door Ford Custom was restored by a retired police officer with the Union County (New Jersey) Police Department. It bears the markings of the Clermont (Florida) Sheriff's Department. The original 312-ci Police Interceptor was rebuilt, bored .030-inch over, and balanced. An even higher-lifter, longer-dwell cam from Crane replaced the factory high-performance cam. This four-barrel engine now produces about the same 270 horsepower that the eight-barrel engine produced. The transmission is a three-speed Overdrive with 3.89 to 1 rear gears.

This Bakersfield (California) Police patrolman is shown keying the mike on the Motrac radio in his 1957 Ford Custom. Other than the door shield, this slick-top Ford would have been hard to pick out of traffic while speeding through Bakersfield. Since this wild-west city is on the high-speed link between southern and northern California, this Custom is probably packing a 245-horsepower, 312-ci four-barrel V-8. Yet it wouldn't be odd if the engine actually turned out to be the 270-horsepower, 312-ci dual quad V-8. After all, the 1957 Dodge Coronet used by the California Highway Patrol was powered by the 285-horsepower, 325-ci four-barrel Hemi V-8.

In 1957, the Los Angeles Police drove the four-door Ford Custom. These black-and-white units were powered by the 144-horsepower, 223-ci one-barrel six. This was not much of an engine compared to the 265-ci V-8 in the 1956 LAPD Chevrolets and the 348-ci big-block V-8 in the 1958 LAPD Chevrolets. Unlike Chicago and New York, where the patrol cars used sixes, from 1956 on, the LAPD cars generally had either a medium-size V-8 or a big-block V-8. Perhaps the department learned a lesson from the wimpy 223-ci six in 1957. This cruiser has LAPD's famous twin soup-can lights with a continuous burning red to the front and a flashing amber to the rear.

The 1957 Kansas City (Missouri) Police cruiser was based on the upscale Ford Custom 300. Most police departments selected the base trim level Custom. Both the Custom and Custom 300 were built on the same 116-inch chassis. This four-door sedan is all-white with black door lettering. Notice the blackwall tires mounted on white wheels. The dog-dish hubcaps also had white accent centers. This KCMO cruiser has twin red lollipop roof lights. Displayed beside the car is all the gear carried in the trunk and passenger compartment. It includes everything from flares and a shotgun to a first aid kit and a crime scene kit.

In 1957, for at least the third year in a row, the Los Angeles County Sheriff's Department used the Ford Custom. These black-and-whites had twin, fender-mounted, clear-lens spotlights. On a single roof-mounted platform were twin forward-facing, continuous-burning red lamps, a mechanical siren, and a rear-facing flashing amber light behind the siren. In 1955 and 1956, the LASD Fords were powered by the 223-ci six. This wasn't the case for 1957. In the middle of the horsepower race, the LASD used the 245-horsepower, 312-ci four-barrel V-8 in its Fords to patrol the "Hot Rod Capitol of the World." These Fords all used the two-speed Fordomatic.

The Chicago Park District Police used this 1957 Ford Custom. The Chicago Park District Police was later combined into the Chicago Police Department. This four-door Ford is jet-black with a red rotator and a clear spotlight. Note the chrome, wraparound pusher bars on the front bumper. For 1957, Fords had front-hinged hoods that opened from the rear, and windshield A-pillars that actually sloped to the rear. The Custom and Custom 300, used to make police cars, rode on a 116-inch chassis. The Fairlane and Fairlane 500, which were retail cars, were built on a 118-inch chassis. Ford police cars would have a 118-inch wheelbase in 1959 and a 119-inch wheelbase in 1960.

In 1957, the Indiana State Police used the Ford Custom like this jet-black two-door sedan. The police identification was a pointed, yellow stripe and a gold and white on blue door shield. The combination red roof light and mechanical siren was still very popular. For 1957, Ford introduced a totally new chassis. This included a new four-way ball-joint front suspension, outboard-mounted rear leaf springs, and a deep-offset rear axle. Other first-time advancements included finned or ribbed brake drums for extra heat dissipation, a manual throttle control, and up to a 100-amp alternator. For 1957, the electrical systems were strictly 12 volt. Notice the low-band whip antenna on the rear quarter panel.

Powered by the 245-horsepower, 312-ci four-barrel V-8, this 1957 Washington State Patrol Ford Custom had a lot of power for the time! Starting in 1957, the WSP ordered automatic transmissions for its cruisers. This was an extremely progressive step at a time when the vast majority of police cars used a three-speed stick. Ford's automatic was the two-speed Fordomatic introduced in 1951. In 1957, the WSP purchased both Fords and Chevrolets. Most of the Fords were blue with a white door and black-on-silver door shield but no lightning bolt. Some of the Ford were painted all-white and fitted with a small red roof rotator. The troopers called these white cars with a black lightning bolt and door shield "gray ghosts."

This Michigan State Police trooper stands proudly with his 1957 Ford Custom. The gold lightning bolt and the deep-blue door shield all make for one of the best-looking state police cars around. This cruiser has twin fender-mounted spotlights and an unusual combination red light and mechanical siren. This cruiser also sports the famous MSP hood-mounted "pull-over" sign. Mounted in the center of the hood, are the words "State Police" in white and the word "Stop" in red. The sign could be illuminated at night. The MSP would continue to use this same hood sign well into the late 1990s, becoming the last agency to use the "pull-over" sign on a police car.

Two officers with the South Bend, Indiana Police stand with their 1957 Studebaker Ambulet. In 1956, the same year as Dodge and one year ahead of Plymouth, Studebaker introduced its formal police package based on the 116.5-inch-wheelbase Champion four-door. This came with a 101-horsepower, 185-ci flathead six. For just $20 extra, the 116.5-inch Commander could be ordered with the 210 horse-power, 289-ci "Sky Hawk" and "President" overhead-valve V-8 upgrade. The police cruiser in 1957 was based on the Commander, which came standard with the President 289-ci V-8. The Ambulet was available as either a 101-horsepower, 185-ci, six-powered Pelham model or as this 180-horsepower, 259-ci V-8-powered, two-door Parkview. For 1957, the all-white SBPD police cars used black door shields with white lettering.

Note this strikingly marked 1958 Chevrolet Delray. At a time of black police cars with white doors and door shields, the Grinnell (Iowa) Police used the new styling of the Delray to completely change the look of a police car. The word "Police," set in a white background on the rear quarter panel, clearly identifies this as a police car, even if the motorist misses the red gumball. In 1958, most city police cruisers were powered by the 283-ci small-block V-8, but a fair number were also powered by the 235-ci in-line six. At 3,442 pounds, the longer, lower, wider, and heavier 1958 Chevrolet was a bit sluggish with the 145-horsepower six.

The Ames (Iowa) Police used an interesting mix of patrol cars for 1958. There was one Ford, one Chevrolet, and two Edsels. It made sense that the Chief, on the far right, received the upscale Edsel. It was, however, extremely unusual for a patrolman to be issued the expensive Edsel, yet this is what appears to be the case. These cars were either white or black, with fender-mounted red lights, and no door shields. The Allen Park (Michigan) Police also used the 1958 Edsel Ranger. The Edsel was powered by either a 303-horsepower, 361-ci V-8 or a 345-horsepower, 410-ci V-8, which was a destroked version of the 430-ci Mercury engine.

Notice the fins on this state police vehicle. This 1958 Illinois State Police Plymouth Plaza used on the Illinois Tollway had a dual exhaust. Most of these powerful cruisers had black hoods, black roofs, and black trunks with a white body. The door shield had white graphics. However, note an all-black with white roof Plymouth is in the background. The "T-27" markings on the trunk stood for Tollway Unit 27.

In 1958, the Indiana State Police drove the Ford Custom 300. The big news for 1958 was the FE-series of big-block V-8s. (FE stands for Ford-Edsel.) The police cars received 332-ci, 352-ci, and 361-ci versions of this new engine. For the first time ever, in 1958 a Ford-marque police engine produced over 300 horsepower with the 303-horsepower, 361-ci four-barrel V-8. Chevrolet and Plymouth also reached this lofty goal in 1958. This Hoosier State cruiser was all-black with a long yellow stripe and reflective blue door shield. This commission had the top-of-the-line 303-horsepower, 361-ci V-8. This was the only year this engine was used in police cars. Note the fender-mounted spotlight and roof-mounted red light and mechanical siren.

The Michigan State Police used this 1958 Chevrolet Delray. In 1958, the Chevrolet police package was based on the two-door and four-door versions of the low-priced Delray and the mid-priced Biscayne. The 1958 Chevrolet was longer, lower, and wider and rode on a new 117.5-inch wheelbase. All the V-8-powered cars received a front stabilizer, or anti-sway, bar. While nearly all 1958 Chevrolets rode on 14-inch wheels, the 15-inch wheels were the indicator of the police package. In addition to the MSP, the Iowa Highway Patrol, Nebraska Safety Patrol, and Ohio State Highway Patrol also drove the 1958 Chevrolet. These were all powered by the 348-ci big block.

The Chicago Police drove this 1958 Ford Custom 300. The four-door patroller has a white roof over a black body with white door lettering, a red rotator, and a fender-mounted spotlight. The big driveline news for 1958 was the introduction of the three-speed Cruise-O-Matic automatic transmission to police cars. This was in response to the Dodge and Plymouth TorqueFlite released in 1957. Chevrolet, however, did not develop its three-speed Turbo Hydra-Matic until 1966! The two-speed Fordomatic was available with all the police engines. However, Ford's three-speed Cruise-O-Matic was only used with the new 332-ci, 352-ci, and 361-ci FE-block V-8s. The Cruise-O-Matic could start off in second gear "for sure-footed, intermediate starts on wet, icy or loose surfaces," according to the Ford advertising literature. This Windy City cruiser, however, had a three-speed stick bolted to a 145-horsepower, 223-ci six.

This 1958 Mercury Monterey was used by the Jefferson County (Colorado) Sheriff's Department in the greater Denver area. The Mercury police package was based on the 122-inch Monterey in both two-door and four-door versions. The standard engine was the 312-horsepower, 383-ci four-barrel V-8. One optional engine was the 360-horsepower, 430-ci four-barrel V-8, normally restricted to the Montclair. Another optional engine was the 400-horsepower, 430-ci with three two-barrel carburetors. This was the first year for triple-deuce carburetors on any Ford product, but not the first year for multiple carburetors. The 1958 model year was the last for multiple carburetion on any Ford or Mercury engine. It was also the first year a FoMoCo police engine achieved 400 horsepower.

Note the roof gear on this 1958 Mercury Monterey station wagon. This Jefferson County (Colorado) Sheriff's Department special-purpose vehicle has twin combination red lights and sirens. The white speaker in the center of the hood is for the public address system. This sheriff's unit has an especially attractive two-tone, black and white color scheme: white roof, black hood, and two-tone fenders and doors. This two-door wagon, called a Commuter, was based on the Monterey trim level. It tipped the scales at 4,400 pounds. Powertrains included the 383-ci and 430-ci V-8s.

The California Highway Patrol operated this 1958 Dodge Coronet. This was an experimental cruiser. First, it was a four-door at a time when most CHP cruisers were two-doors. The reason for the four doors was clear; there was an experimental prisoner cage mounted behind the front seat to protect the driver from passengers being transported in the back. New for 1958 was the famous B-block V-8 displacing 350 ci and 361 ci. These wedge-head engines replaced the Hemi. *Motor Trend* noted the performance from the Hemi but stated, "fancy, free-breathing valve and port layouts are a thing of the past." The 305-horsepower, 361-ci four-barrel Dodge ran the quarter mile in 17.7 seconds at 82 miles per hour. The 320 horsepower, dual quad version did it in 17.3 seconds at 84 miles per hour.

The East Hartford (Connecticut) Police owned this 1958 Plymouth. The Plymouth police package in 1958 was available on the 118-inch low trim, two-door Plaza and the midlevel, four-door Savoy. The original 1958 EHPD patrol car, however, was a top-of-the-line Belvedere! This EHPD patroller is black with "East Hartford Police" in gold letters on the door. A V-8 and a three-speed pushbutton TorqueFlite powered the EHPD cruiser. The V-8s available in 1958 Plymouths were the 225-horsepower, 318-ci two-barrel; the 250 horsepower, 318-ci four-barrel; and the 305 horsepower, 350-ci eight-barrel engines. With the dual quad 350-ci engine, the Plymouth hit 60 miles per hour in 7.7 seconds, which was faster than the dual quad Dodge. This Plymouth ran the quarter mile in 16.1 seconds at 86.5 miles per hour, more than a second faster than the dual quad Dodge.

Of particular interest is this 1958 Chevrolet Bel Air bearing the fictional markings of the Route 66 Highway Patrol. Also note the "V" under the Chevrolet crest on the hood. All V-8-powered Bowties had such a chrome ornament on the hood and trunk. The new V-8 for 1958 was the 348-ci big block. Chevrolet engineers were aware of the new 350-ci and 361-ci B-block Mopar engines and the new 332-ci and 352-ci FE-series Ford engines. They responded with an equally new W-block Turbo Thrust 348. Chevrolet needed a bigger engine to power the much heavier 1958 models and also needed a new truck engine. The 265-ci small block was discontinued by 1958. Three versions of the 283-ci small block, up to 250 horsepower, and three versions of the 348-ci big block, up to 315 horsepower, were available.

The 1958 Chevrolet Delrays were fast with the new 348-ci big-block V-8. The 348-ci engine featured a radical block design. The wedge combustion chambers were built directly into the block instead of the head. The new engine also had a staggered valvetrain and larger valves to take advantage of the new engine layout. All 348-ci engines used dual exhaust. At the beginning of the model year, two police versions were available. One was the 250-horsepower, four-barrel version powering this Los Angeles County Sheriff's Delray. The other was the 280-horsepower version with three two-barrel carburetors. In midyear, a 315-horsepower version of the triple-deuce engine was released with an 11 to 1 compression.

The Michigan State Police used the bright blue 1958 Chevrolet Delray. This two-door cruiser is sporting twin fender-mounted spotlights, a red roof rotator, the famous hood-mounted "pull-over" sign, and a rear whip antenna. The Delray nameplate was used with the base trim level replacing the One Fifty name. The powertrains for 1958 included a 145-horsepower, 235-ci six; three versions of the 283-ci V-8 including a two-barrel, four-barrel, and fuel injection; and three versions of the 348-ci big-block V-8. In 1958, the 250-horsepower, fuel injected, 283-ci small-block Chevrolet was actually faster than the 280-horsepower, triple-deuce, 348-ci big-block car. Chevrolet solved that problem with a mid-year 315-horsepower version of the 348-ci engine.

Note that this 1958 Ford Custom 300 used by the Chicago Police really does share many styling features with the Thunderbird. The quad headlights, honeycomb grille, and fake hood scoop all make this look like the T-Bird's big brother. Ford wanted to capitalize on as much of the Thunderbird's performance image as it could. This four-door CPD Custom has a white roof over a black body. Note that the window pillars are also white. In spite of the ongoing horsepower race between manufacturers, and the availability of 303-horsepower, 361-ci four-barrel dual exhaust engines, this CPD patroller is powered by the 145-horsepower, 223-ci one-barrel single exhaust six.

The biggest engine for 1959 Ford police cars, like this Nassau County (New York) Police Custom 300, was the 352-ci V-8. This four-barrel, dual exhaust engine produced 300 horsepower. The "horsepower race" was finally over. Engines with dual-quad carburetion were gone. The 361-ci V-8 was no longer available. However, the 390-ci FE-block V-8, a bored-out version of the 361-ci, would appear in 1960. This NCPD cruiser is orange over blue with orange lettering and a nonrevolving, red four-way flasher. Note that this is a two-door police cruiser. Nassau County cops patrol the west end of Long Island right up to New York City.

In 1959, the Missouri State Highway Patrol drove these Dodge Coronets. The 1959 Dodge Coronet "Pursuit" was available with just three engines. These included the 255-horsepower, 326-ci two-barrel V-8; the 320-horsepower, 383-ci four-barrel V-8 and the 345-horsepower, 383-ci V-8 with twin four-barrel carburetors. The standard Dodge engine was the 326-ci Red Ram V-8, which was new for 1959. This wedge-head V-8 was totally different from the 325-ci Red Ram V-8 that used a Hemi head. The bore and stroke on these engines were also very different. The new 326-ci mill was actually a bored-out version of the 318-ci big block. This was the only year the 326-ci engine was produced, and Dodge was the only division in all of Chrysler Corporation to use this unique powerplant.

The Missouri State Highway Patrol used this 1959 Dodge Coronet. The patrol car is white with light-blue wings and light-blue body panels below the beltline chrome strip. The 1959 fleet was different from any previous fleet of MSHP cruisers in that some of the cars were two-door hardtops. This particular patroller is a four-door sedan. The formal police package was available on both versions. These MSHP Dodges were purchased at such a low price, and were traded-in at such a high price, that the MSHP replaced the vehicles after just 25,000 miles! They used the patrol cars and traded them in for new ones, all in the same model year!

A California Highway Patrol traffic officer stands confidently next to his 1959 Dodge Coronet. This Coronet was powered by a 320-horsepower, 383-ci four-barrel V-8 bolted to a three-speed TorqueFlite and 3.31 to 1 rear gears. In 1959, the CHP pitted the Dodge Coronet Highway Cruiser against both the Pontiac Catalina, powered by the 300-horsepower, 389-ci four-barrel V-8, and the Mercury Monterey Patrol King with a 345-horsepower, 430-ci four-barrel V-8. In tests conducted at the Palmdale Airport and the Riverside Speedway, the Coronet had the fastest quarter-mile speeds, at 86.9 miles per hour, and the fastest speeds after one mile, at 117.7 miles per hour. The CHP standards were 75 miles per hour and 105 miles per hour, respectively.

With six-shot .38 Special revolvers dramatically drawn, these two uniformed police officers pose with the 1959 Dodge Coronet in a promotional shot for the "Pursuit" police package. The powertrains for 1959 Dodge police cars included three V-8s. These were the 345-horsepower, 383-ci "Super D-500 Pursuit" V-8 with two four-barrel carburetors; the 320-horsepower 383-ci "D-500" V-8 with a single four-barrel carburetor; and the 255-horsepower, 326-ci "Red Ram" V-8 with a two-barrel carburetor. The last Hemi-head police engine available was in 1958. By 1959, the engines would all have the wedge-head. Drivetrains included the pushbutton three-speed TorqueFlite, the pushbutton two-speed PowerFlite, and the three-speed manual shift.

This slick-top 1959 Dodge Coronet was on duty with the California Highway Patrol. In 1959, the CHP required its Enforcement-class vehicles to weigh a minimum of 3,800 pounds and have a wheelbase of at least 122 inches. The two-door Coronet tipped the scales at 3,565 pounds. The engine was required to be at least 380 ci with a compression ratio of at least 9.75 to 1. The 383-ci V-8 in this Dodge had a 10 to 1 compression. The transmission was required to be an automatic. The Dodge's three-speed TorqueFlite is arguably the best automatic transmission ever made.

Notice this dapper 1959 Dodge Coronet with the Hialeah (Florida) Police. This city police car has wide whitewall tires and full-dress wheel covers. The fancy wheel covers were definitely factory options with the police package, but the whitewall tires definitely were not. This black, two-door cruiser has a red roof rotator but no spotlights. Hand-held spotlights were common then and still exist 40 years later. In 1959, Dodge was still posturing itself as the ultimate police car for state police and highway patrol use, while Plymouth aimed at the city police car market. The Dodge image of absolute top-notch vehicle performance, of course, spilled over to the city and county police departments.

These two troopers with the Kansas Highway Patrol are getting ready to put this 1959 Plymouth Savoy through its paces on a handling course. This 305-horsepower, 361-ci "Golden Commando 395" V-8-powered Savoy was faster than the 320-horsepower Dodge Coronet. The 395 stands for pounds-feet of torque from this big-block V-8. The 305-horsepower Savoy hit 60 miles per hour in just 8.5 seconds and ran the quarter mile in 16.4 seconds at 83.3 miles per hour. The nimble, 118-inch Savoy was also quicker around the shorter road courses and tighter handling exercises. In spite of the awesome reputation of the big, bad Dodge, the 361-ci four-barrel Plymouth was the better police car at all speeds under 110 miles per hour. Imagine the Savoy with the Dodge's 345-horsepower, 383-ci dual quad V-8. That would have been an awesome combination!

An award-winning replica of a Maumee (Ohio) Police patroller, this 1959 Chevrolet Bel Air is white over black with a red roof rotator, red fender-mounted light, and clear-lens spotlight. Note the vintage license plate that reads "City-1959-Ohio." In 1959, Chevrolet placed the headlights in the front sheet metal as low to the ground as the law allowed. The 1959 Chevrolets included the low-priced Biscayne, the mid-priced Bel Air, and the high-priced Impala. Only the Biscayne and Bel Air were available with the police-body and police-chassis packages, on both two-door and four-door versions. In 1959, the hood ornament identified the powerplant. The Chevrolet script alone meant the 235-ci six. The Chevrolet script plus a "V" indicated one of the four 283-ci small-block V-8s. A script "V" and crossed flags said one of the five 348-ci big-blocks was under the hood.

This beautifully restored 1959 Ford Galaxie bears the gold, seven-point star of the Santa Clara (California) Sheriff. Santa Clara County includes San Jose and the entire Silicon Valley on San Francisco's South Bay. The Galaxie nameplate was new for 1959 as the top-of-the-line trim level. The police package, however, was restricted to the base trim level Custom 300 and the intermediate trim level Fairlane. Perhaps the sheriff himself drove this black-and-white cruiser because this was too fancy for road deputies. Note the twin forward-facing red light and the rear-facing amber flasher mounted on the package tray. Also note the roof-mounted, moveable spotlight. These were quite common.

A Washington State Patrol trooper stands "at ease" with his 1959 Plymouth Savoy. This four-door sedan is blue with a white lightning bolt, black-on-silver door shield, and black on white "STATE PATROL" door decal. This cruiser has a fender-mounted red-lens spotlight and a padded rollbar behind the driver's seat. The cop gear includes a riot shotgun, a tear-gas gun, a knife, a baton, a spade, a fire extinguisher, blankets, and a rope. The camera-like object is a stationary traffic radar unit. Drivetrains for the 1959 Savoy included the 132-horsepower, 230-ci six; the 230-horsepower, 318-ci two-barrel V-8; the 260-horsepower, 318-ci four-barrel V-8; and the 305-horsepower, 361-ci four-barrel V-8. The "Golden Commando 395" 361-ci V-8 produced more torque per cubic inch than any other engine of any size, 395 pounds-feet from 361 ci.

Notice this 1959 Chicago Police Ford Galaxie used in the T.V. series, *Crime Story,* filmed in Chicago and then Las Vegas. There's something wrong with this picture. Never mind that the police package was based on the Custom 300 and Fairlane, not the Galaxie. This car has a white roof, white front door, white trunk, blue five-point star, blue body, and blue rotator. However, the blue lights and white with blue paint scheme didn't start until 1960. Oops! The 1959 Ford Custom 300 was indeed used by the Chicago Police. This was the last year for the white roof over black body with white door lettering and a red roof light. The 1959 models were the first year for the 118-inch wheelbase. Previous police-package Fords used a 116-inch platform.

Bearing the markings of the Nashville (Illinois) Police, this 1959 Ford Fairlane is immaculate. Compared to the base trim level Custom 300, the midpriced Fairlane had chrome window moldings and a horn ring instead of a button. It also had sun visors and arm rests on both sides instead of just the driver's side and the same side moldings as used on the Galaxie. For 1959, the wheelbase on the Ford police cars was bumped from 116 inches to 118 inches. This was a big deal at a time when longer wheelbases were assumed to have better high-speed stability than shorter ones, all else being equal. The 116-inch platform from 1958 was simply dropped. All trim levels in 1959 used the 118-inch chassis. This Nashville unit was black-and-white with a red rotator.

The South Carolina Highway Patrol used this 1959 Ford Fairlane. The cruiser is all-white with a blue-on-yellow "winged" state seal as a door shield. Of particular note on this Palmetto State cruiser is the slang word "Hi-Way" on the hood instead of "Highway." This cruiser used a combination red light and mechanical siren mounted on the roof. Note the trunk-mounted whip antenna. Powertrains for 1959 Ford police cars included a 223-ci six; a 292-ci V-8; a 332-ci V-8; and a 352-ci V-8. The 352-ci engine was the only engine to use a four-barrel carburetor and dual exhaust.

Notice this clean and straight 1959 four-door Ford Country Sedan station wagon used in Colorado. An extremely common practice in the 1950s and 1960s was to use station wagons as patrol units until they were needed as an ambulance. However, that was not the case with this all-white unit. Note the white-out rear window glass with the cross cut-out. This meant the wagon was clearly used full time for emergency medical transportation. The emergency lights included twin front-facing red flashers on the roof, a red roof rotator, and red lollipop flashers mounted to the front bumper. Note the upscale side trim on this Fairlane-based Country Sedan. Both the Country Sedan and the Custom 300-based Ranch Wagon were sometimes fitted with a police package.

The Iowa Highway Patrol drove this jet-black 1959 Ford Custom 300. The cruiser has a fender-mounted spotlight, which is a lot harder to install than one would think. The roof rotator has a red globe. The door shield has black letters on a yellow background. Note the low-band whip antenna mounted at the base of the back glass. The antenna could be pulled forward to clip in the rain channel near the door opening. Also note the sparse chrome trim on this base level Custom 300. This car came with only one sun visor and one arm rest. The package-mounted amber flasher could actually be seen at a greater distance than the red rotator.

The Lower Merion Township (Pennsylvania) Police used this Ford Custom 300. The all-white cruiser has a red roof rotator as the only piece of visual warning gear. This practice would become more common in the 1960s. Many enthusiasts consider the 1959 models to be the best-styled full-size Fords ever built. At a time when Ford's competitors were excessive with wings and fins and other decorations, the Ford shows stylistic restraint. As a result, 40 years later, it still looks great. The 1959 Fords were long, wide, and low and they had an exceptionally flat hood. For 1959, the Custom nameplate was dropped, replaced by the Custom 300 as the base model.

Notice this mixed fleet of police cars used by the Pinellas County (Florida) Sheriff's Department. These black-and-white cruisers have gold five-point stars on both doors and on the trunk. This lineup includes 1959 Fords, 1958 Fords, 1959 Chevrolets, 1958 Chevrolets, 1957 Chevrolets, and 1958 Plymouths. For 1959, Ford introduced its Equa-Lock limited-slip differential. This was the first for a Ford, and was a badly needed feature with any engine with more than 250 horsepower. With the limited-slip axle, both tires turned at equal speeds rather than one spinning wildly and the other one not spinning at all. While the Ford came with four axle ratios from 2.91 to 3.70, the limited slip was available only with the 3.10 and 3.70 ratios. Pinellas County is on the Gulf side near Tampa-St. Petersburg, Florida.

This 1959 Studebaker "Marshal" was based on the 108.5-inch-wheelbase Lark. After the introduction of the Lark, all the former Studebaker designs, except the Silver Hawk, were dropped. The Lark was new for 1955; however, the term, Marshal, was introduced in 1958. This was the name given to the police-package 116.5-inch Champion model. This all-white Marshal four-door sedan was powered by the 180-horsepower, 259-ci overhead-valve V-8. The 90-horsepower, 170-ci flathead six was also available. This South Bend (Indiana) Police sedan has a red roof rotator, twin red flashers, and an electro-mechanical siren.

In 1959, the Indiana State Police drove the Ford Custom 300. This Ford was especially unique among Hoosier State police cars. The 1959 models were the last of the all-black ISP cruisers and the first of the ISP cars to use a gold "V" underneath the door shield. No other model year had this same color and shield combination. Prior years used a long yellow stripe. Later years had a white roof over a blue body. In 1998, the ISP returned to using all-black Fords, but these had a gold body-long stripe. These 1959 Blue Ovals were powered by the 300-horsepower, 352-ci four-barrel dual-exhaust V-8. In 1959, more than 70 percent of the state police and highway patrols used Fords.

Meticulously restored as a Baltimore (Maryland) Police cruiser, this 1959 Ford Custom 300, jet-black unit has a black and red on gold door shield. In 1959, about half the Baltimore Police fleet were two-door sedans, like this patroller. Sergeants, detectives, and one-man patrol units used the two-door cars. The two-man patrol units used the four-door sedans. This particular Ford is powered by the 200-horsepower, 292-ci two-barrel V-8 teamed with a three-speed stick. The graphics on this restoration came from the same source that supplies graphics to the department in the 1990s. The radio gear came from the basement of the department. Baltimore police cars were solid black through 1967. For 1968, they adopted a white and blue color scheme.

Chapter Five

1960-1964

For 1960, the Ford police sedans were totally redesigned, so they were longer, lower, and wider. The wheelbase was stretched to 119 inches to match the full-size Chevrolet.

For 1960, Dodge turned its attention to "short" wheelbase cars for police work. While the 122-inch Dodge Matador filled the "big" slot for that year, the police package on the long-wheelbase Dodge was, unfortunately, only available on special-order, volume purchases. Instead, Dodge pushed the cops toward its newly introduced, 118-inch-wheelbase Dodge Dart.

This was the wrong direction! Cops, especially state police, were very sensitive about wheelbase length. Dodge promoted the agility of the 118-inch wheelbase. However, many state police and highway patrols were influenced by the California Highway Patrol, and its reliance on a 122-inch wheelbase. At the time, a longer wheelbase was felt to give greater stability at higher speeds.

To a traffic officer who regularly reaches 100 miles per hour, high-speed stability is critical. To a beat cop in a large city, who seldom exceeds 60 miles per hour, the long wheelbase was not an issue. Instead, the shorter wheelbase and its agility at low speeds would be a benefit.

The Clinton County Sheriff's Department in north central Indiana used this 1960 Chevrolet Bel Air. It bears the brown-over-tan markings and gold five-point star used by all Hoosier sheriffs' departments through the early 1990s. This color scheme is still used in the late 1990s; however, the word, "Sheriff" in bold, semi-script has been added along the side of the car. The powertrains in 1960 ranged from the 135-horsepower, 235-ci one-barrel six to the 335-horsepower, 348-ci, three two-barrel V-8. With the commonly used 250-horsepower, 348-ci four-barrel engine, the 3,840 pound Bowtie accelerated to 60 miles per hour in 10.7 seconds. The Indiana State Police and the Ohio State Highway Patrol also ran the Chevrolet in 1960.

Two very different powertrain advancements were available from Chrysler Corporation. At one end of the scale was the criss-crossing runner, ram-tuned intake manifolds used on the D-500 383-ci "Ram Induction" V-8s. At the other end was 225-ci slant six, which was more relevant to police work. This durable work-horse of an engine powered police cars through 1983! The engine, called the 30-D, was canted 30 degrees on its side, thus the name slant six. The 30-degree cant was supposed to allow the

The Nassau County (New York) Police used this orange-over-blue 1960 Ford Fairlane two-door. The police package was also available for four-door sedans. The 1960 Fords had a 119-inch wheelbase, which was one inch longer than 1959 sedans. Every inch added to high-speed stability. This cruiser is attached to the 6th Precinct and is fitted with a nonrevolving, four-way red flasher. In 1960, two versions of the 352-ci V-8 were available: a two-barrel with single exhaust at 235 horsepower and a four-barrel with dual exhaust at 300 horsepower. The orange door shield reads "Police Department, County of Nassau, New York."

Notice the markings of the Arkansas State Police on this 1960 Chevrolet Impala. Trooper Shelby Bodenhamer is standing next to the white-over-blue four-door sedan fitted with a red rotator, back when the ASP used red emergency lights. The police powertrains included one six-cylinder, two 283-ci small-block V-8s, and five 348-ci big-block V-8s. Powered by the 135-horsepower, 235-ci one-barrel six, the Chevy accelerated to 60 miles per hour in 18.6 seconds and ran the quarter mile in 20.4 seconds at 63 miles per hour. With a 280-horsepower, 348-ci V-8 fitted with three two-barrel carburetors, the 0- to 60-mile-per hour time was 9.9 seconds. The quarter-mile time was 17.2 seconds at 81 miles per hour. The 11.3 to 1 high-compression engine with three two-barrel carburetors produced 335 horsepower.

use of a longer intake manifold, again, in an attempt to ram-charge the cylinders. Long after ramcharging was replaced by other more compact induction methods, the slant six remained exactly as introduced.

The 383-ci-powered Dodge Dart was the fastest-accelerating police-package car of 1960, closely followed by the 361-ci-powered Plymouth Savoy, and the 383-ci-powered Dodge Polara. The 348-ci Chevrolet Biscayne was next, followed by the 389-ci Pontiac Catalina, 352-ci Ford Fairlane, 430-ci Mercury Monterey, and 371-ci Oldsmobile Dynamic 88. These full-size police cars had quarter-mile times ranging from 16.3 seconds to 18.3 seconds, with speeds from 75 miles per hour to 86 miles per hour.

For 1961, Ford reacted to the pressure from Dodge in the state police and highway patrol market. The result was the 390-ci FE-block V-8, which became one of Ford's most popular and versatile police engines. The 390-ci V-8, basically a stroked version of the 361-ci V-8, powered full-size and mid-size police cars through 1971 until finally being replaced by the 400-ci "Cleveland" V-8.

For an entire decade, the "Thunderbird 390 Special" and the "Interceptor 390" proved to be durable and reliable police engines. Rated between 265 horsepower and 330 horsepower, the 390-ci V-8 never had the reputation of a high-torque tire-burner like the Mopar 383 or Chevy 396. However, it was powerful enough for a wide variety of traffic enforcement duties.

At Chrysler Corporation, the police package for the upscale Chrysler Newport was introduced, and it was the first Chrysler-marque vehicle to come with a police package. Called the Enforcer, this 122-inch Newport was available in police trim through 1964. The Enforcer was significant because it was the only advertised 1961 Chrysler, Dodge, or Plymouth police-package car with a 122-inch wheelbase.

For 1961, the Dodge Dart Seneca and the Plymouth Savoy carried the police banner for their respective divisions. Both cars were available in engines ranging from the 225-ci slant six to the 383-ci big-block V-8. This was the first year a Plymouth police car was available with the 383-ci V-8.

The ill-fated, rear-engine Chevrolet Corvair, fitted with a genuine police package, was released in 1961. It was available as a retail car from 1960 to 1969 and with a police package in 1961 and 1962. Billed as "America's most advanced thrift car" by Chevrolet and "Unsafe at Any Speed" by Ralph Nader, the controversial and unreliable Corvair was not used by any city, county, or state police department of note.

Ford was law enforcement's number one choice for police vehicles in 1962. The blue oval released two very different police-package cars: the full-size 119-inch, which Ford called the Galaxie, and Ford's first mid-size police-package car, the 115.5-inch-wheelbase Fairlane. The vast majority of cops considered the Fairlane far too small for police work. How times change! The 1999 Crown Victoria used by over 90 percent of America's cops has a 114.7-inch wheelbase! Perhaps the biggest news for 1962 was Ford's first Windsor small-block engine, the 221-ci V-8. Future Windsor V-8s are the 260-ci, 289-ci, 302-ci, and 351-ci engines. Ironically, at 221 ci, Ford's first thin-wall, precision-cast, small-block V-8 had exactly the same displacement as Ford's first flathead V-8. In mid-1962, Ford released a bored-out version of the 221-ci engine, the more famous 260-ci V-8.

At the same time, this was a very awkward model year for Chrysler Corporation police cars. All of the 118-inch police cars were gone, and the only 122-inch police car was the Chrysler Enforcer. The 383-ci V-8 was dropped from the Dodge and Plymouth police cars option list, but the 325-horsepower, 383-ci V-8 was the top cop Mopar engine, and this was only available in the Chrysler Enforcer. That meant Ford's 330-horsepower, 390-ci police engine produced more horsepower than anything from Chrysler Corporation, a situation that had not occurred since Dodge's formal entry into the police market in 1956.

In the horsepower race, Chevrolet was the real police leader in 1962. Its 409-ci big block, introduced in mid-1961, was a bored-and-stroked version of the 348-ci W-block V-8 that had used a single four-barrel to produce 380 horsepower. The new 409-ci was the first Chevrolet police car engine to sport twin four-barrel carburetors, and it produced 409 horsepower. The 409-ci V-8 was the only police engine of any make or vintage to ever produce over 400 horsepower. The 327-ci small-block V-8, a bored-and-stroked version of the 283-ci V-8 became available. The 327-ci was the first of the 4-inch-bore Chevy small blocks that would eventually include the 350-ci V-8. This was also the first of the "big valve" small-block engines. In 1963, Ford was once again America's best-selling make of police car, a streak more or less uninterrupted since 1932. The Ford police fleet was made up of the 119-inch-wheelbase Ford 300 and Galaxie and the 115.5-inch Fairlane. By midyear, the 289-ci Windsor V-8, a bored-out version of the 260-ci V-8 was available in police-package cars.

By 1963, Chrysler Corporation had its wheelbase problems all sorted out. Plymouth remained at 116 inches, Dodge was stretched to both 119 and 122 inches, and Chrysler-marque police cars remained at 122 inches. Under pressure from cops and retail customers alike, Dodge introduced its 122-inch-wheelbase Dodge Custom 880 by mid-1962. The car, literally "thrown together" during the Christmas shutdown, was simply a 1962 Chrysler body with a 1961 Dodge front end. It was produced too late in the model year to be teamed with a police package. For 1963, the Dodge 880 was back with an official police package, but it was still pure Chrysler from the firewall back. However, for 1963, it received a new front end all of its own. For 1963, the 383-ci big block returned to Dodge and Plymouth police cars. Other big news from Chrysler Corporation in 1963 was the 413-ci raised-block, B-engine V-8. This now gave cops the choice of two big blocks in the Dodge line, the 383 ci and the 413 ci. Used in the Chrysler Enforcer and Dodge 880 police cars, the 413-ci V-8 produced 360 horsepower.

Ford retained the distinction of building the most popular police car in America for 1964. Both Dodge and Chevrolet offered more powerful V-8s for pursuit use and more powerful six-cylinder engines for urban patrol, but Ford was powerful enough, reliable enough, and economical enough to get the job done.

In fact, in 1964, Ford began its famous Total Performance theme that alluded to this fact, and the company set out to have the best "overall" performance. They would never accelerate like a Dodge, or brake like a Chevrolet, or corner like a Pontiac, but the Ford's goal was to do well enough in all these categories to attain the best Total Performance. The concept worked, and Ford continued to dominate police sales through 1968.

This 1960 Ford Ranch Wagon was with the Nassau County (New York) Police on Long Island. Like the four-door sedans used by NCPD, this police wagon has an orange roof and a blue body. Following years of tradition, the hood, trunk, and door lettering and numbering is orange, while the door shield is orange and blue. The Ranch Wagon was the base trim level wagon with a level of equipment similar to the base level Fairlane. The Country Sedan and Country Squire were the upgraded wagons. The police wagon and full-size sedans shared the same 119-inch wheelbase. Station wagons were used by shift supervisors, watch commanders, sergeants, K-9 officers, crime scene technicians, and commercial truck regulation enforcement officers. Wagons often had the biggest V-8s and the numerically highest rear gear ratios.

The Washington State Patrol used this 1960 Ford Fairlane. Nearly four decades later, the WSP still marks its cars the same way: all-white with a black lightning bolt and a silver/black door shield. Note the very small red roof rotator. This was a time of experimentation for the WSP. On a trial-run basis, the WSP began to use small red rotators in 1957. The patrol cars used to have a red lens on the A-pillar spotlight. This was replaced in 1960 by twin red flashers in the grille. In 1960, the WSP also purchased Plymouths and Chevrolets, a practice started in 1955. Of the Fords the WSP used, some were blue and some were white. The white Fords were equipped with the small red rotator. New for 1960, the wheelbase grew from 118 inches to 119 inches. These totally new Fords were longer, lower, and wider than the 1959 versions.

If it's a 1960 to 1965 black-and-white Ford, it could be a Mayberry car. Every major police car show has at least one replica from *The Andy Griffith Show*. TAGS enthusiasts are also Ford police-car enthusiasts. Each year the TAGS Rerun Watchers' Club gathers near Dayton, Ohio, for a Mayberry Squad Car Rendezvous and again near Raleigh, North Carolina, for a Mayberry Reunion. Original T.V. cast and crew members actually attend these events. These festivities are a celebration of a much more innocent and wholesome time. Introduced during *The Danny Thomas Show* in February 1960, *The Andy Griffith Show* ran from October 1960 until *Mayberry RFD* replaced it in September 1968. Any 1960 to 1965 full-size Ford Fairlane or Galaxie is a candidate for a Mayberry replica.

The Nashville (Tennessee) Police operated this 1960 Ford Fairlane. Nashville, of course, is the capitol of the Volunteer State. This four-door sedan is white over black with a red rotator and a gold-and-blue door shield. The redesigned 119-inch chassis was 25-percent stronger than 1959. The rear suspension was also redesigned with asymmetric rear leaf springs. Both the front and rear tracks were wider than in 1959. For 1960, a new two-barrel version of the 352-ci V-8 rated at 235 horsepower replaced the two-barrel version of the 1959 332-ci V-8, which was now discontinued. For 1960, the 292-ci V-8 received smaller valves for better fuel economy, but the result was less horsepower. For 1960, the words "Police Special" were embossed in the valve covers of the 300-horsepower, 352-ci Police Interceptor V-8.

Mopar enthusiasts remember the 1964 model for the reintroduction of the Hemi-head engine, now displacing 426 ci. However, unlike the first-generation Hemi, the 426-ci Hemi was never used in police-package cars.

The Mopar police-package fleet was made up of the 122-inch-wheelbase Chrysler Enforcer and Dodge 880, the 119-inch Dodge 330, and the 116-inch Plymouth Savoy. The Enforcer, powered by the same 360-horsepower, 413-ci V-8 as used in the Chrysler 300 K, was in its last year as a police car.

The Chevrolet police package was available on the 119-inch-wheelbase Biscayne, the Chevy II, built on a 110-inch chassis, and, new for 1964, the 115-inch platform Chevelle four-door sedan. This gave Chevrolet three very different police cars to meet a wide variety of law enforcement needs. Chevrolet, currently in a distant fourth place in the police market, had been trying to find a niche. Its continued efforts to develop a specialty police car hit paydirt with the 1975 Nova, Chevrolet's most influential police car.

Notice the "seagull" rear fins on the rear of the Nashville (Tennessee) Police 1960 Ford Fairlane. The Ford also had fins in 1961, but they were much smaller. In 1960, the police-package Fairlane came with either a two-speed Fordomatic or a three-speed Cruise-O-Matic. The Cruise-O-Matic could start off in either first or second gear. New for 1960, the Cruise-O-Matic came with a smaller, 12-inch torque converter. This increased the stall speed and gave greater throttle response without affecting fuel economy. For 1960, Ford increased the width of the rear brake drums and increased the lining area by 25 percent. Taller, 15x5-inch wheels were now used for better brake cooling on the 300-horsepower, 352-ci-powered cruisers. Note the large black-on-gold trunk decal, reading "Nashville Police."

Dodge Division released its police package in 1960 for two very different cars. One was the 118-inch-wheelbase Dodge Dart, such as this unmarked unit from Chicago's south side. Trim levels on the Dodge Dart included the base level Seneca, the midlevel Pioneer, and the upscale Phoenix, such as this patroller. The other car was the 122-inch-wheelbase Dodge. Transmissions included the three-speed T-85 manual, two-speed PowerFlite auto, and three-speed TorqueFlite auto. New for 1960 Dodge and Plymouth police cars was the introduction of a "unibody" construction, which acted as both body and frame. Pioneered as early as 1934, it took decades to work out all the problems. The unibody was 40-percent stronger and the twist rigidity was doubled. However, engine vibration, road noise, and corrosion were problems. By 1960, Chrysler solved these concerns with extrathick side rails, an 11-step corrosion prevention process, and 5,400 welds.

This 1960 Dodge Dart Seneca was with the Los Angeles County Sheriff's Department. The four-door, mid-size sedan used the same torsion bar front suspension and 12-inch drum brakes as the full-size Dodge. The warning signals on this white-over-black LASD cruiser include two red lamps and a mechanical siren bolted to a triangular plate that is bolted to the roof. With a reduction in wheelbase, this 118-inch mid-size was now a direct competitor to the 118-inch Plymouth. The Dodge Dart was available in a wide variety of six-cylinder and eight-cylinder engines, including the 330-horsepower, 383-ci V-8 with dual four-barrels and dual exhausts. With this big-block V-8, the Dodge Dart hit 60 miles per hour in 8.5 seconds. The 3,610-pound cop car ran the quarter mile in 16.3 seconds at 86 miles per hour.

In 1960, the California Highway Patrol used this full-size Dodge Matador. This was the last year for the black-and-white color scheme with a black roof. For 1961, the CHP cruisers would have white roofs. This full-size 122-inch-wheelbase Matador was fitted with twin A-pillar spotlights. The left spot had a red lens. The CHP powertrain in 1960 was a 325-horsepower, 383-ci four-barrel V-8 bolted to a three-speed TorqueFlite and 3.23 to 1 rear gears. Per CHP specs, the Holley four-barrel found on the standard 383-ci engine was replaced with a Carter AFB (aluminum four-barrel) four-barrel. The CHP cruiser hit 60 miles per hour in 9.5 seconds. It ran the quarter mile in 17.3 seconds at 86 miles per hour. From a standing start, this CHP cruiser hit 129 miles per hour in just two miles.

The Suffolk County Police on the east end of Long Island, New York, used this 1960 Plymouth Savoy. The 118-inch-wheelbase, four-door Plymouth is white over blue with a red rotator and white-on-blue police markings. The wheels are black, not blue. This was the fourth year for "Jet Age" fins on the rear of these Plymouths. It would also be the last year. Plymouth police cars were available with four police engines including the 145-horsepower, 225-ci slant six; 230-horsepower, 318-ci two-barrel V-8; 260-horsepower, 318-ci four-barrel V-8; and 305-horsepower, 361-ci four-barrel V-8. The 318-ci V-8 was a polysphere-head, big block introduced to Plymouth police cars in 1957. This was very different from the 318-ci wedge-head, small-block V-8 introduced to Plymouth police cars in 1967. In 1960, the Plymouth police package was used by 523 cities in 38 states.

At a public showing in Chicago, this 1960 Plymouth Savoy received plenty of attention. That's because it was the first year for the Chicago Police to use a white-over-blue police car. The roof is white, as are the trunk and front doors. The rest of the car is blue, along with the five-point star on the front door. This was also the first year for the Chicago Police to use blue emergency lights instead of red lights. In 1960, the CPD used the 352-ci four-barrel V-8-powered Ford Fairlane in its Traffic Division. This 1960 Savoy was with the Patrol Division and was powered by the 225-ci one-barrel slant six, which was also new for 1960. This was the first Plymouth six-cylinder engine with overhead valves. The 225-ci slant six went on to become a Mopar legend. It would serve in police cars through 1983.

Notice the generic markings of a "state police" vehicle complete with white roof letters on this 1960 Plymouth Savoy. One of the troopers directed traffic while the other helped change the tire. Actually, this was a staged publicity shot for Plymouth police-car literature. In four short years since the police package was introduced, Plymouth had indeed captured many high-end state police and highway patrol contracts. Plymouth had shed its taxicab image and instead began to challenge Dodge for the prestigious police-car accounts. The 1960 Plymouth was used by the Texas Highway Patrol, West Virginia State Police, Minnesota State Patrol, Indiana State Police, Washington State Patrol, Wisconsin State Patrol, Ohio State Highway Patrol, and the New York State Police.

This staged shot with a generically marked 1960 Plymouth Savoy police car was for Plymouth police-car literature. Even though the Savoy was fairly heavy at 3,500 pounds, most major cities ordered Plymouths with either the 145-horsepower, 225-ci one-barrel slant six (like the NYPD and Chicago Police) or the 230-horsepower 318-ci two-barrel V-8 (like the LAPD and Houston Police). If a city police department was large enough to have a Patrol Division or Bureau and also a Traffic Division or Highway Patrol Bureau, the Patrol cars had the smallest engines and the Highway cars had the largest engines. Police departments that went with the medium-large engines used the 260-horsepower, 318-ci four-barrel big-block V-8.

In 1960, the Detroit Police selected a fleet of Dodge Seneca police-package station wagons as a replacement for its patrol scout cars. These Detroit Police station wagons served as ambulances at a time when police ambulances were common. In addition to the use as an ambulance, these 1960 police wagons were also used by the Detroit Police for routine patrolling and for responding to emergency radio traffic. These wagons were black with silver door markings and a red rotator. Note the hood-mounted sign, which reads "Police." This was similar to the hood sign used by the Michigan State Police.

In 1960, the California Highway Patrol tested a series of heavy, long-wheelbase, full-size, two-door and four-door sedans. The CHP wanted a car with a minimum weight of 3,800 pounds, a wheelbase of at least 122 inches, and an overhead-valve V-8 engine with a minimum 380 ci. One of the test vehicles was this 1960 Pontiac Catalina Enforcer. This 123-inch Catalina, tipping the scales at 3,850 pounds, was packing the famous 389-ci engine. While the Catalina came standard with the 283-horse-power, 389-ci two-barrel V-8, this Enforcer used the 303-horse-power, four-barrel V-8 from the upscale Bonneville, teamed with the Super Hydra-Matic transmission. The hot Enforcer met all of the CHP performance standards but was outrun by the 383-ci Dodge. The CHP had used the Pontiac as an E-class vehicle in 1956 and 1957.

Menlo Park, California, Police Officer John Lyle drove this 1960 Chevrolet Biscayne. Lyle heard an "all points bulletin" about a red 1959 Ford Thunderbird stolen from nearby Redwood City. Twelve minutes later, he identified the vehicle at Draeger's Supermarket in Menlo Park. He pulled his four-door cruiser behind the T-Bird, blocking its exit. With his .38 Special service revolver drawn, Lyle approached the suspected stolen car. As he approached, car thief Roy Lane fired two 9mm rounds from inside the car, through the back glass, striking Lyle. The wounded officer returned fire four times with his service revolver, striking Lane twice. Lane fled into the shopping center where he was apprehended within four minutes of the shooting by responding Menlo Park Police Officer Richard Donohoe. Officer Lyle, father of four, died of his injuries at the scene. Lane was convicted of murder and later executed at nearby San Quentin Prison. Officer Lyle's badge, Number 3, was retired and placed on permanent display in his honor at the department. This is an actual crime scene photo.

Many "big city" patrol cars suffered damage to some extent during their tenure. This 1961 Plymouth Savoy with the Chicago Police was no exception. The squad car is white over blue with a blue star for the door shield. It has a roof-mounted, blue MARS rotator and blue headlight lenses for emergency gear. While it might look strange, the license plate is not out of place. The Chicago Police Department mounted the license plate on the grille of its patrol cars for at least 30 years. Note the fender-mounted spotlight. That was a tough installation!

The Massachusetts State Police drove the 1961 Ford Fairlane. In 1961, the police package was based on the 119-inch-wheelbase Fairlane in both two-door and four-door versions. This Bay State cruiser is a two-door. The color scheme includes a gray hood, roof, trunk, and doors with dark-blue fenders and a red rotator. In 1961, Ford released its famous 390-ci Ford-Edsel-block V-8. This was basically a stroked version of the 361-ci big block. The 390-ci V-8 powered police cars through 1971. It was eventually replaced by the 400-ci Cleveland V-8. The 390-ci V-8 was available in two versions. One was the 300-horsepower "Thunderbird Special 390." The other was the 330-horsepower "Interceptor." Both had four-barrel carburetors, 9.6 to 1 compression, and dual exhaust. The 330-horsepower version used a higher lift cam and header-type exhaust manifolds.

The Montreal (Quebec, Canada) Police used this 1961 Ford Fairlane to keep the peace among its 1 million residents. Other major agencies to use the 1961 Ford included St. Louis County (Missouri) Sheriff; Baltimore (Maryland) Police; Omaha (Nebraska) Police; and the Atlanta (Georgia) Police. Drivetrains for 1961 included the 135-horsepower, 223-ci six; 175-horsepower, 292-ci V-8; 220-horsepower, 352-ci V-8; and the 300-horsepower and 330-horsepower versions of the 390-ci V-8. The 390-ci engines had four-barrel carburetors and dual exhaust. The other V-8 engines had two-barrel carburetors and single exhaust. A heavy-duty version of the Cruise-O-Matic was developed for the 330-horsepower Interceptor version of the 390-ci V-8. Neither of the big torque 390-ci V-8s were bolted to the two-speed Fordomatic.

This 1961 Ford Galaxie replica show car bears the markings of the Missouri State Highway Patrol. The light-blue cruiser has a red rotator fender-mounted spotlight. The 1961 Ford police package was based on the low trim level Fairlane. However, Ford was willing to put its police package on the intermediate trim level Fairlane 500 or the top trim level Galaxie. In fact, in 1961, Ford offered 25 versions of police vehicles, each with a separate package tailored to specific kinds of duty. These packages included the Police Cruiser V-8 Package based on the 300-horsepower, 390-ci V-8 and the Utility Six Package based around the 135-horsepower, 223-ci in-line six. The Utility Six Package was intended for light urban patrol or use by nonemergency personnel such as detectives and investigators.

The supervisor of the Washington State Patrol Vehicle Maintenance Section used this 1961 solid-blue two-door unmarked Ford Ranch Wagon. This police-package wagon was used for a wide variety of support tasks, not the least of which was hauling spare parts. Three police-package wagons were available. These included the two-door and four-door Ranch Wagon and the four-door, six-passenger Country Sedan, but not the nine-passenger version. The Ranch Wagon had the same base trim level as the Fairlane sedan, while the Country Sedan was equal to the intermediate trim level Fairlane 500. Wagons were more likely to have higher numeric rear axle ratios such as the 3.89 to 1, while the sedans were likely to have the 3.56 to 1. Nearly all police cars with the Cruise-O-Matic had 3.00 to 1 rear gears.

Notice that this 1961 Ford Fairlane is a Mayberry Sheriff replica. The Andy Griffith Show Rerun Watchers Club holds a Mayberry Squad Car Rendezvous in Ohio and a Mayberry Reunion in North Carolina each year. This attracts black-and-white early-1960s Fords from all across America. They even have their own set of rules for judging the cars. To the vintage police-car enthusiast, the original factory literature and period photos are the means to judge what is correct and not correct. Not so TAGS enthusiasts. For this group, the T.V. show is the final authority on what is correct. TAGS watchers scroll frame by frame through each of the 249 episodes trying to get their car as close to the original studio version as possible.

New for 1961, the full-size Chevrolet, including this Oregon State Police Biscayne, received a totally new chassis and totally new sheet metal. The "Safety Girder" X-frame was retained and so was the "big car" 119-inch wheelbase. However, the Chevrolet was downsized overall. The four-door 1961 Biscayne was 1.5 inches shorter and 65 pounds lighter than the 1960 Biscayne. For 1961, the LPO 1105 and 1108 police packages were only available on the Biscayne and Biscayne Fleetmaster in two-door and four-door sedans and Brookwood station wagons. This was the last year for the fleet-oriented Fleetmaster. This Beaver State cruiser is a two-door. Actually, two-door police cars were very common in the fleets of the state police and highway patrols. This commission is jet-black with white door lettering.

The Iowa Highway Safety Patrol was organized in 1935. In 1939, the name was changed to the Iowa Highway Patrol. In 1973, the name was changed again to Iowa State Patrol. This 1961 Iowa Highway Patrol Chevrolet Biscayne was all-black with a yellow door shield. With a 250-horsepower, 348-ci four-barrel V-8, a Turboglide automatic, and 3.08 to 1 rear gears, the 3,980-pound Biscayne reached 60 miles per hour in 10.6 seconds and 100 miles per hour in 28.0 seconds. With this powertrain, the 119-inch-wheelbase cruiser ran the quarter mile in 17.2 seconds at 79 miles per hour. Top speed was 115 miles per hour. The police 348 ci also came in 280-, 305-, 340-, and 350-horsepower versions. The 348-ci V-8 with three two-barrel carburetors and an 11.25 to 1 compression ratio was the first carbureted Chevrolet police engine with one horsepower per cubic inch.

The Big Sandy (Texas) Fire Department, east of Dallas, used this striking 1961 Chevrolet Impala. This fire car has a black roof and a bright-red body. Roof-mounted emergency gear includes twin forward-facing red flashers, a red/clear, four-bulb rotator with a clear globe, and a torpedo-style mechanical siren with red light. The package tray includes twin red flashers. The door shield is the traditional fireman's Maltese Cross. To this day, most fire departments use police-package cars. Most have a medium-size V-8 engine. Fire cars do not do a lot of patrolling, so they don't need to be especially economical. On the other hand, they are not driven at speeds requiring the biggest engines with multiple carburetion. This type of duty typically calls for something like a 283-ci four-barrel V-8 rated at 230 horsepower.

The Indiana State Police drove the Chevrolet Biscayne again in 1961. These were powered by the 305-horsepower, 348-ci four-barrel V-8. This was the most powerful engine available without going to multiple carburetion (three two-barrels) and high compression ratios, such as 11.25 to 1. This two-door Biscayne has a torpedo-style warning device, which is a combination of a red flasher and a mechanical siren. The ISP cruisers have changed color schemes over the years. The 1961 Hoosier cruiser had a white roof over a blue body. This color scheme started in 1960. Prior to 1960, ISP cars were all-black. The white over blue color scheme lasted through 1966. Then in 1967, the ISP drove all-white cars. For the next 30 years, in fact, ISP cruisers were white with either a blue stripe or gold "V."

For 1961, Dodge released a police package for the two-door and four-door Dart Seneca and the four-door Seneca station wagon. This Michigan State Police unit is a two-door. The Seneca was the base trim level Dart. The Dart had a 118-inch wheelbase. This was the only official police-package car from Dodge in 1961. This MSP cruiser is bright blue with a red rotator and red "State Stop Police" hood light. The markings include a blue and gold door shield and lightning bolt, and the gold trunk lettering "State Police." Powertrains included the 330-horsepower, 383-ci eight-barrel, long ram dual quad, V-8; 325-horsepower, 383-ci four-barrel V-8; 305-horsepower, 361-ci four-barrel V-8; 260-horsepower, 318-ci four-barrel V-8; 230-horsepower, 318-ci two-barrel V-8; and the 145-horsepower, 225-ci one-barrel slant six. Transmissions included the pushbutton three-speed TorqueFlite, the two-speed PowerFlite, and the three-speed stick.

In 1961, for the first time ever, a police-package car was released with a Chrysler name tag. Called the Enforcer, the first Chrysler-marque police car was based on the newly reintroduced Newport. The retail version of the Newport was intended as an entry-level Chrysler. Compared to the regular 126-inch-wheelbase Chryslers, the 122-inch Newport was considered a lightweight even though it weighed 4,400 pounds. The retail engine was a 265-horsepower, 361-ci two-barrel V-8 while the police-package engine was a 325-horsepower, 383-ci four-barrel V-8. With a high-performance cam, low-restriction air cleaner, and low back-pressure dual exhaust, Chrysler's first police car was said to "provide sling-shot acceleration." This was the only Chrysler-marque car with this powertrain.

This 1961 Chrysler Newport Enforcer was actually powered by a Dodge Polara D-500 engine. The 325-horsepower, 383-ci four-barrel engine was not available in any other Chrysler-marque vehicle. The 383-ci Newport was advertised as the biggest, brawniest police car ever to lay down the law. It was powered to prowl the turnpikes. The 325-horsepower, 383-ci big block was bolted to a three-speed TorqueFlite with a 3.23 to 1 Sure-Grip rear end. This drivetrain pushed the heavy Newport to 60 miles per hour in an impressive 8.3 seconds and to 100 miles per hour in an even more impressive 24.1 seconds. It ran the quarter mile in 16.9 seconds at 86 miles per hour. The big Chrysler had a top speed of 131 miles per hour.

This 1961 Dodge Dart is pulling out of the basement garage below one of the Los Angeles Police precincts. The LAPD four-door sedan was powered by the 230-horsepower, 318-ci two-barrel V-8 bolted to a two-speed PowerFlite automatic. Unlike some major metro police departments who patrolled in six-cylinder cars, the LAPD went to V-8s in 1958 and never went back. Other LAPD patrol cruisers were powered by the 383-ci Mopar V-8; the 401-ci AMC V-8; and the 429-ci Mercury V-8. The LAPD purchased 337 of these "Municipal Patrol Package" Darts. While these were not "official" police-car engines, *Motor Life* magazine reported that two engines were unofficially available to police departments across the country. One was the "short ram" dual-quad 383 ci rated at 340 horsepower. The other was the in-line, dual-quad 383 ci rated at 330 horsepower. The in-line intake allowed easier access to the valve covers for periodic adjustment of the solid lifters.

The 1961 Dodge Polara was used exclusively by the California Highway Patrol. The black-and-white cruiser has gold door lettering and a gold and blue seven-point star. The fender-mounted spotlight is continuously burning red. This cruiser is powered by the 325-horsepower, 383-ci four-barrel V-8 bolted to a three-speed TorqueFlite and 3.23 to 1 rear gears. This big, bad Dodge ran the quarter mile in the 16-second bracket and had a top speed of just over 130 miles per hour. *Motor Life* tested the 1961 CHP Dodge and wrote, "for chilling performance plus the ruggedness and reliability which has characterized Dodge for years, the Police Pursuit powerhouse was hard to beat. We definitely don't recommend trying to outrun one!"

Sitting on the grounds of the California Highway Patrol Academy in Sacramento, this 1961 CHP Dodge Polara is a "Best of Show" winner. From the front, the 1961 Dodge Dart and 1961 Dodge Polara shared the same sheet metal. From the rear, however, the 122-inch CHP Polara and the 118-inch Dart were very different. While both Dodges had the chrome-trimmed "inverted fin" quarter panels, the Polara had its taillights built into the inverted fins. The Dart did not. Like all Dodge police cars, the CHP Polara had an extra leaf in the rear springs, oversize tires, and 12x2.5-inch drum brakes. The police-package Polara was built only for the CHP, making these cars among the rarest and most unique of any genuine police-package vehicles.

A proud Michigan State Police trooper stands at attention next to his 1961 Plymouth Savoy. The police package was available on two-door and four-door models alike. This MSP cruiser is a two-door. The unit is bright blue in color with a blue and gold door shield and a red roof rotator. The hood-mounted sign says "State Police" in white and "Stop" in red. It could be illuminated. What made the Savoy so attractive to the MSP was the availability of the Golden Commando 435 engine, which was the 325-horsepower, 383-ci four-barrel V-8 used in the Chrysler Newport Enforcer, Dodge Dart, and the CHP's special Dodge Polara. This marked the first time a Plymouth police car was powered by a 383-ci wedge-head, big-block V-8. The name Golden Commando 435 came from the 435 pound-feet of peak torque it produced at 2,800 rpm. With this engine, the lighter Savoy was actually faster than the Newport Enforcer or either of the Dodges.

The Village of Farnham, New York, used this 1961 Plymouth Savoy Fleet Special. This two-door coupe is all-silver with black door lettering and a red rotator. The Plymouth was purchased new by the Village of Farnham and was used as its only police car until 1979. In 1979, enforcement duties were taken over by the Erie County Sheriff and the New York State Police. Remarkably, this cruiser was in service for 18 years! It was powered by the 361-ci "Golden Commando 395" V-8. In its time, it was the fastest car on the road. Even when it was taken out of service, it could still outrun the 1979 crop of cruisers. This cruiser is built on a 118-inch wheelbase, just like the Dodge Dart.

The most famous cop car of the early 1960s, this 1961 Plymouth Savoy is the original car from the T.V. series *Car 54, Where Are You?* starring Joe E. Ross as Officer Gunther Toody and Fred Gwynne as Officer Francis Muldoon. Their beat was New York City's fictional 53rd Precinct in the Bronx. The series aired from September 1961 to September 1963. Hollywood marked the Savoy differently than the NYPD actually marked them. The NYPD cars had "Police N.Y." two places on the side of the hood, and "Police" and the unit number at the center leading edge of the hood, like this T.V. car. The door markings were very different, however. The NYPD had a new door shield on 1961 cruisers instead of the precinct number, which was moved to the rear door. The car number did not appear on the side of NYPD cruisers anytime near this vintage. But the biggest difference is this Hollywood car was white over red!

The Harwood Heights (Illinois) Police used this 1961 Pontiac Catalina Enforcer in the Chicago area. For 1961, the Catalina was downsized from a 123-inch wheelbase to a 119-inch platform thanks to a new, perimeter-frame design. The Catalina was the base trim level. The Catalina Enforcer came standard with a 215-horsepower, 389-ci V-8 as teamed with the Hydra-Matic. Optional versions of the 389-ci V-8 teamed with the Hydra-Matic were rated at 230, 267, 287, 318, 333, and 348 horsepower. The 318-horsepower and 348-horsepower engines used the famous tri-power, three two-barrel setup. The 405-horsepower, 421-ci Super-Duty V-8 with dual four-barrel carburetors was available in two-door Catalinas only. Serving a Chicago suburb, this HHPD Catalina was probably powered by one of the three versions of the 389-ci two-barrel V-8.

Notice this extremely well-restored 1961 Dodge Dart Seneca. The four-door, black-and-white cruiser is generically marked as a Hogg Classic Cars Pursuit Special. It sports twin spotlights, one red and one clear, and red-lens high-beam headlight covers. The roof rotator on this particular Mopar squad car has a blue globe. Blue emergency lights just began to be used on police cars in 1960, especially in the Deep South. In 1961, Dodge produced two very different cars. One was this 118-inch-wheelbase Dodge Dart. The trim levels were the Seneca, the Pioneer, and the Phoenix. Police-package cars were, of course, based on the low-trim Seneca. The other police car was the 122-inch Dodge Polara. The top cop mill in the Dart Seneca was the 330-horsepower, 383-ci dual quad "D-500 Ram Induction" V-8.

This 1962 Ford Galaxie used by the Nassau County (New York) Police was as hot as they came. The car number, extra "wing" flashers on the front fenders, and the extra speedometer mounted on the upper dash indicate this is a Highway Patrol unit. It is powered by a 330-horsepower, 390-ci FE-block V-8 with a four-barrel carburetor and dual exhausts. This cruiser is dark blue with an orange roof and red emergency lights. This was the year for Fords. In 1962, more Ford police cars were sold than all other makes combined.

Twenty-five-year Pennsylvania State Police veteran trooper Mike Novatnak is shown in period-correct dress uniform with his 1962 Chevrolet Bel Air. The PSP used this particular door shield from 1957 through 1963 on Chevrolets and from 1957 through 1962 on Fords. The yellow letters, "State Police," surround Pennsylvania's famous keystone. The outline of the state is in the center of the keystone. Troopers in the Keystone State drove blue-gray cruisers from the 1940s to the early 1960s. Like the California Highway Patrol, the Pennsylvania State Police often ordered very special engines. Chevrolet was as willing to accommodate the PSP as Dodge was the CHP.

There are a number of reasons why this 1962 Pennsylvania State Police Chevrolet Bel Air is special. First, the PSP ordered its patrol cars with the upscale Bel Air trim level instead of the base Biscayne trim level that was used by everyone else. In fact, there is no mention made in police literature of the police package even being available on the Bel Air. Second, this is the first year for the 327-ci V-8, a bored-and-stroked 283 ci. The 327-ci small block replaced the 348-ci big block. All 327-ci police engines had four-barrel carburetors. Two versions of the 327-ci engine were available: the 250 horsepower and the 300 horsepower. The 327 ci was the first of the "big valve" Chevy small blocks.

The only big police car during a year of very small police cars was this 1962 Chrysler Newport Enforcer. If you think these California Highway Patrol and Chrysler Corporation officials look happy, imagine the CHP Traffic Officers! They received a 122-inch, full-size patrol car powered by a 325-horsepower, 383-ci V-8. All the other cops driving a Mopar received a downsized, 116-inch cruiser with a 305-horsepower, 361-ci V-8 as the largest engine. The CHP was absolutely convinced it needed a 122-inch-wheelbase cruiser. If it had to force Dodge to make a police package out of a retail 1961 Polara, the CHP would do it. If it had to buy Chrysler Newports in 1962, the CHP would do it.

Police departments that demanded a full-size, 122-inch-wheelbase police car had very few choices in 1962. The Fords and Chevrolets measured 119 inches. The Dodges and Plymouths were downsized to just 116 inches. The 1961 Dodge Police, the 122-inch retail car that had been pressed into police service by the CHP, had a mere 116-inch wheelbase for 1962. The 122-inch Dodge Custom 880 was not released until midyear. The obvious choice was this 122-inch Chrysler Newport Enforcer. The standard equipment engine for the Enforcer was the 265-horsepower, 361-ci two-barrel V-8. No thanks, said the California Highway Patrol. It went with the optional 325-horsepower, 383-ci four-barrel V-8. This 383-ci engine was not available in any Dodge or Plymouth police car.

The 1962 California Highway Patrol Chrysler Enforcer was based on the retail Newport. In 1961, the CHP began a study of a variety of police gear including bucket seats, roll bars, head rests, and shoulder harnesses. Fifty cruisers were fitted with auxiliary pusher bumpers. This study carried over to 1962. In the end, pusher bumpers became the absolute symbol of the CHP's Enforcement-class vehicles. While it didn't invent them, the CHP certainly popularized them to the extent that it wasn't considered a real police car unless it had pusher bumpers. It did not matter that pusher bumpers were seldom used, or that they added unwanted weight on an already understeering car, nor that they accelerated front wheel bearing wear. The CHP had good reason to use pusher bumpers, but very few other departments did.

In 1962, the Dodge Dart was restyled to become what is thought to be one of the ugliest police cars ever. The 1962 Dart, as seen in this Chrysler promotion photo, was considered so ugly that when it was announced at the new car dealer conference, a dozen Dodge dealers dropped their franchises that day! Cops made fun of the styling on the 1970 Dodge Coronet. The styling on the 1991 Chevrolet Caprice was also the focus of humor. But the 1962 Dart was simply too ugly to even joke about. This Dart was the full-size Dodge for 1962, the flagship of the "performance" division. It sank. Plymouth's police-car market share took a huge leap upward at Dodge's expense.

In 1962, the entire Dodge car line was downsized. The 122-inch-wheelbase vehicles were eliminated. The 118-inch platforms were reduced to a mere 116 inches. The Polara, which was a 122-inch car in 1961, and the choice of the California Highway Patrol, was now an upgraded trim package on the 116-inch Dart. By name, these Dodges were the Dart 330, Dart 440, and Polara 500. Dodge Division tried to put the best possible spin on these much smaller cars. Using the catch phrase "Action-Economy," the concept suggested that with shorter wheelbases and lighter cars, cops would have both better performance and better fuel economy. Maybe they would not miss the 383-ci big block, which was not available in any Dodge or Plymouth police car.

For 1962, the standard-equipment Dodge police engine was the new 170-ci slant six, a destroked 225-ci slant six, rated at 101 horsepower. Optional engines included the 145-horsepower, 225-ci slant six; 230-horsepower, 318-ci two-barrel V-8; 260-horsepower, 318-ci four-barrel V-8; and 305-horsepower, 361-ci four-barrel V-8. The 383-ci V-8 was not available in any Dodge or Plymouth police car. These new pursuit cars had a shorter wheelbase and less total weight. Dodge claimed the 260-horsepower, 318-ci four-barrel V-8 was intended "For jobs that call for rubber-burning acceleration, rapid interception and continuous high-speed operation . . . The jobs where man and machine never get a chance to cool off." The 1962 literature claimed "Dodge Powers The Law of 28 States, as well as 434 city and 101 county police forces."

Cop-flick enthusiasts will recognize this shot as a re-creation from the movie, *In the Heat of the Night*. Chief Bill Gillespie crosses the bridge from Mississippi to Arkansas in a pivotal scene to arrest murder suspect Harvey Oberst before he crosses the state line. This 1962 Plymouth Savoy is marked as a Sparta (Mississippi) Police cruiser. The driver is police historian, Monty McCord, complete with the Sparta uniform. Actually, the black Sparta cruiser in the movie described as a "fine, big, shiny car" was a 1963 Savoy, while the white Sparta cruiser that crossed the bridge was a 1966 Plymouth Belvedere. However, when the car in question is as fully restored and detailed-out as this 1962 Savoy, it just doesn't matter. True of 1962 Plymouth police cars, this Savoy is powered by a 145-horsepower, 225-ci slant six.

Parked in front of the Sparta (Illinois) Police Department, this all-black 1962 Plymouth Savoy bears the vintage markings of the Sparta Police, exactly as seen on the 1967 movie, *In the Heat of the Night*. It's true that the epic cop flick was set in Sparta, Mississippi. But the movie was actually filmed in Sparta, Illinois, a tiny town in the southern part of the state. In fact, the train depot was completely renovated for the 25th anniversary of the filming in 1992. Many of the pivotal scenes in the movie took place at the depot. The city of Sparta is proud of its film heritage. For the record, filming for the T.V. series *In the Heat of the Night* took place in Conyers, Georgia.

This 1962 Plymouth Belvedere was with the U.S. Park Police. The all-black two-door cruiser patrolled the parks in the Washington, D.C., area. The emergency lights include a single roof rotator with a red-and-white lens under a clear globe. Also note the red "pull-over" light on the right front fender. In front of the side-facing fender light is a fender-mounted mechanical siren. It's a little surprising that the Park Police used the mid-trim level Belvedere rather than the base-level Savoy. The stainless-steel strips along the fender feature line identifies the trim level. It's also a little surprising to have optional backup lights on any low-bid government vehicle. The white lenses next to the tail lights are backup lights, available for an extra $11, regardless of trim level.

The Los Angeles County Sheriff operated this 1962 Plymouth Savoy. These new Savoys were undergoing fleet preparation when this photo was taken. The emergency gear includes a mechanical siren, two forward-facing reds, and a rear-facing amber all mounted on a triangular plate, which was bolted to the roof. This cruiser sports dual-exhaust pipes, a sure sign of a four-barrel carburetor and high-lift-cam V-8. In this case, it was the 305-horsepower, 361-ci V-8. In the early 1960s, Los Angeles County purchased Plymouths because exhaust emission controls were available. By 1963, Chrysler had developed the Cleaner Air Package. The CAP included a specially calibrated carburetor and a retarded-ignition distributor. The package also included a six-bladed fan with shroud to overcome any overheating problems caused by lean mixtures and retarded timing. By 1963, the CAP-equipped Mopars met California's 1966 emissions standard.

Notice this fleet of police cars with the Pinellas County Sheriff's Office in Largo, Florida. The front row has black-and-white 1962 Plymouths while the second row has 1961 black-and-white Plymouths. The unmarked cruisers include 1962 Plymouths and 1961 Chevrolets. It was common for marked and unmarked cruisers to be different makes and models. These 1961 and 1962 Plymouths are powered by the 361-ci Wedge V-8. The use of a "V" hood stripe or hood painting dates as far back as the late 1930s and has continued into the late 1990s. These Pinellas County cars have gold stars and red lights.

In 1962, the "interceptor" car used by the Los Angeles Police was the Pontiac Catalina, powered by the 389-ci V-8 with three two-barrel carburetors rated at 345 horsepower. However, the "patrol" car used in 1962 by the LAPD was this Plymouth Savoy. The 230-horsepower, 318-ci two-barrel V-8 bolted to the new TorqueFlite powered most of the four-door sedans. The 0- to 60-mile-per-hour times were 11 seconds, which was mighty slow. Some of the LAPD cruisers had the 260-horsepower, 318-ci four-barrel V-8, which included a high-performance cam, dual point distributor, and dual exhausts. The LAPD's 1962 Savoys were white over black with a roof-mounted mechanical siren and twin soup-can lights. With these lights, the forward-facing reds burned continuously while the rear-facing ambers flashed.

The Greenwich, Connecticut, Police drove this 1962 Plymouth Savoy. A four-way, non-revolving red flasher tops the white cruiser. This was common in the late 1950s and early 1960s. For 1962, Dodges and Plymouths were available with the "new" push-button three-speed TorqueFlite with a new "Park" position. This was the first year TorqueFlites had an aluminum housing. This version was 60 pounds lighter than the cast-iron version. It was also more compact, allowing a smaller transmission tunnel bump and more driver compartment room. Most important, this new transmission still had the push-bottom controls and all the ruggedness cops expected. The three-speed TorqueFlite was the most durable automatic transmission ever built by any auto manufacturer.

In 1962, the Indiana State Police selected the Chevrolet Biscayne as its patrol car. The ISP used these white-over-blue cruisers between 1960 and 1966. The 1962 model year saw the introduction of two of Chevrolet's most famous engines for police cars, the 327-ci small block and the 409-ci big block. The 327-ci was a bored-and-stroked version of the 283-ci engine introduced in 1957. This was the first of the 4.00-inch-bore small blocks. The 409-ci was a bored-and-stroked version of the 348-ci wedge-block engine introduced in 1958. The 409-ci V-8 was the first Chevrolet police-car engine to sport dual-quad (two four-barrel) carburetors, and the only police engine of any make or year to produce over 400 horsepower. This ISP Biscayne is powered by the milder, 380-horsepower version of the 409-ci V-8 with a single four-barrel.

This 1962 Chevrolet Biscayne was with the Harwood Heights (Illinois) Police at the scene of an arson. This four-door sedan has a red rotator and red high-beam lenses. In 1962, the Chevrolet police package was a Regular Production Option (RPO 400) on the Biscayne, Bel Air, and Impala. Of these, only the two-door and four-door Biscayne and the Biscayne station wagon are specifically mentioned in the police literature. The RPO 400 police package included 15-inch wheels, sintered-metallic brake shoes, and a heavy-duty suspension. The police package was also available on the 110-inch-wheelbase Chevy II. This compact police car came standard with a 194-ci six, while a 153-ci four was optional. This was the first four-cylinder engine produced by Chevrolet since the introduction of the six-cylinder engine in 1929.

Notice this 1962 Ford Galaxie with the markings of the Franklin Park Police. Franklin Park is on Chicago's northwest side near Chicago's O'Hare Airport. This all-white cruiser has bold black lettering, a red rotator, and red high-beam lenses. Powertrains for the police Galaxie included the 138-horsepower, 223-ci six; 170-horsepower, 292-ci V-8; 220-horsepower, 352-ci V-8; and both 300- and 330-horsepower versions of the 390-ci four-barrel dual exhaust V-8. Powertrains for Ford's new mid-size police car, the Fairlane, included the 101-horsepower, 170-ci six; 145-horsepower, 221-ci V-8; and the 160-horsepower, 260-ci V-8. The 221-ci engine was the first Windsor small-block V-8. In mid-1962, Ford released the more famous 260-ci Windsor V-8. Future Windsor-based V-8s would be the 289-ci, 302-ci, and 351-ci engines. All these engines have the same 4.38-inch cylinder bore centers.

The Sparta Police in downstate Illinois owned this 1962 Chevrolet Biscayne. Powertrains for 1962 included the 135-horsepower, 235-ci six; 170-horsepower, 283-ci V-8; 250- and 300-horsepower versions of the 327-ci four-barrel V-8; 380-horsepower, 409-ci four-barrel V-8; and the dual quad 409-ci V-8 rated at 409 horsepower. Both 327-ci engines had a 10.5 to 1 compression while both 409-ci engines had an 11.0 to 1. The 409 ci was the first of Chevrolet's bad-to-the-bones "super-stock" engines, designed to compete with the Mopar 413-ci Max Wedge engines. The 409-horsepower, 409-ci V-8-powered Biscayne with a four-speed Synchro-Mesh and 3.36 rear gears hit 60 miles per hour in 6.3 seconds and ran the quarter mile in 14.9 seconds. That was quick for a 3,475-pound cruiser with skinny 6.70x15-inch tires. Chevrolet recommended the twin four-barrel engine for "specialized pursuit duty."

This perfectly restored 1962 Ford Galaxie bears the markings of the Dallas, Texas Police. This award-winning, big-block cruiser is one of the most popular cars on the police-car show circuit. This particular cruiser also appeared in the movie, *The Trial of Lee Harvey Oswald*. The Thunderbird engine emblem on the lower front quarter panel tells would-be scofflaws that this 119-inch Ford is packing a 330-horsepower, 390-ci four-barrel V-8. This was Ford's top cop engine. While Ford joined the horsepower race during the Super Stock era with a 405-horsepower, 406-ci V-8, this bored-out 390-ci engine was never used in police cars. This Dallas cruiser is topped by a red lens, mechanical siren, and twin red flashers. It also has a vintage traffic radar unit.

This 1962 Plymouth Savoy has the markings of the Pope Valley (California) Police. The police package for the 116-inch Savoy included heavy-duty springs, Oriflow shocks, dual electric windshield wipers, a calibrated speedometer, left and right sun visors, a 70-amp battery, a 40-amp alternator, extra heavy-duty 14x5.5-inch or 15x5.5-inch wheels, and the new 3.23 to 1 maximum-duty rear axle. Options included a Sure-Grip axle, power brakes, power steering, and a 60-amp alternator. Advancements for 1962 included a lightweight TorqueFlite automatic, a high-torque starter motor, improved recirculating-ball manual steering, self-adjusting "Servo-Contact" brakes, and longer lubrication intervals. Police engines ranged from the 170-ci slant six to the 361-ci V-8. This was the first, and last, year that the 170-ci six-cylinder was used in police cars.

The Chicago Fire Department used this 1962 Buick LeSabre. Assigned to the 7th Division, this two-door LeSabre is red with a black roof and black wheels. The black roof dates back to a time when the CFD put black rubber on canvas-topped fire cars in order to waterproof them. This 123-inch-wheelbase Buick has plenty of roof-mounted warning gear. There are twin sirens with integral white lights, twin side-facing red lights, and twin forward-facing white lights. Available engines in 1962 included the 265-horsepower, 401-ci V-8; the 280-horsepower, 401-ci V-8; and the 325-horsepower, 401-ci "Wildcat" V-8. Fire departments almost always used police-package vehicles, either two-door sedans, four-door sedans, or station wagons.

Bearing the door markings of the Tulare (California) Police, this 1962 Dodge Dart four-door sedan was judged the "Best Restored 'Novelty' Car" at the 1998 Northern California police car show. The "Novelty" class was designed for nonpolice-package vehicles that have been accurately restored to resemble a genuine police car. Just the front doors on this black-and-white cruiser are painted white. This was the custom of Northern California police agencies, following the lead of the California Highway Patrol. The four-door cruiser has twin forward-facing, continuously burning red lights and a red roof rotator. The TPD door shield has a gold city seal based on the state seal.

The Chicago Police used this 1962 Dodge Dart. The roof, front doors, and trunk are white, while the rest of the Windy City patroller is medium-blue. The roof rotator has a blue globe, as CPD cars had had since mid-1960. The door shield is a blue, five-point star with a gold city seal and gold lettering. The door shield was gold on blue from 1960 to 1965. This particular Dodge sports a rear-facing traffic radar antenna. The 5000-series car number identifies this as a Traffic Division car. This means it was powered by one of the more powerful engines, such as the 260-horsepower, 318-ci V-8 or the 305-horsepower, 361-ci V-8. The Patrol Division cars, with numbers in the 7000, 8000, and 9000 series, were powered by either the 170-ci or 225-ci slant six.

This jet-black 1963 Pontiac Catalina has been meticulously restored as a replica of the police cars used by the Clarkstown Police in Rockland County, New York. Owned by the Clarkstown Police Benevolent Association, this patrol car has been judged "Best-In-Class" at the Washington, D.C., Police Memorial car show. While this police car is based on the base trim level Catalina, it used the 303-horsepower, 389-ci four-barrel V-8 from the upscale Bonneville series. It is fitted with a single red rotator.

The Columbus (Georgia) Police used this Viking Blue 1963 Ford 300. The letters on the doors and deck lid are gold. This beautifully restored vehicle has the original Police Sentinel package. At the beginning of the model year, this package included the 164-horsepower, 260-ci V-8. By midyear, this engine was replaced by the 195-horsepower, 289-ci V-8, which powers this car. Note the right fender-mounted siren. When in service, this police car was assigned to CPD Sgt. David Reed, who would become a 30-year police veteran.

This 1963 Ford Galaxie is one of the extremely popular Mayberry replicas. The formula is easy. Take any 1960 to 1965 full-size Ford four-door sedan. Paint the roof and doors white and the body black. Install a red rotator. Have a local graphics shop make a pair of gold, five-point stars with the words, "Sheriff Mayberry." Get yourself one bullet for your left shirt pocket and you are done.

If that is a black-and-white 1963 Ford Galaxie 500 with a red rotator and gold five-point star, then we must be in Mayberry County, North Carolina. Expect to see this four-door sedan patrolling fictional Route 43, Route 88, Route 31, Route 22, Highway 6, Highway 10, and Highway 1, all of which criss-cross Mayberry County.

Pictured is a 1963 Ford Galaxie 500 Mayberry replica. The Mayberry Fords are extremely popular at police car shows and Mayberry-style reunions alike. About police patrol techniques, you'll hear Barney Fife say, "One of the few differences Andy and me have when it comes to crime fighting is how much modern technology should be used. I'm a hardware man. Andy's not. Ya' either are or ya' ain't. Andy ain't. I am."

With the traditional white-over-black markings, this 1963 Ford Galaxie bears the markings of the Orland Park (Illinois) Police. Notice the black door lettering. The use of lettering to identify a police car as opposed to a door shield or star was popular in the 1950s and carried over slightly in the 1960s. The Chicago Police went from lettering to a five-point star in 1960. The New York City Police went from lettering to a door shield in 1961. This Orland Park cruiser with red rotator is a show and parade car with the Chicago suburb. It is pictured at the annual Memorial Day parade, which honors fallen soldiers and fallen police officers alike . . . lest any may forget.

Many state police and highway patrols used the 1963 Ford 300 and Ford Galaxie. These included the Missouri State Highway Patrol, North Carolina Highway Patrol, Nebraska State Patrol, Pennsylvania State Police, South Dakota Highway Patrol, Washington State Patrol, and New York State Police. The patrol cars with each of these state police or highway patrols were powered by the 330-horsepower, 390-ci FE-block four-barrel dual-exhaust V-8; so was this Missouri State Highway patrol cruiser. This engine was not nearly as powerful as the Chevrolet 380-horsepower, single four-barrel 409-ci V-8. However, it was very comparable to the Chrysler 325-horsepower, 383-ci V-8 and more powerful than the Dodge/Plymouth 305-horsepower, 361-ci V-8.

The Montreal (Quebec) Police operated this 1963 Ford 300. The solid black cruiser with white hood, door, and trunk lettering has a red rotator. For 1963, the 170-horsepower, 292-ci Y-block was replaced by the 164-horsepower, 260-ci Windsor V-8. The 292-ci engine had been used in police cars since 1955. The 260-ci engine was ideal for urban patrol situations such as Montreal. The 260 ci was a bored-out version of the 221-ci V-8 with the same stroke. This was the second in this series of engine blocks using new thin-wall casting techniques for the lightest engine of its displacement. Introduced to police work in 1962, the 260-ci engine had been restricted to the mid-size Fairlane. For 1963, it became the small V-8 on the full-size Ford. This was the only year the 260-ci engine was used in the full-size Ford 300 and Galaxie. By 1964, the small V-8 was the famous 289-ci Windsor engine.

For 1963, the Washington State Patrol kept its loyalty to Ford by using the full-size Ford 300. This four-door sedan is a fully marked patrol car, complete with black door and trunk lettering, a red rotator, and black lightning bolt. These WSP Blue Ovals were powered by the 330-horsepower, 390-ci four-barrel V-8. WSP troopers reported that the 390-ci Fords were not quite as fast as the 361-ci Dodges used in 1962. This was easy to understand. The 119-inch 1963 Ford 300 weighed 3,640 pounds and had 330 horsepower. The 116-inch 1962 Dart weighed 3,170 pounds and had 305 horsepower. This Ford, being cleaned and prepped by mechanics from Fred Lewis Ford in North Bend, Washington, was one of the first all-white WSP cruisers to be widely used for patrol. The white WSP cruisers were assigned to the Seattle area where traffic was heaviest. The light-colored cars with roof lights were highly visible.

In 1963, the Los Angeles Police selected the Ford 300 as its general-duty patrol car. These cruisers were powered by the 220-horsepower, 352-ci two-barrel single exhaust V-8 teamed with the three-speed Cruise-O-Matic and 3.00 to 1 rear gears. Detectives drove unmarked Ford 300s powered by the 138-horsepower, 223-ci six. Investigators and deputy chiefs used Ford 300s with the 300-horsepower, 390-ci V-8. The Fords were not popular among LAPD cops. The use of the siren, red lights, and two-way radio at the same time would drain the electrical system so much that the engine would lose power. In the LAPD's experience, the 1963 Ford did not have the handling, braking, or reliability of the Plymouths and Dodges used between 1960 and 1962.

The Cook County Sheriff Department, surrounding Illinois' Windy City, used this 1963 Ford 300. These full-size Fords have a white roof over a brown hood and trunk with white doors and fenders. The door shield is gold and brown, while the roof rotator is red. The CCSP made a good choice by selecting white wheels. Note the fender-mounted spotlight. Interestingly, the Ford crest in the center of the grille was the hood latch. A few other departments ran the 1963 Ford 300. These included the Pinellas County (Florida) Sheriff; Dallas Police; San Francisco Police; and St. Louis County (Missouri) Sheriff.

The Cook County (Illinois) Sheriff's Correctional Department used this 1963 Ford Country Sedan as a prisoner transport unit. The Country Sedan wagon had the same trim level as the mid-range Galaxie sedan. Jail Unit 4 is white over brown over white with a single red rotator. The entire passenger compartment behind the front seat is lined with chain-link fencing, including the tailgate window. The police-package Country Sedans were available in all police drivetrains from the 223-ci six to the 390-ci Police Interceptor V-8. This transport unit wisely has the big, bad 330-horsepower, 390-ci four-barrel V-8. The police wagon hauled heavy loads and on occasion had to get up and go!

This 1963 Ford Galaxie 500 has been restored as a Lyon County (Nevada) Sheriff's unit. Lyon County is just east of Reno and Carson City. The all-white, four-door Ford has a red rotator and twin, door-mounted red lights. The only other police marking is the black and gold, five-point star. The Thunderbird engine emblem on the front fender denotes this is a 330-horsepower, 390-ci V-8. According to the Ford police car literature, "The Interceptor 4-V/390 V-8 is a specially engineered 330 horsepower powerplant designed exclusively for and sold only to law enforcement agencies." Since this LCSD cruiser is the upscale Galaxie 500, it has the full-dress wheelcovers. However, no self-respecting deputy sheriff would patrol his jurisdiction in a squad car with whitewall tires!

For 185,000 miles, this 1963 Chevrolet Biscayne was on-the-job with the U.S. Park Police. The jet-black cruiser has red and white lights under the clear rotator globe. Mounted on the right front fender are a mechanical siren and a red "pull-over" light. The top speed this Biscayne was claimed to have reached was 142 miles per hour, as verified by radar. Therefore, this unit was probably powered by the 400-horsepower, 409-ci four-barrel V-8. The 409-ci big block came in three versions in 1963: a 340-horsepower, four-barrel engine with 10 to 1 compression; a 400-horsepower, four-barrel engine with 11 to 1 compression; and a 425-horsepower, dual quad eight-barrel engine with 11 to 1 compression. The Iowa State Patrol, Missouri State Highway Patrol, and the Kansas Highway Patrol also drove 409-ci-powered Biscaynes.

Bearing the markings of the Pevely (Missouri) Police, this 1963 Chevrolet Biscayne is an original-condition cruiser. The dark-blue and light-blue door shield with gold lettering is based on the St. Louis Metro Police shield, which is in turn based on the Missouri State Highway Patrol shield. The 195-horsepower, 283-ci two-barrel V-8 bolted to the two-speed Powerglide powers this cruiser. It also has air conditioning! The police package was available on the 119-inch-wheelbase two-door and four-door Biscayne sedan and station wagon and the compact, 110-inch four-door Chevy II. The ill-fated, rear-engine Corvair was no longer available with a police package. A Biscayne powered by the 195-horsepower, 283-ci V-8 hit 60 miles per hour in 10.7 seconds.

The California Highway Patrol originally operated this restored 1963 Dodge 880. For 1963, the CHP was back in Dodges and back in 122-inch-wheelbase Enforcement-class vehicles. The big news was a brand-new big-block V-8, the 413-ci wedge. This raised-block, B-engine had been a Chrysler Corporation engine since 1959. It first appeared in the Chrysler New Yorker as a replacement for the 392-ci Hemi-head V-8. This same year, with in-line dual quads, it also powered the exotic Chrysler 300 E. In 1960 and 1961 the 413-ci was again hot-rodded with dual quad "cross-ram" induction setups. The 1962 413-ci V-8, in Max Wedge form, was Chrysler Corporation's first true drag-racing engine. For 1963, this highly developed big block was detuned to "only" 360 horsepower. It was available only as a Chrysler Enforcer and Dodge 880 police engine.

The 1963 Dodge 880 used by the California Highway Patrol has the back end from a 1963 Chrysler. Only the front sheet metal is new. Dodge sold the long, 122-inch wheelbase sedan for the luxury-car and law-enforcement market. The CHP, in particular, had long insisted on a 122-inch-wheelbase vehicle weighing at least 3,800 pounds, and the 1963 Dodge 880 met that standard. While the CHP selected the 360-horsepower, 413-ci four-barrel V-8, other police engines were available on the big Dodge, including the 305-horsepower, 383-ci two-barrel V-8 and the 265-horsepower, 361-ci two-barrel V-8. The three-speed stick was standard equipment, but the famous "push-button" three-speed TorqueFlite was almost always requested on vehicle fleet orders. The rear gear ratio was 3.23:1, and a Sure-Grip limited-slip differential was optional. The police package included either 8.50x14-inch tires or 7.60x15-inch tires.

In 1963, the California Highway Patrol selected the Dodge 880 as its Enforcement-class vehicle. The Dodge Dart shrank from 116 inches to 111 inches in 1963, but was no longer available with a police package. The new mid-size Dodge was the 119-inch 330, 440, and Polara series. Restyled for 1963 was this 122-inch-wheelbase Dodge 880. The Dodge 880 was a mid-1962 release to fill the gap left by the demise of DeSoto. It had a 1962 Chrysler body with a 1961 Dodge front end. For 1963, the Dodge 880 was still pure Chrysler-marque from the windshield and firewall back. However, the 880 received a newly styled front end and a Dodge identity of its own. This particular Dodge 880 was an original CHP cruiser and has been restored to award-winning condition by California State University Police Corporal John Bellah.

A California Highway Patrol traffic officer stands next to his 1963 Dodge 880 with ticket book in hand. The Dodge 880 was available only as a four-door sedan. The Dodge 880 now had the same 122-inch wheelbase and the same selection of engines ranging from the 361-ci two-barrel V-8 to the 413-ci four-barrel V-8. The police package on this Dodge 880 included 11x3-inch drums. These extrawide brakes were straight off the big Chryslers. Options included a Sure-Grip differential, a seven-blade fan with shroud, and an extrahigh-capacity radiator. Dual-belt-drive alternators of up to 100 amps were also optional. Dodge would even install the fender-mounted spotlights. Full of cop gear, this CHP Dodge with a 360-horsepower, 413-ci four-barrel V-8 ran the quarter mile in the 16-second bracket.

The Chicago Police Department used this 1963 Plymouth Savoy. The police package included a calibrated speedometer, a 40-amp alternator, a 70-amp battery, heavy-duty shocks and springs, either 14x5-1/2-inch wheels or 15x5-1/2-inch wheels, and 11-inch drum brakes. This CPD unit is powered by a 145-horsepower, 225-ci slant six. The police Savoy with a V-8 also came standard with a front sway bar. Three V-8 engines were available. These included the 230-horsepower, 318-ci two-barrel; the 265-horsepower, 361-ci two-barrel; and the 330-horsepower, 383-ci four-barrel. After a one-year absence, the 383-ci big block was back. Forget all the focus on wheelbases. With a 383-ci V-8, the Savoy was faster than the 383-ci-powered Dodge 330 and just as fast as the 413-ci-powered Dodge 880.

This all-white 1963 Plymouth Savoy is with the Milwaukee (Wisconsin) Police. In a snowstorm, all you would see are the black wheels, black door lettering, and red rotator. The door markings are very simple, "Milwaukee" in small letters and "Police" in big letters. A mechanical siren is mounted in front of the red gumball. These kind of general-purpose patrol cars were probably powered by one of the medium-sized V-8s, either the 318-ci two-barrel or the 361-ci two-barrel. Remember, the 318-ci engine was still the polysphere-head, big-block V-8. The 318 ci was a big block from 1957 through 1966. For 1967, the 318 ci became the third engine to benefit from thin-wall, high-precision casting techniques to make it a small block. The first engine was the 1964 273-ci V-8 and the second was the 1966 440-ci V-8.

In 1963, the Nevada Highway Patrol opted for the 119-inch Dodge 330 instead of the larger, 122-inch Dodge 880. Then-Superintendent Robert Stenovich (left), Chief of the Patrol, accepted the keys to the first of 33 white-over-black Dodges from Phil Roventini of State Motors in Carson City, Nevada. These Dodge 330s were powered by the 330-horsepower, 383-ci four-barrel V-8. At 3,253 pounds, the mid-size Dodge 330 with 330 horsepower was actually faster than the full-size, 3,790-pound Dodge 880 with the 360-horsepower, 413-ci four-barrel V-8. This just fueled the long-standing rivalry between the Nevada Highway Patrol and the California Highway Patrol. The NHP Dodge had a gold-and-blue seven-point star and a large, roof-mounted red flasher with forward- and rearward-facing lenses.

This photo captures Los Angeles County Sheriff's mechanics doing fleet preparation on their new 1963 Plymouth Savoy. From left to right: Apply door shield-Check; Install passenger-side spotlight-Check; Wire the roof-mounted red lights-Check; Remember, this is California: be sure the twin red lights illuminate but do not flash-Double check; Mount the driver-side spotlight-Check.

For 1963, Dodge extended its 116-inch wheelbase to 119 inches and 122 inches. With the 119-inch models came a new series beginning with this Dodge 330, upon which the police package was based. Other trim levels in this mid-size series were the Dodge 440 and the Polara. This cruiser from a Chrysler promotional piece is a four-door sedan; however, two-door versions were also available with the police package. The base police engine was the 145-horsepower, 225-ci slant six, while the 230-horsepower, 318-ci V-8 was a no-cost option. Other optional police engines included the 265-horsepower, 361-ci two-barrel V-8; 305-horsepower, 383-ci two-barrel; and the 330-horsepower, 383-ci four-barrel V-8. The three-speed stick came with either 3.23 or 3.55 rear gears. The push-button, three-speed TorqueFlite came with either 3.23 or 2.93 rear gears. Only the four-barrel engine had dual exhausts.

The factory used this 1963 Studebaker Lark Marshal as a demo police car. The 289-ci V-8, available as a 210-horsepower, two-barrel engine or as a 225-horsepower, four-barrel mill, powered this particular Marshal. The 170-ci six and 259-ci V-8 were also available with the police-package Studebaker. The South Bend, Indiana-based car company had big powertrain news for cops in 1963. Two Jet-Thrust engines used in the Avanti were now an option. Based on the 289-ci V-8, the naturally aspirated four-barrel version produced 240 horsepower. The supercharged version of the same 289-ci engine was rated at 289 horsepower. The Avanti was Studebaker's fiberglass-bodied, two-seat sports coupe.

This 1964 Ford Galaxie 500 represents the car driven on the T.V. series *The Andy Griffith Show,* and is one of dozens of Mayberry replicas seen at car shows from coast to coast. One look at this black-and-white Ford and one can almost hear Barney say, "We're just plain, simple men fighting organized crime with raw courage . . . strong, determined, rugged and fearless." Or, "There's a little hayseed in all of us . . . some of us cover it up better than others."

The Pennsylvania State Police used this 1964 Ford Custom. The Galaxie nameplate was used with police-package cars only in 1962 and 1963. It disappeared in 1964 and resumed in 1969. The police package was available on both two-door and four-door versions of this 119-inch-wheelbase cruiser. This PSP patrol car has a red rotator mounted on a white vehicle with a bright-green hood and trunk. In 1964, Ford was once again the most popular brand of police car in America.

This 1964 Ford Galaxie 500 has the easy-to-recognize markings of the Mayberry County (NC) Sheriff's Department.

The 1964 Ford Custom with the Manteca Police in Northern California, south of Stockton, was a very simply marked unit. The all-white, four-door sedan has a fender-mounted spotlight with a red lens and both red and amber flashing lights on the driver's side of the package tray. It has no roof-mounted lights. As the base trim level, this Custom also lacks some of the side chrome found on the upscale Custom 500. Both the Custom and Custom 500 came with the police package. Powerplants for the full-size Ford included the 138-horsepower, 223-ci Police Special six; 195-horsepower, 289-ci two-barrel Challenger V-8; 250-horsepower, 352-ci four-barrel Thunderbird V-8; 300-horsepower, 390-ci four-barrel Thunderbird V-8; and the 330-horsepower, 390-ci four-barrel Police Interceptor V-8. For traffic enforcement along California's Highway 99, this Manteca unit packed the Police Interceptor V-8.

The Iowa Highway Patrol drove this tan 1964 Ford Custom 500. The Iowa Highway Patrol changed its name to Iowa State Patrol in 1973. Emergency lights used on this 119-inch cruiser consisted of a single red roof rotator. In 1964, Ford began the "Total Performance" promotional theme. This was an emphasis on balanced performance, not necessarily the most performance. The Ford police car may not accelerate like a Dodge, or brake like a Chevrolet, or corner like a Pontiac. However, Ford's goal was to be sufficient in all categories in order to give the best "Total Performance." Ford did not have 360-horsepower police engines like Dodge, let alone 425-horsepower police engines like Chevrolet. The 330-horsepower, 390-ci four-barrel dual exhaust V-8 was good enough to get the job done for the state police or highway patrol in at least a dozen states. Note this two-door sedan. The formal police package was available on two-door sedans and four-door sedans alike.

The North Carolina Highway Patrol used the 1964 Ford Custom to enforce laws in the Tar Heel State. The Washington State Patrol and Texas Highway Patrol also prowled around in the 1964 Custom. All were powered by the 330-horsepower, 390-ci four-barrel dual exhaust V-8 teamed with a three-speed Cruise-O-Matic and 3.00 to 1 rear gears. This 330-horsepower version was the Police Interceptor engine. The Custom with either 390-ci engine had the Thunderbird-style engine emblem on the lower front fender. The 390-ci V-8 was still considered a Thunderbird engine, but so was the 250-horsepower, 352-ci four-barrel V-8. The two-speed Fordomatic was no longer available in the full-size Custom. The NCHP kept this black-over-silver paint scheme until the 1980s.

This restored 1964 Ford Custom 500 is marked as a Chillicothe, Ohio, Police cruiser. The 119-inch Ford sports a red rotator and a white-over-black color scheme with a gold door shield and eagle. The 289-ci small-block V-8 was released for police cars in mid-1963. For 1964 it was available in both the full-size Custom and the mid-size, 115.5-inch-wheelbase Fairlane. This engine was basically a bored-out version of the 260-ci V-8. The 195 horsepower, 289-ci two-barrel V-8 was intended for routine patrol in urban areas where fuel economy was a concern. Ford claimed this combination gave "thrifty performance."

In 1964, the Chevrolet Z04 police-chassis package and B01 police-body package were based on the Biscayne trim level like this Ankeny, Iowa, Police cruiser. The police package was available on the two-door, four-door, and station wagon. This cruiser is black-and-white with a gold door shield and door lettering. The warning equipment includes a rectangular siren speaker in front of a red rotator. The 195-horse-power, 283-ci two-barrel V-8 with two-speed Powerglide and 3.36 rear gears was a popular powertrain for urban enforcement. With this drive line, the 119-inch Biscayne hit 60 miles per hour in 12.7 seconds. It ran the quarter mile in 19.2 seconds. The top speed from this two-barrel small-block V-8 was 108 miles per hour. Police engines with more than twice that horsepower were also available in the Biscayne.

It's interesting to note that this 1964 Ford Fairlane is a replica of the mid-size Fords used by patrol constables in New Windsor, New York, during the early 1960s. New Windsor is on the Hudson River just north of New York City. Restored by NWPD Officer Greg Gaetano, this mid-size, four-door sedan has a 115.5-inch wheelbase. The cruiser has a black roof over a white body and sports a red rotator. Part-time patrol constables staffed the NWPD until the department became a full-time agency in 1966. The pre-1966 constables used six-cylinder-powered Fords. When the agency went full time, the police officers used eight-cylinder-powered Dodges and Plymouths. The police-package Fairlane was available with two small-block V-8s and two in-line sixes.

This restored 1964 Chevrolet Bel Air wins some kind of trophy every time it attends a police car show. Whether the show judges are cops or rodders, the result is the same. This Vermilion County (Illinois) Sheriff's cruiser is as good as it gets. The black-and-white patroller has a white, blue, and black five-point star and a window-mounted, stationary traffic radar unit. The headlight high beams, fender-mounted spotlight, and roof rotator are all red. Of course, it has a low-band radio frequency "whip antenna." Inside is a period-correct Motorola radio and Federal Signal siren controller. This beautiful piece of Chevrolet and Illinois police history is powered by a 195-horsepower, 283-ci V-8 teamed to a two-speed Powerglide. It cruises down the road like Grandma's car.

In 1964, the Indiana State Police drove the Plymouth Savoy Police Special. These cars had a white roof over a solid-blue body. The door shield was deep-blue and silver with white lettering and a gold "V." Note the roof-mounted "torpedo," a combination red light and mechanical siren. These cruisers also had a red lens in the A-pillar-mounted spotlight. These Hoosier State squad cars were powered by the 330-horsepower, 383-ci four-barrel V-8. This "Commando 383 V-8" was standard equipment with the Pursuit Special police package. Other go-fast goodies with this package included the heavy-duty, three-speed TorqueFlite with a high-speed governor. This was still the famous "push-button" automatic, but it was the last year.

The Missouri State Highway Patrol operated this 1964 Chrysler Newport Enforcer. This was the second year for this front-end styling. It was also the last year a police package was available on the big, 122-inch-wheelbase Newport, ending a 4-year run. For 1964, the 360-horsepower, 413-ci four-barrel wedge-head V-8 was the one and only Chrysler-marque police engine. This 360-horsepower V-8 was shared only with the Dodge 880 pursuit cars and the Chrysler 300K personal luxury car. This jet-black Enforcer has the very latest emergency lights. New for 1964, Federal Signal released its soon-to-be-legendary Visibar lightbar. This would be the lights system of choice for well into the next decade.

Adorned by a generic door shield, this all-black 1964 Chrysler Newport Enforcer had a classic red Federal Beacon Ray. According to Chrysler, "The Chrysler Enforcer will meet the demands of any emergency and be first on the scene. There's power to spare in its big 413 cubic inch Police Engine, and it's teamed with a special high-performance (3.23 to 1) axle for lightning acceleration to interceptor speeds. Whether on tight city turns or over unpaved roads, control is sure and easy with Chrysler's exclusive heavy-duty torsion bar suspension. A front sway eliminator shaft (anti-roll bar) adds to the Enforcer's outstanding cornering ability. Fast straight-line stops from high speeds are provided by the Enforcer's fade resistant heavy-duty brakes."

In 1964, the Missouri State Highway Patrol ran the Dodge 880 powered by the 360-horsepower, 413-ci four-barrel V-8. This 122-inch Show Me State cruiser is all-white with a gold, blue, and gray door shield. A progressive new kind of emergency light system is mounted on this Dodge 880. Federal Sign and Signal, later to become Federal Signal, invented this double rotator lightbar, called the Visibar. Federal took two of its ever-popular Beacon-Ray rotators and mounted them on a bar that also accepted an external siren speaker. Interestingly, one of Visibar's lights was powered while a silent chain from the powered unit drove the other light. By mechanically indexing the two lights, one geared to rotate slightly faster than the other, Federal was able to produce the first variable-flash warning signal. This revolutionized police emergency equipment.

In 1964, Dodge celebrated 50 years of auto production by capturing the California Highway Patrol contract for Enforcement-class vehicles with this Dodge 880. John Francis Dodge and Horace Elgin Dodge were major players in the auto industry long before Dodge Brothers Motor Car Company incorporated on July 14, 1914. The Dodge Brothers supplied transmissions to Oldsmobile in 1901 and engines, transmissions, and axles to Ford from 1904 to 1914. John Dodge was once the director of Ford Motor Company. Dodge Brothers was sold to Walter P. Chrysler in 1928. This 1964 CHP Dodge 880 is powered by the 360-horsepower, 413-ci V-8. And yes, it snows in California.

The California Highway Patrol used this 1964 Dodge 330 station wagon for commercial vehicle enforcement. The official police package was available for station wagons just like the official police package was available for two-door sedans and coupes. This all-white wagon was the truckers' worst nightmare. Like the two-door and four-door Dodge 330 sedans, the Dodge 330 police wagon was available in a wide variety of engines from the 145-horsepower, 225-ci one-barrel slant six to the 330-horsepower, 383-ci four-barrel V-8. The police package included a heavy-duty suspension. As a rule, this meant one more leaf in the rear leaf springs. That's why this station wagon had a balanced and even stance even though the back end was fully loaded with instruments of trucker torture, including portable scales.

This 1964 Plymouth Savoy has been accurately restored right down to the period-correct, four-way flashing, not rotating, red light. Patrolman Mark Wilson of the Greenwich (Connecticut) Police did a lot of research and searching for parts to make the squad car with his agency's name a true representation of the past. Among the most accurate, but least understood, aspects of this 116-inch-wheelbase Savoy is the drivetrain. This two-door cruiser has what many urban police patrollers had, a 225-ci slant six bolted to a "three on the tree." This may shatter some images of older police cars. The facts are, more police cars, of all makes and models, were sold with a six or a small V-8 than with the big-block V-8. This Savoy is true-to-form right down to the 7.00x14 four-ply blackwall rayon tires.

Restored as a Santa Monica (California) Police unit, this 1964 Plymouth Savoy has the Los Angeles County Sheriff-style emergency lights. These include two continuously burning red lights to the front and a mechanical siren mounted on a triangular roof plate. Behind the siren, and facing the rear, is an amber flashing light. This white-over-black Patroller Special was formerly a Los Angeles County Sheriff detective unit. In 1964, both the Los Angeles Police Department and the Los Angeles County Sheriff ran the Plymouth Savoy. The LAPD patrol cars were powered by the 305-horsepower, 383-ci two-barrel V-8. The Los Angeles County Sheriff's cars were powered by the 330-horsepower, 383-ci four-barrel V-8. Detectives and investigators with both Los Angeles agencies drove Plymouths with a variety of powertrains from the 225-ci slant six to the 383-ci four-barrel V-8.

The 1964 Plymouth Savoy was the patrol car driven by agencies large and small, from coast to coast. This particular Plymouth is a restored cruiser with the Santa Monica Police in Southern California. This black-and-white patroller is fitted with Los Angeles County Sheriff-style emergency lights. Two forward-facing, continuous reds, one rear-facing, flashing amber and a mechanical siren, are all mounted on a triangular plate bolted to the roof. This particular unit was originally a LASD detective unit, powered by a 265-horsepower, 361-ci two-barrel V-8. California cops, being no different than cops from the other 49 States, pulled the two-barrel engine during the restoration. They dropped in a 330-horsepower, 383-ci four-barrel V-8. Look closely to see the dual exhausts on this real "California cruiser."

The sharply dressed trooper with the Virginia State Police operated this 1964 Plymouth Savoy. This blue-over-gray 116-inch-wheelbase Plymouth sports a roof-mounted, combination red light and mechanical siren, a fender-mounted, low-band whip antenna, and an A-pillar-mounted spotlight. The Old Dominion State cruiser is powered by the 330-horsepower, 383-ci four-barrel V-8, a three-speed, push-button TorqueFlite, and 3.23 to 1 rear gears. That was a powerful-enough combination to overtake just about any vehicle on the road. Note the antique sidearm on this trooper's belt. For those used to automatic pistols, this trooper's handgun is a 6-shot revolver. Extra ammunition was stored in belt loops, the police version of a bandoleer.

The South Bend (Indiana) Police used this 1964 Studebaker four-door wagon as an ambulet. Cpl. Don Cornelis, shown as the driver, eventually became the SBPD historian. This was the last year Studebaker offered a police or taxi package. The South Bend assembly plant was shut down in December 1963. For 1964, the Challenger replaced the Lark name at the low trim level. The powertrain options included the 112-horsepower, 170-ci six; the 180- and 195-horsepower, 259-ci V-8; and the 210- and 225-horsepower, 289-ci V-8. In 1964, Studebaker produced just 280 police-package vehicles. Of these, 20 were roll bar–equipped factory demonstrators. They were sent to cities such as New York City, Metro-Dade County, Seattle, and Los Angeles. Thirty of the four-door sedans were powered by the Avanti 240-horsepower, 289-ci V-8. One of the 1964 Marshals, a two-door sedan, was powered by the Avanti 289-horsepower, supercharged 289-ci V-8.

Chapter Six

1965-1969

F ord was on top of the police market, and it had been for three decades by 1965. For this year, Ford expanded its police fleet to a total of 41 different "kit-priced Police Packages." This included the Custom and Custom 500 in five different engines, the Fairlane with three different engines, and three kinds of police station wagon with five different engines. The 240-ci six was available for the full-size Ford, and the Fairlane was bumped to a 116-inch wheelbase, and a four-barrel version of the 289-ci V-8 was now offered.

All of Ford's police cars were converted from a generator-based electrical system to an alternator-based system. At an idle, the generator simply could not keep up with emergency lights going and the two-way radio keyed. At extended emergency scenes, the battery actually ran down while the car was running! Alternators produce peak amp output at much lower engine speeds than generators and were a significant step forward.

Meanwhile, the full-size Dodge Polara was reduced from 122 inches to a 121-inch platform, but there was a problem. Many city, county, and state cops, especially the CHP, really wanted a 122-inch cruiser, and 121 inches was not enough. By January 1965, in time to secure the CHP contract, Dodge released an optional "Special Handling Package," which included special torsion bars, special leaf springs, and a 122-inch wheelbase!

In 1965, the Michigan State Police used this Ford Custom to enforce the laws of the Great Lakes State. This Custom is bright blue with a deep-blue shield, gold lettering, and a gold lightning bolt. Of particular interest is the single rotating beacon. Federal Signal had already released the twin-beacon Visibar, and would eventually release the fully enclosed Twinsonic, the sleek Aerodynic, the even more aerodynamic JetSonic, the radically progressive Vector, and the radical, individual-pod Vector and the enclosed pod Vista lightbars. During the next 35 years of technological advances in emergency warning signals, the MSP would remain with the single rotator. No one ever proved to the MSP that the newfangled lightbars were more effective at making stops or preventing accidents.

By March 1965, the 122-inch-wheelbase Dodge Polara Pursuit was standard. Dodge Division produced the police Polara with a 122-inch wheelbase and the retail Polara with a 121-inch wheelbase in 1966. By the following year, Dodge stopped resisting the police, and the full-size Dodge had a 122-inch platform that remained that way for the next decade. Plymouth released its first "long"-wheelbase patrol car, the 119-inch Fury. This gave Plymouth a full-size police car, the Fury, and a mid-size police car, the Belvedere.

Chevrolet started the 1965 model year with a wide-stance

The Montreal (Quebec, Canada) Police used this 1965 Ford Custom. This unique Montreal cruiser was Car 1 from District 1, according to the blue numbers on the wide white stripe. The cruiser itself is blue with a nonrevolving, red four-way roof-mounted flasher. Note that this police car is a two-door sedan. The two-door police-package patrol car was much more common than many enthusiasts realized. Ford made full-size, two-door police-package sedans through 1982.

In 1965, the Ford police package was available only on the Custom and Custom 500, not on the Galaxie 500, according to Ford's police-car literature. But in the case of the vast array of Mayberry replicas, the final authority is the T.V. series, *The Andy Griffith Show.* Mayberry enthusiasts scroll frame by frame through episodes with the squad car, looking for the finest details. In 1965, the Mayberry County, North Carolina Sheriff's Department (Andy and Barney) drove a Custom, not a Custom 500, and not a Galaxie 500. Jack Fellenzer's 1965 Ford Custom pictured is closer to the one on the T.V. series than any other replica in the nation. His car would be perfect except for the square-top, oversize red rotator. The Mayberry car had a Federal Beacon-Ray with a round globe.

look using a new "girder-guard" frame. The track of the Biscayne was widened, but the 119-inch wheelbase remained unchanged. At the beginning of the model year, Chevrolet police engines ranged from the 140-horsepower, 230-ci six to the 340-horsepower 409-ci V-8. The big news came as midyear releases. First, the 230-ci six was stroked to 250 ci, and the mill would power many urban police cars from 1965 to 1971. The 396-ci big-block V-8, complete with the "porcupine head" canted valvetrain, hit the market. The first of the legendary Chevrolet "rat" motors, the 396 ci would eventually be bored, stroked, or both to displace 402 ci, 427 ci and 454 ci, all of which became police engines. At least as important as the 396 ci, a three-speed automatic transmission, the famous Turbo Hydra-Matic was released. All things considered, the two-speed Powerglide was simply not a good police transmission, in spite of being a popular retail option. Chevrolet desperately needed an automatic to compete with the market-leader Ford Cruise-O-Matic and the bullet-proof Mopar TorqueFlite, and the Turbo Hydra-Matic completely filled this demand!

Ford was the police car of choice for 1966. The 428-ci version of the FE-block V-8 was released, and many police-car enthusiasts consider the 428-ci V-8 Ford's best big-block engine, in spite of the hype about the 429-ci and 460-ci engines. The 428-ci gave Ford what they needed to compete against Dodge for the state police contracts: 360 horsepower! Ford released its new "C6" big-block version of the three-speed Cruise-O-Matic to handle the torque from the 428-ci V-8. Up to 1966, the "C4" trans had been used for all Ford engines, from the six to the big-block V-8. Ford had been lagging behind the competition in the stopping-power department, but front disc brakes were added to the lineup. The Dodge Polara got them at the beginning of 1965, while the Plymouth Fury got discs as an option in mid-1965. Chevrolet did not offer front discs until 1967.

The 1966 model year will forever be etched in the memories of Dodge, Plymouth, and Chrysler enthusiasts, both police and retail alike. The retail 426-ci Hemi V-8 hit the streets, and the legendary 440-ci wedge V-8 was dropped into police cars to chase the kids driving the Hemis. The 440-ci V-8 was never intended

This black-and-white 1965 Ford Custom 500 with a gold star and red rotator is a Mayberry replica. It is owned by Bob Sheib, owner of Wally's Service Station, the site of the Mayberry Squad Car Rendezvous each year in Bradford (Dayton), Ohio.

to be a high-performance, competition engine. Instead, it was developed as a luxury-car engine. It was a massive, slow-revving, big-block V-8 that provided huge amounts of torque, maximum smoothness, and minimum maintenance. It didn't have fancy-breathing heads with complex rocker arms, mechanically progressive, multiple carburetion, or extremely high-compression ratios, just simple engine displacement. The 440 ci was a entirely conventional engine that produced gobs of power but was well-mannered enough for a luxury car. It was an ideal police-pursuit engine, and it was the largest engine ever used in Dodge, Plymouth, or Chrysler police cars. In 1966, the California Highway Patrol once again was the exception to the rule. The Polara used by the CHP was powered by the 426-ci wedge, which was never listed as an official Dodge police engine! No, this was not the 426-ci Hemi. The wedge-head engine was a bored-out version of the 413-ci V-8, and it was introduced as a retail engine for the 1963 Chrysler 300J.

For 1966, Chevrolet offered both a 325-horsepower, 396-ci V-8 and a 390-horsepower, 427-ci V-8, which were available with a wide variety of transmissions. The 396-ci and 427-ci engines were nearly identical and used the same porcupine-head canted valvetrain and high-compression ratio. The 427 ci was much more powerful, and in fact, it was far more powerful than even the Mopar 440-ci V-8. Most cops opted for the 396-ci engine!

By 1967, the song had remained the same, and Ford still was the most popular make of police car for city, county, and state law enforcement. The Bronco 4x4, a vehicle way ahead of its time and 30 years ahead of the craze, was released with a police package. For the first time, all Ford police cars came with dual-chamber master cylinders, and radial tires were used as original equipment on a Ford police car.

This powder-blue 1965 Ford Galaxie 500 was the winner of the "Best Restored Ford" police-car class at one of the Police Car Owners Of America national conventions. Restored by a corporal retired from the Missouri State Highway Patrol, this full-size Ford has all the goodies. It sports the Federal Visibar with twin red globes and bar-mounted siren speaker. During the mid-1960s there was a transition from electro-mechanical "growler"-style sirens to fully electronic sirens such as this one, where only the siren speaker was mounted on the vehicle. However, it would be the early 1970s before the fully electronic siren was used exclusively. This particular cruiser has been retro-fitted with a mid-1970s traffic radar antenna.

Notice this 1965 Ford Custom restored cruiser with the Watsonville (California) Police. Black-and-white cars came in two styles in California. The Northern California version was modeled after the California Highway Patrol. Just the front door was white. The rest of the body was black like this cruiser. The Southern California version was modeled after the Los Angeles Police. Both front and rear doors and the roof were white, while the rest of the body was black. By the late 1960s, the roof of all California police cars would be white. However, the differences in the doors existed into the late 1990s. This Watsonville cruiser has a red spotlight as the only visual warning signal to the front. Other cop gear includes a dash-mounted shotgun and a wire-screen partition between the front and rear seats. The engine, as noted on the fender emblem, is a 330-horsepower, 390-ci V-8.

In 1965, Ford offered 41 different "kit-priced" police packages. This included the two-door and four-door Custom and Custom 500 with five different engines. Powertrains ranged from the 150-horsepower, 240-ci six to twice that power with the 330-horsepower, 390-ci Police Interceptor V-8. This Indiana State Police Ford Custom is a two-door. Many state police and highway patrol cruisers had two doors up through the early 1980s. This white-over-blue cruiser with red and white bulbs under a clear globe is built on a 119-inch platform. Like most full-size 1965 police-package Customs, this one is powered by the 330-horsepower, 390-ci V-8. The Indiana State Police patrolled the Hoosier State in black cars until 1960 when it changed to this white-over-blue color scheme. The ISP adopted all-white cars in 1967.

A Battalion Chief with the San Francisco Fire Department uses this 1965 Ford Custom. This all-red Ford has a red roof rotator and twin red roof lights. Typical for a fire car, this full-size, four-door sedan is fire-engine red, including the red interior and red wheels. Notice the whitewall tires. This is perfectly okay for a fire car, but it is not an accepted practice on a police car. This Battalion Chief's car has the gold city seal as a door shield. Interestingly, it has no other identifying markings at all. There may be a reason for this. The Battalion Chief may not want to be identified with San Francisco Fire. The City of Wood has burned to the ground on many occasions. The most notable was "The Big One" in 1906 when an 8.5 Richter Scale earthquake started 52 fires in one morning.

One of the autoworkers who assembles the Crown Victoria owns this 1965 Ford Custom. This shot was taken at the St. Thomas, Ontario, Assembly Plant, which has produced the police-package Crown Vic since 1983. This black-and-white Custom sports a red, A-pillar spotlight. Notice the license plate, POL OVR (Pull Over). New for 1965, the full-size Custom received a larger, in-line six as its base engine. The old 223-ci six with only four crankshaft bearings was replaced with the 240-ci six, which had seven crank bearings. The 223-ci six and the 240-ci six were totally different! The new, 150-horsepower, 240-ci six was a bored-and-stroked version of the 200-ci six used in the police Fairlane. Compared to the 223-ci six used in the 1964 models, the 240-ci six had a larger bore and shorter stroke.

Chrysler Corporation applied its thin-wall, precision-casting techniques to the 318-ci V-8, and it became a wedge-head, small-block V-8. It had the same bore and stroke, and the same horsepower and torque. The LA-block 318-ci V-8 would be in constant police use from 1967 until the demise of the police-package Dodge Diplomat and Plymouth Gran Fury after 1989. By 1982, the 318-ci V-8 was the primary Dodge and Plymouth police-car engine. The 375-horsepower "special cam" version of the 440-ci mill, designated the "440 HP" (high performance), won the hearts and minds of cops everywhere. This was the first year for a Plymouth police car to get the 440-ci King Kong motor, and the Fury was the lucky recipient. From this time on, with rare exception, the Dodge Police Pursuits and the Plymouth Police Specials would have access to the same drivetrains and chassis components. Kelsey-Hayes front disc brakes were optional on all four Dodge and Plymouth police-package cars. In addition, all Mopar police cars were upgraded to dual-chamber master-cylinder brakes.

For 1967, Chevrolet joined the rest of the automakers in offering front disc brakes on its police cars. It was easy to spot Chevrolet cop cars with front disc brakes because the wheels were aggressively slotted and vented.

For the previous 30 years, more U.S. law enforcement agencies selected Ford than any other make of police-package vehicle. While 1968 was a milestone for Ford, it was also the end of an era. It would be a long time before Ford would dominate the police-car market again. The 302-ci V-8 Windsor small block was created by stroking the 289-ci V-8. The new powerplant had very humble beginnings and remained a two-barrel police engine between 1968 and 1983. The 302-ci powered all of the legendary special-service package Mustangs, the first fuel-injected Ford

For 1965, Chevrolet dropped the police package for the 110-inch-wheelbase Chevy II. The police package was still available for this 115-inch Chevelle; however, the choice of engines was dropped from four in 1964 to just one in 1965. In 1964, the first year of the police Chevelle, the mid-size patroller was powered by everything from the 194-ci one-barrel six to the 283-ci four-barrel V-8. In that first year, Chevrolet discovered detectives and other non-emergency personnel used the Chevelle strictly as a taxi. The V-8 engines were overkill for the dull duty performed by these four-door mid-size cars. For 1965, the Chevelle was available only in the thriftiest, taxi-class engine, the 120-horsepower, 194-ci six. This was the last year for the police Chevelle until 1969.

police engine, and would be the urban police engine of choice on full-size Fords for all of the 1980s.

Although Ford had been the top-selling police car in America for more than 35 consecutive years, in 1969 Plymouth surpassed Ford, claiming the No. 1 spot in market share. The mid-size, 116-inch Belvedere and the full-size, 120-inch Fury could be tailored to any job with powertrains from the economical 225-ci slant six, to the versatile 383-ci V-8 to the awesome 440-ci V-8. The Fury switch from a 119-inch wheelbase to a 120-inch platform was an important aspect to its ascendance. It had a range of powerful engines, the bullet-proof TorqueFlite, and braking as well as suspension parts from the Dodge Polara. It was priced right.

For 1969, Ford released the 429-ci V-8 police engine, the first engine in the 385-series of big blocks. Oddly, the canted-valve, high-compression, big-block V-8 designed for optimal breathing was choked by a two-barrel carb and a single exhaust! Ford's top cop engine remained the 360-horsepower 428-ci V-8. The wheelbase of the full-size Ford grew to 121 inches and remained at 121 inches through 1978, only to be downsized to 114.4 inches for 1979. The 1969 to 1978 Fords were the longest and heaviest police cars ever built by Ford.

In 1969, Chevrolet's four-barrel 350-ci V-8 entered the police market and replaced the 327-ci four-barrel. In addition, the 116-inch, four-door Chevelle returned to the police lineup and was powered by engines ranging from the 250-ci six to the 396-ci V-8. That's right. At the height of the musclecar craze, cops could ride around in 396-ci Chevelles, and some may have been looking to drag race the cops in the nearby towns who were driving 383-ci Belvederes.

The Chevrolet Biscayne was restyled for 1965. The old Safety-Girder X-frame used since 1958 was replaced with a full-perimeter "girder-guard" frame that was basically full-length box rails and four cross-members. The new platform had a true wide-stance look. The track of the Biscayne was 2.2 inches wider at the front and 3.1 inches wider at the rear. This made the cars more stable at higher pursuit speeds. New angled strut rods in the front suspension improved control over bumps and potholes. The new link-type rear suspension with a Panhard rod improved roll stiffness without making the ride harsh. The new frame, suspension, and track only added 75 pounds to the four-door Biscayne, which now weighed 3,380 pounds. The police package in 1965 was based on the low trim level Biscayne in two-door and four-door sedan and four-door station wagon.

This all-white 1965 Chevrolet Bel Air is unmarked. In fact, the only clue that this cruiser had a law enforcement role is a red, dash-mounted Federal "Fireball" rotator. While the police package was based on the Biscayne, the Z04 police-chassis package and the B01 police-body package were, in fact, Regular Production Options (RPO). This meant the cop gear could be added to the Bel Air and Impala. This Bel Air is powered by the 327-ci V-8. In 1965, this small block came in three versions for police use: a 230-horsepower, two-barrel; a 250-horsepower, four-barrel; and a 300-horsepower, four-barrel. Note that the grille on the 1965 full-size Chevrolet is similar to, but still different from, the 1966 models.

For 1965, the 119-inch wheelbase on the mid-size Dodge 330 was reduced to 117 inches. The resulting new car was renamed Coronet, a name last used by Dodge in 1959. The Coronet was longer than the Chevrolet Chevelle and Ford Fairlane but shorter than the Dodge Polara. As in the past, the mid-size, patrol-oriented sedans had a different selection of engines than the full-size pursuit-oriented sedans. The standard engines for the Coronet were the 145-horsepower, 225-ci slant six and the 180-horsepower, 273-ci V-8. The optional engines were the 230-horsepower, 318-ci big-block V-8; 265-horsepower, 361-ci V-8; and 330-horsepower, 383-ci V-8. The 273-ci V-8 was a mid-1964 release. This was the first of the LA-series of small-block V-8s made by lightweight casting techniques. The first big-block engine to benefit from this technology was the 440-ci V-8.

The Colma Fire District on the San Francisco peninsula operated this 1965 Plymouth Belvedere. The Colma Fire Department, along with the fire departments in Broadmoor, Daly City, and Brisbane make up the four most important fire departments in all of California. Colma is just south of San Francisco, which is also known as the City of Wood. Every couple of years, or so it seems, the city catches on fire due to an earthquake. On more than one occasion, the entire city has burned to the ground. The Colma Fire Department is the only defense between the city of San Francisco and the rest of the peninsula. This Colma Fire Department Belvedere packed the 265-horsepower, 361-ci two-barrel V-8. It needed a big engine. Colma Fire has a big responsibility.

The Greenwich (Connecticut) Police used this 1965 Plymouth Belvedere. This two-door cruiser sports one of the last four-way flashing red lights. These became obsolete, along with the torpedo-style light with siren, with the addition of the rotating light within a year or so. For 1965, the Belvedere replaced the Savoy nameplate. Both, however, shared the same powertrains, with one exception. For 1965, the 180-horsepower, 273-ci two-barrel small-block V-8 was the standard-equipment engine on the Pursuit-package Belvedere. This was Chrysler Corporation's first thin-wall, high-precision small-block V-8. The 1965 model year was the only time a police-package Belvedere or Dodge Coronet was powered by the 273-ci V-8.

Pictured is a fire-engine red 1965 Plymouth Fury I, an original unit with the Millbrae Fire Department on the San Francisco peninsula. Millbrae is right on top of the San Andreas Rift Zone. Earthquakes break natural gas mains, which cause fires. In fact, fires due to earthquakes cause more damage than earthquakes themselves. It's no wonder firefighters have such a special status in California. For the first time in the history of Plymouth police cars, Plymouth fielded two different police cars in 1965. One was the mid-size Belvedere. The other was the full-size Fury I. At a 119-inch wheelbase, this was the longest Plymouth police car to date. This all-red Fury I has a red rotator. Door markings include the city seal in gold and in gold lettering, "Battalion Chief."

The 1965 Dodge Polara used by the California Highway Patrol is proof that Dodge Division would do almost anything to keep the CHP business. In 1965, the 121-inch-wheelbase Polara replaced the 122-inch 1964 Dodge 880. By January 1965, Dodge developed the Special Handling Package, which included special rear springs, special front torsion bars, and a 122-inch wheelbase. Instead of altering the wheelbase forward for better weight transfer under acceleration, Dodge altered the wheelbase rearward for better high-speed stability. So many cops ordered the 122-inch option that Dodge re-released the Polara as a 1965 1/2 model. For 1965, Dodge produced two police brochures. The early version had the 121-inch wheelbase with the 122-inch Special Handling Package. The midyear version had the 122-inch wheelbase boldly noted, with no mention whatsoever of the 121-inch wheelbase. The CHP philosophy on high-speed handling altered an entire car line. By March 1965, the 122-inch Polara Pursuit replaced the 121-inch Polara Pursuit. The full-size Dodge would have a 122-inch wheelbase through the 1977 model year.

This 1965 California Highway Patrol Dodge Polara is parked on the skid pad at the CHP Academy in Sacramento. According to *Rodder & Super Stock* magazine, the Polara Pursuit with the Special Handling Package "handles as well as most of the so-called sporty-type cars and better than any of the full-size jobs. The specially engineered suspension components convert this bulbous brute into an agile cornering demon. Beefier torsion bars, special front and rear [export] shocks, larger front stabilizer bar, widely-spaced Mack truck-type leaf springs, and special spring bushings are all part of the package. If equipped with a radio [radios were deleted from all of these cars], slightly tamer suspension, and power steering, the Polara Pursuit CHP Special would qualify as the ultimate GT vehicle."

Notice the front pusher bar on this 1965 California Highway Patrol Dodge Polara, fresh out of Motor Transport and ready for service. The CHP had experimented with front pusher bars as early as 1962. By 1965, they were standard equipment on Enforcement-class vehicles. Dodge pre-set the front torsion bar height to account for the 75-pound pusher bars. The CHP wanted the greater ground clearance and the improved brake cooling that comes from 15-inch wheels. As many as half of the CHP Polaras came with front wheel discs, which required 15-inch wheels. The CHP did not want to inventory both 14-inch and 15-inch tires. The CHP also continued to experiment with high-back bucket seats and head rests on bench seats. This cruiser has the headrests designed to protect the driver from whiplash in the event of a rear-end collision.

The dual exhausts on this restored 1965 California Highway Patrol Dodge Polara are quite obvious. On a 1965 Polara, the dual exhaust meant only one thing: the 360-horsepower, 413-ci four-barrel V-8 with the special cam. The standard cam version of the 413-ci and the 383-ci V-8 both used single exhaust. This white-over-black four-door sedan has gold lettering both on the doors and under the trunk lid. During 1965, the CHP experimented with rear-window defrosters. The CHP patrol areas vary from the hot, desert areas of Southern California to the snowy, mountain areas of Northern California. On slick-top CHP cruisers, the driver-side flashing light on the package tray is red, while the passenger-side flasher is amber.

This Dodge Division promo photo shows the 1965 Polara. The Polara Pursuit package included a 270-horsepower, 383-ci two-barrel V-8, three-speed manual transmission, and 3.23 to 1 rear gears. The brakes were 11x3-inch drums, front and rear, while the standard-equipment tires were 8.25x14-inch 4-ply. Four optional engines, including the 360-horsepower, 413-ci V-8 used in the Chrysler 300L, were available. The heavy-duty three-speed TorqueFlite was also an option. This was the first year for the non-push button, column-shifted automatic. A Sure-Grip, limited-slip differential was available, and so were power front disc brakes. When discs were ordered, the rear drums changed to the 11x2-1/2-inch size and 15-inch tires were required to clear the front rotors. The early-1965 Polara Pursuit came with a 121-inch wheelbase. By midyear, a Special Handling Package with a 122-inch wheelbase was optional. By year end, the Polara Pursuit came standard with a 122-inch wheelbase.

The Township of Toronto Police in Ontario, Canada, owns this 1966 Chevrolet Biscayne. This was one of five police departments that combined in 1974 to form the Peel Regional Police. The Metro Toronto Police, organized in 1957, was a combination of all police departments inside the Toronto metropolitan area. The Peel Regional Police would serve the area surrounding and outside the Metro Toronto area. This all-white Biscayne has a red rotator and blue door and fender lettering. Notice the "pull over" light mounted on the right front fender. This light faced the driver when the squad car overtook the violator. When illuminated, the red fender light highlighted the black lettering on the lens reading, "Police." This Biscayne is powered by one of the two versions of the 327-ci four-barrel V-8.

This 1966 Chevrolet Biscayne served the New York City Police Department's 120th Precinct at Staten Island. The NYPD used McDermott auxiliary emergency lights for the first time in 1966, in addition to the red rotator. The McDermott light-rack consisted of two long, folding arms, each holding two to four red/amber flashing lights. With the arms raised, motorists could see the warning signal from blocks away in heavy traffic. When the problem was resolved, the officer simply lowered the arms, which folded flat. With the arms down, the McDermott lights looked like a bulky lightbar. With the early manual models, the officer held the arms in a raised position with a hinge pin. Later models had tiny hydraulic pistons, which raised and lowered the arms. Although this light-rack makes perfect sense for major cities with heavy, congested traffic that obscures the emergency vehicle visibility, only the New York metro area used McDermott lights. These were still in use well into the late 1990s in the Big Apple.

A Cook County (Illinois) Sheriff's Deputy and a police dog stand by a fleet of emergency vehicles during inspection. A 1966 Ford Custom is in the foreground, and a 1966 Chevrolet Biscayne police wagon is in the background. The Cook County Police powered its wagons with the biggest engine available. In 1966, this meant the brand-new Chevy 427-ci "porcupine-head" canted-valve V-8. The 427 ci was a bored-out 396-ci V-8 available in two versions: the 390-horsepower "street" version used by the cops, and a 425-horsepower "special" version used by the kids the cops chased. A 3,510-pound four-door sedan powered by the 390-horsepower, 427-ci V-8 with a three-speed Turbo Hydra-Matic and 3.07 to 1 rear gears reached 60 miles per hour in 7.6 seconds. This 1966 Biscayne wagon is white with a brown-and-gold door shield and an all-red Visibar lightbar.

Shown here is the rear view of a perfectly restored 1966 Chicago Police Chevrolet Bel Air. The car number appears in blue lettering on both the trunk and the front doors. The first digit, number 8, identifies this as a Patrol Division car. In the 1960s and most of the 1970s, this meant the cruiser was powered by a six-cylinder or very small V-8. This particular CPD Bel Air is on its way to a special appearance at a Chicago car show. These special events and police car shows themselves are definitely family events. Kids of all ages enjoy seeing the emergency lights and hearing the wail, yelp, and hi-lo pitches of both mechanical and electronic sirens. That explains the unrestrained "prisoner" in the back seat of this four-door cop car.

Pictured here is a perfectly restored 1966 Chicago Police Chevrolet Bel Air parked in front of the downtown Chicago Police headquarters. The CPD headquarters proudly displays both the American flag and the Chicago flag. The Chicago flag, which also appears on the CPD uniform, has two blue bands and four red stars set on a white background. The first digit of the car number, in this case 8, identifies this as a Patrol Division car. Patrol Division cars began with a 7, 8, or 9. The Traffic Division had the 5000 series. Trucks, vans, motorbikes, and station wagons start with 6. Patrol Division cars were generally powered by a six-cylinder for maximum economy. In mid-1965, the 155-horsepower 250-ci six was introduced as a replacement for the 230-ci six. The newer engine had the same bore but a longer stroke.

In 1966, the Arkansas State Police used the two-door Ford Custom. The Tennessee Highway Patrol and Washington State Patrol also prowled in the 1966 Custom. A 315-horsepower 390-ci four-barrel V-8 powers this ASP cruiser, although a 275-horsepower 390-ci two-barrel V-8 was also available. Both 390-ci engines were detuned from their 1961–1965 golden era; this was the first time a two-barrel was offered on a police 390-ci engine. At least it still had dual exhausts. In 1967, this once-great big block was insulted by both a two-barrel carburetor and a single exhaust. This Bear State Custom with the three-speed Cruise-O-Matic and 2.80 to 1 "economy" gears reached 60 miles per hour in 9.2 seconds. This white-over-light-blue Custom has a blue rotator.

The Cook County (Illinois) Sheriff's Police and the Illinois State Police used the 1966 Ford Custom. In 1966, the Ford police package was based on the 119-inch-platform Custom and Custom 500 in two-door and four-door versions. New for 1966 was the 428-ci Police Interceptor V-8. Like the Interceptor version of the 390-ci V-8, the 428-ci V-8 had a four-barrel carburetor, solid lifters, high-lift cam, high-rpm valve springs, dual exhausts, and low back-pressure mufflers. This was the last year for maintenance-intensive solid lifters. The 428-ci engine was available with either a four-speed stick or a three-speed C6 Cruise-O-Matic transmission. A retail version of the 428-ci V-8 with hydraulic lifters and standard lift cam producing 245 horsepower was not available in police cars until 1967.

The Washington, D.C., Metro Police used this 1966 Ford Ranch Wagon. One of these Custom-based police wagons was issued to each of the 14 precincts. These all-white wagons had a single, A-pillar-mounted spotlight, and a red-and-clear two-bulb rotator with a clear globe. These 3,963-pound, six-passenger, four-door wagons had a genuine police package. The precinct could use them in any manner it saw fit. This particular police wagon is completely empty. The lack of engine emblems on the fender means the powerplant was either the 240-ci six or the 289-ci V-8. In 1966, Ford was the number one make of police car. The police-car market averages about 60,000 cars per year. Ford led police-car sales through 1968, although Plymouth took the top honors for sales in 1969.

The 1966 Dodge Polara pictured comes with an interesting story. This particular police-package Polara went into service with the Police Reserve of Monroe County, Pennsylvania, in April 1966 and remained in continuous service with the county outside Philadelphia until 1992! When it was taken out of service it had only 51,000 miles on the odometer. It was purchased by Don Miller, a retired police officer with the Tredyffrin Township (Pennsylvania) Police. All the new owner did was clean and detail the police Polara. Still without any restoration, this cruiser has the original paint and interior. It also has the original red rotator, siren, and police radio. It is currently registered as an antique vehicle. Instead of chasing bad guys, it now collects trophies at car shows and applause during parades and cruises.

A 1966 Dodge Coronet is being prepped for the Chicago Heights (Illinois) Police Department. The Coronet and Plymouth Belvedere shared drivetrains for 1966. At 117 inches, the Coronet had a 1-inch-longer wheelbase. Both mid-size Mopars got new, reinforced unibodies for 1966. *Motor Trend* magazine tested a 1966 Coronet with the 383-ci four-barrel V-8 on the Emergency Vehicle Operations Course (EVOC) at the CHP Academy. "With heavy-duty components all the way around, it handled like a sports car. The 0- to 60-mile-per-hour time was a short 7.7 seconds and it went from 0-100 miles per hour in 21.6 sec-

onds. It was not, however, an all-out, race-type machine, which would be too temperamental for around-the-clock use. On city streets, the ride was noticeably stiff, but in the way it took the corners at Riverside Raceway, one could see the advantage of a rugged suspension over soft, especially when the difference could mean the apprehension of a law breaker.

The unmistakable look of a former Los Angeles Police cruiser permeates this unmarked black-and-white 1966 Plymouth Belvedere. It doesn't need a door shield; the roof-mounted siren and red/amber soup-can lights tell it all. In 1965, the LAPD ran the Plymouth Belvedere. By 1966, the Los Angeles County Sheriff also used the Belvedere. The 330-horsepower, 383-ci four-barrel dual exhaust V-8 bolted to a three-speed TorqueFlite powered all these cars. During LAPD-LASD joint testing, the 330-horsepower 383-ci Belvedere was pitted against a 375-horsepower, 425-ci Olds Jetstar 88; 330-horsepower, 383-ci Dodge Coronet; 325-horsepower, 396-ci Chevrolet Biscayne; 310-horsepower, 330-ci Olds Cutlass F-85; and a 360-horsepower, 428-ci Ford Custom. This lineup was the exact order of finish around the 2-mile sports-car course laid out at the Los Angeles County Fairgrounds in Pomona. The 383-ci Belvedere came in 4-1/2 car lengths ahead of the much more powerful Olds 88.

The Greenwich (Connecticut) Police used this 1966 Plymouth Belvedere. Located close to New York City, the city's influence can be seen in the selection of the emergency light on this Belvedere. Rather than a rotating light, there is a four-way, stationary flasher under the red globe. The Nassau County (New York) Police, across the Long Island Sound from Greenwich, made these four-way flashers famous in the region. In 1966, a variety of engines powered the police-package Belvedere. These included the 145-horsepower, 225-ci slant six; 230-horsepower, 318-ci V-8; 265-horsepower, 361-ci V-8; and the 330-horsepower, 383-ci four-barrel dual-exhaust V-8. The 1966 model year was the last for the 361-ci V-8. It was also the last year for the big-block polysphere-head version of the 318-ci V-8.

In 1966, the Indiana State Police Department drove both this Dodge Polara four-door sedan and the Plymouth Fury I two-door sedan. The last year for this color scheme, this 122-inch Polara is white-over-blue with a red rotator. The big news for 1966 was the 440-ci big-block V-8. Unlike the 426-ci Hemi-head V-8, the 440-ci wedge-head V-8 big block was developed as a large luxury-car engine. The 440-ci engine gained horsepower the old-fashioned way: cubic inches. There were no fancy, high-flow heads with complex valvetrains; no diesel-like compression ratios; and no mechanically linked multiple carburetion. Instead, the 440 ci used a conventional valvetrain and a wedge-head design. The 440 ci was simply a large-displacement luxury-car engine that produced a lot of horsepower and torque without revving the engine too high.

The 1966 slick-top Dodge Polara pictured here is with the Nevada Highway Patrol. The cruiser has a silver roof over a medium-blue body with gold door and trunk markings and a wide silver stripe. This Polara is powered by the 440-ci V-8, a big-block engine made possible by new, high-precision casting techniques that minimized core shifting and allowed more control over the cylinder-wall thickness. The 440 ci was basically a bored-out 413-ci raised-block B-engine. In 1966, the 440-ci four-barrel V-8 was available in two versions for the police Polara: the 350-horsepower engine with single exhaust developed in 1965 for the Chrysler New Yorker, and the 365-horsepower engine with a twin snorkel air cleaner, wider camshaft, stronger valve springs, and a free-flowing, larger-diameter dual exhaust. In 1966, the 440-ci V-8 was only available in the Polara.

The California Highway Patrol used this 1966 Dodge Polara, a white-over-black four-door sedan. It has all the traditional California cruiser cop gear, from the front pusher bars to the twin A-pillar spotlights. Also note the red rotating light. The CHP is constantly researching new equipment for its Enforcement-class vehicles. In the early 1960s alone it evaluated front disc brakes before the automakers ever offered them, four-wheel disc brakes that were never offered on a Dodge or Plymouth police car, bucket seats, headrests, pusher bars, and shoulder harnesses. This red rotator was just another CHP experiment. The CHP checked the effects on fuel consumption and on top speed. It also checked to see whether it reduced rear-end collisions with CHP cruisers and whether it resulted in traffic violators noticing the "pull-over" signal sooner. The CHP conclusions are evident in its modern cruisers, most of which are slick-top with no roof lights.

In 1966, the California Highway Patrol used the Dodge Polara as its Enforcement-class vehicle. What was surprising about this 1966 CHP Polara was the engine, a 365-horsepower, 426-ci wedge-head V-8. Not to be confused with the 426-ci Hemi, which was never used in police cars, the 426-ci wedge was the first of the raised-block B-engines with a 4.18-inch bore and a 3.75-inch stroke. The 426-ci wedge was the same basic block bored out to 4.25 inches. With the casting technology in 1963, this was the largest bore possible. By 1966, casting improved enough to allow a 4.32-inch bore, resulting in the 440-ci wedge V-8. Even though the 440-ci V-8 was available in 1966, the CHP chose the 426-ci V-8 for its purchase of Polaras. The second purchase of 1966 CHP Polaras, however, involved the 365-horsepower, 440-ci V-8.

Shown here is a rear view of the 1966 Dodge Polara used by the California Highway Patrol. Restored by San Mateo County Sheriff's Deputy Phil Moser, this cruiser is in award-winning condition. It is correct right down to the white ivory white steering wheel and spotlight handles. The dual exhausts on this Polara denote a big-block V-8, but not the one many enthusiasts expect. The 440-ci V-8 was introduced in 1966 police Polaras, but this CHP cruiser has a 426-ci V-8. What makes this unusual is that the 426-ci V-8 was not listed as an official police-package engine in 1966. In fact, the 426-ci V-8 was never an official police engine! The same engineers at Dodge who made a police package for the 1961 Polara, when none officially existed, also made the 426-ci wedge V-8 a police engine, when none officially existed. Dodge went to great lengths to keep the CHP business.

Although four-door models seem much more common, the two-door sedan and coupe have always been available with the official police package. The 1966 Plymouth Fury I shown here was used by the Nebraska Safety Patrol. This all-white Fury I has a red rotator. Note the red light on the right fender. When illuminated to pull over a driver, black letters on the lens, which read, "Stop," become visible. The Fury I clearly played a secondary role to the Dodge Polara in 1966. The 122-inch Polara received the 440-ci big-block V-8 while the engine in the 119-inch Fury I was limited to the 383-ci big-block V-8. In 1965, the Polara got front disc brakes six months before the Fury I. By 1967, when the Fury I received the 440-ci V-8, the two models made improvements at the same pace. From this time on, both mid-size and full-size Dodges and Plymouths were comparably equipped.

The rear-quarter view of the 1966 Nebraska Safety Patrol Plymouth Fury I is displayed here, showing another example of the police package on a two-door. Note the black lettering, "Safety Patrol," under the trunk lid. This was the last year for that name. In 1967, the state police in the Cornhusker State changed their name to the Nebraska State Patrol. They did, however, keep their all-white cruisers at least to the 1999 model year. The Special Police Handling Package includes a heavy-duty front sway bar, heavy-duty torsion bars, extraheavy-duty rear springs, and heavy-duty shock absorbers. The Fury I was built on a 119-inch wheelbase. Even though the Dodge Polara had the 122-inch-platform supposedly favored by the state police and highway patrols, more officers used the Fury I than the Polara.

The Indiana State Police Department used this 1966 Plymouth Fury I. This cruiser had a 119-inch wheelbase, while the Dodge Polara that year had a 122-inch wheelbase. This ISP two-door sedan has red and clear rotating lights under a clear globe. The roof is white and the rest of the body is medium-blue. The ISP used all-black cars from its formation in 1933 through 1959. From 1960 through 1966, the cruisers were white over blue. In 1967, the ISP adopted all-white patrol cars. This lasted more than 30 years until the cruisers were painted all-black in 1998. From the 1940s through 1958, the door shield included a gold stripe, which, in most years, ran from the rear fender to the headlight. From 1959 through at least 1981, the door shield included this gold "V."

This extremely well-done 1966 Plymouth Belvedere bears the markings of the Jackson (California) Police Department. Jackson lies in the foothills of the Sierra Nevadas, east of Sacramento. This cream-colored four-door sedan has the traditional seven-point gold star as a door shield. This car makes an excellent entry at a police show. All of the cop gear is correct for the period. The fender-mounted, electro-mechanical siren is correct. So is the red, roof-mounted rotator. The twin, forward-facing, continuous reds and the rear-facing red and amber flashers were all required in California. Even the dog-dish hubcaps are correct. Far too many Mopar cop car restorations have the vented hubcaps long before they were available. Despite the whitewall tires, this Belvedere cop car gets "two thumbs up."

The 1967 New York City Police Plymouth Fury I pictured here was assigned to Motorcycle Precinct 1. Today, this group is called Highway Patrol Unit 1. This Radio Motor Patrol is equipped with special gear to handle the civil disturbances of the mid- to late 1960s. This special equipment includes metal screens over all side windows and a Plexiglas shield insert mounted behind the windshield. NYPD Highway Patrol cars did not have the hood decals common to most NYPD patrol cars. Also unlike most other NYPD police cars, the Highway Patrol units got the largest engines. This one almost certainly had either the urban-oriented 350-horsepower, 440-ci V-8 or the famous 375-horsepower, 440-ci V-8.

Police cars in big cities must endure a great deal of abuse, often as much as big-city taxis. This 1967 Buick Special with the Hudson County (New Jersey) Police Department shows some battle scars. This cruiser has a red hood and red roof over a black body. It has a red rotator and red flashers along with a roof-mounted siren speaker. The police powertrains included a 210-horsepower, 300-ci V-8; 220-horsepower, 340-ci V-8; and 340-horsepower, 400-ci V-8.

The Texas Department of Public Safety (Highway Patrol) operated this 1967 Plymouth Fury. This was the second and last year for the odd color scheme of a white car with black front doors. More important, this was the first year for some of the Texas Highway Patrol cars to receive lightbars. This commission has twin red-lens emergency lights mounted on a crossbar, hence the name lightbar. Also note the chromed front pusher bar. The 119-inch-wheelbase Fury I was available in police engines ranging from the 225-ci slant six to the 440-ci "Super Commando" V-8.

In 1967, the Washington State Patrol selected the Ford Custom, as it had done the year before. These 1967 Customs are remembered for both their attributes and drawbacks. The attributes include two options of driver comfort. First, the WSP began ordering power steering in all of its cruisers. Second, six-way power seats were also ordered. The drawback was the engine. Due to an apparent error in ordering, the 1967 WSP Customs were powered by the 345-horsepower, 428-ci "Thunderbird" 4-barrel V-8 instead of the 360-horsepower, 428-ci "Interceptor" 4-barrel V-8. WSP troopers had been spoiled by the 360-horsepower, 428-ci 4-barrel V-8 engine in the 1966 Custom. A full 30 years after these Customs went out of service, veteran WSP troopers still remember the lack luster performance. This WSP Custom is all blue with a white lightning bolt door emblem and has twin red flashers mounted behind the grille.

The Massachusetts State Police used this 1967 Ford Custom in all weather conditions. Note that this is a two-door police car. These were common among the state police and highway patrol. This MSP Custom has a gray hood, roof, trunk, and front doors (in the case of a four-door) over dark-blue front and rear fenders. This cruiser was powered by the 360-horsepower, 428-ci Police Interceptor four-barrel dual-exhaust V-8. This engine was only available with the three-speed Cruise-O-Matic and 2.80 to 1 rear gears. According to Ford Fleet, this combination produced a "top speed well in excess of 120 miles per hour." To help control these top speeds, disc brakes were recommended but remained optional. Power-assist was also optional with front discs. Manual disc brakes required such a strong pedal effort that, by 1968, disc brakes were always power-assisted.

Although this 1967 Ford Custom now bears the markings of the Spring Grove, Illinois, Police Department, the car originally came from the Oklahoma City, Oklahoma, Police Department. This clean and straight all-white Custom has a Federal Visibar with two red globes. In 1967, radial tires were used for the first time as original equipment on a Ford police car. However, these innovative tires were restricted to the full-size Custom and were only available with the 240-ci six and 289-ci V-8 engines. The big-block Customs got 4-ply "Tyrex" rayon cord bias tires. In 1967, all Ford police cars came with a dual-chamber master cylinder. This marked as big a safety improvement over the single-chamber master as ABS brakes were over their non-ABS predecessors. While a leak in the single-chamber brake caused the entire system to fail, the dual-chamber system could withstand a leak and still allow either both front or both rear brakes to work.

The Hudson County (New York) Police owned this 1967 Ford Custom. Hudson County is between the Hudson River and the Newark Bay. This cruiser has a red roof over a black body. The twin lollipop lights have red lenses to the front and amber lenses to the rear. The rotator is red. In 1967, two versions of the 390-ci V-8 were available. The 315-horsepower version had a four-barrel carburetor, 10.5 to 1 compression, and dual exhausts. The 270-horsepower version had a two-barrel carburetor, 9.5 to 1 compression, and single exhaust. Ford police cars with two-barrel big blocks frequently competed against police cars powered by a four-barrel big-block V-8. A full-size Ford powered by the 315-horsepower, 390-ci four-barrel V-8 hit 60 miles per hour in 9.2 seconds. It ran the quarter mile in 17.4 seconds at 82 miles per hour.

In 1967, the Indiana State Police used two very different police cars: the Chevrolet Biscayne two-door sedans and the Dodge Polara four-door sedans. The all-white Biscaynes pictured here were used only for traffic enforcement on the Indiana East West Toll Road. The Biscaynes were powered by the 325-horsepower, 396-ci four-barrel dual-exhaust V-8 teamed with the three-speed Turbo Hydra-Matic and 2.73 to 1 rear axle. This powertrain propelled the Biscayne to 60 miles per hour in 9.1 seconds. The 396-ci Biscayne ran the quarter mile in 17.0 seconds at 83 miles per hour. New for 1967 police Chevrolets were front disc brakes, which, when specified, also required power-assisted brakes. The disc brake–equipped Biscaynes also came with special 15x6-inch steel wheels, which were slotted for extra cooling. Disc brake cars also came with 8.15x15-inch tires. The Toll Road Biscaynes spent all day in one of three modes: hard acceleration, hard braking, or idling.

Mopar experts will quickly notice a problem with this promotional shot of a generic 1967 Plymouth Belvedere. The 1966 and 1967 Belvederes were similar but not identical. This Belvedere has the correct 1967 grille and dual headlights instead of single headlights with large diameter, grille-mounted turn signals. However, this car has a 1966 front bumper! For 1967, the parking lights and turn signals were moved from the grille to the bumper. This early prototype of the 1967 Belvedere has no turn signals! Errors like this are common with police cars, which are tested before the models are available to the public and sometimes before the final fascia is approved. The blue rotator on this Plymouth police brochure cover model is an example of the growing use of blue lights on police cars.

In 1967, the Indiana State Police used this Dodge Polara as its primary patrol vehicle. This was the ISP's second year of the 440-ci-powered, 122-inch-wheelbase Polara. Two versions of the 440-ci wedge V-8 were available. The 350-horsepower engine had the standard cam, which was used in the 413-ci big block. The 375-horsepower mill had a high-lift cam and less-restrictive exhaust. Both engines used the Carter AFB four-barrel and the distinctive dual-snorkel air cleaner developed for the 1966 Chrysler 440 TNT. New for 1967 was the all-white color scheme of the ISP cruisers. The ISP started off in 1933 using black cars. Then it went to white over blue in 1960, all-white in 1967, and all-black in 1998. This cruiser has a blue door shield with a gold "V."

Stationed here is a fleet of white-over-black 1967 and 1968 Dodge Polaras. The name, "Polara," was placed on the rear fenders in 1967 models and the front fenders in 1968 models. The 1968 Polara also had the small turn signal and parking light in the side of the fender. These cruisers are all equipped with twin red/amber lollipop flashers and a roof-mounted mechanical siren. In 1967, the 122-inch-wheelbase Polara was available in one of five police-spec engines. These were the 270-horsepower, 383-ci two-barrel V-8; the 325-horsepower, 383-ci four-barrel V-8 in single and dual exhaust versions; and the 350-horsepower and 375-horsepower versions of the 440-ci four-barrel Magnum V-8. The police 440-ci big-block V-8 always came with a four-barrel. The state police or highway patrol in Alaska, California, Mississippi, Missouri, Nevada, New Mexico, Pennsylvania, Tennessee, and Wisconsin used the Dodge Pursuit.

The rear view provides a good perspective of this 1967 Mineral County (Nevada) Sheriff Dodge Coronet. In 1967, the 117-inch-wheelbase Coronet came standard with the new, small-block 318-ci V-8. In 1957, the 318-ci engine was originally released as a big block, or Y-block, using polysphere heads. The new, small-block version used a wedge head with in-line valves. The old big-block 318 ci came with dual quad carbs in 1957 producing 290 horsepower. The new small-block 318-ci would remain a two-barrel engine until 1979, after the demise of the big-block engines. In 1967, two transmissions were available for the Coronet. One was the three-speed manual, which was not available with the 383-ci engine. The other was the bulletproof three-speed TorqueFlite, one of the toughest automatic transmissions ever made.

The Rockford (Illinois) Police used this 1967 Dodge Coronet. This photo shows the car prior to restoration. Still visible on the door is the area where the shield was scraped off before the patroller was sold. When in service, this white-roof over blue-body Coronet had a red rotator. This unit was powered by the 383-ci big-block V-8. The 383-ci engine was available in the Coronet and Plymouth Belvedere in two versions. The two-barrel, single-exhaust engine produced 270 horsepower. Ford was not the only one to put a two-barrel on a big-block V-8 in a false attempt to get power with economy. The four-barrel, dual-exhaust engine produced 325 horsepower. This Rockford Police Coronet has the popular four-barrel version. Note the correct hubcaps for a police-package Coronet.

The 1967 Plymouth Belvedere I pictured here has all the correct markings of a Kansas Highway Patrol cruiser. Troopers in the Sunflower State drove 383-ci-powered Belvederes back-to-back in 1966 and 1967. The 1967 models had dual headlights on each side with the turn signals in the bumper. The 1966 version had large-diameter turn signals in the grille. Other than that, these two models were very difficult to tell apart. The big news for the 1967 mid-size Belvedere and Dodge Coronet was the availability of Kelsey-Hayes 11-inch-diameter front disc brakes. Vacuum-assisted power brakes and 15-inch tires were mandatory with the optional front discs. The full-size Dodge Polara and Plymouth Fury I received front discs in 1965.

The markings on this 1967 Plymouth Fury I identify it as serving with the Ottawa (Ontario, Canada) Police. This beautifully restored cruiser is jet-black with a white door, black door lettering, and a red rotator. Powertrains for the 1967, 119-inch-wheelbase, police-package Fury I include the 225-ci slant six, the 318-ci small-block V-8, two versions of the 383-ci big-block V-8, and two versions of the 440-ci big-block V-8. This represents the widest range of powertrains for any Mopar police car. The 122-inch-wheelbase Dodge Polara was not available with the slant six. The 117-inch Dodge Coronet and the 116-inch Plymouth Belvedere I were not available with the 440-ci V-8. Vented wheel covers, such as those on this 1967 Ottawa patroller, were not available until 1974.

The Michigan State Police used the Plymouth Fury I in 1967. This Great Lakes State cruiser is powered by the 350-horsepower, 440-ci four-barrel "Commando" V-8. This engine was only teamed with the three-speed TorqueFlite transmission. This was the first year that the 119-inch Fury I was available with the 440-ci V-8. The "Commando V-8" fender emblem on this deep-blue MSP Fury I stood for one of three V-8 engines: the 270-horsepower, 383-ci two-barrel V-8; the 325-horsepower, 383-ci four-barrel V-8; or the 350-horsepower, 440-ci four-barrel V-8. The 375-horsepower version of the 440-ci V-8 was a "Super Commando." This MSP Fury I has two unique pieces of cop gear. One is the hood-mounted "pull-over" sign that reads "State Police" in white letters and "Stop" in red letters. The second unusual feature is the lightbar. A red rotator is mounted on one side and a public address speaker on the other.

In 1967, the Indianapolis-area Marion County Sheriff's Department used the Plymouth Fury I. These two sergeants pause alongside their "county brown" cruisers, one car bearing a red rotator. In Indiana, all marked sheriff's department cars have a brown hood, roof, and trunk over a tan body with a gold five-point star. This unchanged body-color scheme continues through the turn of the century. Subtle differences exist between departments. A few have the county name on the door like these MCSD units. A few have a wide brown stripe running from fender to fender. The majority simply have a gold star that reads "Sheriff Indiana." These units are powered by the 325-horsepower, 383-ci four-barrel "Commando" V-8 teamed with a three-speed TorqueFlite and 3.23 to 1 rear gears. This cruiser hits 60 miles per hour in 9.6 seconds. It runs the quarter mile at Indianapolis Raceway Park in 17.4 seconds at 81 miles per hour.

In an unusual move, the California Highway Patrol selected the Oldsmobile Delmont 88 as its 1967 Enforcement-class police vehicle. This broke the long streak of CHP Dodge and Chrysler police cars, dating back to 1956. The 123-inch-wheelbase, police-package Oldsmobile Delmont 88 was available with three engines: the 250-, 260-, and 320-horsepower, 330-ci V-8; the 350-horsepower, 400-ci V-8; and the 300-, 310-, 365-, and 375-horsepower, 425-ci V-8. The CHP made an exception in the selection of the 365-horsepower "Super Rocket" 425-ci V-8 for its Delmont 88. The CHP usually selected the most powerful of the single four-barrel engines, and this was a single-exhaust, 10.25-to-1 compression version of the four-barrel engine. A dual-exhaust, 10.5-to-1 compression, 375-horsepower "Police Apprehender" version was available.

Five years of use and abuse with the New York City Police show through on this 1968 Plymouth Fury I. It experienced the kind of hard life typical for any big-city police car. It is now a part of the Motor Transport Division assigned to the 103rd Precinct, as noted by the white letters "MT" on the rear door. This was a motor pool of semi-retired but still operational police cars. The tri-color white-over-green and black cruiser has a fair number of dings and dents but is still in service three years after most patrol cars are sold off. The almost indestructible 225-ci slant six almost certainly powers this Radio Motor Patrol.

The Dayton (Ohio) Police operated this 1968 Chevrolet Biscayne. The squad car is blue with a white stripe and yellow lettering. For emergency gear, it has a red-and-white single rotator and red lenses in the headlights. Note the "Special Operations" license plate and Corvette-style hubcaps. This was the only model year the 307-ci V-8 was available in a full-size police car. This was also the year the Chevy small-block V-8 was upgraded to large-diameter rod and main-bearing journals.

The 1968 Ford Custom shown here provides an example of the first year that the San Antonio (Texas) Police sported white-over-light-blue squad cars. They kept this same color scheme through the 1980s. The doors are white on this two-door sedan, and all four doors were white on the four-door cars. San Antonio used police-package two-door sedans through 1969. Ford police engines for the 119-inch-wheelbase Custom included the 240-ci six, 302-ci small-block V-8, and both 390-ci and 428-ci FE-block V-8s. This was the first year for the 302-ci V-8 in police cars. It remained a police engine on the full-size Ford until 1992 and on the police Mustang until 1993.

The chrome front pusher bar completes this 1968 Texas Highway Patrol Plymouth Fury I. Police engines for the 119-inch-wheelbase Fury I included the 225-ci slant six, 318-ci small-block V-8, and 383-ci and 440-ci big-block V-8. The Plymouth Fury I had the same selection of police engines as the Dodge Polara, including the 375-horsepower, 440-ci Super Commando. The Fury I, however, had a 3-inch-shorter wheelbase and weighed less. Plymouth police literature bragged that the 440-ci V-8 got the Fury I "from 0 to 60 in short order."

The roadside chat is a hallmark of law enforcement. Here's one between a New York City Police motorcycle cop and an officer seated in a 1968 Plymouth Fury I. What makes this shot historic is the then-new "Dial 911" decal on the rear of the patrol car. The 911 emergency number replaced the seven-digit phone number, 440-1234. The word "Police" on the left side of the trunk has a green background. This 1968 Radio Motor Patrol was probably powered by the 145-horsepower, 225-ci slant six, which was standard equipment on the Fury Patroller package. It also could have had the 230-horsepower, 318-ci two-barrel V-8, which was standard equipment on the Dodge Polara and on the Fury Pursuit.

An attractive variation of the old black-and-white theme, this 1968 Ford Custom 500 is with the Menlo Park (California) Police in the San Francisco Bay area. The hood and roof are black, while the rest of the car is white. The door carries a gold and green, seven-point star. In keeping with California statute, the two outboard red roof lights burn a continuous red instead of flashing. The red, four-bulb light in the center of the roof is extremely interesting. Instead of rotating, the platform with the four bulbs oscillates back and forth. Oscillating emergency lights were re-invented 30 years later. Note the chromed traffic radar antenna mounted to the rear window. This cruiser is powered by the new-for-1968 302-ci V-8. The 210-horsepower, 302-ci two-barrel V-8 pushed the Custom 500 to 60 miles per hour in 13.2 seconds and had an EPA city fuel-economy rating of 15.3 miles per gallon.

On active duty, this 1968 Ford Custom is with the Milpitas (California) Police Department at the southernmost tip of the San Francisco Bay. This "semi-marked" patroller does not bear all of the usual California Police Department markings. It does not have the department's gold and blue seven-point star on the door. It does, however, have a red roof flasher, twin lollipop lamps that burn continuous red, and rear-facing red and amber flashers on the package tray. This four-door sedan could be powered by the 150-horsepower, 240-ci six, but it probably has the 210-horsepower, 302-ci V-8. This V-8 was a stroked version of the 289-ci V-8. The 302-ci Windsor V-8 replaced the 289 ci in both the Custom and the Fairlane.

Pictured is a 1968 Mercury Monterey with the Indiana State Police Department. One inch longer than the 1968 Dodge Polara, this police-package Merc had a 123-inch wheelbase. This, the longest wheelbase available with a genuine police package, may have persuaded Hoosier State cops to join the Missouri State Highway Patrol in selecting the Monterey. Mercury had not yet been a major player in the police market. All this changed, as, for the next ten years, the Monterey became a rather common choice for some state police and highway patrol departments. The Monterey was long, comfortable, and extremely powerful. All police-package Mercs came with the 360-horsepower, 428-ci four-barrel dual-exhaust V-8. This 1968 cruiser is all-white with a red rotator under a clear globe. The door shield is deep blue with a gold "V."

The St. Louis County (Missouri) Police used this 1968 Ford Custom. This four-door sedan is white over blue with a red triangle on the door. The bold lettering "Police" on the door denotes a county police car. In contrast, some sheriffs' departments serve only the county court system. This SLCPD cruiser has a Federal Visibar with twin red globes. The fender-mounted engine emblem marks it as a quick car. These 428-ci-powered cruisers run the quarter mile in the low 16-second bracket and have top speeds between 125 and 130 miles per hour. This was the last model year with Ford as the number one make of police car. The crown went to Plymouth in 1969.

The screen mesh on the rear windows identifies this 1968 Chevrolet Biscayne as a K-9 (canine) unit with the Suffolk County (New York) Police on Long Island. This cruiser is white over blue with blue door lettering and a red rotator. Note the public address speaker on the right front fender. The officer barks through the PA while the police dog barks from the back seat. This cruiser is powered by the 327-ci four-barrel V-8. In 1968, this mill again came in two versions, 250 horsepower and 275 horsepower. The 327-ci V-8 was the smallest engine to be teamed with the three-speed Turbo Hydra-Matic. For 1968, all Chevrolet small-block V-8s were upgraded with larger-diameter rod and crankshaft bearings. This "large journal" design produced the now-legendary durability and reliability of the Chevrolet small-block V-8.

Bill Hackley, a retired Baltimore City police officer, restored this 1968 Chevrolet Biscayne to Baltimore (Maryland) Police Department specs. The patroller is powered by the 307-ci V-8, an engine new to police service in 1968. This was the only model year this engine was used in a full-size Chevrolet. The 307 ci did, however, see use in the police Chevelle through 1969. The 307-ci V-8 was never hot-rodded by the factory like the 283 ci and 327 ci. In fact, the 307-ci V-8 never came with a four-barrel carburetor. Perhaps the biggest drawback to this particular V-8 is the automatic transmission bolted to it. The 307 ci was only available with the two-speed Powerglide. The 200-horsepower, 307-ci two-barrel V-8 teamed with the two-speed Powerglide and a 3.08 rear axle took 14 seconds to reach 60 miles per hour.

The Sunnyvale (California) Public Safety Department used this 1968 Dodge Coronet. This black cruiser has a white door with the city seal. The word "Police" appears nowhere on the vehicle! Sunnyvale was one of the nation's first Public Safety departments where police, fire, and medical emergencies were combined into one agency. The Sunnyvale Coronet has a roof-mounted red rotator, a roof-mounted forward-facing red light, and a trunk-mounted rear-facing amber flasher. The police Coronet was simply a four-door version of the Dodge Super Bee, the famous two-door musclecar from the late 1960s. Both had the same chassis and Spartan interiors. Just as 93 percent of the Super Bees came with the 335-horsepower, 383-ci four-barrel engine, most police Coronets came with the 330-horsepower, 383-ci four-barrel V-8. While many Super Bees had the four-speed stick and up to 4.10 rear gears, the police-package Coronets typically had the three-speed TorqueFlite and 3.23 rear gears.

The Pasadena (California) Police Department outfitted this all-white 1968 Dodge Coronet. Notice the massive pusher bumpers and the riot helmet worn by the driver. This was a common sight from Los Angeles to Chicago in the late 1960s. It was the toughest time for law enforcement since the Roaring Twenties. The Coronet Pursuit had a 116-inch wheelbase and was available in engines from the 145-horsepower, 225-ci slant six to the 330-horsepower, 383-ci four-barrel V-8. This Pasadena Coronet has four roof lights and a mechanical siren. The two forward-facing lights burn continuously red while the two rear-facing lights are amber flashers. A ticket for speeding or an unsafe start didn't seem to hurt so bad coming from a cop driving a four-door Super Bee.

Dressed out as a Los Angeles Police Department cruiser, this 1968 Plymouth Belvedere is a replica of the one used on the T.V. series *Adam-12* starring Martin Milner and Kent McCord. This crime drama ran from September 1968 to August 1975. The first episode used a 1967 Plymouth Belvedere. This was followed by 1968 and 1969 LAPD Belvederes, 1971 Plymouth Satellites, and 1972 AMC Matadors. The "1-Adam-12" unit designation can be decoded as follows. There are 18 stations in the City of Los Angeles. Station "1" is the Central Division. Two-officer patrol units were designated as "Adam" units, as opposed to an "L" unit which was a solo officer unit and an "X" which was an extra car. The identification "12" would be the assigned work area, a census-tract area of a particular division. The even-numbered units worked the mid-day watch, while the odd-numbered units worked the early watch.

The Battalion Chief with the Milwaukee (Wisconsin) Fire Department used this 1968 Plymouth Belvedere. The cars used by fire departments across the United States are almost always police-package vehicles. Fire cars have some of the same demands on the drivetrain as police cars. Specifically, they must remain cool during long periods of idling and must have enough electrical capacity to power lights, siren, and radio gear. Fire departments typically piggyback on the state contract for police cars, because it is the least expensive way to buy their heavy-duty vehicles. This Milwaukee Fire Belvedere probably has the 230-horsepower, 318-ci small-block V-8. This unit, of course, is all red from the siren speaker and rotator to the wheels. The door and fender lettering is gold.

The Pulaski County (Missouri) Sheriff's Department maintained this sharp 1968 Plymouth Satellite. Pulaski County includes a piece of the Mark Twain National Forest and a 25-mile stretch of Interstate 44. This part of the historic U.S. Route 66 held plenty of opportunities for law enforcement. In 1968, the Plymouth mid-size cars started with the Belvedere. Next up the trim level came the Road Runner, then the Satellite, the Sport Satellite, and the GTX. Only the Belvedere and Satellite were available as a four-door. This beautifully restored cruiser is white over medium-blue with a red/red Visibar and electronic siren. The vented hubcaps look good on this 1968 Satellite, although they were not introduced until the mid-1970s. Police markings on this 116-inch-wheelbase Satellite include a white and brown five-point star and brown on white fender lettering.

An inspection is underway for this fleet of 1968 Plymouth Fury I sedans and the sheriff's deputies with the Cook County (Illinois) Sheriff's Police. Uniforms are freshly pressed. Brass is polished. Guns are cleaned. Shoes are polished. Same thing for the all-white patrol vehicles. Engines are steam-cleaned. Cars are washed and waxed. Interiors are vacuumed. Rubber mats (not carpeting) are washed. Trunks are straightened out with a place for everything and everything in its place. Belts and hoses are checked. The underside of the trunk lid is even waxed. Inspections vary in frequency from agency to agency. More and more, the yearly inspection coincides with Police Memorial Week in the middle of May, and the local press and general public are invited. These Cook County cruisers have brown and gold door shields and twin red/white lights under clear globes.

A new coat of paint adorns this 1968 Plymouth Fury I. The car is being restored as a Chicago Police patroller and the color scheme is white over blue with a blue five-point star. As finishing touches, the wheels need to be painted argent (silver), and the lettering, "We serve and protect," needs to be added to the front doors. This started in 1965. This cruiser also needs a blue four-digit car number on the upper edge of the doors near the front fender. Since this Fury I is packing a 375-horsepower, 440-ci Super Commando V-8, the unit number will be in the 5000 series. The Chicago Police Department is the second largest municipal police agency in the nation, behind the New York City Police Department. The emergency lights on CPD cruisers have been blue since 1960.

The Nebraska State Patrol owned this 1968 Plymouth Fury I. When founded in 1937, the original name of the department was Nebraska Safety Patrol. The name was changed to Nebraska State Patrol in 1967, making this Fury I just the second year with the revised door-shield lettering. The NSP Fury I is all-white with a blue-and-gold door shield. Except for a brief period in the early 1970s, NSP cruisers have been all-white since 1963. Prior to 1963, the patrol cars were black with either all-white or partially white doors. Note the red "pull-over" light on the front fender of this Fury I. The 1968 Fury I was built on a 119-inch platform and this side shot makes it look quite long. A two-door police-package Fury I such as this was common among state police and highway patrols.

Deputies with the Los Angeles County Sheriff are putting this Plymouth Fury I through its paces on an Emergency Vehicle Operators' Course (EVOC). The EVOC course is laid out on the huge parking lot of the Los Angeles County Fairgrounds in Pomona. The LASD ran the Fury I powered by the 330-horsepower, 383-ci four-barrel V-8 from 1968 to 1970. These black-and-whites all had the three-speed TorqueFlite and 3.23 to 1 rear gears. These 119-inch-wheelbase cruisers came with engines from the 145-horsepower, 225-ci slant six to the 375-horsepower, 440-ci V-8. The standard engine on the Fury Pursuit was the 230-horsepower, 318-ci two-barrel V-8. This was a popular choice for urban police departments, which emphasized economy and yet wanted to keep a V-8. With 2.94 to 1 "economy" gears, the 318-ci Fury I accelerated to 60 miles per hour in 11.2 seconds and got 14.7 miles per gallon.

Pictured is a 1968 Dodge Polara with the California Highway Patrol. This white-over-black 122-inch-wheelbase Dodge is equipped with what the CHP calls its "A" lightbar. In fact, it does have emergency gear bolted to a very-low-profile bar. The two forward-facing lights have red lenses. These do not flash. Instead, per California Vehicle Code, they burn continuously. The two rear-facing lights are amber flashers, similar to the LAPD setup. The package tray also has red and amber flashers. This CHP Dodge is powered by the 375-horse-power, 440-ci four-barrel dual exhaust Magnum V-8. Some CHP veteran traffic officers recall that the 1968 Polara was the fastest patrol car the CHP ever used. This honor is actually a toss-up between the 1968 Polara and 1969 Polara, but it certainly was one of those two.

Pinellas County, Florida, ran Plymouths and Dodges throughout the 1960s, 1970s, and 1980s. Here's the back end of a 1968 Plymouth Fury I with the Pinellas County Sheriff's Department. By this time the color scheme had changed from black and white to the now-familiar green and white. The lettering and five-point star appear on both doors and the trunk lid. The dual exhausts on this Fury I could mean the powerplant is the 330-horsepower, 383-ci V-8; the 360-horsepower, 440-ci V-8; or the 375-horsepower, 440-ci V-8. At this time, the four-barrel version of the 383-ci big block was selected. For 1968, the 383-ci wedge-head V-8 was upgraded from the 325-horsepower "Commando" to the 330-horsepower "Super Commando," thanks to a larger four-barrel carburetor and larger exhaust valves. The police-package Fury I was available in four-door and two-door versions.

The 1968 Dodge Polara shown here is restored as a Keene (New Hampshire) Police unit. Keene is in the southwest corner of the Granite State. The four-door sedan is medium-blue with a blue roof light and a gold door shield. Odd though it seems, police-package Polaras were available with full-dress wheel covers, although no self-respecting police officer would mount the white-walls out. The factory did not even offer whitewalls on police-package cars. No real explanation can be offered for this unit's twin orange glass-pack mufflers. You can find restored police cars from Maine to California and Florida to Washington State.

The Cleveland (Ohio) Police used this 1968 Ford Custom. The all-white, four-door, 119-inch-wheelbase cruiser has twin clear-globe rotators and a rectangular siren speaker mounted on an open-air light rack. The door shield is blue on gold with the words "Cleveland Police." The department's logo on the door under the shield is different from most: "Our Men Serve All Men," an acknowledgment to the racial and political tension in all big cities during the late 1960s. This cruiser was the last of the all-white or black-and-white CPD police cars. In late 1968, all Cleveland emergency vehicles, police, fire, and EMS, were painted "Safety Green." This horrible but unique shade of lime green lasted until late 1978, when the CPD mercifully returned to the traditional black-and-white.

The pair of roughneck 1969 Buick Specials sitting here are with the Hudson County (New Jersey) Police in Jersey City. They are painted with a red hood, roof, and trunk over a black body. The emergency lights include a red rotator and red/amber lollipop flashers. Buick was a major player in the 1950s, but its use for police cars rapidly declined until the police package was dropped in the early 1980s. These four-door sedans had a 116-inch wheelbase. These patrol cars were almost certainly powered by the optional 280-horsepower, 350-ci Buick big-block V-8. However, a 155-horsepower, 250-ci V-6 was standard equipment and a 230-horsepower version of the V-8 was available. These cars also may have had the big-block Turbo Hydra-Matic 400 transmission, an option with the 350-ci V-8.

The District Chief with the San Antonio (Texas) Fire Department drove this 1969 Plymouth Fury I, painted white over a flashy red. Note that this is a two-door sedan. Also remarkable are the twin fender-mounted sirens. The emergency light is, of course, red. The door shield has yellow lettering. Other SAFD cars in the background have white roofs and doors on a red body with red roof rotators. Fire departments almost always use police-package vehicles and were actually more likely than some city police cars to have the largest engines.

Pictured here is a 1969 Dodge Coronet in service with the Dayton (Ohio) Police Department. This medium-blue, 117-inch-wheelbase cruiser has gold lettering and a white stripe. The Coronet was rare in police work. Just as the Plymouth Belvedere-based Road Runner outsold the Dodge Coronet-based Super Bee on the civilian market, a similar thing happened in police work. Engines available for the police Coronet included the 225-ci slant six, 318-ci small-block V-8, and two versions of the 383-ci big-block V-8. The 330-horsepower, 383-ci V-8 police Coronets ran a 15-second quarter mile and had a top speed of 126 miles per hour. Note the 1968 Chevrolet Biscaynes in the background.

In 1969, the Nevada Highway Patrol used the Dodge Polara, one of the fastest and most popular police cars ever produced. The NHP cruisers were silver over blue with a silver stripe, gold lettering, and gold seven-point star. This unit has a Federal Visibar with twin red lenses and twin spotlights. Powered by the 440-ci "Magnum" V-8 with 375 horsepower, these 122-inch-wheelbase squad cars ran the quarter mile in 14.3 seconds at 99 miles per hour.

The most noteworthy aspect of this 1969 Plymouth Fury I marked for the North Las Vegas (Nevada) Police is its paint scheme. The police cruiser has stark black doors on an otherwise all-white body. Also note the two-way, bullet-style red flasher mounted beside the siren speaker on the lightbar. There is no mistaking this as a police car, but it also qualifies as a public eyesore. The citizens of North Las Vegas had to endure at least three years of this paint scheme.

The 1969 Plymouth Fury I parked here is marked with the gold lettering and gold star of the San Antonio (Texas) Police Department. This was the first of just two years when the cars had a white roof over a solid medium-blue body. For most years, the doors were painted white. This was also the first year for San Antonio cops to get power steering, power brakes, and air conditioning. The 1969 Plymouth Fury I also changed in terms of its wheelbase, which was lengthened from 119 inches to 120 inches.

The New York City Housing Police used the 1969 Chevrolet Biscayne. Still based on the 119-inch platform, these were significantly restyled and grew in overall length and weight. The full-size Chevrolet continued to gain length and weight every year through 1976. This NYC Housing patroller, like NYC Transit and most New York City Police patrollers, was powered by a six-cylinder engine. This six is the 155-horsepower, 250-ci one-barrel "Turbo-Thrift" engine. The small-block V-8s were called "Turbo-Fire," while the big-block V-8s were named "Turbo-Jet." The 250-ci six was used in police cars from 1965 through 1971. It reappeared in downsized 1977 to 1979 models. This was the last of the in-line six-cylinder engines. In 1980, the 250-ci I-6 would be replaced by the 229-ci V-6. Full-size Chevrolet police cars were available with a six-cylinder engine from the 1955 release of the police package through 1990.

The 1969 Chevrolet Biscayne and Bel Air were easy to recognize by the massive, wraparound, integrated bumper-grille. In 1969, with no fanfare, the greatest police and retail engine of all time made its appearance in police-package Chevrolets. This, of course, was the incredible 350-ci small-block V-8. This "mouse motor" (as opposed to the big-block "rat motor") was the primary Bowtie police engine from 1977 through 1996. After the demise of the Caprice, this legend continued to power the police Camaro and police Tahoe into the twenty-first century. The 350-ci V-8 was simply a stroked version of the 327-ci small block. For 1969, 255-horsepower and 300-horsepower versions of the 350 ci quietly filled the spots once held by the 250-horsepower and 275-horsepower versions of the 327-ci V-8.

The Traffic Division of the Newark (New Jersey) Police used this 1969 Chevrolet Biscayne. Traffic enforcement normally means the use of a big-block V-8 or, at the very least, the most powerful small-block V-8. In a different move, Newark chose a light engine for the weight. This 119-inch-wheelbase, 3,590-pound Bowtie was powered by the 155-horsepower, 250-ci six. Note the public address speaker on the front fender. In addition to the 350-ci V-8, the other big driveline news for 1969 was police cars with smaller displacement engines: the availability of the three-speed Turbo Hydra-Matic. This legendary automatic transmission, second only to the Chrysler TorqueFlite, was previously restricted to engines with 250 horsepower and above. In 1969 it was available with all powerplants.

The Islip Police Department of Long Island used this 1969 Chevrolet Biscayne station wagon. Notice that the hood and doors read, "Town of Islip," with no mention of the word "Police." The rotator with red and white bulbs under a clear globe made that part clear! This police wagon was powered by the 235-horsepower, 327-ci two-barrel V-8. This was the last year for the 327-ci engine to be used in police-package vehicles. For 1969, the once-great 327-ci small block was demoted to mere two-barrel status and replaced almost completely by the 350-ci V-8. In reality, the 327-ci mill did the duties in 1969 that the 307-ci V-8 had done in 1968. The 327 ci was the base V-8 for all Chevrolet police cars. This was the first time the heretofore-powerful police version of the 327-ci V-8 was humbled with a two-barrel.

For 1969, the Chevrolet Chevelle 300 was billed as "The Concentrated Chevrolet." The B07 police package was available in only the 116-inch-wheelbase four-door sedan. Powerplants for the police version included the 155-horsepower, 250-ci six; the 200-horsepower, 307-ci V-8; the 255-horsepower, 350-ci V-8; the 300-horsepower, 350-ci V-8; and the 325-horsepower, 396-ci V-8. The 300-horsepower and 325-horsepower versions used 3.07 to 1 rear gears. All other police Chevelles had 3.31 cogs. The 396-ci V-8 that came in the Chevelle was more powerful than the two-barrel version in the Biscayne and Bel Air. The Chevelle came with a rear sway bar when the 350-ci or 396-ci engine was specified. With the power disc brakes and special tires, the 325-horsepower, 396-ci-powered Chevelle was very quick.

This 1969 Ford Custom is with the New York City Police. The NYPD calls all their police cars RMPs, which stands for Radio Motor Patrol. This particular RMP is assigned to the First Traffic District. The color scheme is the famous tri-color used from 1961 through 1972: white roof and trunk, black front fenders, and dark-green body. Check out the roof gear. In the front is an electro-mechanical siren. Behind it is a four-bulb rotator with alternating red and amber lenses under a clear globe. Behind that is the NYPD's famous McDermott light-rack. Used since 1966, this folding lightbar has arms that unfold into a vertical position. Each arm has from two to four red or amber flashers. The McDermott bar is widely used in the New York metro area, but almost nowhere else.

The dents and dings in this 1969 Ford Custom show the tough life on the streets of New York. The rear door of this New York City Police Department RMP reads "MT." That stands for Motor Transport Division, which means this poor old Ford is a loaner car or a pool car. Loaner police cars are often treated as "beaters," and treated worse than rentals. Patrol cars get demoted to MT status once they are too old or have too many miles for primary duty, but they run too well to be sold off. In fact, so many police cars in the biggest cities are so banged up that this particular Ford really does not stand out! This NYPD patroller is almost certainly powered by the 150-horsepower, 240-ci six with a one-barrel carburetor, single exhaust, and 3.25 axle.

The 1969 Ford Custom shown here is with the North Carolina Highway Patrol. This cruiser was restored to period-correct condition by the maintenance section of the NCHP fleet garage in Raleigh. The four-door sedan has the color scheme used until the early 1980s: a silver roof, black hood, and trunk, each with white State Patrol lettering, black-topped fenders, and doors with silver bottoms. The roof-mounted torpedo-style, combination mechanical siren and flashing light has twin blue lenses, one front-facing, one rear-facing. Nearly all state police and highway patrols using the Custom opted for the 360-horsepower, 428-ci four-barrel V-8. However, two other big blocks were available, the 265-horsepower 390 ci and the 320-horsepower 429 ci. Unfortunately, a two-barrel carburetor and single exhaust weakened both engines. This was the first year for the 429-ci engine in police cars.

The 1969 Ford Galaxie 500 pictured is marked as a South Carolina Highway Patrol cruiser. This particular cruiser is green, with blue-on-gold fender and trunk decals and door shields, and a blue rotator. Note the window-mounted, external traffic radar antenna. For 1969, the police package was available on the Custom, Custom 500, and Galaxie 500 in both two-door and four-door versions. The big news for 1969 was an increase in wheelbase from 119 inches to 121 inches, the longest wheelbase ever attained by the Ford-marque. It had grown to 119 inches in 1960 and, following the 1969 gain, remained at 121 inches through 1978. In 1979, it shrank back to 114.4 inches. The 1969 to 1978 models were the longest and heaviest police cars ever produced by the Ford Division. This SCHP cruiser is powered by the 360-horsepower, 428-ci Police Interceptor V-8.

The Indiana State Police Department used the 1969 Mercury Monterey. The Iowa State Patrol also drove 1969 Monterey cruisers. The 360-horsepower, 428-ci V-8 powered these cars. That was Ford's top cop engine even though the 429-ci big block was introduced to police work this year. The 428-ci and the 429-ci engines shared the same 10.5 to 1 compression ratio. The 428-ci mill used a four-barrel carburetor and dual exhaust, while the 429-ci engine was surprisingly fitted with a two-barrel carburetor and single exhaust. This gave a 20-horsepower advantage to the 428-ci engine. The 429-ci powerplant was again restricted to a two-barrel carburetor in 1970 full-size Fords. It did not come with a four-barrel carburetor and dual exhaust until it replaced the 428-ci V-8 in 1971. This 428-ci-powered ISP cruiser is all-white with a red rotator, blue door shield, and gold "V."

In 1969, the Virginia State Police Department was among the many state police and highway patrols to select the Plymouth Fury I. For approximately 37 years in a row, Ford had been the number-one-selling make of police car. This all changed in 1969 when Plymouth became the top-selling make of squad car. Plymouth continued to dominate the U.S. police car market and, by 1978, it had 80 percent of this market. Except for the 1979 model year, when Plymouth did not make a full-size police car, Plymouth kept the number one title until the mid-1980s. At that point Chevrolet captured the top spot. Ford regained the honor of number one police car after 1996.

A Chrysler Corporation promotional shot displays the 1969 Dodge Coronet Police Pursuit. In 1969, the Coronet was available in four different trim levels: Coronet, Coronet 440, Coronet 500, and Coronet R/T. The police package was based on the low-trim level Coronet. This trim level also included the famous Super Bee musclecar. When both were equipped with the 383-ci four-barrel engine and three-speed TorqueFlite, the police Coronet and Super Bee had similar performance. One of the few differences was the rear axle ratio. The police Coronet could have an axle ratio from 2.93 to 3.55 but it was typically the 3.23. The Super Bee came standard with 3.23 rear gears, but many came with ratios as snappy as 4.10 to 1. As a result, the musclecar usually ran 5 miles per hour faster in the quarter mile, while the police car had a 15-mile-per-hour higher top speed.

Parked here is a slick-top 1969 Dodge Coronet. This all-black, 117-inch-wheelbase police car was available with a wide variety of heavy-duty engines. The powerplants included the 145-horsepower, 225-ci six; the 230-horsepower, 318-ci V-8; the 290-horsepower, 383-ci two-barrel V-8; and the 330-horsepower, 383-ci four-barrel dual exhaust Super Commando V-8. The police-package Coronet and the Dodge Super Bee musclecar had the potential for a great deal of similarity. When each was equipped with the 383-ci four-barrel engine and three-speed TorqueFlite, one of the few differences between these two cars was the weight. At 3,440 pounds, the two-door Super Bee actually weighed 264 pounds more than the four-door Coronet Pursuit. Despite the Super Bee's Spartan reputation, this comparison shows that other cop cars also received few frills.

The St. Louis County (Missouri) Police used this 1969 Dodge Polara. The 1969 Polara was one of the most popular Mopar police cars, according to a 1991 survey of 250 city, county, and state police departments. In a tie for third overall of all Mopar police cars ever made were the 1969 Dodge Polara with the 440 Magnum, the 1969 Plymouth Belvedere, and the 383 Super Commando. Car Craft magazine took a nostalgic look back at all police cars and concluded: "Up until 1980, when they introduced the pathetic 318-powered St. Regis, Chrysler practically owned the police vehicle market. But of all the great Chrysler cop cars, the 1969 Polara is the one that stands out. The 1968 Polara was too ugly and the 1970 Polara lost power."

The California Highway Patrol traffic officer standing here is keying the mike on the radio in his 1969 Dodge Polara. By 1969, the CHP had toughened its minimum performance standards. In order to qualify for the CHP contract, the squad car had to reach 115 miles per hour from a standing start in 1 mile, 125 miles per hour in 2 miles, and 130 miles per hour in 3 miles. This standard would have disqualified every police sedan built from 1979 to 1993! This is an acceleration and top-speed standard all rolled into one. The 375-horsepower, 440-ci V-8-powered Polara easily met this standard. Note the rear flashers and the dash-mounted shotgun on this slick-top Dodge.

The 1969 California Highway Patrol Dodge Polara is one of the most famous police cars ever. It was the fastest, officially timed, full-size, police car of all time. With a 375-horsepower, 440-ci V-8, a Dodge Polara was clocked at Chrysler's Chelsea Proving Grounds doing 147 miles per hour around the 4.1 mile banked oval. No other full-size police car at the time, or since, equaled the 1969 440-ci Polara. The LT-1-powered Chevrolet Caprice peaked at 141 miles per hour in 1994. The Chevrolet Camaro reached 159 miles per hour, but that was not a patrol sedan. Among full-size police-package cars, the 1969 440-ci Polara remains the top gun. The 440-ci Polara hit 60 miles per hour in 6.3 seconds and 100 miles per hour in 14.3 seconds. It runs the quarter mile in an astonishing 14.2 seconds at 99 miles per hour.

This 1969 Plymouth Fury I remains one of the nicest police cars in the country. The Fury I Police vehicle served with the Kansas Highway Patrol. The light-gray over deep-blue Fury has a gold door shield. The fender-mounted decal commemorates 50 years of service, from 1937 to 1987, for the KHP. The Fury I has a red roof rotator and a red, A-pillar spotlight. Vented wheel covers were not available until the mid-1970s, but they look good on this long-wheelbase Plymouth. This cruiser is powered by the same 375-horsepower, 440-ci V-8 that pushed the Dodge Polara to 147 miles per hour. No official top speeds were published for the 440-ci Fury. Both the Fury and the Polara have a similar front-end shape, and the Fury weighs 123 pounds less than the Polara. It is entirely possible that the Fury could have reached 148 miles per hour.

"Best-Of-Show" is a difficult title to win. This is especially true when the police car show is judged by California cop car experts, former Best-Of-Show winners, and authors of police car books. This 1969 Plymouth Belvedere was the unanimous choice for best overall at the Ripon, California, Emergency Vehicle Show. The Commissioner of the California Highway Patrol even signed the trophy! Recognition such as that makes the effort even more worthwhile. This cruiser has been restored as a Chino (California) Police unit by Chino PD Sergeant Fernando Tomicic. The forward-facing emergency lights are twin red-globe rotators and twin "continuous burn" red lights. Note the dash-mounted shotgun. The Belvedere was one of the most popular Mopar squads of all time.

Displayed here is an accurately restored 1969 Plymouth Belvedere with the Los Angeles Police Department markings. This car is LAPD-correct from the markings on the soup-can lights to the wheel covers. The LAPD Belvederes were powered by a 330-horsepower, 383-ci four-barrel V-8 and three-speed TorqueFlite. Belvederes used for surface street patrol had 3.23 to 1 rear gears and top speeds just under 120 miles per hour. Belvederes set up as freeway interceptors had 2.91 to 1 rear gears and top speeds around 126 miles per hour. In October 1969, the California Highway Patrol assumed jurisdiction of all freeways, thus ending the need for LAPD freeway interceptors.

The front end is displayed in this photo of a 1969 LAPD Plymouth Belvedere. The forward-facing visual signal is simply two "continuously burning" red lights. In some cases, when the overhead reds came on, the headlights were also wired to come on. Just as the reds did not flash, the headlights then did not wig-wag. By 1969, the LAPD began to phase out the old, electro-mechanical "growler" siren. Most, but not all, 1969 LAPD Belvederes used the new Federal electronic sirens as seen on this cruiser. The siren speaker also doubled as a public address system speaker.

The rear view shows the back attributes on this 1969 Plymouth Belvedere. This unit is with the Bell (California) Police Department in Southern California. This patroller has LAPD-style markings and emergency lights. The rear-facing amber lights do indeed alternate or flash. It's interesting to note that episodes of the *Adam-12* television series are so accurately filmed that you can hear the heavy-duty flasher relay alternate between left and right amber lights during an emergency response. The LAPD cars, and many others in Southern California, came with a rear sway bar. This virtually eliminated understeer at all speeds and made the cruiser especially nimble when patrolling city streets.

Shown here is a 1969 Plymouth Belvedere with the Bell, California, Police Department. Engines available in the Belvedere include the 145-horsepower, 225-ci slant six; the 230-horsepower, 318-ci V-8; the 290-horsepower, 383-ci two-barrel V-8; and the 330-horsepower, 383-ci four-barrel V-8. With the 330-horsepower engine, three-speed TorqueFlite, and 3.23 to 1 rear gears, the police Belvedere reached 60 miles per hour in 7.5 seconds. It ran the quarter mile in 15 seconds flat with speeds through the traps of 93 miles per hour. The top speed was 126 miles per hour. The Road Runner, with basically the same engine, but a four-speed stick and lower rear gears, hit 60 miles per hour in 5.1 seconds. The two-door Road Runner ran the quarter in 14.7 seconds at 100 miles per hour but had a top speed of only 112 miles per hour. The police Belvedere and the Road Runner musclecar were surprisingly similar.

On-the-job with the St. Petersburg, Florida, Police, this is a 1969 Plymouth Belvedere four-door sedan. In the background are two 1968 Chevrolet Biscaynes. The police cars in this Tampa Bay-area city are white over dark green. The door shield is an unusual eight-point star including the city seal complete with palm tree. The front fender and trunk lid lettering is in gold. The roof rotator uses a red globe. The 1968 SPPD cars used a round globe rotator while the 1969 units used the new oversize, square-top rotators. The 116-inch Belvedere came standard with either a 145-horsepower, 225-ci slant six or a 230-horse-power, 318-ci V-8. A 330-horsepower, 383-ci V-8 would get these Belvederes to 60 miles per hour in 7.5 seconds with a top speed of 126 miles per hour.

In 1969, the Missouri State Highway Patrol used the impressive Mercury Monterey as its primary police car. The 1969 Mercury can be distinguished from the 1970 Mercury by the more-solid grille on the 1969 version. The nearly identical 1970 Merc has the grille split horizontally in two. In 1969, the 320-horsepower, 429-ci, 385-series big-block V-8 was introduced to police work. However, this used a two-barrel carburetor and single exhaust. The overwhelming police powerplant choice was the 360-horse-power, 428-ci V-8. With the same 10.5 to 1 compression as the new 429-ci V-8, the 428-ci engine used a four-barrel carburetor and dual exhaust to achieve a 360-horsepower rating. This gold cruiser has a Visibar lightbar with twin red globes.

Chapter Seven

1970-1974

P lymouth was the top-selling brand of police car for 1970. In response to tightening emissions standards, lower-compression ratios for police and retail engines entered the market. This trend reinforced the fact that police-package engines and retail engines are often more similar than some enthusiasts care to realize. In general, it was the beginning of the end for big-block, high-performance police engines. The police 440-ci V-8s dropped from 10.1 to 1 to 9.7 compression ratio, and it would continue to fall in the coming years.

In 1970, Ford had lost its crown and was no longer king of the police-car hill, but it showed no signs of giving up. A new 117-inch-wheelbase mid-size patrol car, which was called a Torino, was released, but in reality it was not a Torino. It was a Fairlane 500 (the intermediate trim level in the Fairlane/Torino series) equipped with a police package. Ford released two completely different 351-ci V-8 engines, one built in Windsor, Ontario, and the other built in Cleveland, Ohio. The Windsor was a wedge-head engine in the Windsor series of small blocks, and the Cleveland was considered a big-block engine. Both used the same bore and stroke and were available in both two-barrel and four-barrel versions. However, the Cleveland had the incredible, free-breathing canted valvetrain that was used in mid-sized cars, while the Windsor was used in the full-size Fords.

The only police-package Mercury ever used by the California Highway Patrol as an Enforcement-class vehicle was this 1970 Monterey. This unquestionably makes the 1970 Monterey the single most historic and most collectible Mercury police car. The black-and-white CHP Mercury was powered by a fast-revving 360-horsepower, 428-ci FE-block, four-barrel V-8. The Monterey had front and rear sway bars, power front disc brakes, and the comfortable ride that comes from a 124-inch wheelbase. This CHP Mercury represents a legendary piece of California and automotive history.

The California Highway Patrol selection of the Mercury Monterey as its Enforcement-class vehicle was one of the year's most significant developments. Mercury captured both the influential CHP contract and the LAPD contract with the mid-size Montego. This took some of the sting out of Ford losing the police market to Plymouth. Mercury had not been used by the CHP since the late 1940s, and the 1970 Monterey was one of just five non-Mopars to be CHP E-class cruisers between 1956 and 1988. That fact alone earns the 1970 Monterey a special place in police-car history!

Chevrolet offered its largest police engine ever, the 454-ci V-8, and the 454 was one of the four "porcupine" head, canted-valve

The now-defunct Long Island State Parkway Police Department of New York once used this 1970 Plymouth Fury I as a traffic enforcement and pursuit car. The all-white battle cruiser has red and amber rotating lamps inside a clear globe. These white cruisers had the word "Police" lettered on all four sides of the car. They also held a spotlight. The siren speaker mounted on the hood is particularly intimidating. It was probably extremely loud; siren speakers were frequently mounted well away from the driver to reduce damage to the officers' ears from long-term exposure. This car also sports a pusher bumper big enough to make California Highway Patrol traffic officers envious.

In 1970, the Nassau County (New York) Police used four-door sedans such as this Ford Custom as Highway Patrol units. The regular patrol units were orange over blue while the Highway Patrol units were typically all-white. As a Highway Patrol unit, this police car was powered by the 360-horsepower, 428-ci Police Interceptor. This was the only four-barrel police engine offered in 1970 full-size Fords. This 10.5-to-1-compression engine was the same as the retail 428-ci Super Cobra Jet. The 428-ci engine had lighter reciprocating parts than the 429-ci V-8 and, as such, the 428-ci mill "wrapped up" faster and gave quicker acceleration. It did this even in cases where both engines were rated at the same horsepower and torque. Note the second NCPD Highway Patrol unit in the background, a 1968 Chevrolet Biscayne.

big blocks affectionately called "rat" motors. The others were the 396 ci, 427 ci, and the 402 ci. The 1970 model year was the last year for high-compression engines from General Motors.

The 1971 model year is best remembered as the year the horsepower rating system changed from SAE gross, or brake, horsepower to SAE net horsepower. With only minor changes, the same horsepower rating system continues to be used today. Net horsepower averages about 75 percent of the brake horsepower, but this varies widely from engine to engine. To provide some perspective between net and brake horsepower ratings, the 1971 Mopar 440-ci HP engine was rated at 370 brake horsepower and at 305 net horsepower. The Chevrolet 454-ci "rat" motor produced 365 brake horsepower and 285 net horsepower. Ford held onto the old brake horsepower rating system until 1972, but eventually the entire industry converted to the new net horsepower system.

In 1971, Chrysler Corporation introduced the 360-ci small-block V-8. Compared to the 318-ci LA-block, the 360 ci had a longer stroke and a slightly larger bore and became a potent police engine. In the late 1970s and early 1980s, the Mopar 360-ci V-8 far outpowered the Ford 351-ci Windsor and the Chevrolet 350-ci V-8s. The 360 ci was available through 1979 in California cop cars and through 1980 in the other 49 states.

In 1971, Ford introduced its 400-ci Cleveland V-8, which replaced the 390-ci big-block V-8. A stroked version of the 351 Cleveland, the 400 Cleveland was a true "square" engine design, which required the block deck be raised by more than 1 inch. The bore and the stroke were both 4 inches. As with all Cleveland engines, the 400 used a canted valvetrain. It was a police engine from 1971 through 1978.

Chevrolet stretched the full-size police pursuit car wheelbase from 119 inches to 121.5 inches, and it was based on the GM B-body. It would keep the 121.5-inch wheelbase through 1976, and it was as long as any Chevrolet would ever get. It was a significant development, for Chevy full-size cars had had a 119-inch wheelbase since 1959. During the "great downsizing" in 1977, the wheelbase shrank to 116 inches and stayed there through 1996. The "long wheelbase" Chevrolets hold a special place in the hearts of police-car collectors.

In 1970, Chevrolet pushed its small block to the absolute limit by releasing the 400-ci V-8. The "giant" small block was much more than a bored-and-stroked 350-ci engine. Engineers actually removed the water jacket from between the cylinders to get large bores with the same bore centerlines. This was a mistake! The 400 ci suffered from overheating problems, of course. The "siamese"-cylinder, 400-ci engine had the largest bore and longest stroke of any Chevy small block. It was used in police cars from 1971 through 1976. All Chevrolet police engines had a newly lowered compression ratio of 8.5 to 1. The combination of lower compression, leaner carburetor calibrations, less-aggressive cam grinds, and the now-heavier vehicle lowered the top speed of a 454-ci-powered police Biscayne to just 115 miles per hour!

By 1972, emissions standards had lowered the compression ratios, carb calibrations, ignition timing, and cam grinds to the point where all police-engine performance was feeble. Mopar police engines ranged from a compression of 8.2 to 8.6 to 1. Chevrolet and other General Motors police engines were all based around 8.5 to 1. FoMoCo police engines varied from 8.0 to 8.6 to 1. Many of the cars still had four-barrel carburetors and dual exhaust, but performance had dramatically decreased. Chrysler Corporation responded by putting the 440-ci big-block V-8 in its mid-size Dodge Coronet and Plymouth Satellite for the first time. Plymouth was the largest-selling brand of police car in 1972. Mopar's 400-ci wedge-head, big-block V-8 was introduced. It was a bored-out 383-ci V-8, and it replaced the smaller big block in this year's police cars. The incredible success and police acceptance of the AMC Matador was the biggest police car news of 1972. The 118-inch-wheelbase Matador came from nowhere to capture the Los Angeles Police Department contract. The Wisconsin State Patrol also used the 1972 AMC Ambassador riding on a 122-inch platform. By 1973, the Los Angeles County Sheriff had also adopted the Matador. The Dallas Police later joined in. In most cases the Matador was powered by the 255-horsepower, 401-ci V-8. The 401-ci Matador was very fast for the times, but it did not hold up as well as other makes in police service. As a result, the success it achieved in the police market was short-lived. The Matador returned to obscurity after 1974, but not before starring in the Adam-12 television series! Just as revolutionary, in 1972, the Alabama State Troopers drove the AMC Javelin. This indeed was a specially prepared police-package vehicle, and the first such pony car to be used for law enforcement. These Javelins were powered by the 255-horsepower, 401-ci V-8.

In 1972, Ford's hottest police engine was not the 400-ci Cleveland nor the 429-ci big block; it was the 351 Cleveland. Although the 429 held a slight torque advantage, the 351 Cleveland had the most horsepower of any Ford engine, and it was available only in the mid-size Torino and Mercury Montego. The 351 Cleveland-powered Torino and Montego were the fastest FoMoCo cruisers of the otherwise bleak year.

In 1972, Chevrolet police cars put on enough weight for the low-trim level four-door Biscayne to break the 2-ton weight bracket for the first time. Chevrolet released a Turbo Hydra-Matic 350 for use with small-block V-8s and a Turbo Hydra-Matic 400 for use with big-block V-8s. In 1970, Chevrolet bored out the "porcupine head," canted-valve 396-ci big block to a 402-ci V-8. It was such a subtle change that most enthusiasts still refer to this 402-ci engine as a "396" engine, and for 1972 the 402 ci was available on police-package cars. And it was the only

The Las Vegas (Nevada) Police used this 1970 Ford Ranch Wagon as a supervisor's car. A twin red beacon Visibar tops off the white-over-blue station wagon. Supervisors and sergeants typically carry a larger and more diversified payload of emergency equipment: everything from riot shields and tear gas equipment to rope ladders and battle-pack first aid gear. These police wagons often had the most powerful pursuit engines just to handle the weight of the extra emergency equipment.

The Nevada Highway Patrol used this 1970 Dodge Polara. The cruiser has a silver-blue roof over a deep-blue body with a silver-blue stripe and gold lettering. The Federal Visibar has twin red rotators. It also has an aluminum plate attached to the center of the lightbar. This acts like an airfoil to reduce or eliminate the high-speed vibrations that were a problem with this lightbar and mounting system. The 440-ci Magnum V-8, rated at 375 horsepower, powered this intimidating 122-inch-wheelbase Dodge battle cruiser. The compression ratio, however, was lowered from 10.1 to 9.7 for 1970.

Left — The Montreal (Quebec, Canada) Police Department used this 1970 Ford Custom Ranch Wagon as a police ambulance. This police wagon was photographed at St. Justine Hospital. Police officers are often the first on the scene of most traffic accidents. It only made sense to combine the ambulance service with police duties. Police station wagon ambulances were extremely common in the 1950s and 1960s. They were later used as supervisor cars, K-9 vehicles, SWAT wagons, and commercial enforcement vehicles. The heritage of the police station wagon, however, is as an ambulance.

In 1970, the Los Angeles Police Department used the mid-size Mercury Montego as its primary patrol vehicle. The powerplant was the 370-horsepower, 429-ci, four-barrel V-8. These LAPD cruisers had an unusual list of equipment. They used the three-speed Cruise-O-Matic transmission and had air conditioning and power front disc brakes. This was the first year for an air-conditioned LAPD patrol car. In an odd departure, however, these cars had manual steering. That may have been okay for highway patrol cars, but bossing the big-block cruiser around the city streets with manual steering would have taken tremendous effort. One of the Montegos was built with power steering by mistake; it became the LAPD's favorite Mercury.

The twin pipes from the dual exhaust are easily visible in this rear-quarter shot of the 1970 CHP Monterey. In 1970, dual exhaust on a full-size FoMoCo cruiser meant just one thing: the 360-horsepower, 428-ci big-block V-8. All the other powerplants used single exhaust, even the 390 and 429 big blocks. The black-and-white 1970 CHP Mercury used red and amber flashing deck lights and a forward-facing, "continuously burning red" spotlight. In case the motorist misses the dual exhaust, the white letters, "Highway Patrol," on the trunk indicate this is not the right car to pass.

year this rat motor was used in a police car. Chevrolet did not even bother to make die cast fender emblems for the 402-ci engine size. Instead they used the same "400" emblems for both the 400-ci small block and the 402-ci big block. New for 1972, the police package was once again available for the mid-size, 116-inch-wheelbase Chevelle.

In 1973, Plymouth retained its grip on the police market as number-one-selling brand of police car, followed by Ford, Dodge, and Chevrolet. The AMC had secured contracts with the Los Angeles County Sheriff and the Los Angeles Police Departments to use the Matador. Since 1966, the awesome Mopar 440-ci big block had been available in standard-cam and special-cam versions, but in 1973, only the special-cam "HP" version was offered for police sedans. As it turned out, the special cam, designed for high performance, was also very good at reducing emissions.

Ford responded to the industrywide horsepower loss by releasing its largest police engine ever, the 460-ci V-8. The 460 was simply a stroked version of the 429-ci V-8 and the only other engine in the 385-series of Ford big-block engines. This 7.5-liter overhead-valve, big-block V-8 was only rated at 219 horsepower. In comparison, the 1999 4.6-liter overhead-cam, modular V-8 was rated at 215 horsepower! But the torque was the big difference. Cops everywhere would love to have 460-ci V-8s in their 1999 Crown Vics, even though the horsepower is the same! By 1974, the United States was in the middle of an energy crisis brought about by the oil embargo. Thus, gasoline prices skyrocketed and fleet managers scrambled for ways to save gasoline. Cops insisted on long-wheelbase cars, and it took thirsty big-block V-8s to provide a reasonable level of performance.

John Cristy, Motor Trend editor and Los Angeles County Sheriff technical reserve, woke up the law enforcement community with a series of articles that explained how to improve performance and fuel economy as well as reduce vehicle weight. He devised a test procedure and incorporated it into the annual LAPD/LA Sheriff vehicle tests to prove his point. His work paved the way for mid-size cars to replace full-size cars in many patrol areas.

The Motor Trend/Los Angeles Sheriff testing also led to the nationwide popularity of the Chevrolet Nova. A 1974 350-ci-powered Nova with a three-speed Turbo Hydra-Matic impressed the law enforcement community at the annual testing. It had the best handling, acceleration, braking, and fuel economy. If compact and mid-size police cars provided better performance than full-size sedans, cops didn't mind smaller cars.

Plymouth was America's most popular make of police car for 1974. In spite of the energy crisis, Plymouth released its first-ever 122-inch-wheelbase sedan, and Dodge and Plymouth offered a radial police tire as an option for the first time.

Ford dropped the 429-ci big block, but two versions of the Ford 460-ci were available—a 460-ci Police and a 460-ci Police Interceptor. The Interceptor had an 8.0 to 1 compression ratio, pumped out 260 horsepower, and was worthy of its name. At 260 horsepower, the FoMoCo 460-ci Police Interceptor produced nearly the 275 horsepower of the Mopar 440 HP and far more than the 235 horsepower from the Chevrolet 454-ci rat motor. In addition Ford introduced steel-belted radials as options on all police-package cars, including those powered by the 460-ci Police Interceptor.

Chevrolet's High Speed Pursuit package was required running gear for the 454-ci V-8 police pursuit car. The package included more durable control arm bushings, a rear stabilizer bar, severe-duty front and rear brakes, and H78x15 nylon police high-speed tires. Chevy introduced radial tires as options on all cars, except units powered by the 454-ci V-8. Interestingly, the rat-engined Chevy never came from the factory with radials. Radial-tired Chevy police cars came with General Motor's famous Radial Tuned Suspension, that included a rear stabilizer bar, heavier front anti-sway bar, modified shock valving, and a larger power-steering gear for better on-center handling and road feel. In 1974, the COPO (central office purchase order) 9C1-package Nova was jointly developed by Chevrolet, the Los Angeles County Sheriff, and Motor Trend magazine. This turned out to be the most important police car ever made by Chevrolet. The 9C1 Nova revolutionized the police use of mid-size patrol cars in much the same way as the special service package 1982 Mustang.

Law enforcement's most famous Mercury is this 1970 CHP Monterey. The Monterey used a 124-inch wheelbase. For decades, the CHP required its Enforcement-class vehicles to have at least a 122-inch wheelbase and to weigh at least 3,800 pounds. With no police equipment whatsoever and without the heavy front pusher bars, the four-door Monterey sedan weighed 3,940 pounds. The cop gear added up to 400 pounds.

The 1970 Mercury Monterey was the first FoMoCo product used as a CHP Enforcement-class vehicle since the 1952 Ford Mainline. The next was the 1984 Ford Crown Victoria. In spite of its obvious place in police car history, the CHP experience with the 1970 Monterey was not entirely positive. Problems during rugged police duty included separated motor mounts, broken ball joints, cracked wheels, and cracked transmission housings. All police cars have fleet maintenance problems. In fact, only the police cars with a higher-than-normal downtime record are even remembered. Unfortunately, the Monterey was one such car. This might explain why it was a dozen years before the CHP ran a Ford police car again.

The 1970 CHP Mercury Monterey was powered by a 360-horsepower, 428-ci V-8. This powerplant was unique to the police-package cars. No retail Mercury came with this engine. Instead, the retail Cyclone, Marauder, and Marquis were available with the 429-ci V-8 while the Monterey was only available with the 390-ci V-8. Only the police Monterey received the 428-ci "Super Cobra Jet" V-8. Of the 29,432 Mercury Montereys produced in 1970, a total of 1,820 went to the CHP. The bid price was $2,478 each.

Left — The beautifully restored 1970 Ford Custom shown here bears the brown and olive two-tone markings of the Maryland State Police Department. The two-bulb rotator has a red lens. The full-size Ford state police and highway patrol cars used one of three big-block V-8s. These included the 265-horsepower 390 ci, the 320-horsepower 429 ci, and the 360-horsepower 428-ci V-8. Only the 428-ci engine had a four-barrel carburetor and dual exhausts. The Maryland State Police Department was organized in 1920. The 1970 police cars marked the 50th year of service.

In 1970, Ford released a 351-ci Cleveland V-8 for mid-size police cars and a 351-ci Windsor V-8 for full-size police cars, such as this San Antonio, Texas, Police Custom. The 351-ci Windsor was the largest displacement made from what was originally a 221-ci small block. The Windsor V-8 had a wedge-style head and parallel valves. The 351-ci Cleveland used an entirely different block but exactly the same bore and stroke. The Cleveland V-8 used the exotic canted-angle valvetrain. This four-door sedan has a white roof over a powder-blue body with a gold-and-brown door shield. The roof rotator is red.

Shown here is a side view of the 1970 Philadelphia (Pennsylvania) Police Department Ford Custom. The cruiser has the very unusual color scheme of a white roof over a red body with all-red emergency lights. The leading edge of the hood and the trailing edge of the trunk are marked with the word, "Police," to keep out-of-towners from confusing it with a fire chief's car. This unit also has the missing hubcaps typical of all big-city police cars, frequent victims of theft or potholes. The emergency phone number, 231-3131, which predates 911, appears on both rear quarter panels.

The tri-color paint scheme of the New York City Police Department is displayed on this 1970 Ford Custom. The roof and trunk are white, the front fenders are black, and the rest of the car is dark green. Oddly enough, this 1970 Custom has a 1970 car number. The trunk decals are white on green for the word "Police," and green on white for the number "911." Note the helicopter-visible number on the trunk. Like most NYPD units, this cruiser has a red/white rotator and a red/amber McDermott light rack. This patroller is attached to the 103rd Precinct.

The 1970 Chevrolet held the largest police engine ever produced: the 454-ci Turbo Jet V-8. This canted-valve, "porcupine head," big block came in 345-horsepower and 390-horsepower versions. The 454-ci, 427-ci, 402-ci, and 396-ci big-block Chevrolet engines are all closely related. The 454 is a stroked 427 with the same bore. The 427 is a bored-out 396 with the same stroke. The Chevrolet 454-ci V-8 was designed to take on the Chrysler 440-ci V-8, and would eventually compete against the Ford 460-ci V-8. The 1970 Bel Air with the milder 345-horsepower 454 ci and super-economy 2.56 rear gears still ran the quarter mile in the 16-second bracket. The 454-ci big block was a high-compression engine only in the 1970 model year. After 1970, the compression and horsepower both dropped dramatically.

The heavy use and frequent abuse typical of any big-city police department is evident on these two 1970 Chevrolet Biscaynes. Both are powered by the thrifty 250-ci in-line six. Both the six and the 350-ci, two-barrel V-8 were considered standard equipment for 1970. Both engines ran on regular-grade gasoline during an era when most police engines required premium fuel. All 1970 Chevrolet police cars were available with either the two-speed Powerglide or the three-speed Turbo Hydra-Matic, regardless of the engine. This was the last year for the 119-inch wheelbase. The 1971 Chevrolets to follow were built on a 121.5-inch platform.

By 1970, the 350-ci small block, introduced in 1969, caught on among cops. One of these powers this Redding (California) Police Department Chevrolet Biscayne. This all-white, semi-marked, slick-top unit was used as a detective's car. A fully marked white-over-blue Redding Police Department traffic unit is in the background. This car has a four-barrel carburetor and just 3.07 rear gears. Even still, the perky 300-horsepower, 350-ci V-8 gets this 4,205-pound, four-door sedan down the quarter mile in the 16-second bracket. A 250-horsepower, 350-ci two-barrel V-8 was also available. The 300-horsepower version uses a 10.25 to 1 compression compared to 9.0 to 1 for the 250-horsepower version. The 350-ci V-8 was the largest standard-equipment V-8 ever put in a full-size Chevrolet. The two-barrel version was new for police cars in 1970, replacing the 235-horsepower, 327-ci two-barrel V-8.

An excellent example of a beautifully restored, perfectly correct 1970 New York City Police Department Plymouth Fury I is pictured here. This is one of the famous NYPD tri-color Cruisers with a white hood and trunk, black front fenders, and dark green body with either green or white lettering. These cars had black wheels and the lower half of the rear quarter panels painted black. This police car from the 54th Precinct is equipped with a roof-mounted electro-mechanical siren and a red and white lens rotator under a clear globe. These NYPD units had either the 225-ci slant six or the 318-ci V-8. Both were considered standard equipment.

A deep-blue 1970 Michigan State Police Department Plymouth Fury I makes a roadside stop. The two-bulb rotator is under a red lens. The light is visible from the front over the roof-mounted speaker. Note the famous hood-mounted, illuminated sign, which reads, "State Stop Police." For 1970, the compression ratios on all Mopar police engines, except the slant six, were lowered by about 1/2-point. The intimidating 440-ci V-8 in this MSP cruiser had a 9.7 to 1 ratio compared to 10.1 to 1 in 1969. Oddly enough, even though the 1969 and 1970 engines had the same carburetors, cams, and heads, the engines had the same horsepower rating in spite of the compression loss.

A good side view of the 1970 North Carolina Highway Patrol Plymouth Fury I is available here. The NCHP was organized in 1929. The NCHP cruisers have kept a black and silver color scheme from the 1940s through the 1990s. The letters, "State Patrol," appear on both the trunk lid and leading edge of the hood of this unit. The oversize roof rotator is blue. This was the first year for the more modern rotator. Prior to 1970, the NCHP used a roof-mounted, torpedo-style combination siren and blue light.

Parked just off the road in the brush, this white-over-deep-blue 1970 Lakewood, Colorado, Police Department Plymouth Fury I, looks as though it is just waiting to pounce on the next lawbreaker. This unit has a combination of red/amber soup-can lights and a four-bulb red rotator. The inconspicuous siren speaker is located in the lower housing of the rotating light. This beautifully restored cruiser has it all, right down to the twin, A-pillar spotlights, dash-mounted shotgun, and whip antenna.

This 1970 Berkeley, California, Police Plymouth Belvedere was essentially a four-door version of the Road Runner musclecar. The slick-top, all-white cruiser has a red driver's spotlight as the only forward-facing emergency light. The mid-size Belvedere and Dodge Coronet were popular among urban police departments. These units were available with the 225-ci slant six, 318-ci small-block V-8 and both two-barrel and four-barrel versions of the 383-ci big-block V-8. With the 330-horsepower, 383-ci four-barrel V-8, the only differences between the police Belvedere and the retail Road Runner were the different cam and rear gear ratio. The cop cam was 5 horsepower milder. The cop gears were 3.23 compared to 3.55, 3.91, or 4.10 in the musclecar.

A sketch from the Chrysler Corporation police-vehicle literature shows a four-door 1970 Dodge Coronet, complete with Federal Visibar lightbar. The 1970 Coronet was a transition from the square styling of the late 1960s to the Coke-bottle fuselage styling of the early 1970s. The wild nose job for 1970 produced two basic reactions among cops; either they loved it or they hated it. This 117-inch-wheelbase, mid-size Dodge and the 116-inch-wheelbase Plymouth Belvedere shared the same police drivetrains. The Plymouth-marque was so popular among cops, in both full-size and mid-size cars, that a 1970 police Coronet was extremely rare.

A most unusual duty awaits this 1970 white over blue-gray San Jose, California, Police Biscayne. Although it seems an odd use for one, police cars also make the best demolition cars. They have the stiffest suspensions, heaviest-duty transmissions, longest wheelbases, heaviest-duty radiators, and even reinforced frames with heavier frame gauges or extra welds at stressed areas. Police cars are designed to cut through medians at full-pursuit speeds, and remain cool in both traffic jams and after 100 miles with a wide-open throttle. The bad news is that demo derby drivers and police car restorers look for exactly the same kind of car. Every year, in every county, in every state, dozens of candidates for restoration as a police car are demolished. It is a great shame and waste for the restoration aficionados.

In 1970, the Chevrolet Biscayne patrolled the streets and alleys of Chicago. The vast majority of these Windy City cruisers were powered by the 250-ci Turbo-Thrift six rated at 155 horsepower. The color scheme on this Chicago Biscayne is white over medium-blue with a blue roof-mounted rotator and a blue-and-white five-point star as the door shield. All lettering is blue. The 1970 model year brought a greater loss than gain for Chevrolet. The 327-ci, 396-ci, and 427-ci V-8s were all discontinued. The wheelbase for the full-size Chevrolet, however, remained at 119 inches for this one last year. The Bowtie police package was limited to the Biscayne and Bel Air. For the first time in the history of the Chevrolet cop cars, the B07 police package was limited to four-door sedans unless the department put in a special order.

Responding to a fire scene is a 1970 Oldsmobile Delta 88 with the Chicago Fire Department and a 1970 Chevrolet Biscayne with the Chicago Police Department. The CFD Olds has a black roof over a red body with the novel combination of green and red warning lights. The door reads "Deputy Chief Fire Marshal," along with the CFD symbol. The CPD Chevrolet has a white roof, front doors, and trunk lid over a blue body with a blue roof rotator. The 7,000-series unit number on the Biscayne indicates it is with the Patrol Division. That means it is powered by the 155-horsepower, 250-ci six. Only the 5,000-series Traffic Division cars got the 454-ci V-8. The CFD Olds Delta 88, almost certainly a police-package vehicle, came standard with a 310-horsepower, 455-ci V-8.

The Chicago Fire Department almost certainly used a police-package vehicle with this 1970 Buick LeSabre. The two-door and four-door sedans used by fire departments need to be as durable, reliable, and fast as the sedans used by police departments. The police-package, 124-inch-wheelbase LeSabre came standard with a 370-horsepower, 455-ci V-8. Incredibly, a three-speed stick was standard. Thankfully, the rugged Turbo Hydra-Matic 400 was optional. Rear gears were either 2.78 or 3.23 to 1. No other engine was available and, with the 455-ci V-8, none other was needed! This CFD Buick is red with a black roof. The high beams have red lens covers. The twin roof lights are green, a CFD trademark.

The 1971 AMC Matador pictured is with the Yonkers Police Department in Westchester County, New York. This four-door sedan has traditional East Coast markings: blue hood, roof, and trunk over a white body. The Federal Visibar has two red globes. The 1971 Matador was based on the now-discontinued 1970 Rebel. For 1971, the wheelbase grew to 118 inches. That was long enough to be considered by cops at the time. The power-train for these relatively successful AMC police cars were a 135-horsepower, 258-ci six; 210-horsepower, 304-ci V-8; 245-horsepower or 285-horsepower, 360-ci V-8; and the famous 330-horsepower, 410-ci V-8.

The mark of credibility and acceptance for a vehicle is for the state police or highway patrol to adopt the vehicle as its patrol car. AMC gained this acceptance in 1971. The Alabama State Troopers used the AMC Javelin, and the Arizona Highway Patrol used this 1971 AMC Matador. The front quarter panel reads "SST," which was the middle trim level. AMC attempted to enter the police market in the late 1960s with only limited success. The 1971 model year began its glory era. Matadors were taken seriously by the state police, although still not widely used. However, they became the "car to beat" for urban police departments from 1971 through 1975. This 1971 Arizona Department of Public Safety Matador was powered by the 330-horsepower, 401-ci, four-barrel V-8.

The first pony car officially used as a police pursuit vehicle was not the 1982 Mustang, but this 1971 AMC Javelin. Long before the California Highway Patrol experiment with the 1979 Camaro Z28, Alabama State Troopers used this 1971 Javelin with a factory Police Interceptor package as a regular patrol vehicle. The Javelin has a 110-inch wheelbase like the Dodge Challenger, compared to a 108-inch wheelbase on the Camaro, Mustang, and 'Cuda of the time. The Alabama Javelins were powered by the 330-horsepower, 401-ci, four-barrel V-8 and three-speed TorqueCommand automatic. Restyled for 1971, the Javelin featured an integral rear spoiler. These pony pursuit cars were gray with a single blue rotator mounted on the roof. Only 100 of these 1971 Javelins were made.

In 1971, the New York State Police used the Plymouth Fury I. These cruisers had a dark-blue hood and dark-blue roof but a white trunk, fenders, and doors. The simple block lettering on the front doors was black. This unit has a Federal Strat-O-Ray, which is a version of the Beacon Ray. Packing a 370-horsepower, 440-ci V-8, these 120-inch Furys were extremely fast. They hit 60 miles per hour in just over 7 seconds and had a top speed over 130 miles per hour. In 1971, the Mopar police package was based on the 120-inch Plymouth Fury I, the 122-inch Dodge Polara, the 118-inch Dodge Coronet, and the 117-inch Plymouth Satellite, replacing the Belvedere.

Shown is a rear-quarter view of a 1971 Plymouth Fury I with the New York City Police. Again, the color scheme is white over green with black front fenders. The off-center location of the trunk lock caused the NYPD to rearrange its rear markings. The letters "Emergency Dial 911" were moved to the roof and the "Police" decal was centered on the trunk, while the four-digit car number was moved from the license plate frame to the trunk. The helicopter-readable car number on the trunk, in this case "19," was part of a short-lived experiment. This Radio Motor Patrol is attached to the 103rd Precinct, which is the Jamaica district. This patrol car has a four-bulb roof-mounted rotator with red and amber lenses.

The setting for this scene is downtown Manhattan. The pictured traffic patrol car is a New York City Police Department 1971 Plymouth Fury I. This car provides another example of one of the last "tri-color" NYPD police cars. The color ensemble includes a white roof and trunk, black front fenders, and green body. Notice the presence of both a siren and a public address speaker. Since the roof-mounted siren was electro-mechanical, as opposed to electronic, a separate roof-mounted speaker was needed for the public address system.

A 1971 Nevada Highway Patrol Dodge Polara is parked along a desert stretch of road. This silver-over-blue pursuit sedan has a 370-horsepower, 440 Magnum V-8. Note the strange little feature mounted on the lightbar between the two red rotators. The device is an airfoil. At speeds over 100 miles per hour, the lightbar would vibrate due to the air turbulence. The airfoil helped silence the noise.

The Palisades Interstate Park Commission Police used this pair of Plymouth police cars. The all-white wagon is a 1971 Fury Suburban, almost certainly powered by the 300-brake-horsepower, 383-ci big-block V-8. The dark-blue-over-white four-door sedan is a 1973 Fury, almost certainly powered by the 280-horsepower net, 440-ci big-block V-8. The Emergency Wagon has the word "Police" in black letters on two places of the hood, and one place each on the front fenders and tailgate. The Fury sedan has the word, "Police," in white letters in two places on the dark-blue hood, and in black letters on each fender and trunk lid. Both vehicles have a four-bulb rotator with red and white bulbs inside a clear dome.

For 1971, the wheelbase on the full-size Chevrolets, such as this Pompton Lakes (New Jersey) Police Department Biscayne was increased from 119 inches to 121.5 inches. The Chevrolet police sedan was never lengthened any further. The GM "B-body" had used a 119-inch wheelbase during the previous 12 years. The 1971 Biscayne was 18 inches longer overall, 6 inches wider, and had a 6.5-inch-longer wheelbase than the 1956 Chevy One Fifty. And at 3,888 pounds, it outweighed the older Chevy by 750 pounds. This weight gain continued until the 1977 model year.

The all-black 1971 Lyman (South Carolina) Police Department Ford Custom 500 pictured sports a blue, four-bulb rotator. By about this time, a blue light was widely used by law enforcement in the Deep South. Northern police departments continued to use red emergency lights. Even after much of the country converted to combinations of red and blue, many Southern departments retained their blue emergency lights. Blue is especially effective at night. This 429-ci-powered four-door sedan performed superbly on the hills and hollers of South Carolina.

All-back Ford Customs were the standard for the New York City Transit Police Department in 1971. The markings on this cruiser include a gold door shield and gold trunk lettering. A red rotator completes the package. These cruisers were powered by the 351-ci "Windsor" V-8. This was the standard-equipment engine available in 1971, and also the smallest police engine for full-size Fords. A 250-ci six and 302-ci V-8 were available in 1971 but were limited to the mid-size, 117-inch-wheelbase Torino.

A 400-ci, two-barrel V-8 rated at 260 brake horsepower powers this beautifully restored 1971 Haysville (Kansas) Police Department Ford Custom. This engine represents a big change. The 400-ci Cleveland V-8 was new for 1971 police cruisers. This was a 351-ci Cleveland stroked by a full half-inch. It was a true "square" engine design. The bore and stroke were the same at 4 inches. The 400 Cleveland had a block-deck height one inch taller than the 351 Cleveland. The 400 Cleveland was the second engine in the 335-series of engines. In 1974, the raised-deck 400 Cleveland was de-stroked back to 351 cubic inches. The result would be the 351 Modified, the third 335-series engine.

In 1971, the Indiana State Police prowled the Hoosier State in this all-white Mercury Monterey topped with a red, four-bulb rotator. The door shield is deep-blue with a gold, forward-pointing "V." These 4,028 pound, 124-inch-wheelbase, four-door sedans were powered by the 429-ci V-8. This big block had an 11.3 to 1 compression ratio, four-barrel carburetor, dual exhausts, and 370 horsepower. ISP troopers still talk about this patrol car 20 years later. Many troopers consider it the most comfortable and powerful cruiser of their careers.

The California Highway Patrol went back to the Dodge Polara as its Enforcement-class vehicle in 1971. The CHP ran the Dodge Polara, Monaco, Coronet, St. Regis, and Diplomat with just three exceptions from 1971 through 1988. The 1971 CHP Polara was powered by a 370-horsepower, 440-ci V-8. Even with the compression lowered from 9.7 to 9.5, the 440 High Performance V-8 produced plenty of power and torque. Top speeds may have gone from the 140-mile-per-hour bracket to the 130-mile-per-hour bracket, but no one complained. These cars were so fast, almost no one got away. With the CHP's reputation of not calling off pursuits, anyone attempting to outrun one of these cruisers needed an engine with enough cooling capacity to run at wide-open-throttle for as long as a full tank of gas would last.

In the lead of a special parade is a 1971 Illinois State Police Dodge Polara. The all-white Polara has a twin red-lens Federal Visibar. The high-beam headlight on each side is also fitted with a red lens cap. Although it seems as though there are a lot of state troopers for a parade, the black Lincoln limousine behind the ISP Polara explains their presence. The limousine's passenger, President Richard Nixon, is the person on the passenger side shaking hands. A career in law enforcement involves a lot of very special memories.

The 1971 Chicago Police Dodge Polara pictured here served in the Traffic Division. As such, it was powered by one of the larger V-8s, probably the 300-horsepower, four-barrel version of the 383-ci big block. A 275-horsepower, two-barrel version of the 383-ci engine was also available, as was a 255-horsepower, 360-ci small-block V-8. This CPD unit is white over blue with a blue door shield and a single blue rotator. The color of the wheels, however, is argent (silver) and not blue.

The Chicago Police Department used this 1971 Dodge Polara as a patrol unit. Routine patrol CPD units normally used a six-cylinder engine for maximum economy. In 1971, the smallest engine available for the Polara was the 230-horsepower, 318-ci two-barrel small-block V-8. The 1971 model year also marked the transition from gross (or brake) horsepower to the net horse-power rating used ever since. The net horsepower rating varied widely from engine to engine, but was an average of 75 percent of the brake horsepower reading. This 318-ci V-8 produced 155 net horsepower. This patroller is white over blue with a blue star and argent (silver) wheels. The blue door shield script lettering reads "We serve and protect."

A close-up shot of the 1971 Dodge Polara shows a good front perspective. This Golden State black-and-white cruiser has a red, four-bulb rotator, twin red/amber soup-can lights, and a roof-mounted spotlight. This was the last model year for the 383-ci big-block V-8. From 1959 through 1971, over 30 million 383-ci "low block" wedge-head V-8s were built. In fact, many cops who drove a 383-ci-powered cruiser claim it was the best law-enforcement engine ever. The 383-ci V-8 was more fuel-efficient than the 440-ci V-8 and just as reliable. Most important, it could provide a good dose of big-block torque when it was needed.

In 1971, the wheelbase of the mid-size Mopar police cars was bumped up by 1 inch. The Plymouth Satellite, such as this Miami, Florida, Police unit grew from 116 to 117 inches. The name Satellite replaced the name Belvedere. The Dodge Coronet grew from 117 to 118 inches. Both mid-size Mopars took on the Coke-bottle or fuselage body style that lasted through the late 1970s. The full-size Plymouth Fury I and Dodge Polara were available only as four-door police sedans. The police package on the mid-size Satellite and Coronet was available on both the four-door sedan and four-door station wagon. This Miami police car is white with green lettering and a blue rotating light.

After years of service as a pursuit car with the Arizona Highway Patrol, this 1971 Dodge Coronet, unit number B234, is now a cherished daily driver. The pride and joy of a U.S. Capitol Police officer, this all-white Coronet is powered by the 300-horse-power, 383-ci four-barrel V-8. It is one of only 1,594 Coronets with that drivetrain. The four-door, 118-inch-wheelbase mid-size has factory air conditioning. In 1971, Chrysler introduced the 360-ci V-8. This was an LA small block similar to the nonpolice 340-ci V-8. The 360-ci engine had a different bore and different stroke than the hot 340-ci V-8. It also had a more substantial web area to accept larger main bearings. With 175 net horse-power, the 360-ci two-barrel V-8 was midway between the 155-horsepower, 318-ci two-barrel and the 190-horsepower, 383-ci two-barrel engines. The 360-ci engine would gain fame power-ing the 1979 to 1981 R-body Newport, St. Regis, and Gran Fury.

The vehicle maintenance supervisor and a mechanic with the Pinellas County (Florida) Sheriff's Office check the engine of this 1971 Dodge Polara. Parked next to the Polara is the incredibly popular 1970 Plymouth Fury I. Pinellas County is on the Gulf side of Florida in the Tampa-St. Petersburg area. These PCSD Mopars are white over dark-green with red rotators. The hood bears an obvious "V"-shaped graphic. In 1970, the 440-ci V-8 in the Fury I had a 9.7 to 1 compression and a 375-horsepower rating. For 1971, the 440-ci V-8 used in the Polara had 9.5 to 1 compression and a 370-horsepower rating. This was the beginning of the lower-compression ratios that ended up at just 7.8 to 1. SAE net horsepower dropped from 305 net horsepower to just 225 net horsepower (Federal) by 1978.

A 1971 Plymouth Satellite displays the accurate markings of a Chicago Police unit. It was built for the Hollywood movie, *Back-draft*, starring Kurt Russell. In a Chicagoland setting, one of the early scenes of the movie portrayed a flashback to the time when Russell's father was a Chicago fireman. The CPD Satellite was used to block the road to keep motorists from running over fire hoses. In 1971, the mid-size Satellite was available with the 225-ci slant six, 318-ci V-8, and 383-ci V-8. Had this 117-inch-wheelbase Satellite been a true Chicago Police patroller, it would have the slant-six one-barrel engine.

New to the service of the Chicago Police is this 1971 Dodge Polara. The four-door cruiser is white over blue with argent wheels. The MARS lightbar includes a chromed siren speaker, twin blue-globe rotators, and twin rear-facing red lights. The 5,000-series car number indicates this unit is assigned to the Traffic Division. Patrol Division cars used 7,000, 8,000, and 9,000-series numbers. Trucks, vans, motorcycles, and station wagons used 6,000-series vehicle numbers. Unmarked district tactical or area detective division cars are numbered from 2,800 to 4,500. The 5,000-series Traffic Division cars had larger engines and were generally assigned to Chicago's expressways and the famous Lake Shore Drive.

A rear-quarter view of the 1972 AMC Matador used by the Federal Protection Service Police Department is shown here. The two most popular AMC police engines were the 360-ci four-barrel V-8 and the 401-ci four-barrel V-8. These engines were powerful, but their reliability under severe duty was not as good as the competition. The AMC Matador enjoyed incredible success and acceptance among police. The 118-inch-wheelbase Matador captured the Los Angeles Police Department contract. By 1973, the Los Angeles County Sheriff's Department had also adopted the Matador. The Dallas Police Department later joined in.

The Alabama State Troopers used 401-ci-powered 1972 AMC Javelins such as this as regular patrol cars. AMC specially prepared 100 Javelins with the race-inspired Police Interceptor package. The 401-ci, four-barrel V-8 produced 255 net horsepower. The 1972 Javelin was available with a three-speed Torque-Command automatic or a four-speed manual with a floor-mounted Hurst shifter, but these patrol cars used the automatic. The Alabama Javelin had a blue hood and trunk over a gray body. The single roof-mounted rotator was blue, and so was the background of the Alabama-shaped door shield which proudly read "State Trooper, Alabama." The fender bears the impressive red emblem "401."

The 1972 Plymouth Fury pictured here served the citizens of Suffolk County (New York). The color scheme is deep-blue with a white roof and front door. The emergency gear includes a red Federal Beacon Ray and a pair of red/amber "lollipop" roof flashers. The siren speaker mounted on the passenger-side front fender indicates that this impressive Plymouth belongs with the Highway Patrol Bureau. This four-door sedan is powered by a 285 net horsepower, 440-ci V-8 HP (high performance). A 230 net horsepower version of the 440-ci V-8 was also available. This cruiser had a three-speed TorqueFlite and a 3.23:1 ratio Sure-Grip rear end. Semi-metallic linings were standard with the front disc brakes. The entire package made for an imposing police car.

The Newtown (Connecticut) Police Department operated this beautiful 1972 Plymouth Fury. The four-door sedan is deep-blue with a gold door shield. The front fenders and trunk lid have the word "Police" in gold lettering. The impressive-looking urban patroller is topped off with twin red rotators. While this cruiser could have been powered by a 285 net horsepower, 440-ci V-8 HP engine, the 110-horsepower, 225-ci slant six and the 150-horsepower, 318-ci small-block V-8 were standard equipment on 1972 police-package Furys. A one-barrel six just doesn't fit the image.

The 1972 Ambassador station wagon parked here is on duty with the Contra Costa County (California) Sheriff's Department near San Francisco. Given the prisoner cage, the roof-mounted spotlight, the modest red flashers, and lack of a visible siren, this police wagon was probably used to transport prisoners from one lockup to another. Carpet cargo areas, rooftop luggage racks, and H78x14 tires were standard. A 304-ci, 360-ci, or 401-ci V-8 could power the Ambassador wagon. The wagon and four-door sedan shared the same 122-inch wheelbase. Other uses of a police wagon include K-9, shift supervisor, special response team, crime-scene technicians, and commercial carrier enforcement.

It seemed the AMC police cars were everywhere in the early 1970s, and this 1972 Wisconsin State Patrol Ambassador provides another example. The 118-inch-wheelbase Matador took some contracts while the 122-inch-wheelbase Ambassador took others. In 1972, the Wilmington (Delaware) Police and the Missouri State Highway Patrol were among many agencies to patrol in the 401-ci Ambassador. The color scheme on this cruiser is white over deep-blue with red/red rotators. The door shield is red, white, and deep-blue.

An era ended for the New York City Police with this 1972 Plymouth Fury. This was the last year for the tri-color paint scheme. This Radio Motor Patrol has a white roof and trunk, a green hood, doors, and rear quarter panels and black front fenders. This was also the last year that the NYPD door markings were configured in the shape of a police officer's badge. Commonly referred to as a badge in most places, it is called a shield in the Big Apple. This door shield reads "City of New York" and "Police." In the future, the door markings took on the appearance of the NYPD shoulder patch. The car colors were changed to white over medium-blue. This unit was with the 105th Precinct serving the cities of Queens Village and Bellerose.

The Palisades Interstate Park Commission of New York and New Jersey made use of this 1972 Plymouth Fury. This cruiser has a black hood and roof over a white body with overlaid gold leaves configuring the door shield. The four-bulb, roof-mounted rotator has red and white lamps inside a clear dome. While it may look like this Plymouth Cruiser has a huge wheelbase, it is actually just 120 inches. The 1972 Dodge Polara had a 122-inch wheelbase. This was the first model year for the 400-ci V-8, which was a bored-out 383-ci V-8. Larger engine sizes were needed to make up for lower compression ratios. The 400-ci V-8 was released with an 8.2:1 ratio. This was the lowest-compression police engine in the history of the Plymouth police package.

A rare shot of a 1972 Plymouth Fury holds a special significance for the Keystone State. This was the only year the Pennsylvania State Police used this gold-over-blue color combination and the only year this particular door marking was used. The 1972 door decal is similar to that used from 1957 through 1963, except this one has the state seal instead of the state profile inside the famous keystone. The beautiful gold-over-blue patrol cars used a red, roof-mounted rotator and a wide gold pinstripe.

The Maryland State Police maintained this very clean and crisp-looking all-white 1972 Dodge Polara. The door shield, hood lettering, and identical trunk lettering are the only markings. The oversize, single roof rotator has a clear globe with four alternating red and blue lamps. The use of both red and blue lenses was just beginning in the early 1970s. By the late 1980s, the majority of police cars across the United States would have red and blue lights. The only major exceptions were the blue lights used by the Chicago Police Department and police departments in the Deep South.

The 1972 Chevrolet Bel Air shown here served the 245 citizens of Frohna, Missouri, for 24 years. The mayor sold the car with just 25,600 original miles. His father was the mayor when the car was originally purchased new. The Sequoia Green cruiser is powered by a 402-ci "porcupine head," big-block V-8. In 1972, Chevrolet produced three different engines they called a "400." The first was the 170-horsepower Turbo-Jet 400, which was a 400-ci, two-barrel small-block V-8. The second engine was the 210-horsepower Turbo-Jet 400, which was a 402-ci, four-barrel big-block V-8 with single exhaust. The third was the 240-horsepower Turbo-Jet 400, which was a 402-ci, four-barrel big-block V-8 with dual exhaust. The police cars with all three 400-ci and 402-ci engines wore 400 fender emblems. The 402-ci engine was only available in 1972 Chevrolet police cars.

Many 1972 Chevrolet police cars, like this Frohna (Missouri) Police Bel Air, used a fender-mounted spotlight. The spotlight runs through the front fender, through the firewall, and through the dash. This particular Bowtie cruiser has a window-mounted, Kustom MR-7, which was the first of the moving-radar units. Before this, police cars had to be stationary to use a traffic radar unit. This 1972 Bel Air is equipped with the High Speed Pursuit Package, which included bias-belted police-spec tires. Even though radial tires were introduced in 1974, and big blocks were used through 1976, no Chevrolet big-block police car ever came from the factory with radials. This Sequoia Green Bel Air is topped off with a red/red Federal Visibar. The whip antenna connects to a trunk-mounted power pack for the two-way police radio.

In 1972, the Chicago Police Department cruised along the streets of the Windy City in the Chevrolet Bel Air. The police package was also available on the Biscayne and Impala and all three station wagons: the Brookwood, Townsman, and Kingswood. For the first time since Chevrolet produced the police-package car, a six-cylinder engine was not available in the full-size, four-door sedan. Urban police departments wanting an economical engine had the choice of only two small-block V-8s: the 350 ci and 400 ci. Nearly every Bowtie urban patroller used the venerable 350-ci two-barrel V-8 rated at just 165 horsepower.

There is no question whatsoever about what type of emergency vehicle this 1972 Chevrolet is or the jurisdiction of its riders. This Jersey City (New Jersey) Police cruiser has the word "Police" in large block letters on the rear quarter panels and on the trunk. In the absence of a fender-mounted engine decal, this JCPD unit packs a 350-ci, two-barrel V-8. The wheelbase for 1972 continued to be 121.5 inches, the longest ever for a Chevrolet four-door sedan. These cars were simply too big to use the 110-horsepower, 250-ci six.

The bumps and bruises typical of any big-city police cruiser are evident on this 1972 Elizabethtown (New Jersey) Police Chevrolet Biscayne. The emergency gear includes twin bar-mounted gumballs and a rectangular siren speaker. Spotlights were not common on these Bowtie patrollers because they had to be mounted on the fender, which made for a difficult and expensive installation. For 1972, Chevrolet changed its police-package designation. Regular production order B07 was the Police Chassis Equipment while BY2 specified the Police Body Equipment. In addition to some big cities, the West Virginia State Police, Arizona Highway Patrol, and Maine State Police used the full-size Chevrolet.

The Kentucky State Police used this 1972 Ford Custom. The all-gray cruiser has a blue rotator and gold, blue, and white door shield. The state police in Maryland, Kansas, Montana, and Florida also used the full-size Ford. All these state police and highway patrol cars are powered by the 212 net horsepower, 429-ci Police Interceptor four-barrel V-8 with dual exhaust and a 3.00 to 1 rear gear. That was the hot setup in the full-size Ford. Even so, the performance was markedly different from the 370 brake horsepower version used in 1971. The difference was a drop in compression ratio from 11.3 to 1, to 8.5 to 1. The Kentucky State Highway Patrol, formed in 1936, changed its name to the Kentucky State Police in 1948.

The Massachusetts State Police Department used this 1972 Ford Custom. The state police or highway patrol in Connecticut, South Carolina, and Georgia also used the full-size Ford. The Massachusetts State Police Department was organized in 1921. The color scheme includes a gray hood, roof, trunk, and front doors over dark-blue fenders and rear doors. For 1972, the compression ratios on all police engines followed the exact path of the retail engines. In that same year, the compression ratio fell to an average of 8.5 to 1. No police engine had compression higher than 8.6 to 1. In comparison, the average compression in 1971 was 9.7 to 1, with a high of 11.3 to 1.

The streets and alleys of Suffern, New York, were patrolled using this 1972 Ford Custom. The compression ratio was dropped from a 1971 average of 9.7 to 1, to a 1972 average of 8.5 to 1. This allowed the use of regular gasoline. The 153 net horsepower, 351 Windsor was standard on the 121-inch full-size Ford while a 163 net horsepower, 351 Cleveland was an option on the 118-inch mid-size Torino. This Suffern Police unit has a medium-blue roof over a white body. Both the four-bulb rotator and the twin flashers use red lenses.

Before being sold to a police-car collector, this powder-blue 1972 Plymouth Fury I was used by the Altenburg (Missouri) Police for 25 years. This photo was taken the year it went out of service with its original paint. All of the emergency lights and the radio are also original. Best of all, this Mopar cruiser had just 19,000 original miles on it, and the documentation to back it up. This Plymouth and the 1972 Chevrolet from Frohna, Missouri, were both in service for more than 20 years, both had under 30,000 miles, both sold to collectors, and both served towns within 5 miles of the other. Even better, both hit the police-car show circuit without making any mechanical repairs other than preventative maintenance. Those real finds are still out there!

For 1972, the Ford Torino, like this New York City Health and Hospitals Police unit, was restyled. It acquired an even more pronounced Coke-bottle or fuselage shape. The hottest Ford police engine in 1972, the 351 Cleveland four-barrel V-8 was available only in the mid-size Torino. Rated at 248 horsepower, the 351 Cleveland had more horsepower than the 429 Interceptor, which was rated at just 212 horsepower. The 429-ci big block, of course, produced more torque. The fastest police car in Ford's 1972 fleet was the mid-size Torino with the Cobra Jet-inspired 248-horsepower, four-barrel dual exhaust 351 Cleveland V-8.

A New Jersey State Police Department inspection is about to take place for this line of 1972 Plymouth Fury Is. In the mid-1970s, the NJSP used a striking variation of the old black-and-white color scheme. Its battle cruisers had a white roof and doors, and a black hood, trunk and fenders. However, the doors included a wide, bold blue stripe and corresponding gold stripe through the triangular door shield, which was blue with yellow lettering. The white wheels dramatically accent the overall black-and-white graphics. The NJSP, founded in 1921, ran solid-red Twinsonic lightbars.

The New York City Police Department set the pace for every urban police department in New England when it comes to police cars. In 1972, the NYPD ran the Plymouth Fury I. This particular cruiser is with the 105th Precinct. This was the last year for the tri-color NYPD cars, the cars with the color scheme that replaced the all-black cars in 1961. These NYPD cruisers have a white roof and trunk, black front fenders, and a green body. The pedestal-mounted red/white rotator and electro-mechanical siren complete the cop gear. The door shield is white with green lettering. These NYPD cruisers used either the 225-ci six or 318-ci V-8. Neither of these engines made for a fast car, but that was not a problem.

Sporting an orange-over-deep-blue paint job, this is a 1972 Plymouth Fury I with the Nassau County (New York) Police Department. Red deck flashers bolster the twin red emergency rotators. The siren speaker is not the typical chrome. Instead, it has the less expensive, and less attractive, black paint. This Long Island-area cruiser has white-outline orange lettering and an orange lion as a door emblem. The unusual appearance makes it clear that this is not a normal passenger car. The powertrain for this county patroller was probably one of the small-block V-8s, either the 150-horsepower, 318-ci or the 175-horsepower, 360-ci.

Half Moon Bay (California) Police Officer Guy Reimche is shown with his pride and joy: a fully restored 1972 Dodge Polara. This beautiful, all-white cruiser has a blue and gold door shield. The emergency lights include a red, four-bulb rotator and twin red/amber flashers. Actually, the forward-facing red does not flash, but the rear-facing amber does. This squad car is complete with twin, A-pillar spotlights, prisoner cage, and front pusher bars. Note the off-center, rectangular siren.

A rear, quarter view of the 1972 Half Moon Bay (California) Police Dodge Polara is displayed here. Notice how well the white wheels set off the all-white cruiser. This Bay-area police car is powered by the 400-ci big-block V-8. This was a bored-out 383-ci engine with the same stroke as the 383 ci. In the Polara, the 400 ci was available in two power levels using California emissions. One was the 181-horsepower, two-barrel version. The second, a four-barrel engine produced 241 horsepower. The California version had 9 horsepower and 5 pound-feet of torque less than the Federal version. In 1972, the four-barrel carburetor was switched from the Carter AVS (air valve secondary) to the Carter ThermoQuad with a phenolic-resin main body and float section. This allowed the carburetor to insulate the fuel from the ever-increasing underhood heat.

The Canine Patrol unit of the Benicia (California) Police Department used this 1972 Dodge Polara. The white-over-black four-door sedan has a black and gold seven-point star and gold lettering. The emergency lights make this Bay-area California cruiser a little unusual. It has red/amber soup-can lights and separate left and right alley lights. Also noteworthy is the four-bulb center rotator with a blue globe. Red globes were the convention of the time. None of this legally matters to the motorist, however, since the soup-can lights glow continuously red, and that is all it takes to satisfy the state statute.

California Highway Patrol battle cruisers have looked like this for 50 years. In fact, the white roof and front door over a black body so defines the identity of a police car that California citizens are not allowed to drive a black, private vehicle with a white roof and front door. This 1972 Dodge Polara shows off everything we expect from a 1970s police car: whip antenna, roof lights, A-pillar spotlights, dash-mounted shotgun, and front pusher bars. Without a doubt, the CHP sets a standard for law enforcement vehicles that continues to this day. Only the Michigan State Police Department rivals the prestige of the CHP when it comes to police patrol vehicles.

In 1972, the California Highway Patrol cruised across the Golden State in the Dodge Polara. Other state police and highway patrol departments that used the 122-inch Polara included Oklahoma, Iowa, Idaho, Illinois, Nevada, New Mexico, and Washington. CHP-specs required a 440-ci engine with a Holley carburetor, even though most 440-ci engines came with the Carter ThermoQuad. These Dodges had the three-speed TorqueFlite and a 3.23-ratio Sure-Grip. Also specified were front disc brakes with semi-metallic pads and a special front-to-rear proportioning valve to reduce the possibility of rear-wheel lock-ups on severe stops.

A promotional photo displays this generically marked, 1972 Plymouth Fury Pursuit. Given the success and domination of Plymouths in the 1970s, no promotion campaign was necessary. Quite literally, the performance from the 440-ci V-8, the durability of the three-speed TorqueFlite and the high-speed stability of the front torsion-bar suspension sold the Mopar police car to cops without any sales effort from Chrysler Corporation. New for 1972 was the availability of the 400-ci big-block V-8. This was essentially a 383-ci V-8 bored out to 400-ci. Dodge and Plymouth used cubic inches to partially make up for lower compression ratios. Of course, an extra 17 cubic inches does not make up for a compression drop from 10:1, to 8.5:1. Nearly all full-size Dodge and Plymouth police cars used the 440-ci V-8 instead.

You can almost hear this Georgia State Patrol trooper saying, "You're in a heap of trouble." When you have a finger from the long arm of the law pointing at you, surely you will have chills going up your spine. This GSP trooper has the southbound lane of U.S. 41 blocked with his 1972 Ford Custom. This four-door Ford has a gray-over-blue color scheme. By 1972, the Peach State cruisers made the transition to a blue roof rotator instead of red. The fender, door, and trunk lettering, however, remained orange, as it had been since 1937. The lettering was changed to gray by the 1980s. It is hard to swallow the presence of white-wall tires on this GSP cruiser. Note the rear seat prisoner cage, possibly intended for those motorists who question the GSP use of whitewalls.

A Chrysler Corporation promotional photo provides a great twilight shot of a 1972 Plymouth Satellite. The big news for the 1972 Satellite and Dodge Coronet was the availability of the 440-ci big-block V-8. Even so, the horsepower ratings for engines used on the Mopar intermediates was slightly lower than the same basic engine used in the full-size Mopars. For example, the 440-ci "HP" V-8 was rated at 280 horsepower when used in the 117-inch Satellite, but 285 horsepower when used in the 122-inch Fury. The mid-size Satellite and Coronet with either a 400-ci or 440-ci big block came standard with a rear anti-sway bar developed by the Los Angeles Police Department. The use of optional 15-inch wheels and tires also added to its pursuit capabilities.

If this is Southern California in the early 1970s, it must be an AMC Matador. In fact, it is a 1973 Los Angeles Police Matador, sporting a new grille for this model year. Cops everywhere used the 401-ci-powered Matador, including LAPD SWAT Team 75. Note the officer with the shotgun and the binoculars on the hood. This Matador is a far cry from the average Rambler. It has a full police suspension including front and rear anti-sway bars and disc brakes strong enough to let the driver go deeper into turns than most cruisers of the day. The three-speed AMC TorqueCommand transmission was Chrysler's version of the bulletproof TorqueFlite. And the 255 net horsepower 401-ci, four-barrel V-8 pushed the Matador well over 120 miles per hour.

The lineup pictured here comprises a virtual big-block heaven for any police car enthusiast. These cars are all with the Arizona Department of Public Safety, Arizona Highway Patrol: a silver 1973 AMC Matador with the 401-ci V-8, a medium-brown 1972 Mercury Marquis with the 429-ci V-8 and a white 1972 Chevrolet Bel Air with the 454-ci V-8. Each squad car is equipped with a lightbar sporting one red and one amber rotator. The Bel Air has a bar-mounted siren speaker. Each four-door sedan is fitted with a heavy-duty front pusher bar. AMC police cars were discontinued after 1976. Mercury dropped its police package after 1981, and the last full-size Chevrolet police car was produced in 1996.

The Nevada Motor Carrier Division of the Nevada Highway Patrol used this 1973 Plymouth Fury I. While the traffic patrol cars were silver over blue, these commercial enforcement vehicles were white over brown. They were also labeled with a traditional door shield instead of a seven-point star. This commission is equipped with a federal Visibar using one red and one blue lens, and rear-facing deck flashers. The driver-side spotlight has a clear lens, while the passenger-side spotlight has a red lens. The police Polara was available with 318-ci and 360-ci small-block V-8s, and 400-ci and 440-ci big-block V-8s.

In 1973, the Pennsylvania State Police changed from blue and gold patrol cars to the medium-blue and bright yellow of this Plymouth Fury I. The Keystone door shield was deep blue. In 1974, the color scheme was changed once again, this time to deep-blue hoods and trunks on white bodies, as evidenced by the Plymouth Fury I in the background. The PSP retained this white-and-blue color scheme until 1991. The 1974 model represented the first time that the PSP used a siren built into the base of the red, roof-mounted rotator, a feature used into the 1980s.

The New York City Police ushered in a complete change in color scheme, body markings, and emergency equipment with this 1973 Plymouth Fury I of the 103rd PCT. The older NYPD cruisers in the background show the contrast. The vehicle colors were changed from a white roof and trunk, black front fenders, and green body to a white roof, blue body, and wide white stripe. The change was in keeping with then-new recommendations from a federally funded study, which stipulated bold and simple markings that kept clutter to a minimum. Emergency gear was upgraded from a single, pedestal-mounted, four-bulb rotator and roof-mounted bullet-style mechanical siren to a lightbar with twin, four-bulb rotators, twin-can light flashers and an electronic siren speaker. In the later years, the word "Police" was added back to the trunk lid, the precinct number or command to the rear doors, and the car number to the rear fender.

The Highway Patrol Bureau of the Suffolk County (New York) Police Department, used this long-wheelbase 1973 Chrysler New Yorker. The term "Highway Patrol" appears on the door. The white-and-blue cruiser has a red/white rotator and twin red flashers. It also has a passenger-side spotlight and a siren mounted above the headlights on the fender. For normal patrol work, the SCPD used Plymouth Furys in 1973. The New Yorker is powered by a 215-horsepower, 440-ci V-8. Even with this fairly strong engine, at 4,460 pounds, it is a lot of work to get it moving down the highway. These cars were not available with a factory police package.

A 350-ci V-8 powers this 1973 Kearny (New Jersey) Police Chevrolet Bel Air. The full-size, small-block-powered Chevrolets were available in either 3.42 or 3.08 rear gears. This was an attempt to give either better performance or better fuel economy, knowing that the cops could not have both. The 350-ci two-barrel with single exhaust was rated at 145 horsepower. The 350-ci four-barrel with dual exhaust achieved 175 horsepower. This four-barrel engine was also available in the 112-inch two-door and 116-inch four-door Chevelle. This was the only Chevelle engine.

The 1973 model year was one of low performance for the Chevrolet Bel Air and Impala. Oddly enough, the 175-horsepower, 350-ci-powered police Chevelle was about as fast as the 245-horsepower, 454-ci-powered police Bel Air. This was especially true if the Chevelle was the shorter and lighter two-door version. Even with a comparison such as this, it was not until 1975 that the 454-ci V-8 hit bottom. From then, it was more than 20 years, more than an entire police career, until a Chevrolet police sedan had an engine with more than 250 horsepower.

New for 1973 Ford police cars, including this South Carolina Highway Patrol Galaxie 500, was the 460-ci, 335-series, big-block V-8. This was a retail engine in 1972. Ford needed the extra cubic inches to make up for yet another reduction in compression. The 460-ci V-8 was made by stroking the 429-ci V-8 while keeping the same bore. The new engine was called the 460 Police Interceptor. Unlike the 429-ci big block, the 460-ci big block always came with a four-barrel carburetor. This 7.5-liter, 460-ci V-8 was the largest police engine ever built by Ford Motor Company. This white SCHP Galaxie 500 has a large blue rotator, window-mounted radar unit, A-pillar spotlight, and gold markings with blue lettering.

Pictured is the rear-quarter view of a 1973 South Carolina Highway Patrol Ford Galaxie 500. This cruiser is powered by the 219-horsepower, 460-ci Police Interceptor. In comparison, the 281-ci single overhead cam (SOHC) V-8 used in the police Crown Victoria produced 210 horsepower, and it was developed 20 years later. What a difference fuel injection, overhead cams, and computer technology made. The 460-ci engine included an engine cooler and an auxiliary power steering oil cooler. New for 1973 were 80-amp batteries, 90-amp alternators, and a coolant recovery system.

A light-blue 1973 Ford Custom is shown on duty with the Hoboken (New Jersey) Police Department. It is topped with a red, four-bulb rotator and twin blue flashers on a strap-style lightbar. In 1973, the Ford Police Special package was available for the Custom 500 four-door pillared hardtop, the Galaxie 500 two-door hardtop, and four-door pillared hardtop. The full-size Ford was built on a 121-inch wheelbase. All 1973 Ford police engines had an 8.0 to 1 compression ratio, and all ran on regular-grade gasoline. This Hoboken cruiser is almost certainly powered by the 156-horsepower, 351 Windsor. That was the smallest engine available in the full-size Ford.

The citizens of Danbury, Connecticut, were served by this all-white 1973 Ford Custom. The powerplant is either a 351 Windsor or a 400 Cleveland. Both came with two-barrel engines using single exhaust. For 1973, the full-size police package included larger 15x6.5 wheels and H78x15 tires, except for 460-ci-powered cruisers, which used J78x15 rubber. In 1973, all Ford police engines had lower compression ratios. At 8.0 to 1, this was the lowest compression ratio since 1955. The 429-ci V-8 was also available but this was its last year. The 1973 Ford was honored as *Motor Trend's* "Full-size Sedan of the Year."

The Police Special package was available for the Ford Torino in a 114-inch, two-door hardtop and a 118-inch four-door pillared hardtop in 1973. Torinos like this gold Leon Valley (Texas) Police unit were available in a wide variety of engines including the 250-ci six, 302-ci V-8, 351-ci and 400-ci Cleveland V-8s, as well as 429-ci and 460-ci big-block V-8. This was the last year for a Ford police six-cylinder engine until the Fairmont in 1979. The 460-ci, four-barrel Torino four-door weighed 4,530 pounds. Even with 3.00 rear gears, the big-block Torino still ran a 16.5 second quarter mile at 85 miles per hour.

The Arizona Highway Patrol used this maroon 1973 Mercury Montego MX. The door shield is a blue, seven-point star. The Federal Twinsonic has one red and one amber lens, with a red lens in the driver's spotlight as well. Note the massive front pusher bumper. This four-door pillared hardtop is powered by the 266-horsepower, 351-ci Cleveland four-barrel V-8. The 351 Cleveland was only available in the Montego and Ford Torino, not the full-size police cars. The Cobra Jet–inspired Cleveland V-8 had a special carburetor, intake manifold, cam, and 2-1/2-inch-diameter pipes. This was the only Ford police engine to use four-bolt main bearing caps. The four-barrel 351 Cleveland used in police cars truly was the 351 Cobra Jet, or at least what was left of it. All 1973 Ford engines had an 8.0 to 1 compression ratio.

The Indiana State Police became famous for its use of Mercury police cars, like this 1973 Monterey. The 460-ci V-8 engine in this commission was the largest police engine ever built by Ford Motor Company. It was not, however, the most powerful. That honor goes to the 1970 and 1971 429-ci four-barrel V-8 with 370 brake horsepower and roughly 280 net horsepower. The difference was compression; the 429-ci engine had an 11.3 to 1 ratio compared to 8.0 to 1 for the 460-ci big block. This 460-ci engine was never a high-compression engine, unlike the Chevrolet 454 and Mopar 440, both of which enjoyed high compression during at least some of their police careers. This all-white Monterey has a red rotator, blue door shield, and gold "V." Note the full-dress wheel covers.

When the 1973 Mercury Monterey was not quite plush and large enough, there was always the 1973 Mercury Marquis. Built on the same 124-inch wheelbase as the Monterey, this Stockton (California) Police Marquis outweighed the Monterey by 322 pounds at a total of 4,547 pounds. This fender-skirted cruiser did not come from the factory with a Police Special package. It did, however, have a very powerful optional engine. The base engine was the 198-horsepower, 429-ci V-8. The optional engine was a 267-horsepower, 460-ci V-8. Strange as it seems, it had one horsepower more than the 351 Cleveland. It just would not do to have a small-block V-8 produce more horsepower than a big-block V-8 in the division's most prestigious luxury sedan.

New York police car enthusiast Frank Goderre restored this "Best of Show" award-winning 1973 New York State Police Fury I. This 120-inch NYSP cruiser is perfect to the finest detail, including an orange "NY State Police NY" license plate. This cruiser has a glass-black hood and roof with black door lettering over a white body. This is a different paint scheme than the NYSP Thruway units. The Thruway cruisers have a dark-blue hood and roof. The outline of the state marks the doors of the Thruway vehicles. The New York Thruway Commission, which pays the salaries of the NYSP Thruway patrol, also owns the vehicles. The state owns the non-Thruway police cars, which patrol statewide.

The New Jersey State Police used the Plymouth Fury III in 1973. This 120-inch-wheelbase commission has a white roof and doors over a black body with white wheels and dog-dish hubcaps. A blue triangle with gold lettering configures the door shield on this NJSP cruiser. The Federal Twinsonic has twin red lenses. Note the license plate, which starts with the letters "SP" for State Police. The powertrain, of course, is the 280-horsepower, 440-ci four-barrel V-8 with the three-speed TorqueFlite and a 3.23 Sure-Grip. This is one of the most famous police drivetrains of all time.

In 1973, the Michigan State Police used the Plymouth Fury I. This cruiser is a beautiful, deep blue. The exact shade of blue was restricted to use by the Michigan State Police for decades. The door shield and lightning bolt are painted gold. Note the famous, hood-mounted "State Stop Police" sign, which could be illuminated at night. This cruiser was powered by the 440-ci V-8. Since 1966 for Dodge, and since 1967 for Plymouth, cops had their choice between a standard-cam 440-ci V-8, or the special-cam version of the engine, called the 440-ci HP V-8. For 1973, the standard-cam version was restricted to police station wagons, and only the 440-ci HP was available in police sedans.

The 1973 Dodge Polara pictured here is fully restored as a Missouri State Highway Patrol unit. The Missouri State Highway Patrol itself was formed in 1931. A Federal Twinsonic tops the deep-blue cruiser with red and white lights under clear lenses. The door shield and fender emblems use gold letters on a light-blue background. The protruding rubber bumperettes introduced in 1973 are clearly visible. This is one sharp-looking restoration.

This 1973 California Highway Patrol Dodge Polara is being put through its paces at the emergency-driving course at the Academy. Note that the driver is wearing a helmet and the wheel covers have been removed. The CHP sergeant in tan utilities is explaining something about the rear tires or brakes, perhaps the fact that CHP cruisers had brake-proportioning valves to prevent the rear drum brakes from locking up even during extreme braking. The CHP Polara with a 440-ci HP V-8 ran a 15.5-second quarter mile at 89 miles per hour, and had a top speed of 129 miles per hour. The 0- to 60-mile-per-hour time was 7.7 seconds.

A New York State Police sergeant is standing next alongside his "Sunoco" cruiser. The cruiser is a 1974 Dodge Monaco with a bright-yellow over deep-blue color scheme. The wheels are painted the same deep blue as part of the body. The massive gumballs perched on top of the roof have red globes. This cruiser needs a 440-ci engine just to push those oversize rotators through the air. The 8.2:1 compression big block was rated at 275 horsepower, still enough to produce plenty of tire-melting torque.

The Peel Regional Police, responsible for enforcing the laws in suburban Toronto, Canada, used this 1974 Plymouth Fury. The car is painted "chrome yellow," or taxicab yellow, which is the same color used by the Metro Toronto Police. Note the large red light on the right fender, which reads "Police Stop" when illuminated. The cruiser uses a red, four-bulb rotator, which sits high enough to be seen over the roof-mounted siren speaker. Although this car is a Fury, the Canadian version had the Plymouth emblem mounted on the front fenders under the Fury emblem. The A38 Police Package was available on U.S. versions called the Fury I, Fury II, and Fury III. While the civilian version of the Fury I and Fury II had a 120-inch wheelbase, the 1974 Plymouth police car was based on the 122-inch Fury III and Gran Fury, regardless of the actual trim level.

The beautiful 1974 Plymouth Satellite shown was in service with the Nassau County (New York) Police Department. The color scheme is orange over bright blue, with the orange color extending well onto the rear quarter panel. Over the years, Nassau County has had some of the most strikingly marked cruisers. From black cars with orange wheels in the 1950s, to white cars with broad blue and orange stripes in the 1980s, the Nassau County cars have always stood out. This cruiser from the 5th Precinct has a four-bulb rotator inside a clear lens, and red/amber flashers. In 1974, the door emblem mimics the shape of the police officer's shield, or badge, hence the term "door shield." The door shield reads "Nassau County Police" along with the car's unit number.

The Arkansas State Police used this 1974 Chevrolet Bel Air. The color scheme includes a white roof over a medium-blue body, with a blue/blue Federal Twinsonic lightbar. Note the fender-mounted driver-side spotlight. The 22-inch control shaft for the light went through the front fender, firewall, and dash. The A-pillar was too small to drill for a spotlight. These patrol cars were all powered by a 454-ci big-block V-8, which, in turn, required the "High Speed Pursuit Package" This included severe-duty brakes, a rear anti-sway bar, and nylon, high-speed police bias-belted tires. The 454-ci engine was never available with radial tires.

It appears that the Los Angeles Police put this 1974 AMC Matador station wagon to good use. Again, the color scheme is white over black with red/amber emergency lights. In spite of the Matador's replacement by other makes of police cars after 1974, the AMC workhorses continued to perform a wide variety of official police duties. This four-door, six-passenger station wagon was built on a 118-inch wheelbase and weighed 3,957 pounds before any cop gear. The 258-ci six was standard equipment while 304-ci, 360-ci, and 401-ci V-8 engines were optional.

A 1974 LAPD Matador is parked in front of a 1978 Plymouth Fury being used as a detective unit. The Matador was something of a Southern California legend. These cars remained in service for years after other cars were put out to pasture in the hands of detectives and administrators. Some Matadors were still in use well into the late 1980s. This cruiser has the traditional LAPD markings: white roof and doors over a black body with roof-mounted soup-can lights and siren. The emergency lights display a continuous burning red to the front and a flashing amber to the rear.

Anthony Kovic, the chief fleet manager of the Chicago Police, checks out the proposed graphics on this 1974 Chevrolet Bel Air. The change involved a transition from white over blue to all-white with a wide blue stripe and red numbers and letters. The red, white, and blue theme was designed in anticipation of the nation's Bicentennial. The 1974 Chevrolet was a big, comfortable police car. The B07 and BY2 police packages were available for the Bel Air and Impala four-door sedans and for the Impala two-door coupe.

Pictured is a 1974 Mount Prospect (Illinois) Police Dodge Monaco. This is the car and the police agency that eventually ended up as the sold-at-auction "Bluesmobile" Monaco. The gold, five-point star and the white "P1" were almost completely sanded off before the car was shamefully auctioned off. These markings are still visible on the movie car. The real Mt. Prospect cruiser has been perfectly restored right down to the twin red rotators, twin red can lights, and red high-beam headlight lenses. Mount Prospect is a Chicago suburb.

A rear-quarter view is shown of the 1974 Ventura (California) Police Dodge Monaco. Note the prisoner cage between the front and back seats. This black-and-white cruiser has gold lettering on the trunk and doors, and a gold city seal as the door shield. This Ventura police car has all the gear that typifies a true California cruiser, including twin A-pillar spotlights and auxiliary alley lights mounted on the Federal Twinsonic. The Twinsonic has red lenses to the front and red lenses to the rear with the exception of a small amber section on the left side.

Famous for its Dodge police cars, the California Highway Patrol ran the Dodge Monaco in 1974. Posed by the black-and-white cruiser is then-Sergeant Maury Hannigan. Hannigan went on to become the commissioner of the CHP, as well as the host and narrator of the T.V. series *Real Stories of the Highway Patrol*. Hannigan is a real "car guy" and frequently attends police car shows held in the Golden State. This CHP cruiser has the famous pusher bars, twin A-pillar spotlights, and low-band whip antenna. The Twinsonic lightbar has one red and one blue lens. Now retired from the CHP, Hannigan was one of the CHP's most popular commissioners and one of law enforcement's best spokespeople.

New for 1974 were the yellow-over-blue graphics that this New York State Police Dodge Monaco shows off. The hood, trunk, lower body panels, and wheels are blue. The new color scheme was voted upon at county fairs in the Empire State prior to its adoption by the NYSP. The big, 122-inch-wheelbase Monaco sports twin oversize red rotators. It is, of course, powered by the 440-ci V-8, now rated at 275 horsepower. This is the "special cam," four-barrel HP engine that absolutely ruled the roads in the 1970s. This particular Monaco is virtually perfect; it is a class winner or best-of-show winner everywhere it goes.

These two Pennsylvania State Police cruisers, parked side by side, are white with blue hoods and blue trunks. One is a 1974 Plymouth Gran Fury and the other is a 1977 Ford LTD II. 1974 was the first year for this color scheme, as well as the first model year for the Gran Fury nameplate. This name was used for police cars until the demise of the police car line in 1989. Plymouth made a distinction between the Police Special package, which was a police car from the ground up, and the A38 Police package, which was a retail car with police bolt-ons. The Police Special was based on the Fury I. This Gran Fury had the A38 police package.

Although it seems wrong for 1974, this Iowa Highway Patrol cruiser is a Chrysler Newport. In 1974 Chrysler was not back in the police car business, but many full-size 1974 Chrysler Corporation sedans were available with a bolt-on A38 Police package. The A38 package included one of the police-spec engines, in this case a 275-horsepower, 440-ci V-8. It also included the bulletproof TorqueFlite, beefed-up steering, suspension, brakes, wheels, and tires. The package included heavy-duty cooling and electrical components. Finally, it included heavy-duty interior fabric and police-only dash instrumentation. About the only thing the A38 package did not include was extra welds on the unibody. This IHP cruiser is all-white with red/red emergency lights and a red-lens fender-mounted light.

West Coast police-car expert and veteran police-car show judge, traffic officer Darryl Lindsay stands proudly next to his cruiser, a 1974 Plymouth Satellite Custom. This all-white San Mateo (California) Police unit is clearly marked as a Traffic Safety vehicle. It packs a 275-horsepower 440-ci HP V-8 to get the job done. Lindsay's patrol unit accelerated to 60 miles per hour in 7.7 seconds, and ran a 15.0-second quarter mile at 96 miles per hour. In the bleak performance era of the mid-1970s, this cruiser was a genuine rocket sled. It was much faster than the mid-1970s crop of Camaros, Mustangs, and Corvettes.

The Lawton (Oklahoma) Police Department used cruisers such as this 1974 Plymouth Satellite. This particular unit is powered by a 360-ci V-8, a common police engine for urban scenarios. This was the first model year the 360-ci V-8 was available in the mid-size Satellite and Dodge Coronet. The 200-horsepower, 360-ci four-barrel pushed the mid-size Mopars to 60 miles per hour in 9.5 seconds. The 360-ci-powered, 117-inch-wheelbase Satellite ran the quarter mile in 16.6 seconds at 85 miles per hour. This beautifully restored and strikingly marked Lawton cruiser is white with a wide red stripe. The Federal Visibar has red and blue globes. The word "Police" on the rear door is in blue lettering. The exceptional graphics on this cruiser rank it among the all-time most attractive police cars.

In 1974, the Dodge Coronet was available in six police engines, which ranged from the 105-horsepower, 225-ci slant six to the 275-horsepower, 440-ci HP V-8. This all-white Coronet was with the Alamo Heights (Texas) Police Department. A 400-ci four-barrel V-8 probably powers this cruiser. The standard-cam, single-exhaust version was rated at 205 horsepower, while the special-cam, dual-exhaust version achieved 250 horsepower. The 250-horsepower Coronet hit 60 miles per hour in 9.0 seconds. It ran a 16.3 second quarter mile at 86 miles per hour. Note that the clear-lens Twinsonic has only two rotators. Most Twinsonics had four rotators.

The Santa Clara, California, Police used this 1974 Chevrolet Bel Air. Santa Clara is near San Jose. Due to restrictive emission laws, the only police engine certified for full-size Chevrolets in California was the 454-ci four-barrel V-8 with dual exhausts. This 235-horsepower V-8 was teamed with the 3.08 axle, making it a great high-speed pursuit car. However, the big engine prevented Chevrolet from bidding on urban police contracts that required smaller engines. That explained why Chevrolet worked so hard on the 350-ci Nova. This Santa Clara cruiser is white over medium-blue with a red/blue Twinsonic and a roof-mounted spotlight. The fender-mounted spotlights were very difficult to install.

The 235-horsepower, 454-ci V-8 powers this 1974 Walhalla (North Dakota) Police Chevrolet Bel Air. Plymouth historian Jim Benjaminson was issued this beast, and he recalls that it could pass anything on the road (which was true) except a gas station (which was also true). The 4,373-pound, 121.5-inch cruiser had a 0- to 60-mile-per-hour time of 9.6 seconds. It ran the quarter mile in 17.9 seconds at 82 miles per hour. With 3.08 gears, the Bowtie battle cruiser was just getting started at the end of the quarter mile. The Pembina County (North Dakota) Sheriff's Department also ran the 454-ci Bel Air. The 454-ci Bel Air was quicker than the 460-ci Ford Custom to the 60-mile-per-hour mark, but not as quick as the 440-ci Plymouth Fury I.

In 1974, the police package was available on the 118-inch Torino four-door sedan and the 114-inch Torino two-door hardtop. This 1974 Reno (Nevada) Police Torino sports the 255-horsepower, 351 Cleveland V-8. This was the last year for this engine. In 1975, the 351 Cleveland was replaced by a destroked, raised-deck 400 Cleveland, known as the 351 Modified. Torino powertrains ranged from the 140-horsepower, 302-ci two-barrel V-8 to the 260-horsepower, 460-ci Police Interceptor V-8, including the 351 Cleveland, 400 Cleveland, and 460-ci Police. This Reno patroller is all-white with a red-and-blue Twinsonic and gold door lettering. The city seal forms the door shield.

A 118-inch wheelbase supports this 1974 San Francisco Police Ford Torino. For 1974, a V-8 powered all police Torinos. The 250-ci six was no longer available. At 4,530 pounds, the cars were too heavy and the emission controls robbed too much power. Among four small-block V-8s and two big-block V-8s, the Torino was powered by the 195-horsepower, 460-ci Police, or the 260-horsepower, 460-ci Police Interceptor. The non-police 220-horsepower, 460-ci V-8 pushed the Torino to 60 miles per hour in 8.9 seconds. It ran the quarter mile in 16.5 seconds at 85 miles per hour. The EPA city mileage rating of 14.3 miles per gallon was surprisingly good for such a large-displacement engine.

An awesome 1974 Dodge Monaco Custom was used by the Washington State Patrol. Of course, it has the 275-horsepower, 440-ci V-8 teamed with a TorqueFlite and 3.23 rear gears. For 1974, Dodge and Plymouth aggressively pushed the A38 police package. The Dodge Police Pursuit and Plymouth Police Special were available only on low trim level, four-door sedans. Introduced in 1971 but emphasized in 1974, the A38 package could be added to literally any full-size Mopar, like this Monaco Custom. The A38 package included one of the police-spec engines and the most heavy-duty TorqueFlite. It also included the beefed-up suspension, heavy-duty cooling, heavy-duty interior fabric, and police instrumentation. This impressive Dodge has a blue roof rotator with twin red flashers as an auxiliary warning signal.

The discreet 1974 Mercury Montego shown here is very much a police-package four-door sedan. It was used by the Washington State Patrol. Notice the license plate: WSP 982. Of course, by the time you are close enough to read the license plate, the WSP trooper would have the traffic summons half filled out. This all-brown Montego is unmarked except for the spotlight. Either the spotlight has a red lens, or red flashers are mounted behind the grille. The WSP started using hidden red grille lights in 1960. The WSP cruiser was powered by the impressive, 255-horsepower, 351-ci four-barrel "Cleveland" V-8. This canted-valve V-8 produced just 5 horsepower less than the 460-ci Police Interceptor V-8. All 1974 Ford police engines had an 8.0 to 1 compression ratio.

Only a few exterior markings identify this 1974 Ford Torino as an unmarked cruiser with the Washington State Patrol. The visible markings include a license plate, which reads "WSP 988" and an A-pillar-mounted spotlight. Also note the roll cage! In 1974, the WSP purchased the mid-size, 118-inch-wheelbase Ford Torino and Mercury Montego in an attempt to cut back on fuel use. The problem was that at 3,793 and 4,092 pounds, respectively, the mid-size FoMoCo four-door sedans were nearly as heavy as the 4,175 pound, full-size Dodge Monaco Custom. The 255-horsepower, 351-ci Blue Ovals may have had better gas mileage than the 440-ci Mopar, but not necessarily. Except for symbolism over substance, the WSP could have performed equally well using the 240-horsepower, 400-ci V-8 in its Monacos.

The Chicago Police Department used this long-wheelbase, 1974 Chevrolet Bel Air as a Radar Patrol unit. The white-over-blue four-door sedan has twin blue rotators and twin blue flashers mounted along with an electronic siren on the light rack. In all of Illinois, only the Chicago police are authorized to run blue emergency lights. Note the fender-mounted spotlight. The A-pillars on the 1971 to 1976 Chevrolets were simply too narrow to allow them to be drilled through and through with a half-inch bit. The 9,000-series car number would normally mean that this was a Patrol Division vehicle. We cannot explain it other than to confirm that this was indeed a regular traffic car from the Traffic Division. In police work, the "Radar Patrol" decal above the driver's door latch is considered a clue.

Notice this beautifully restored 1974 Dodge Coronet that bears the markings of the Long Beach (California) Police. The white-over-black, four-door sedan is built on a 118-inch platform. This particular squad car is powered by the famous 275-horsepower, 440-ci V-8 with the special camshaft, four-barrel carburetor, and dual exhaust. The 1974 model year was the first that Dodge and Plymouth offered a police-spec radial as an option. The police-spec tires for the mid-size Coronet and Satellite were still G78-15 bias-belted tires. In 1975, the mid-size Mopars could be ordered with GR70-15 radials. Note the fixed-position, fender-mounted red light on this California cruiser. This Coronet is fitted with chromed pusher bars. The red and blue Twinsonic has been retrofitted with auxiliary alley lights.

Chapter Eight

1975-1979

Emissions controls continued to dominate police car news in 1975. For Dodge and Plymouth police cars, this was a year of transition from leaded gasoline to unleaded gas. Cars that ran on leaded gas were required to have an air pump to pump fresh air into the exhaust, which reduced emissions. The air pump was another belt-driven engine accessory and had little effect on engine performance.

Police cars that ran unleaded gas required the use of a catalytic converter, and the catalytic converter had the same effect as a highly restrictive muffler. Often, dual-exhaust engines ran all their exhaust through one catalytic converter, and the result was the choked-off engine performance. The 318 V-8 was the standard powerplant for all Mopar squads. However, it really took a 400-ci-powered cruiser to make an acceptable patrol-class police car.

In 1975, Chrysler produced just four engines for police cars called the "special endurance police engines": the 318-ci two-barrel, the 360-ci four-barrel, the 400-ci four-barrel, and the 440-ci four-barrel. All other available engines were available for the retail market. In 1975, Plymouth sold more police cars than any other automaker.

Ford's raised-block 351 Modified replaced the 351 Cleveland in mid-size cars while the full-size cars continued to use the

Chicago Police Lt. Lee Hamilton stands proudly next to his 1975 Chevrolet Bel Air. This all-white police car with a wide blue stripe and red lettering is topped by the trademark MARS lightbar sporting twin blue globes. The soup-can lights have blue flashing elements facing forward and red lights, hooked into the brake and turn-signal circuit, facing rearward. The B07 and BY2 police packages were based on the four-door Bel Air and the two-door and four-door Impala. This was the last year for the Bel Air nameplate, which was introduced in 1953. In 1975, all Chevrolet police cars had catalytic converters, which required unleaded gasoline.

351 Windsor for 1975. The 460-ci Police Interceptor was the top cop engine, and it was available in two-door and four-door alike. Every Ford police engine ran on unleaded gasoline, and every powertrain included a catalytic converter.

The 1975 Chevrolet Nova made police car history; few police cars have had the instant acceptance or the impact. The Los Angeles County Sheriff's Department, along with many urban police and sheriff's departments, chose the incredible 9C1 Nova. During a time of bleak police car performance, the 350-ci-

A 1975 Dallas (Texas) Police Matador is shown here. Even though the front end was softened and made less radical than the 1974 version, the overall length of the 118-inch-wheelbase cruiser did not change. Of course, overall length does not mean too much when the agency promptly installs a huge pusher bar. Not much was heard of AMC after 1975. In 1976, the 401-ci engine was restricted to law enforcement and only 20 were sold. No mention is made in literature of an AMC police package after 1976, or even of a 401-ci engine.

The 145-horsepower, 350-ci V-8 powered this 1975 Chicago Police Chevrolet. The 121.5-inch-wheelbase Bowtie was a little sluggish with the two-barrel small block, but was economical for heavy urban-police use. The 155-horsepower, 350-ci four-barrel, the 175-horsepower, 400-ci four-barrel, and the 215-horsepower, 454-ci four-barrel were also available. This was the low point for the Chevrolet big-block, "rat motor." The compression on the 454-ci V-8 was reduced to an all-time Chevrolet low of 8.15 to 1. The dual exhaust was choked through a single catalytic converter. Just four years earlier, this same basic engine, still with low compression, had produced 285 net horsepower. The 1970 high-compression version cranked out an estimated 300 net horsepower. Things improved slightly in 1976, the last year of any Bowtie big-block V-8 in a cop car.

powered Nova was fast. Its 155-horsepower V-8 was specifically developed for maximum horsepower and maximum torque under the constraints of the California emissions laws. The carb jetting, ignition timing, valve sizes, cam profiles, and axle ratios were all tweaked to get the most from a California-compliant engine. Suspension components came from the Nova SS and the Camaro Z28, while the brakes came from the full-size Bel Air. The 111-inch-wheelbase 9C1 completely changed the way cops thought about compact police cars.

Chevrolet had always been a third-place competitor in the police market behind Ford and Plymouth, but the Nova 9C1 changed Chevy's status. It initiated Chevy's rise to the top of the police market and established Chevy as a source for highly developed patrol cars specifically engineered for police duty.

In 1975 the market rapidly turned away from steel-belted radials toward fabric-belted radials for police use, because early steel-belted radials' belts separated at high speeds. The use of fabric-belted radials would continue for the next decade.

In 1976, Plymouth maintained its top sales position in the police-car business, and the compact Dodge Dart and Plymouth Valiant hit the streets, largely in response to the acceptance and success of the Nova. Unlike the highly developed Nova 9C1, the Dart A38 and the Valiant A38 were rushed into production for police work, and releasing a police package for the last year of a platform was an extremely uncommon move. With the incredible success of the Nova 9C1, Chrysler Corporation could not wait any longer. The Dart and Valiant were powered by a array of engines, including the 225-ci one-barrel slant six; the 318-ci two-barrel V-8; and the 360-ci four-barrel V-8. The compact Mopars with the slant six were very economical, while the 360-ci V-8 was very fast, but the cars weren't durable.

For 1976, Ford offered a braking package with rear-wheel disc brakes that was almost 20 years ahead of Chevrolet. From 1976 through 1978, four-wheel discs were available with either standard organic brake pads or with police-spec, heavy-duty, semi-metallic brake pads and were an option on the full-size Ford police sedan. This four-wheel disc brake police-package setup was quite an engineering accomplishment. In spite of the popularity of the Mopars, a Custom 500 with the 460 Police Interceptor, police-package suspension, radial tires, and four-wheel disc brakes was an industry-leading pursuit car.

Chevrolet offered police packages for the 111-inch Nova, the 112-inch two-door, and 116-inch four-door Malibu and Malibu Classic, and the 121.5-inch Impala for 1976. The police Nova was accepted from coast to coast as perhaps the ultimate urban police car, and it forged an entirely new segment of the police market. For Chevrolet, it was the last year for the long, 121.5-inch wheelbase. In 1977, the full-sized cars were downsized to a 116-inch platform. The 1976 model year was also the last year for the 400-ci "giant" small-block V-8 as well as the last year for the 454-ci big-block V-8. After 1976, the largest Chevrolet police engine would be the 350-ci small-block V-8. Ford's 460-ci V-8 and Chrysler's 440-ci V-8 led the market with big-inch performance.

In 1976, America celebrated its Bicentennial anniversary. Many police departments used this as an opportunity to change color schemes to a red, white, and blue patriotic format, or to add red and blue body stripes to already existing white cars, or to add American flags to fenders or C-pillars.

For 1977, the police emphasis was on overall performance and on smaller size. Buick, Chevrolet, Dodge, Ford, Mercury, Plymouth, and Pontiac had police packages based on 111-inch to 116-inch-wheelbase vehicles. Ford and Chrysler were in hot pursuit of the Chevrolet Nova 9C1.

Plymouth still dominated the police market in 1977. Chrysler Corporation responded to the Chevy Nova challenge with the Plymouth Volare and Dodge Aspen. Unlike the 1976 Plymouth Valiant and Dodge Dart, the new 1977 F-body Volare and Aspen were genuine police cars, not add-on A38 police-package cars. The two compact Mopars rode on a 112.7-inch wheelbase that would be used throughout the 1980s. The Aspen and Volare's most significant design element was the radical "transverse" torsion-bar front suspension. Instead of straight torsion bars, the F-body used torsion bars bent in the shape of an "L" to provide a lever arm. At the time, these bent torsion bars were deemed to have the same characteristics as the straight torsion bars introduced in 1957. The fact is, these transverse torsion bars would become the center of an intense controversy in the mid-1980s. In 1977, the Royal Monaco was the last of the long-wheelbase Dodge police cars and the Gran Fury was the last of the long-wheelbase Plymouths. The Plymouth had only had a 122-inch wheelbase since 1974, and the Dodge had wheelbases longer than 121 inches ever since 1957 with the exception of 1962.

Ford's best-kept police-car secret in 1977 was a genuine police package available for the compact Maverick. Available with either a 250-ci six or a 302-ci V-8, the 109.9-inch-wheelbase Maverick was supposed to be a competitor to the Chevy Nova, Dodge Aspen, and Plymouth Volare, and it wasn't.

In mid-year, the LTD II was released as a replacement for the Torino. The driveline and chassis for the LTD II-series was the same as the Torino series with one exception: the 460-ci big-block V-8. The largest engine available in the 1977-1/2 LTD II was the 400 Cleveland.

For Chevrolet, this was the year of the "great downsizing". The 1977 Impala was 5.5 inches shorter in wheelbase, 10.6 inches shorter overall, 4 inches narrower, 2.5 inches taller, and 700 pounds lighter than the 1976 Impala. The 350-ci four-barrel was the largest engine available in the 1977 Impala and propelled

The New Hampshire State Police used this 1975 Pontiac Catalina. A copper hood, roof, and trunk over a dark-green body comprise the color scheme of this cruiser. Twin blue strobe lights mounted along with rear-facing halogen flashers adorn the lightbar on the roof. This represents an early use of strobe emergency lights on police cars instead of halogen lights. Also note the roof-mounted spotlight.

The 1975 Mercury Montego MX came with cop gear like its Ford counterpart, the Torino. The Belmont (California) Police used this all-white cruiser. The Montego MX shared the Torino police powertrains, including the 351 Modified, 400 Cleveland, 460 Police, and 460 Police Interceptor. In 1975, for the first time since 1968, the 302-ci V-8 was not available in either a full-size or mid-size police car. At a mere 129 horsepower in retail trim, the 302-ci small block did not have the power to push these heavy police cruisers. This Belmont patroller had a red/blue Twinsonic, auxiliary alley lights, and a roof-mounted spotlight. The Belmont door shield was actually a black and gold map, showing the city of Belmont as the "Hub of the Peninsula" between San Jose and San Francisco in the Bay area.

Left — In 1975, the formal police package was available on the Torino and Gran Torino two-door hardtop and four-door hardtop. The two-door Torino was based on a 114-inch platform while the four-door version had a 118-inch wheelbase. Ford's police package was also available on a variety of station wagons, vans, and the Bronco. The police in Englewood, Colorado, used the Torino. This blue cruiser bears a diagonal white stripe across the doors. A Federal Visibar with twin blue globes tops it off.

The pictured white-over-blue 1975 Ford LTD is on-duty with the San Pablo (California) Police. The Twinsonic has red and blue lenses. Note the rear-facing, window-mounted radar unit. When facing to the rear, the officer would park by the roadside and clock traffic approaching from the rear. This could not be done with the cruiser moving. Turning the antenna forward allowed the officer to drive and clock oncoming traffic at the same time. In 1975, Ford developed a dash-mounted "Fuel Sentry" vacuum gauge. This was intended to help departments get the most out of their fuel dollar by indicating when the drivers were getting the best mileage (high vacuum). This undoubtedly had the opposite effect on some cops who would punch the throttle wide open to see how low a vacuum reading they could get.

The Leon Valley (Texas) Police Department used this 1975 Ford Custom. This four-door sedan has a white roof over a deep-blue body with a white door shield. The emergency lights are red/white rotators under a clear lens Twinsonic. The Twinsonic has a takedown light bolted on top of the siren speaker wire screen. Police engines for the full-size Ford included the 351 Windsor, 400 Cleveland, 460 Police and 460 Police Interceptor. The standard equipment, urban-oriented 351 Windsor was rated at just 148 horsepower.

it to a top speed of 117 miles per hour. The 350-ci four-barrel V-8 produced about the same acceleration as a 400-ci four-barrel V-8 in a 1976 Impala.

Cops wanted nothing to do with the downsized Impala, and the darling of the Chevrolet police fleet continued to be the awesome Nova 9C1. In the late 1970s, the well-equipped police officer drove either a 440-ci-powered Plymouth Gran Fury or a 350-ci-powered Chevrolet Nova. The Plymouth suited state cops and rural county sheriffs, and the Nova suited city cops and urban county police. The Nova totally dominated urban law enforcement around the United States. It simply was the mid-size police car.

In 1977, 17 of the 50 state police departments and highway patrols drove mid-size cars, even though full-size cars were available from Dodge, Plymouth, and Ford. It proved to be a valuable learning tool for the police car manufacturers, because in 1978, the only remaining full-size police car would be the Ford LTD.

The 1978 model year will forever be remembered as the last year of the big-block cop engines. It was the last year for the Mopar 440-ci big block, the last year for the Mopar 400-ci big block, the last year for the Ford 460-ci big block, and the last year for the Ford 400-ci Cleveland. And many remember it as the year that the torque died.

The loss of these large-displacement engines wasn't noticed by many city police and urban sheriffs departments, because those departments had transitioned to small-block mid- and compact-sized cars in the early 1970s. Many of these departments used a six-cylinder engine or the smallest V-8 available, and the Los Angeles Police and Los Angeles County Sheriff Departments, for example, stopped using engines with displacements over 400 cubic inches in 1975. However, the loss of the big block after 1978 would have a great effect on rural sheriffs' departments and especially the nation's state police departments and highway patrols. For 1978, the only true "full-size" police car was the 121-inch Ford LTD, and this was its last year! In fact, the Louisiana State Police and Rhode Island State Police Departments selected the Ford LTD this year, in part, for its long wheelbase. The Missouri State Highway Patrol went with the Mercury Monterey for much the same reason, but it was in its last year.

In 1978, Plymouth police cars had an incredible 80 percent of the police market, and it would be almost 20 years before another make of police car took the reins on the police market. In 1978, the competition was formidable. Plymouth still had to compete against Dodge, Mercury, Ford, Chevrolet, Buick, and Pontiac, which were all making police cruisers.

As a sign of the times, in mid-1978 Ford released a brand-new kind of police car, the 105.5-inch Ford Fairmont and Mercury Zephyr. These compact cars were powered by either a 200-ci six or 302-ci V-8 and were used by urban police departments such as the Kansas City (Missouri) Police. The patrol officers hated them for their lackluster performance.

In 1978, the Michigan State Police began a series of performance-based police-car tests. The Los Angeles Police and Los Angeles County Sheriff's Departments had conducted joint police car tests since 1956. However, these were qualifying tests. The prospective police car had to "pass" the LASD/LAPD tests in order to bid. Once the car passed, the contract went to the lowest bidder, regardless of how high or low the performance was.

In other words, high performance was not rewarded. The Michigan State Police changed all that.

Under their test protocol, a certain percent of the bid price is "adjusted" based on prorated results of vehicle testing. The Michigan State Police gave better performance a monetary advantage. From 1978 through the turn of the century, the MSP method found the one police car with the most bang for the buck. The LAPD/LASD method produced qualifiers. The MSP method produced winners. For 1978, the 440-ci-powered Plymouth Fury won the first MSP police car run-offs.

The 1979 model year was one of full denial, shock, and disbelief by traffic officers with the nation's state police, highway patrols, and county sheriffs' departments. Big-block V-8 pursuit engines were gone, and rapid-catch times for speed violators was a thing of the past. The bottom-end torque that made long-wheelbase police cruisers viable and desirable pursuit cars was totally missing. Top speeds above 125 miles per hour simply were not possible. This was the first year in which no long wheelbase existed and no engine over 360 ci was used in a police car.

Instigated by all the changes in the police vehicles, the California Highway Patrol conducted the single most influential test ever performed on police vehicles. The CHP is constantly conducting tests on cop gear and vehicles; its 18-month study on 1979 police vehicles, however, changed the shape of the average police fleet through the turn of the 20th century. The 1979 CHP Special Purpose Vehicle Study involved the kinds of cars the automakers "thought" would be available in the mid-1980s, and the CHP concept was to break up the "one-car" police fleet into different kinds of cars for different kinds of police duties. The CHP Study involved the 108-inch wheelbase and 305-ci V-8-powered Chevrolet Malibu; the 105.5-inch-platform 302-ci V-8-powered Ford Fairmont; the 112.7-inch chassis and 318-ci V-8-powered Plymouth Volare station wagon; and the 108-inch wheelbase and 350-ci V-8-powered Chevrolet Camaro Z28. The study involved 12 units of each car, and three of each were sent to four very different patrol districts in the Golden State. The CHP averaged 57,000 miles per car during the study. In the final analysis, the CHP learned a great deal about small-block-powered, mid-size sedans. They would put that knowledge to use when they adopted the 318-ci-powered Dodge Diplomat in 1981 and 302-ci-powered Ford Mustang in 1982.

Making a quick stop is a polished white Lincoln County (Kentucky) Sheriff's Department unit. In 1975, the Ford police package was based on the Custom 500 four-door hardtop and the LTD two-door sedan and four-door hardtop. This was the first year that an LTD, such as the one pictured here, had a police package. This cruiser has a Twinsonic with twin blue lenses. South of the Mason-Dixon Line, blue emergency lights typically meant "police."

Foster City is a suburb of San Francisco in San Mateo County, California. The city's police cruisers in 1975 were the famous Dodge Monacos. Many California city and county police departments piggybacked with the CHP statewide contract to get the best price on a cruiser. Dodge was the police car of California, while the other 49 States had a preference for Plymouth. Note the mid-size Dodge Coronet in the background. The Foster City (California) Fire Department used this all-red unit, which was, in all probability, purchased with the state bid.

Left — The Sacramento (California) Police used this powerful 1975 Dodge Monaco. New for 1975 on police-package cars was the choice of "special endurance" police engines, or regular passenger-car retail engines. The choice of police-specification engines was very narrow. In addition to the 318-ci two-barrel V-8, they included the 360-ci four-barrel with California emissions only, the 400-ci four-barrel with Federal emissions only, and the 440-ci four-barrel engine available with either emission package. Other engines were available in police cars, but these were all retail engines and lacked the heavy-duty police features. It was simply too expensive for Chrysler Corp. to get emissions certifications for a larger variety of police engines. The certification issue provided a great excuse to choose a 440-ci V-8 for all police cars.

In 1975, the Pennsylvania State Police ran the Plymouth Gran Fury. This cruiser from the Pocono Mountain area is white with a blue hood and trunk and gold lettering. A one-piece siren, speaker, and red rotator sit in the middle of the roof, along with two red flashers, one facing forward and one facing rearward. In 1975, Plymouth used the "Fury" name, once the full-size car, on its mid-size police car. The full-size, 121.5-inch-wheelbase Plymouth became the Gran Fury. By mid-1975, a rear anti-sway bar became an option on full-size cruisers. The sway bar was recommended when radial tires were used, but not recommended when bias-belted tires were used.

In 1979, Chrysler Corporation released a totally new vehicle, the 118.5-inch "R-body" known as the Chrysler Newport and Dodge St. Regis. In 1979, Plymouth, which had owned 80 percent of the police market in 1978, didn't have any full-size police car and didn't have access to the new R-body! The largest Plymouth police car was the 112.7-inch Volare. The 1979 Mopar police-package cars were the "regular-size" Chrysler Newport, last seen in 1976, and the Dodge St. Regis. The two so-called mid-sized police cars were the Dodge Aspen and Plymouth Volare. By 1982, this same 112.7-inch-wheelbase would be considered full-size! The Newport and the St. Regis fitted with 360-ci Mopars were much faster than the 350-ci Chevrolet Impala and the 351-ci Ford LTD and LTD II according to Michigan State Police testing. Thus, the Mopars were the clear choice of American cops.

The 118.5-inch R-body was produced for only three years, but it would be used by Chrysler in 1979, by Plymouth in 1980 and 1981, and by Dodge from 1979 to 1981 for police-package cars. In that brief time, the R-body polarized law enforcement. Many cops still consider the Newport, St. Regis, and Gran Fury "R" as the best Mopar police cars ever. The cars had a good balance of power, handled well, and were roomy and comfortable. However, a vocal minority of cops considered the cars as "dogs" with sluggish power and blamed them for morale problems. Many in this latter group drove the California-version of the St. Regis!

The 1975 Dodge Coronet, like this Broadmoor (California) Police cruiser, was available in a wide variety of engines. Starting in 1975, Chrysler classified its engines into one of two emission equipment categories: Federal and California. The California engine produced 5 to 10 horsepower less than an otherwise identical Federal engine due to the California Emissions Control package. All Mopar police engines, regardless of emissions gear, had either air pumps or catalytic converters, or both. This Broadmoor unit is traditionally equipped with twin A-pillar spotlights. On this black-and-white cruiser, the right lens is blue on the Twinsonic lightbar.

In 1975, the California Highway Patrol began a test of mid-size patrol cars involving this 118-inch-wheelbase Dodge Coronet. This was the first CHP Enforcement-class patrol vehicle with a wheelbase shorter than 122 inches since 1956. The CHP had long required its E-class cruisers to have at least a 122-inch wheelbase and to weigh at least 3,800 pounds. The four-door Coronet weighed 3,710 pounds. This move was such a radical departure from long-standing CHP policy that it made the headlines of the *Los Angeles Times*. Of the 1,100 Dodges ordered by the CHP for 1975, 1,000 were the full-size Monaco and 100 were the mid-size Coronet. This CHP black-and-white is a slick-top unit with a red driver-side spotlight and deck-mounted red and amber flashers.

In 1979, Ford made a monumental change and downsized its LTD from a 121-inch to a 114.4-inch wheelbase. In a curious move, the 1979 LTD II remained at 118 inches, but this meant the 1979 "full-size" Ford LTD was both shorter and lighter than the "mid-size" LTD II. The 302-ci V-8 or the 351-ci V-8 powered both police sedans. The LTD used the 351 Windsor while the LTD II used the 351 Modified in its last year.

In 1979, Chevrolet fielded two police-package cars, the 116-inch full-size Impala and the 108.1-inch Malibu. Although the Malibu, which replaced the legendary Nova, was on a smaller wheelbase, the Malibu in fact had more interior room and a larger trunk. As hard as it is to believe, the Malibu was actually a better police car than the Nova.

A clean and straight 1975 Dodge Coronet, this unit is a patrol car with the South San Francisco (California) Police Department. The Coronet has a gold seven-point star like the SFPD, but includes the seal of the city inside the star. The Twinsonic had red and blue lenses and auxiliary alley lights. This all-white cruiser clearly shows off its vented police wheels. These 6.5-inch extra-width, heavy-duty steel wheels were new for 1975. Also for 1975, all mid-size Mopar cruisers came standard with 15-inch wheels. For the first time, these mid-size cars were available with GR70x15, police-spec, 70-series radials. Only fabric-belted radials were approved for pursuit use, not steel-belted radials.

The mid-size cruiser pictured here, a 1975 Plymouth Fury, patrolled the streets of Hialeah, Florida. In 1975, Plymouth dropped the name Satellite for its intermediate-size squad car. The 117.5-inch-wheelbase mid-size took the name Fury, which was formerly the name of the full-size car. The 1975 121.5-inch-wheelbase full-size cruiser was upgraded to Gran Fury. Cops would drive the Gran Fury police car for every year from 1975 to 1989, except for 1978 and 1979.

The Los Angeles County Sheriff's Department made a major change in police vehicles for 1975. It dropped the AMC Matador and split its purchases between this 1975 Plymouth Fury and the Chevrolet Nova. In its favor, the 350-ci Nova soundly won the *Motor Trend*-inspired LASO vehicle tests. The Nova, however, was untested in actual police service. The LASO hedged its bet with half a fleet of durable and proven Plymouths. These Fury police cars were powered by the 190-horsepower, 360-ci four-barrel V-8. This four-barrel E58 engine was only available in California. The closest Federal engine was the 190-horsepower, 400-ci four-barrel single exhaust V-8.

Left — The traditional trademarks adorn this 1975 Michigan State Police Plymouth Gran Fury: deep-blue paint; blue shield with gold lightening bolt; and red, four-bulb Federal Beacon Ray. It also has twin A-pillar spotlights and the low-band whip antenna. The 1975 model year was the last that Mopar police cars used leaded gasoline. This was also a transition year in which both leaded and unleaded gas engines were available. Cars that used regular, leaded gas got air pumps on their engines. Cars that used unleaded gas got catalytic converters. This was the first year for these converters on a Mopar. Note the famous, hood-mounted MSP "Stop" sign. Still used in the late 1990s, the sign could be illuminated at night.

In 1975, Ford introduced the Granada as a replacement for the Maverick. Built on a 109.9-inch wheelbase, the Granada and the four-door Maverick shared the same platform. The Granada was available is a wide variety of engines, including the 75-horsepower, 200-ci six; 72-horsepower, 250-ci six; 129-horse-power, 302-ci V-8; and, incredibly enough, the 143-horsepower, 351 Windsor V-8. At the time it was a popular retail car but not well received as a police car. With the 351 Windsor V-8, however, the 3,355-pound four-door sedan was clearly one of the fastest 1975 police Fords. In reality, the Granadas used for police work, such as this stark and basic California unit, were powered by the 250-ci six. Four-wheel power disc brakes were introduced as a significant mid-year option.

The 1975 Chevrolet Nova, such as this Metro St. Louis Police sedan, was built from the ground up as a heavy-duty, high-performance police car. Chevrolet started with the California Emission Package on the 350-ci V-8 and then adjusted carb jetting, ignition timing, valve sizes, and cam profiles for the absolute optimum performance. Chevrolet used the heaviest-duty Nova SS and Camaro Z28 suspension parts. The brakes actually came from the full-size Bel Air. The tires were E70x14 Firestone "Wide Oval" bias-belted tires mounted on a special 14x7 heavy-duty steel wheel. During Los Angeles County Sheriff's Department testing at the Pomona Fairgrounds, the Nova thrashed the competition on the EVOC road course. It out-handled the bigger sedan on evasive maneuvers and actually produced more than 1 g of braking power.

Chevrolet, the Los Angeles County Sheriff's Department, and *Motor Trend* magazine completely re-defined and popularized the compact-size, urban police car with this 1975 Nova. The 111-inch Nova was rapidly accepted as the ideal urban police car for the times. The 350-ci-powered Nova was the nation's first compact car built specifically for severe-duty police work. It was designed for the entire spectrum of police work, from routine patrol to high-speed pursuit. Advantages of the Nova included lower initial costs, lower operating costs, improved fuel economy, and better overall acceleration, handling, and braking than nearly every other police car, including the long-wheelbase, big-block cruisers. The Nova's 155-horsepower, four-barrel V-8 was specifically developed to produce maximum horsepower and torque under the constraints of California emission laws.

Pictured is a fully marked, 1975 Ford Custom 500 with the Washington State Patrol. The roof rack has an oversize, four-bulb rotator under a blue globe. Twin red, outboard flashers face to the rear. This 4,298-pound behemoth was powered by the equally awesome 226-horsepower, 460-ci Police Interceptor big-block V-8. WSP troopers recall that the big Ford had strong and fade-resistant brakes. They also remember the propensity for the nose-heavy sedans to understeer in tight curves and the lack of torque to correct it. For all it was or was not during its duty years, the tough Ford made one of the WSP's best pursuit-driving school cars. It took years of abuse, outlasting many newer, de-commissioned cars. The big Ford worked harder, and better, during its retirement than when on duty.

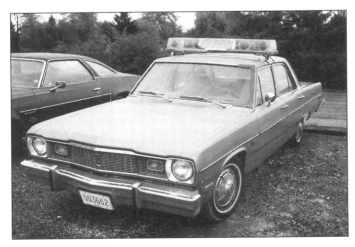

This brown 1976 Plymouth Valiant with a red/red Twinsonic is equipped with the A38 police package. The 1976 Plymouth Valiant and Dodge Dart were available with a wide variety of police engines. These included the 100-horsepower, 225-ci slant six; 150-horsepower, 318-ci V-8; 170-horsepower, 360-ci two-barrel V-8; and 220-horsepower, 360-ci four-barrel V-8. The 360-ci four-barrel versions were very fast for their era. With a 0- to 60-mile-per-hour time of 10.6 seconds, the 360-ci Dart and Valiant were faster than a 360-ci Plymouth Fury. The 360-ci, four-barrel dual exhaust Valiant ran the quarter mile in 16.4 seconds at 84.6 miles per hour.

The fate of old T.V. and movie cars is the same as that of most other used cars; they get sold at auction. This is the car driven by Bobby Hill and Andy Renko in the T.V. series, *Hill Street Blues*. The T.V. show had the real Chicago Police Department Hill Street Precinct as the setting. The inside acting was done in Hollywood, but the surface street scenes were in the Chicagoland area. T.V. and movie studios get authentically marked police cars from movie-car rental companies. The 1975 Plymouth Fury has the look of a 1975 CPD cruiser with its white body, wide blue stripe, and large red lettering. Only the CPD and Hollywood insiders know why the car says Metro Police instead of Chicago Police. The prohibition was CPD's reaction to how its image was portrayed in the movie, *The Blues Brothers*.

One of the rarest patrol cars in the history of the New York City Police Department is caught here on film. It is a very unusual 1976 Pontiac LeMans. This was the only year the NYPD purchased Pontiacs for patrol use. This commission was used in the 112th Precinct, which is Forest Hills. From 1973 to 1978, the famous PCT number did not appear on NYPD cars. The NYPD patrol car is white over light blue with a wide white stripe. The emergency lights are white and red lamps inside clear globes. The 116-inch-wheelbase 1976 police LeMans could have been powered by a 110-horsepower, 250-ci in-line six; 110-horsepower, 260-ci V-8; 160-horsepower, 350-ci V-8; 170-horsepower and 185-horsepower 400-ci V-8; or 200-horsepower, 455-ci V-8.

To commemorate the bicentennial in 1976, the Illinois State Police added one wide red stripe and one wide blue stripe to its 1976 Plymouth Gran Fury cruisers. The hood of these white cruisers also had a wide red, white and blue stripe in the shape of a large "V." These were among the best looking of the patriotic squad cars.

The Idaho State Police used this 1976 Plymouth Gran Fury Brougham. The colors include a white roof and front doors combined with a powder-blue body and blue emergency lights. Note the separate siren speaker mounted off-center on the passenger-side roof. The door shield is a gold profile of the state of Idaho. These cars were all powered by the E86, 255-horsepower, 440-ci V-8 which had both dual exhausts and dual catalytic converters.

The 1976 Los Angeles County Sheriff's Department Chevrolet Nova was the most influential car of the 1970s. The 1976 Nova and the 1982 California Highway Patrol Ford Mustang are the two most influential police cars in the history of law enforcement. Each changed the way cops felt about patrol cars. Each paved the way for an entire generation of cruisers that were completely different from their predecessors. For its part, the LASO Nova made compact, 111-inch-wheelbase police cars legitimate for urbanized law enforcement. This particular black-and-white is on display at the LASO museum in Whittier. It remains a must-see part of law enforcement, Chevrolet, and California history.

The placard in the rear window of this 1976 Chevrolet Nova tells it all: The 1976 four-door Nova Chevrolet radio car was the product of many conversations between the Los Angeles County Sheriff's Department and John Christy, executive editor of *Motor Trend* magazine. This mystical ultimate police car was built to the following specifications: a 210-horsepower V-8 engine, front-wheel power disc brakes, rack-and-pinion steering, extrawide tires, heavy-duty suspension, heavy-duty radiator, power steering, heavy-duty Delco electrical system, modified valve system, positraction rear end, and air conditioning. The California Nova, as it became known, permitted a reduced maintenance level, which in turn saved the county of Los Angeles nearly a million dollars during its first year of operation.

The 1976 Chevrolet Nova blew away the competition from Dodge, Plymouth, Pontiac, Ford, and Mercury during the annual Los Angeles County Sheriff's Department vehicle tests. The light and nimble Nova outran them all on the Pomona Fairground road course. Then it outran them all down the famous Pomona Drag Strip. It was quicker than the 400-ci Torino and Montego, quicker than the 400-ci LeMans, and quicker than the 360-ci Dart and Fury. At 9.5 seconds, it had a faster 0- to 60-mile-per-hour time. With trap speeds of 82.9 miles per hour, it posted the fastest speed during the cop-car drags. Among the cars best suited for patrol in heavily urbanized jurisdictions, nothing could approach the reputation of the Nova 9C1.

The Broward County (Florida) Sheriff's Department used this 1976 Chevrolet Nova in the service of the Ft. Lauderdale area. The four-door sedan is all-white with a wide green stripe. The door shield is an ornate, gold five-point star. Two blue rotators top the compact-size cruiser along with a rectangular siren speaker. While this was a genuine compact car, it was rated for six passengers and weighed 3,720 pounds. To answer the questions of observant viewers, no, this cruiser is not parked in a handicap spot and yes, the time on the parking meter has expired.

In 1976, the Chevrolet Nova was everywhere, including on the force with the San Francisco Police. This four-door Nova is a white-over-light-blue unit. In the early 1970s, a new police chief tried to soften the image of the SFPD police cars. Black-and-white became baby blue and white, and a gold city seal with the lettering "Police Services" replaced the seven-point star with SFPD. When the chief left after a few years, the SFPD returned to black-and-white cruisers. The SFPD removed the Twinsonic's integral center siren speaker and replaced it with an external, rectangular siren speaker between the red and blue lenses of the Twinsonic. Note the roof-mounted spotlight.

The 1976 Chevrolet Impala, like this Missouri State Highway Patrol unit, was the last of the 121.5-inch-wheelbase Chevrolets. After 1976, the B-body Chevrolet was given a 115.9 to 116.0-inch wheelbase until its demise after 1996. For the first time since its introduction, the Chevrolet police package was available only on a four-door sedan, and not the two-door coupe. For 1976, the Bel Air nameplate was dropped. Of the full-size cars, the police package was available only on the Impala and not the Caprice. This MSHP unit is all-white with full-dress wheel covers and a clear-lens Twinsonic.

A sharp-looking, all-white 1976 Chevrolet Chevelle Malibu shown in-service with the Dallas (City) Police. This four-door, mid-size cruiser has white wheels with bright chrome, dog-dish wheel covers. Also in chrome is the pusher bumper with crossbar. This Big D cruiser has a red/red Federal Visibar and external siren speaker. The engines on the Chevelle 9C1 included the 105-horsepower, 250-ci six; 145-horsepower, 350-ci V-8; 165-horsepower, 350-ci four-barrel V-8; and 175-horsepower, 400-ci V-8. The police Chevelle used in California was restricted to either the 350-ci four-barrel V-8, the same engine used in the Nova, or the 400-ci four-barrel V-8.

Leon Valley, Texas, is home to this 1976 Chevrolet Chevelle Malibu patrol car. This 116-inch, mid-size cruiser is black with a white roof, and black-on-silver door shield. The Federal Twinsonic has clear lenses covering red and white rotators. Note the lightbar-mounted takedown light. Also note the rear-facing antenna of the traffic radar unit. In 1976, all police Chevelles came with the 350 Turbo Hydra-Matic, 2.73 or 3.08 rear gears and single exhaust. The police Chevelle came standard with H78x15 bias-belted police-special tires, while HR70x15 fabric-belted police radials were optional. As a traffic enforcement vehicle, this Leon Valley unit is almost certainly powered by the 175-horsepower, 400-ci four-barrel V-8. This was the last year for this "giant" small block.

The ever-popular red/blue Twinsonic emergency lights top the white-over-blue body and gold lettering of this Bay-area 1976 Chevrolet Chevelle. Note the body moldings and the full-dress wheel covers. The only two engines certified for use in California were the 350-ci four-barrel V-8 and the 400-ci four-barrel V-8. Chevrolet specified 2.73 rear gears for all 350-ci V-8s knowing any agency that selected this Chevelle engine did so for the superior fuel economy. Likewise, the 400-ci came only with 3.08 gears, which provided better acceleration. Ratios as low as 2.41 to 1 were used to improve economy. The 3.08 rear gear became standard on mid- and full-size Chevrolets through 1988.

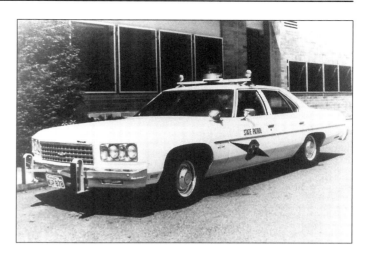

The 225-horsepower, 454-ci four-barrel dual exhaust V-8 teamed with a 400 Turbo Hydra-Matic and 2.73 rear gears powers this menacing 1976 Chevrolet Impala. In addition to the Washington State Patrol, the South Dakota Highway Patrol and Wyoming Highway Patrol also ran the big-block, long-wheelbase Bowtie cruiser. The 454-ci V-8, introduced in 1970, was dropped after 1976. The largest police V-8 after 1976 was the 350-ci small block. In its career, the 454-ci rat motor was rated at a high of 390 brake horsepower (1970) and a low of 215 net horsepower (1975). For 1976, the 454-ci engine was back up to 225 horsepower, but saddled with 2.73 rear gears. This made it no faster than the 1975 version, which was teamed with 3.08 gears. The WSP emergency lights are blue.

The 1976 Chevrolet Impala, like this Northfield (Ohio) Police unit, had a front end identical to the 1975 retail-only Caprice, but different from that of the 1976 retail Caprice. Introduced in 1971, this proved the final year for the 400-ci "giant" small block that used cubic inches to make up for emissions controls. While it always produced more horsepower than the 350-ci, the 350-ci clearly proved the better engine. In retrospect, it was not a good idea to eliminate the water passages between the cylinder heads of the 400-ci engine to keep the same small-block bore spacing. Ford's 400 Cleveland and the Mopar 400-ci big block really were better police engines. The long-wheelbase 1976 Impala weighed 4,222 pounds.

In 1976, the Iowa State Patrol ran the 121.4-inch-wheelbase Dodge Monaco. These all-white sedans had gold door shields with brown lettering, and the 255-horsepower, 440-ci four-barrel V-8 powered them all. The emergency lights were all red, including the one mounted on the right fender. The 1976 Monaco and the 1977 Royal Monaco really did have hide-away headlights. In 1976, the A38 police package was also available for the 124-inch Chrysler Newport. The last Newport that came with factory police gear was the 1964 Enforcer. The next Chrysler-marque police cars were the 1979 Newport, and then the 1981 Chrysler LeBaron.

The Cleveland-area Cuyahoga County (Ohio) Sheriff's Department used this 1976 Plymouth Gran Fury. This white-over-black cruiser has a gold five-point star, gold lettering, and red/blue emergency lights. While the 360-ci small-block V-8 was the standard engine, nearly all police Gran Furys came with either the 400-ci big block or the 440-ci big block. This long-wheelbase Gran Fury was typical of the cruiser run by most sheriffs' departments in the Buckeye State.

The Missouri State Highway Patrol frequently ran different makes of patrol car within the same model year. In 1976, it ran the Chevrolet Impala and this Plymouth Gran Fury. This is a light-blue, four-door sedan with a 121.5-inch wheelbase. The wheelbase is equal to the Impala. The 255-horsepower, 440-ci four-barrel V-8 produced 30 horsepower more than the Impala's 454-ci four-barrel V-8, though the Bowtie rat motor produced more torque. This cruiser is complete with full-dress wheel covers and an A-pillar spotlight. The Twinsonic has twin red lenses. The door shield and the fender decal have gold letters against a blue background.

The Ohio State Highway Patrol ran the Plymouth Gran Fury in 1976. This explains why so many county sheriffs' departments and city police departments in the Buckeye State also drove the Gran Fury. In 1976, Plymouth maintained its top sales position in the police-car business. This all-white cruiser has a black-and-gold winged tire, gold lettering, and all-red emergency lights. The Ohio State Highway Patrol was organized in 1933. The OSHP cars started off as black, but in the late 1960s they made the transition to white. Then, in the 1980s, the OSHP adopted metallic-silver cruisers. The winged tire has always been their door shield.

A police department in Northern California used this 1976 Dodge Coronet on the job. The patroller has the California classic white roof and front door with a black body. The red/blue Twinsonic is fitted with auxiliary alley lights. In spite of the California Highway Patrol's interest in the Dodge Coronet, this mid-size, 117.5-inch-wheelbase police car was not as popular as the mid-size Plymouth Fury. However, with 3,852 police cars sold, the Coronet sold far more than the full-size Dodge Monaco. In California, engines ranging from the 318-ci two-barrel V-8 to the 440-ci four-barrel V-8 powered the Coronet. The 440-ci V-8 was not available in the Coronet/Fury in the other 49 states.

The California Highway Patrol tested the mid-size 1975 Dodge Coronet and liked what it saw. In 1976, the CHP ordered 1,511 Coronets like this one. This order was influential for two reasons. First, the single CHP order comprised nearly half of all the 3,852 police Coronets sold in 1976. Second, as the CHP entered the mid-size police car market, the rest of the city, county, and state police departments seriously considered the mid-size. The *Los Angeles Times* ran the story under the headline, "CHP Will Switch To Smaller Car." Inside two years, the nation's largest sheriff's department (Los Angeles County Sheriff) switched from mid-size to compact patrol cars, and the nation's largest highway patrol (CHP) switched from full-size to mid-size patrol cars.

In 1976, the Los Angeles Police Department ran the Plymouth Fury powered by the 175-horsepower, 360-ci four-barrel V-8. This was the first year the LAPD ordered power steering. It had avoided power steering up until this point because the Mopar power steering generally over-assisted, which caused too light a wheel and too little feel. The LAPD also saved money each year it did not have to order the optional power steering. Giving a final push to the decision, the automakers stopped making cars with manual steering! Even the Firm-Feel power steering was not really firm. It was only as firm as the Ford and Chevrolet retail steering.

The New York City Police Department patrolled the streets of the Big Apple in the Plymouth Fury in 1976. This cruiser is white over blue with a white stripe and lettering and a shoulder patch as a door shield. The emergency lights on this NYPD Fury include a combination of red flashers and red/white rotators under clear domes. These cars were powered by the 150-horsepower, 318-ci two-barrel V-8. This was a genuine retail engine and not one of the "added endurance" police-spec engines. Some of these cruisers may have been powered by the 100-horsepower, 225-ci slant six. This durable six-cylinder was not available with the California emissions package.

The police department in Saegertown, Pennsylvania, near Erie patrolled its small town in this 1976 Ford LTD. The patroller is deep blue with a white roof and doors. The door shield is colored gold and blue, while the lightbar has blue and red lenses. In 1976, the Ford police package was based on the Custom 500 four-door pillared hardtop and the LTD two-door and four-door pillared hardtop. The 1976 Ford police cars were a straight carryover from the 1975 models.

This 1976 Ford LTD served the citizens of Bath, New York, in the upstate Finger Lakes region. The four-door pillared hardtop is deep blue with a red and blue Twinsonic. In 1976, Ford engineers developed a braking package that was nearly 20 years ahead of Chevrolet: rear disc brakes. From 1976 through 1978, four-wheel disc brakes were a regular production option on the full-size cruiser. These were available with either standard organic pads or with police-spec, heavy-duty, semi-metallic pads. The organic pads gave better cold-stopping performance, making this a good choice for urban scenarios. Alternately, the semi-metallic pads gave the best performance under abusive conditions such as a high-speed pursuit. With four-wheel discs and semi-metallic pads, this cruiser had the best brakes of any full-size police car.

The St. George Police Department, located in the far southwest corner of Utah, used this 1976 Ford Torino. The cruiser is all-white with a flowing blue stripe and bold blue lettering. The Twinsonic is red and blue. The front pusher bar looks well used. The full-dress wheel covers pass muster much more easily than the whitewall tires. The 114-inch two-door and 118-inch four-door Torino was powered by the 351 Modified, 400 Cleveland, 460 Police or 460 Police Interceptor. When equipped with the 158-horsepower, 400-ci Cleveland two-barrel V-8, the 4,362-pound four-door Police Torino took an embarrassing 12.2 seconds to reach 60 miles per hour—a clear indication that it needed a 460-ci big block!

One of the most recognizable T.V. police cars in the history of T.V. cops shows is shown here in its current Colorado home. This is the car from the 1970s cult classic, *Starsky and Hutch*, starring Paul Michael Glaser and David Soul. With the T.V. show long past, a police-car collector in Colorado owns this 1976 Ford Gran Torino. The infamous T.V. show aside, however, the Ford police package was indeed available for both the Torino and the upscale Gran Torino in two-door and four-door pillared hardtops.

The Forreston (Illinois) Police near Rockford used this 1976 Ford Torino from 1976 to 1998. When taken out of service, it had just 65,000 miles on the certified odometer. This all-brown cruiser still has the original cage, radio, and working traffic radar unit. The 351 Modified-powered Torino was photographed in Genoa, Illinois, at the annual parade held each May to commemorate Police Memorial Week. The combination police and VFW memorial service attracts hundreds of cruisers with uniformed officers from all over Illinois, Indiana, and Wisconsin. A prized find like this vintage Torino serves as a reminder not to give up hope of still finding cars like this.

In 1976, the Illinois State Police ran the Plymouth Gran Fury. These were all-white cars with a red/red Twinsonic. The door shield has white letters on a brown background, a gold six-point star and a mostly blue state seal. During the nation's bicentennial, one state police car per post had red and blue body stripes. This was generally the Public Information Officer's cruiser. The rest of the patrol cars were white. This was the last year of the full-size 121.4-inch-wheelbase cars driven by the ISP. A total of 7,953 police-package Gran Furys were sold in 1976.

The Georgia State Patrol used this 1976 Pontiac LeMans as its primary enforcement vehicle. The Peach State cruiser has a grey hood, roof, and trunk over a blue body. The only warning light is an oversize, four-bulb rotator under a blue globe. The GSP would switch to blue strobe lights by the 1980s. This cruiser has "State Trooper" in orange letters on the front fenders and "Georgia State Patrol" in orange letters on the front doors and trunk lid. The doors also included the seal of the state of Georgia. Prior to the early 1950s, the state seal was the only marking on the doors. Unlike some easily confused motorists in California, who have to have police cars marked "just so," NO ONE was ever confused when a GSP trooper initiated a vehicle stop. There is nothing like Georgia law enforcement!

This big, bad police sedan was actually used by the Chicago Fire Department. It's a 1976 Ford Custom 500. Following a tradition more than 50 years old, this CFD four-door sedan has a black roof, red body, and black wheels. The fender and door lettering, symbols, and numbering are in gold. The "C.F.D." lettering on the hood moved to the front fenders in 1956 and became "Chicago Fire Department." This 1976 Ford retains that marking. The lightbar has twin red rotators and red and GREEN can lights. The passenger side lens is green, dating back to a nautical protocol from the 1800s. Beneath all of the cat-saving exterior trim lurks the heart of a genuine police-package cruiser. Powertrains ranged from the 148-horsepower, 351 Windsor to the 226-horsepower, 460 Police Interceptor.

The Clark County (Nevada) Sheriff's Department used this white 1977 Chevrolet Nova. With 750,000 people, Clark County is the most populated county in Nevada. The major cities in Clark County include Las Vegas, North Las Vegas, and Henderson. This sheriff's cruiser has a red/amber and blue Twinsonic, similar to the California setup. The Novas have a wide blue stripe with a blue six-point star containing gold lettering. Once again, the police-package Nova was available as a four-door sedan or two-door coupe. For the first time, the 145-horsepower, 305-ci two-barrel V-8 was available in the Nova as an alternative to the 170 horsepower (Federal), 350-ci four-barrel V-8. Both engines came with single exhaust even though they used dual tailpipes.

Chevrolet dramatically downsized its 1977 Impala. Compared to the 1976 Impala, the 1977 Impala had a 5.5-inch-shorter wheelbase, was 10.6 inches shorter overall, and 4 inches narrower. The 1977 four-door sedan was an average of 700 pounds lighter. Chevrolet claimed more overall headroom, rear legroom, and a larger trunk in the downsized version. However, gone were the 400-ci giant small-block and 454-ci big-block V-8s. Engines for the full-size 1977 Impala now included the 170-horsepower, 350-ci four-barrel V-8; the 145-horsepower, 305-ci two-barrel V-8 and the 110-horsepower, 250-ci one-barrel six. Contrary to police opinion, the theory was that lighter cars could match performance with smaller, economical engines. This 1977 Impala is a unique Enforcement-class test vehicle with the California Highway Patrol.

In 1977, Chevrolet really pushed the success of the Los Angeles County Sheriff Nova. Ads with a fully marked police Nova appeared in *Motor Trend* and *Popular Science* with headlines like "Announcing a Cut in Government Spending" and "Last year Chevy Nova captured the Los Angeles Sheriff's Department This year we're after you." One ad pictured police Novas from a dozen different departments across the country. Another ad bragged, "Last year the Los Angeles Sheriff's Department tested a specially-equipped 1976 Chevy Nova against five cars submitted by other car makers. They put the Nova through 24 different tests of durability and performance. When all the tests were over, the LASD decided to order 222 Novas, the largest single order for compact police cars in U.S. history."

Lincoln, California, is a small town just north of Sacramento. The Lincoln Police used this 1977 Chevrolet Impala. It is white over medium-blue with a red and blue Twinsonic and a black-on-silver seven-point star. It has twin clear-lens, A-pillar spotlights, a dash-mounted shotgun, and a prisoner cage. The big news for 1977 was the reduction in the Impala wheelbase from 121.5 inches to 116 inches. The big-block and giant small-block V-8 engines were all gone. The most powerful Chevrolet police engine in 1977 was the 170-horsepower, 350-ci four-barrel V-8. This 3,564-pound 1977 cruiser with a 350-ci four-barrel V-8 accelerated as fast as a 4,222-pound 1976 Impala with a 400-ci four-barrel V-8.

In mid-year 1977, the mid-size LTD II, such as this Brown County (Indiana) Sheriff's Department commission, replaced the mid-size Torino. The LTD II and the Torino shared the same 118-inch wheelbase. This "county brown" Hoosier cruiser has a brown hood, roof, and trunk with tan fenders and doors. All Indiana sheriff's departments have the same markings, or at least the sheriff's association dictates that the cars are supposed to be identical. The gold five-point star on the front doors says simply, "Sheriff, Indiana." The Hoosier sheriff's cars ran red/red Visibars well into the 1980s. Brown County is the resort area of Indiana. Its Hoosier National Forest and state park attract tourists from the surrounding five states. This explains why a small and rural sheriff's department has such a big and modern jail.

For an all-white car, this 1977 Reno (Nevada) Police Ford LTD II looks pretty good. The markings are simple but clear: the word "Police" in black-outlined gold lettering and the city seal on the door. A red and blue Twinsonic and twin A-pillar-mounted spotlights take care of the rest. The 1977 LTD II was styled dramatically different from the 1976 Torino. The vertically stacked, rectangular headlights and wraparound, fender tip-mounted turn-signal lights clearly separate the new model from the old. Ford's goal with the new LTD II was to combine "LTD's traditional high level of workmanship with Mustang's sporty spirit." At 3,894 pounds, it's tough to be sporty, but with the 351 Modified and 400 Cleveland V-8s, the LTD IIs did just fine as police cruisers.

The Traffic Division sergeant with the Bakersfield, California, Police Department used this 1977 Ford LTD II. Bakersfield is located on CA-99 in the central portion of the state. Along with I-5, CA-99 is literally the high-speed link between Northern and Southern California where traffic control is a serious issue. This black-and-white LTD II has the traditional red/amber and blue Twinsonic with auxiliary alley lights. The gold, blue, and white door shield is an exact copy of the police officer's badge. This traffic-enforcement vehicle is powered by the 166-horsepower, 400 Cleveland two-barrel V-8. That was the largest LTD II engine available. The 460-ci big block was restricted to the full-size LTD.

Something unusual stands out about this 1977 Ford LTD II with the Milpitas (California) Police. It's actually a Ranchero. The Ford police package was available for the LTD Wagon, the Econoline vans, and the Bronco, but not for the Ranchero or the LTD II station wagon. This San Jose suburb pressed a retail Ranchero into police service. The two-seater Ranchero has some advantages over an LTD or LTD II station wagon, but only for very specialized assignments. With the rear vents on the topper, this may be a canine unit. The Milpitas cruisers are white with a striking red stripe and a gold seven-point star inside a blue circle.

Shown here is a professionally marked 1977 Ford LTD II with the Burlingame (California) Police Department. Burlingame is a city of 27,000 people in the Bay area midway between San Francisco and San Jose. The city's Ford cruisers are all-white with a double-pinstriped, wide blue stripe running from headlight to taillight. The blue, gold, and green octagonal door shield reads "City of Burlingame, California, Incorporated 1908." The Burlingame cruiser has a large blue center rotator and roof-mounted spotlights. Note the three-lamp cluster on each side of the roof. Continuous red faces forward, red and amber face rearward, and white alley lights face outward. Notice the right pusher bar showing evidence of some altercation.

The Greenfield (California) Police used this 1977 Ford LTD II. The name Greenfield belies the medium-green color of the body panels joined with the white roof and doors. The 1977 LTD II used a red and blue Twinsonic, while the lightbar on the 1978 Fairmont in the background is a red and blue Aerodynic. For 1977, the rear gear ratio on the 351 Modified-powered LTD II was lowered from 3.25 to 1 to an all-time low of 2.50 to 1 in an attempt to improve gas mileage. It backfired; police cars with such low gearing were given full-throttle more of the time to make up for the sluggish acceleration from low gear ratios. These low-gear-ratio police cruisers got horrible mileage. Because they constantly accelerate, police cars seldom operate at a constant speed like retail cars where a lower ratio would improve mileage.

Despite its lack of markings, this largely unmarked 1977 Mercury Cougar is nonetheless a genuine police car. While the word "Police" appears in gold lettering, the agency that operated this dark blue Cougar remains unknown. The Cougar was built on the same 118-inch platform as the Ford LTD II and used the same powerplants. For 1977, these were the 134-horsepower, 302-ci V-8; the 152-horsepower, 351 Modified; and the 166-horsepower, 400 Cleveland. All of these engines were two-barrel, single-exhaust V-8s. Such weak engines did not make for very quick police cars. Note the bumper-mounted grille lights. In a tricky twist, these lights appear clear until activated, when they appear red and blue.

In 1977, the Lovelock Police patrolled this western Nevada town in the Ford LTD. This model year marked the return of the 302-ci small-block V-8 to both the full-size Custom 500 and LTD and the mid-size Torino and LTD II. The last time a 302-ci engine was even available in a full-size Ford police car was 1969. The 302-ci mill was a reasonable choice for small towns where a barking dog or a loud neighbor are the police officer's most common calls. This all-white Lovelock patroller has a gold-and-black seven-point star and a red and blue lens Visibar. During slow evenings, perhaps the police made their way to nearby I-80. That is, after all, a traffic radar antenna mounted in the center of the dash.

From late 1968 to late 1978, all Cleveland, Ohio, emergency vehicles were the most obnoxious shade of lime green, called "Safety Green." That included police, fire, and ambulance. This was in response to a federally funded study during the early 1970s, which called for emergency vehicles to be more rapidly recognized as emergency vehicles. The city of Cleveland interpreted this guideline with the color Safety Green. Its police cars were marked with white-on-blue police fender decals and a white-on-blue and gold door shield. The emergency lights included blue flashers and red/white rotators under a clear-lens Twinsonic. The high beams on this CPD Ford have red lenses. Police and violators alike probably considered it cruel and unusual punishment to be seen in these green cars.

The big news in 1977 from Chrysler Corp. was the brand new F-body Dodge Aspen (shown) and Plymouth Volare. Unlike the earlier Dart and Valiant, these 1977s were genuine police cars, not just bolt-on A38 police-package cars. The new Aspen, such as this Redding (California) Police cruiser, was built on a 112.7-inch wheelbase, which used a new transverse torsion-bar front suspension. This suspension was different from the longitudinal torsion-bar suspension used by Mopars since 1957. The Aspen and Volare were solid police cars and were a much greater challenge to the Chevrolet Nova. At the minimum, the Aspen and Volare greatly expanded the police acceptance of the so-called compact police car. In five short years, the 112.7-inch-wheelbase Mopar came to be considered a full-size cruiser!

Simple yet striking markings adorn this 1977 Dodge Monaco. This cruiser is with the Contra Costa County (California) Sheriff's Department. CoCoCo includes San Pablo and the northeast corner of the San Francisco Bay, called the San Pablo Bay. Unlike many states, the sheriffs' departments in California do not have uniform and consistent vehicle markings. These all-white CoCoCo units have a brown-and-gold seven-point star on twin brown diagonal stripes on the front doors. The word "Sheriff" on the front fenders and the term "K-9 Patrol" on the rear fenders are also brown lettering. This cruiser has a red and blue Twinsonic, twin A-pillar spotlights, and a dash-mounted shotgun. The venting on the heavy-duty steel wheels is obvious in this photo.

The King City (California) Police operated this 1977 Dodge Monaco. King City is well south of San Jose in central California and located on the famous U.S. Highway 101. The white-over-black cruiser has a red and blue Twinsonic. The door shield is a gold crown set against a red background. This cruiser has all the right cop gear: pusher bars, twin, A-pillar spotlights, rear deck flashers, dash-mounted shotgun, and prisoner cage. In 1977, Dodge sold 4,963 police-package Monacos. Power-trains included everything from the 135-horsepower, 318-ci two-barrel V-8 to the 245-horsepower, 440-ci four-barrel V-8. Many enthusiasts feel the 1977 and 1978 Monacos were the best police cars ever made by Chrysler Corporation.

This 1977 Dodge Monaco is with the Cotati (California) Police Department. The city of Cotati is near Santa Rosa and right on the famous U.S. Highway 101. These all-white cruisers have a pale green stripe, which follows the contour of the upper body panels. Note the word "Police" in the stripe on the rear fender. These cruisers have a roof-mounted spotlight in lieu of twin A-pillar spotlights. The emergency lights are red and blue Twinsonics or Aerodynics. New for 1977, the Monaco and Plymouth Fury received restyled front ends. Instead of a single round headlight per side, like the 1975-1976 cruisers, the 1977 mid-size Mopars have dual, rectangular headlights, stacked vertically.

A blue city seal inside a gold seven-point star marks the door of this all-white 1977 Dodge Monaco with the South San Francisco, California, Police. Note the chromed pusher bumpers. In 1977, California-certified engines for the Monaco included the 135-horsepower, 318-ci four-barrel; the 160-horsepower and 170-horsepower 360-ci four-barrel; and the 230-horsepower, 440-ci four-barrel. For 1977, Chrysler Corporation increased the number of police-service, added-endurance engines from three to six. The 160-horsepower, 360-ci was a heavy-duty engine while the 170-horsepower 360 ci was not.

The slick-top Dodge Monaco, such as the one pictured, was the legendary Enforcement-class vehicle used by the California Highway Patrol in 1977. The only forward emergency light is simply a red spotlight. The rear-facing warning lights include red and amber, deck-mounted flashers. The 230-horsepower, 440-ci four-barrel V-8 powering this battle cruiser has a special California emissions package. The dual exhaust includes dual catalytic converters and a separate mini-converter. The mini-converters were only used on California cars. This 440-ci engine was not available on the larger, Dodge Royal Monaco in California. The 440-ci-powered police Monaco accelerated to 60 miles per hour in 8.1 seconds. It ran the quarter mile in 16.3 seconds with a speed of 88 miles per hour. The top speed was an impressive 126 miles per hour.

The Foster City (California) Police used this sharp-looking 1977 Dodge Monaco. This was the last year for the blue-and-white color scheme. In 1977, the California Vehicle Code was changed to require that any police car used specifically for "traffic enforcement" must be painted two contrasting colors. The roof and doors had to be different (light) from the body color (dark). The only exception was the use of an all-white "traffic enforcement" vehicle. Since no one was absolutely sure what a legally contrasting color scheme was, nearly all traffic cars were painted white after 1977.

Pictured is a 1977 Plymouth Fury that patrolled Bakersfield, California. The black-and-white sedan has a gold-and-blue door shield. While most of the BPD Pontiac Catalinas in the background have either a red/red or red/blue Twinsonic, the Fury is sporting the sleek red/blue Aerodynic. Starting in 1966, Mopar police-package cars were identified by "K" as the second digit in the VIN. The 1977 model year was the last for this coding method. In 1978, the police cars were identified by "A38" on the fender tag.

The Daly City (California) Police used this 1977 Plymouth Gran Fury. Daly City is the first city south of San Francisco. Take a good look at this full-size Plymouth since it has two very unusual features. First, the roof is black. This may be the only black-and-white police car in all of California with a black roof. Second, note the lack of symmetry with the cop gear on the roof. There is a center red rotator with a siren speaker to the right side and a red/amber light on the left side. For those who want to call the emergency number used in 1977, printed on the rear quarter panels is "Emergency 992-1225."

In 1977, the Indiana State Police used the 121.4-inch-wheelbase Dodge Royal Monaco to patrol the Hoosier State. Notice the impressive wheels. These cruisers were solid white with a blue door shield and gold "V" through the shield. The emergency lights were twin red rotators. The New Jersey State Police, Utah Highway Patrol, Washington State Patrol, and West Virginia State Police also drove the 1977 Gran Fury. All of them were powered by the 245-horsepower, 440-ci four-barrel V-8. Just 2,206 police-package 1977 Royal Monacos were made.

A proud and confident Virginia State Police trooper stands next to his 1977 Plymouth Gran Fury. These VSP cars had a blue hood, roof, and trunk over a gray body. The four-bulb rotating roof light had a red globe. The VSP later made the transition to blue emergency lights. These full-size Gran Furys were powered by the 245-horsepower, 440-ci four-barrel V-8. Significantly, this was the last year for the 121.4-inch "long"-wheelbase Mopar. After 1977, the longest wheelbase was 117.4 inches, then 118.5 inches, then just 112.7 inches. The first Plymouth with a wheelbase over 120 inches had been the 1974 Fury.

This gorgeous 1977 Dodge Royal Monaco is a restored Chicago Police cruiser. The white with blue stripes and red letter Royal Monaco is parked in front of the Chicago Police Department headquarters. This Windy City four-door sedan has twin blue globe rotators, Chicago's famous MARS lights. The lightbar-mounted can lights have blue flashers facing forward and red lenses facing rearward. The red lights are tied into the brakelight and turn-signal circuits. In the background, CPD headquarters flies the American flag and the Chicago Police Department flag. Found on the police officer's uniform and rear quarter panels of the cars, the CPD flag has two blue stripes and four red stars.

Standing next to his 1977 440-ci-powered Dodge Royal Monaco is Chicago Police Lieutenant Lee Hamilton. This is a vintage shot from 1977 when the Royal Monaco was actually used for traffic enforcement and other police duties. The Chicago Police force is the second-largest city police force behind only the New York City Police Department. The CPD has 13,500 sworn law-enforcement officers. In 1977, the 440-ci V-8 was available in all Royal Monacos, except those used in California. The one and only engine used in the Golden State Royal Monacos was the 360-ci four-barrel small-block V-8.

As a virtual reflection of Lt. Hamilton's cruiser, Chicago Police Officer Greg Reynolds is shown with his fully restored, 1977 Chicago Police Dodge Royal Monaco. Notice that this car number, 5415, is exactly the same as CPD Lt. Hamilton's 1977 issue cruiser. Lt. Hamilton supports the legitimate restoration and display of old police cars, and this unit was marked in such a way to acknowledge his support. Like the original, this CPD Royal Monaco is powered by a 245-horsepower, 440-ci four-barrel V-8. The 155-horsepower, 360-ci two-barrel and 190-horsepower 400-ci four-barrel HD V-8s were also available. However, nearly all of the Royal Monaco police cars had the King Kong 440.

The Indiana State Police Department is famous for running full-size Mercurys and full-size Dodges, such as this 1977 Royal Monaco. Like many state police departments, the ISP selected the biggest cruisers with the most powerful V-8 engines. The 245-horsepower, 440-ci four-barrel big-block V-8 powers this menacing Dodge. The lightbar has twin red globes. Note the concealed headlights. The rear end of this Royal Monaco is squatted down and the front end raised up as this cruiser is in wide-open-throttle pursuit of a traffic violator. The rear gear on these impressive cruisers was 2.71 to 1, while a 3.21 to 1 was optional.

A New Jersey State Police trooper stands "at ease" next to his 1977 Dodge Royal Monaco. At 121.4 inches, the 1977 Royal Monaco was the last Dodge police car with a wheelbase over 120 inches. Dodge police cars had had 120-inch or longer wheelbases since the release of the formal Dodge police package in 1956. All that ended after 1977. And by 1982, the full-size Dodge police car had a wheelbase just 112.7 inches long. This NJSP cruiser is all-white with gold and a blue diagonal door stripes. The blue triangle door shield has gold letters and the Twinsonic has all-red lenses.

The Chaplain with the Chicago Fire Department used this 1977 Oldsmobile Delta 88. This serves as a reminder that, like police work, fighting fires can be extremely dangerous. Also like police work, fire scenes often involve dealing with people who have suffered a profound loss or tragic injury. At times like this, there is only one source of comfort. The false hope of men is no match for the eternal hope in God. Although the Chaplain probably does not need a police-package interceptor to do his job, a state-bid, police-package vehicle was the least expensive way to get any sort of a two-door or four-door sedan or station wagon. This 1977 CFD Olds has a black roof over a red body with twin red rotators. The trademark CFD green light is missing. The base engine of the downsized, 116-inch Delta 88 was the 231-ci six. The 260-ci V-8 and 350-ci V-8 were options. The most powerful Olds police engine in 1977 was the 185-horsepower, 403-ci V-8.

The 1977 and 1978 Plymouth Fury and Dodge Coronet are among the most valuable and collectible of all police cars. This Michigan State Police cruiser is a 1977 Plymouth Fury powered by the 245-horsepower, 440-ci "HP" V-8. As the last of the 440-ci-powered Dodges and Plymouths, these big-block, 117.4-inch-wheelbase Mopars are legendary. The 440-ci engine, perhaps more than anything else, was responsible for the Mopars wresting the police car sales title away from Ford. Remember that Ford got its dominating edge over Chevrolet and Plymouth due to its flathead V-8. Just so, the 440-ci engine was behind the great Mopar run from 1966 to 1978. Any full-size, four-door police sedan that runs a 15- to 16-second quarter mile and has a top speed of 126 to 133 miles per hour is worthy of notice.

The Nassau County (New York) Police commandeered this fleet of police cars. Each is white with a blue door shield and wide orange stripe over a blue one. In the foreground is a 1978 Plymouth Fury. Behind this classic 117.4-inch-wheelbase cruiser is a 1979 Plymouth Volare and a 1980 Plymouth Volare. The 112.7-inch-wheelbase F-body Volare was never fully accepted as a legitimate police cruiser as long as any of the older Plymouth Furys were in the fleet. The perception soon changed; after 1981, the longest-wheelbase Dodge or Plymouth police cars were the 112.7-inch M-body Diplomat and Gran Fury. And the largest Mopar police engine was a 318-ci small-block V-8. Changes such as these amounted to a cop culture shock.

The sheriffs' departments in the state of New York are famous for their red-and-white cruisers. This 1978 Plymouth Volare was with the Franklin County (New York) Sheriff's Department in far upstate New York. This four-door, F-body has a red hood, front doors, and trunk on a white body with a black-and-silver six-point star. The roof rotator has red and white lenses inside a clear dome. Note the bumper-mounted red flashers and prisoner transport screen behind the front seat. It was not uncommon for big-city cops to hassle the sheriff's deputies for their use of "red" police cars.

Shown here is a 1978 Delano (California) Police Chevrolet Impala backed in and ready to go. Delano, north of Bakersfield, is on famous California Highway 99. This all-white cruiser has a red and blue Twinsonic with auxiliary alley lights and a takedown light mounted in front of the siren speaker. The plain-marked cruiser simply has the word "Police" on the front doors in black letters and a gold city seal. For 1978, the axle ratios on the 250-ci six and 305-ci V-8 were lowered from 3.08 to 2.73 and from 2.56 to 2.41, respectively, in an attempt to improve gas mileage. The 2.41 to 1 ratio is among the lowest gear ratios ever used in a police car. This made for extremely sluggish acceleration.

A close-up shot shows off this semi-marked 1978 Los Altos (California) Police Chevrolet Impala. The 1977 and 1978 Impalas had only a slightly different grille. The biggest difference is the location of the bowtie. The 1977 model places the bowtie in the grille, while the 1978 version has it on the leading edge of the hood. Note the low-profile pusher bumpers on this Los Altos cruiser. The only emergency lights are the bumper-mounted red and blue grille lights. The 160-horsepower (California) to 170-horsepower (Federal) 350-ci four-barrel V-8 pushed the police Impala to top speeds between 112 and 115 miles per hour. The Impalas all used 3.08 rear axles.

During the Los Angeles County Sheriff's Department testing, the red-hot 1978 Chevrolet Nova blew the doors off the competition from Dodge, Ford, Mercury, and Plymouth. The 160-horsepower, 350-ci four-barrel V-8-powered Nova hit 60 miles per hour in 9 seconds flat. It broke the light beam at the end of the quarter mile at 83 miles per hour. Around the skid-pad handling course, the Nova generated a lateral force of .83g. This was far better than the second-place Aspen and Volare. While the police Nova turned in the best acceleration and cornering and nearly the best braking, it also turned in the best gas mileage at 14.1 miles per gallon. The 9C1 police-package Nova was available as a four-door sedan and as a two-door hardtop. Nearly all police Novas, like this LASO EVOC unit, were four-door sedans.

The Napa County (California) Sheriff's Department operated this 1978 Chevrolet Nova. The patrol jurisdiction is Northern California's Napa Valley, also shared with Sonoma County, famous for its vineyards and beauty alike. This particular cruiser has the traditional black-and-white markings with gold lettering on the front fenders and trunk lid. As a slight variation to the blue-and-gold seven-point star, this door shield has the word "Sheriff" in white and blue across the top of the star. Note the three-lamp cluster of emergency lights that are red to the front, red/amber to the rear, and white alley lights to the side. In 1977 and 1978, when the Impala did not have a big block but the Fords and Mopars did, the Nova was Chevrolet's flagship.

Originally a Louisiana State Police cruiser, this 1978 Ford LTD is one of the best-restored police cars on the show circuit. Keeping its Louisiana identity, the all-white four-door sedan has a blue marking the shape of the state containing the state seal and red door lettering. The emergency lights have twin red lenses. Note the clear-lens, remote-control takedown light mounted on top of the Twinsonic. This LSP cruiser packs a 202-horsepower, 460-ci Police Interceptor big-block V-8. This was the last year for the 460-ci big block and the last year for the 400 Cleveland. After 1978, the largest Ford police car engine was the 351 Windsor, which carried the flag until 1992. As the last of the big-block Fords, this 460-ci-powered LTD is as important, as collectible, and as valuable as any of the 440-ci-powered Mopars.

This 1978 Ford LTD patrolled the streets of Brooklyn, Ohio, a suburb of Cleveland. The four-door cruiser is silver with gold fender lettering and a gold door shield. The unit has a red/blue Twinsonic with auxiliary front takedown lights in addition to the twin A-pillar spotlights. There is seldom any idea of too much light. The best feature, however, may be the blue lenses mounted in the high-beam side of the headlights. With every light activated, including take-downs and spots, this big Ford would be very imposing. It is uncertain, however, whether the whitewall tire in the rear is the spare of the blackwall tire. The whitewall ought to be removed.

The South Carolina Highway Patrol used this 1978 Ford LTD as a patrol car. The cruiser is white with blue stripes and a blue-and-gold door shield. The words "Highway Patrol" appear as blue letters on a gold background on the front fenders and the trunk lid. The emergency light is a single blue rotator. The highway patrol in the Palmetto State was formed in 1930. The wheelbase on the 1978 Ford was 121 inches. Prior to 1969, the wheelbase on the full-size Ford was 119 inches, and, after 1978, it shrank to 144.4 inches. The powerplant in this SCHP unit was a 202-horsepower, 460-ci Police Interceptor V-8.

The Cuyahoga County (Ohio) Sheriff's Department operated this 1978 Ford LTD. This unit was assigned to one of the court duties, probably prisoner transportation. The white-over-black Ford has an all-red Twinsonic with bar-mounted takedown lights. The sheriff's cruiser has a blue-on-gold five-point star and gold fender lettering. Urban sheriff's department cars like this frequently had smaller engines than their rural sheriff's department counterparts. In 1978, the smaller engines for the full-size Ford included the 137-horsepower, 302-ci V-8; the 149-horsepower, 351 Windsor V-8; and the 173-horsepower 400 Cleveland.

A reserve deputy sheriff with the Mohave County Sheriff's Department in northwest Arizona used this 1978 Ford LTD. Pool cars for reservists are nearly always high-mileage cars that are taken out of regular patrol duty. Although the cars used by reserve deputy sheriffs and police officers may have as little as 50,000 miles, the reserve's pool car usually has 100,000 miles or more. Reservist officers play a critical role in emergency situations, as well as filling in vacant positions. Some reserves bring special technical skills to a department too small to afford a staff member with that ability. It is common to require a reserve to ride with a full-time officer, or with another reserve, while patrolling. Only in the rarest cases will a reserve officer be granted "single unit status." Complete with prisoner cage, this Ford has red and blue rotators with blue and red high-beam headlight lenses.

Two sharp-looking cruisers with a sheriff's department in the Golden State sit idle for the moment. The white-over-dark-blue Ford is a 1978 LTD II. The all-white Dodge is a 1979 St. Regis. Both have chromed pusher bars, prisoner partitions, and red/blue Twinsonics with auxiliary alley lights. Note the electronic device on the dash of the Ford. That is the display unit for the traffic radar. The antenna for the traffic radar is mounted on the driver-side rear window. With moving radar, the cruiser can travel in one direction at freeway speeds and clock oncoming traffic. However, this vintage radar could not clock traffic pulling away from the cruiser. All moving radar units can also be used in a stationary mode. This allows the officer to clock all traffic, either approaching or leaving the cruiser in both directions.

Pictured is a bright and clean 1978 Ford LTD with the Pittsburgh Police Services near the Suison Bay in Northern California. With twin, A-pillar spots and a lightbar full of red, blue, amber, and white lights, the location of the pusher bar that identifies this as a police car is unclear. During vehicle testing by the Michigan State Police, an LTD II with a 166-horsepower, 400 Cleveland two-barrel V-8 took 41 seconds to reach 100 miles per hour. This ranked among the slowest vehicles tested. In fact, even with the largest available engine, this cruiser was disqualified for acceleration that was too slow. The 400-Cleveland-powered LTD II had a top speed of 115 miles per hour.

Ford's police package was available on the 1978 Mercury Cougar. The Cougar and the Ford LTD II shared the same 118-inch wheelbase and all powertrain options. The Cougar was easy to distinguish from the LTD II. Both had quad, rectangular headlights. The LTD II had them stacked vertically, while the Cougar had them horizontally, side by side. Oddly enough, even though both the Cougar and LTD II were available with the same 166-horsepower, 400 Cleveland two-barrel V-8, during Los Angeles County Sheriff's Department testing, the Cougar hit 60 miles per hour more than a second faster than the LTD II did. Of course, even an 11.2-second blast to 60 miles per hour is nothing to brag about. The police Cougar was also available with the 302-ci V-8 and the 351 Modified V-8.

The 1978 model year was the last for the full-size, 121-inch-wheelbase Ford police car. It was also the last for the full-size, 124-inch-wheelbase Mercury police car, such as this Missouri State Highway Patrol Marquis. This Mercury is on display at the MSHP museum on the grounds of its Academy in Jefferson City. The MSHP museum is one of the five best police museums in the United States and is well worth a special effort to see. This 1978 MSHP cruiser is all-white with an all-red Federal Aerodynic. The markings are gold letters on a blue, or blue and gray, background. The Marquis was available in one of three police-spec engines. These included the 173-horsepower, 400 Cleveland; the 197-horsepower, 460 Police; and the 202-horsepower, 460 Police Interceptor.

The Pittsburgh (California) Police used this 1978 Ford Granada. The all-white four-door sedan has a wide blue stripe with white lettering and the California-spec red/amber and blue Twinsonic. What makes this 109.9-inch-wheelbase cruiser noteworthy is the full-dress wheel covers. That was unusual for a police car in the 1970s. Of course, the PPD Granada has front pusher bars. You wonder if these were ever used until you see one that was bent—then you wonder how it got bent. In 1978, the Granada police cars were powered by a 97-horsepower, 250-ci six or a 134-horsepower, 302-ci V-8. The 351 Windsor that had made the Granada a rocket sled in 1977 was no longer available. New for 1978, the Granada was upgraded from round headlights to rectangular ones.

Ford released a brand-new police car, its Fairmont, in mid-1978. Mercury also released a police package for its Zephyr. Both cars were built on a 105.5-inch wheelbase. The Fairmont, like this South Lake Tahoe, Nevada, four-door sedan, was intended for general patrol, ordinance enforcement, investigations, and other nonhigh-speed and nonpursuit assignments, according to Ford Fleet. Ford claimed the Fairmont had 90 percent of the head, leg, and shoulder room of most large cars. The Fairmont was Ford's top-selling retail car in 1978, but was not at all well received by law enforcement. This SLTPD Fairmont is medium-blue with white front doors. The red and blue Aerodynic looks big on this otherwise tiny cruiser.

In mid-1978, a police package was released for the 105.5-inch-wheelbase Mercury Zephyr and Ford Fairmont, such as this Milpitas (California) Police unit. This cruiser from the San Jose suburb is powered by the 85-horsepower, 200-ci six. A 139-horsepower, 302-ci V-8 was optional. The all-white Fairmont has a wide red stripe running from headlight to taillight. In a very odd twist on the police-marking theme, the blue, white, and gold seven-point star with city seal is on the rear quarter panel. The Federal Aerodynic has twin red lenses and twin red grille lights. With all that red, and almost nothing that identifies this as a police car, the car could almost be confused with a fire vehicle. The confusion ends, however, with the presence of the dash-mounted 12-gauge shotgun.

The U.S. Park Service used this clean-looking 1978 Plymouth Volare. The all-white Volare has a broad green stripe with green lettering. The Twinsonic has all-blue lenses. This four-door sedan was photographed in its natural setting at the Rock Creek Park in Washington, D.C. The Volare rode on a 112.7-inch wheelbase. Retail versions of the Volare included the Street Kit Car and Road Runner. These hot rods shared many police components. With the 360-ci V-8, all these cars ran a 16-second quarter mile with top speeds around 110 miles per hour.

A simple yet effective color scheme identifies this 1978 Plymouth Volare with the Livingston (California) Police. Livingston is near Modesto in Northern California. The blue cruiser has an extremely wide white band running the full length of the car. The term, "Livingston Police 394-2211," is in bold, blue, block letters. The Aerodynic has red/amber and blue lenses. Note the roof-mounted spotlight. In 1977, the 112.7-inch Volare was considered a compact car. That was when the 117.4-inch Fury and the 121.4-inch Gran Fury were available. With the Gran Fury no longer available, the Volare was considered a mid-size. By 1982, the same 112.7-inch wheelbase came to be considered full-size!

The Sacramento (California) Police used this 1978 Plymouth Volare. This cruiser is very traditionally marked with white-over-black body colors, a red/amber and blue Twinsonic, and black, silver-and-gold door shield. While this four-door sedan does not have an A-pillar spotlight, it does have auxiliary alley lights. Note the tall, front pusher bumper. In California, the police Volare was available with just two engines, the 90-horsepower, 225-ci slant six and the 160-horsepower, 360-ci V-8. Notice that the rear door is black. In California, there were two main schools of thought on black-and-white cruisers. The CHP-style had a white roof and white front doors. The LAPD-style had a white roof and white front and rear doors. The difference remains to this day.

The fully equipped 1978 Plymouth Volare shown here was with the San Juan Bautista (California) Police. San Juan Bautista is a small community near Monterey Bay in Northern California. This cruiser has everything that makes a police car: pusher bars, A-pillar spots, auxiliary alley lights, rear seat partition, and red/amber and blue Twinsonic. The seven-point star is black on silver but it is still visible on this all-white sedan. The police package in 1978 was noted by an A38 on the fender tag. It was no longer a part of the Vehicle Identification Number as it had been since the 1950s. The bolt-on A38 police package was introduced in 1970, while Plymouth's "ground-up" police cars were available since 1957.

The Long Beach Police Department south of Los Angeles used this 1978 Dodge Aspen. In fact, this black-and-white cruiser is marked exactly like a Los Angeles Police Department unit with just two exceptions. The city of Long Beach seal is used, of course, and the word "Police" appears on top of the seal instead of below it. With the California-spec 160-horsepower, 360-ci four-barrel V-8, the Aspen with the A38 police package had a 0- to 60-mile-per-hour time of 10.7 seconds. Its speed through the quarter-mile lights was 78 miles per hour. This was exactly the same performance as the 350-ci Chevrolet Impala but much slower than the 350-ci Chevrolet Nova. Note the chromed pusher bars. The Aerodynic had red/amber and blue/amber lenses with integral alley lights. Note that these Long Beach cars have a passenger-side, A-pillar spotlight but not one on the driver's side.

The Long Beach (California) Police Department on the San Pedro Bay operated this 1978 Dodge Aspen. This black-and-white police wagon has a red and blue Aerodynic with integral alley lights, but it also has a driver-side, A-pillar spotlight. Station wagons are often used by K-9 officers, shift supervisors, tactical teams, and other nonpatrol officers who are on a mission and need to carry a bunch of cop gear. Sure enough, the rear quarter panel of this Long Beach unit is clearly marked "Sergeant." When you get promoted, they take away your big-block V-8 battle cruiser and give you a mom-and-pop station wagon with a six or a small block.

In 1978, the police in Sausalito, California, used this Dodge Aspen to enforce the laws. The first city north of the Golden Gate Bridge on the south end of the Marin Peninsula is Sausalito. Often compared to the French Riviera, Sausalito is a wealthy area where the mountains meet the sea, where a wooded hillside meets the Richardson Bay, and where the number of yachts and houseboats almost outnumber the cars. In fact, the door shield on this Aspen tells the story of the city; it is a white sailboat against a sea-blue background. The lettering on this all-white cruiser is also medium-blue. Note that this is a supervisor's car.

The rear-quarter view of a 1978 Dodge Aspen used by the Stockton (California) Police displays the black-and-white color scheme of Northern California patrol cars. Two features set these cruisers apart. The first is a door shield identical to the officer's shoulder patch, as opposed to a six-point or seven-point star. The second feature is the siren. An external siren speaker replaced the integral speaker on an otherwise stock Twinsonic. This cruiser, of course, has California-spec lenses. Both the red lens and the blue lens have amber inserts facing the rear. Amber passes much more light than either red or blue.

In 1978, the Indiana State Police used this Dodge Monaco to patrol everything from the interstates to the gravel roads in the Hoosier State. This four-door, 117.4-inch Monaco weighed 3,885 pounds. These all-white cruisers were powered by the 225-horsepower, 440-ci four-barrel V-8. The cruisers were marked with a silver-and-gold-on-blue door shield, with a gold "V"-shaped spear behind the shield. A red rotator and twin red deck flashers make up the emergency lights. Note the rear fender-mounted, low-band whip antenna. This cruiser was able to accelerate to 60 miles per hour in 9.2 seconds. That was pretty quick for a car geared to run over 130 miles per hour

A red and blue Federal Aerodynic sits atop this 1978 California Highway Patrol Dodge Monaco. This lightbar is a streamlined version of the very square Twinsonic. The center section of the Aerodynic has the integral siren speaker, just like the Twinsonic. With this lightbar, both A-pillar spotlights have clear lenses. This CHP Fury is packing the California-spec 240-horsepower, 440-ci four-barrel V-8. This engine includes dual exhausts and dual catalytic converters, plus a mini-converter. While the 1977 model year was the last for the 440-ci V-8 in a retail car, the 1978 model year was the last for this big block in a police car.

This is the rear-quarter view of the 1978 Dodge Monaco with the Foster City (California) Police. For 1978, Foster City traffic-enforcement cars were changed from white over blue to solid white. The lettering on the trunk lid was changed from the words "Foster City" in gold, to the words "Traffic Safety" in black. The door shield was also changed. It went from a blue and gold shoulder-patch-style shield to a blue and gold seven-point star. The rear deck of this four-door sedan has one amber and one blue flasher. With the 440-ci V-8, the police Monaco had a top speed of 133 miles per hour. That beats the Corvette, Camaro Z28, and Datsun 280Z.

These four recent graduates from the Indiana Law Enforcement Academy stand proudly next to a 1978 Dodge Monaco on their first day with the Lafayette (Indiana) Police Department. The LPD Monaco has a white roof and doors over a black body. The black-on-silver door shield is in the form of the police officer's badge. The city seal includes Lafayette, the French general. The Twinsonic lightbar has a red lens and a clear lens with red and white rotating lights. This Twinsonic has been fitted with dual, forward-facing takedown lights in addition to the A-pillar spotlight. This cruiser was powered by a 440-ci big-block V-8 in the last year it was available. The second officer from the left, B.L. Pritchett, went on to become a multiple-term sheriff in nearby Benton County, Indiana.

The 1978 Ford LTD II with the New Jersey State Police is an all-white, mid-size cruiser with a gold and blue diagonal stripe on the front doors. This stripe accents the symbol of the NJSP, which contains gold lettering on a blue triangle. Back in the 1930s the colors were reversed—the triangle was gold and the lettering was blue. Note the "SP" license plate, meaning state police. Powered by a 400-ci Cleveland V-8, this 4-door sedan took 12.3 seconds to reach 60 miles per hour, and 41 seconds to reach 100 miles per hour. That acceleration was deemed too slow by the Michigan State Police. The top speed for this 400-ci LTD II was 115 miles per hour in slick top condition. The Twinsonic's all-red lenses lowered the top speed by as much as 10 miles per hour. This was an era of generally poor police-car performance, and it would get much worse before it got any better.

Displayed is an extremely sharp 1978 Sacramento (California) Police Dodge Monaco. This cruiser was restored in exhaustive detail by a Sacramento police officer. The Sacramento Monaco is powered by a 175-horsepower, 400-ci four-barrel V-8. With this big-block engine, the Monaco reaches 60 miles per hour in 11.1 seconds, 100 miles per hour in 34.4 seconds, and has a top speed of 117 miles per hour. This was the last year for both the 400-ci big block and the 440-ci big block. This cruiser is white over black with the California-spec red/amber and blue Twinsonic. The front pusher bumper is prominent but sees little use on a valuable show car.

The 1978 Dodge Monaco shown was with the Ventura (California) Police Department. It is tough to stand out from the crowd when the overall appearance of the police vehicle is as regulated as it is in California. However, the black-outlined gold lettering and the city seal in gold, blue, and red make for an attractive and distinctive appearance. Almost all the proper CHP gear is here: twin A-pillar spots; Red/amber and blue Twinsonic; Dash-mounted shotgun; Auxiliary alley lights; Partition between the back seat; Dog-dish, vented hubcaps; and a white-over-black color scheme. The only missing feature is the front pusher bars. How does an officer patrol U.S. Highway 101 in Southern California without pusher bars?

One of the best restored and best maintained of all the police cars on the show circuit is this 1978 Nevada Highway Patrol Plymouth Fury. This NHP Fury was driven in service and is now owned by Trooper Jeff Leathley. He drives it to the West Coast police-car shows and drives home with a trunk full of well-deserved trophies. The gray-over-blue Fury has a gray stripe and gold lettering and blue, white, and gold seven-point star. Of course, it is powered by the 440-ci four-barrel V-8 in its last year. This NHP Fury has a red A-pillar spotlight and chromed pusher bumpers. As the last of the 440-ci-powered highway patrol cars, this Fury is among the most valuable and most collectible police cars in existence.

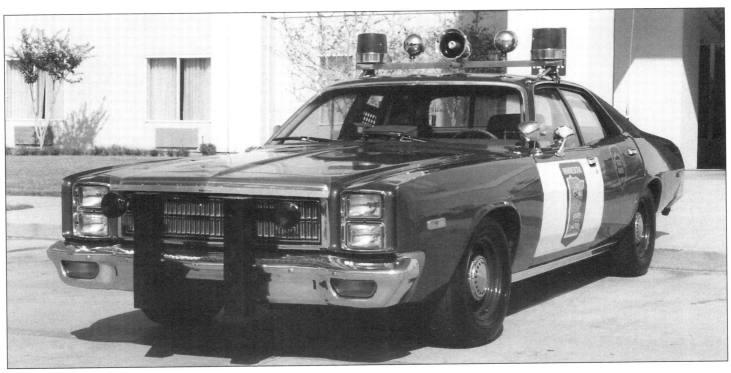

This 1978 Plymouth Fury appears exactly as it did during its days with the Minnesota State Patrol. The four-door sedan is maroon-cinnamon in color with a red/red Federal Visibar. It has a single A-pillar spotlight and an unusually massive pusher bumper. Mounted on the pusher are twin red flashers. Mopars like this will always be remembered as the champions of the era when police officers gave pursuit in almost any circumstances. These cruisers could run at wide-open-throttle all day long. No musclecar of the 1960s or 1970s could do that. These cars had top speeds of 133 miles per hour. In their last year, the 440-ci Fury and Dodge Monaco pounded the competition from Ford, Pontiac, Buick, Mercury, and Chevrolet. The reputation of these big-block Mopars was passed on from one generation of cops to the next.

The Litchfield Fire Department in down-state Illinois operated this fire-engine-red 1978 Plymouth Fury. This Fury is all red, from the Visibar to the wheels. The 117.4-inch Fury was available with six different Federal engines including the 140-horse-power, 318-ci V-8; 155- and 175-horse-power, 360-ci V-8; 190-horsepower, 400-ci V-8; and the 225-horsepower, 440-ci V-8. This fire car probably had the police-spec, "heavy duty" 318-ci two-barrel V-8. It was very common for fire departments to order police-package vehicles. This A38 package Fury had structural reinforcements and extra welds on the unibody. This was the first year the A38 police-package cars had upgrades to the main chassis itself.

What patrol car did the Los Angeles Police Department use in 1978? The LAPD cruised the freeways and surface streets in this Plymouth Fury. This 1978 white-over-black cruiser was powered by the Califor-nia-spec, 160-horsepower, 360-ci four-bar-rel V-8. Even for the time, these were not fast cars. The top speed, which held little importance, was around 112 miles per hour. The 0- to 60-mile-per-hour time, which did matter, was in the 12-second bracket. Many LAPD officers considered these small-block-powered Furys to be "dogs." Compared to the 401-ci AMC Matador and 383-ci Belvedere, the late-1970s Plymouths were indeed slow. Com-pared to most other urban police cars in the late 1970s, the 360-ci Furys gave rea-sonable performance.

A distinctive-looking 1978 Plymouth Fury with the Brisbane (California) Police Department is shown here. Brisbane is a tiny suburb of San Francisco. This Fury has all the right California-style cop gear, everything from the red/amber and blue Twinsonic to the oversize pusher bumpers. What sets this cruiser apart from a sea of black-and-whites is a broad and bold black body stripe. This is reminiscent of the graphics on Mopar musclecars from the late 1960s and early 1970s. The door markings on this striking police car are a gold-outlined, blue seven-point star. Note the black roof letters.

The Wasco Police Department in central California near Bakersfield used this 1978 Plymouth Fury station wagon. It has all the cop goodies and then some. Note the wire screen over the rear side windows. This white-over-medium-blue police wagon has a blue center rotator and twin red/amber can lights. The gold door lettering accents the gold, white, and blue city seal. The dash-mounted shotgun sends a very clear, visual warning all its own. For all the gadgets visible on this wagon, it is doubtful that gear meant much to the prisoners hauled inside.

During the annual Michigan State Police Department vehicle tests, the 1978 Plymouth Fury 440 ci, like this MSP cruiser, proved itself to be the fastest car produced in North America. It was not just the fastest police car, four-door sedan, or full-size car. The 440-ci-powered Fury was simply the fastest car. With the 225-horsepower big block and 2.71 rear gears, the Fury accelerated to 60 miles per hour in 9.2 seconds but kept up the pace to hit 132.7 miles per hour. The 440-ci Fury accelerated like the Corvettes of its day but had top speeds like the Ferraris. It was 16 years before a full-size police car showed this kind of performance again.

The Mason County Sheriff's Department in western West Virginia used this dark-blue 1979 Ford LTD-S with an all-blue Twinsonic. The fender and door lettering is blue on white, as is the six-point sheriff's star. The LTD was available with just two engines, the 302-ci and the 351-ci V-8. These two engines would power the full-size Ford through all of the 1980s until replaced by the 4.6L SOHC in mid-1992. The 1979 Ford LTD was the most downsized of the Big Three police cars. The 1979 Chevrolet rode on a 116-inch wheelbase while the 1979 Dodge used a 118.5-inch wheelbase. Note the orange plug sticking out the grille of this sheriff's patroller. Although the block heater seems a trivial feature, it works well enough to find widespread use.

The Brooklyn (Ohio) Police used this 1979 Ford LTD-S to patrol the Cleveland-area suburb. The cruiser has a red and blue Twinsonic and twin A-pillar spotlights. This solid-silver police car has gold fender lettering and a gold, red, and blue door shield. The 1979 to 1982 police-oriented LTD-S had a different front end than the retail-oriented LTD. The LTD-S had only one headlight per side. As a spotting guide, the 1979 and 1980 LTD-S had single headlights and cooling slots in the bumper. The 1981 LTD-S had single headlights and a solid bumper. The 1982 LTD-S had single headlights, a solid bumper, and the blue Ford oval in the grille.

This all-white 1979 Ford LTD II is with the Prince George's County (Maryland) Police Department. Prince George's County forms the eastern border of Washington, D.C., and is an extremely active enforcement area. In 1979, the LTD II was available in just two powertrains. One was the 133-horsepower, 302-ci two-barrel V-8 with 2.47 to 1 rear gears. This was not much power nor gearing to get a 3,844-pound four-door sedan moving. The other engine was the 151-horsepower, 351-ci Modified two-barrel V-8. Unfortunately, this was also teamed with the extremely sluggish 2.47 to 1 rear gears. Ford's 351 Modified was much milder than either the 170-horsepower Chevrolet 350-ci four-barrel V-8 or the 195-horsepower Mopar 360-ci four-barrel V-8. The use of a two-barrel carb was only part of the problem. Cam grind, ignition timing, and head design accounted for the rest of the differences.

The appearance of a lime-green police car in the 1970s means that this must be Cleveland, Ohio. Famous for unsightly green emergency vehicles, this Cleveland Police car is a 1979 Ford LTD II. The cars were immediately recognizable as emergency vehicles, albeit unsightly ones. This cruiser is marked with white-on-blue police decals. The fire vehicles were the same color except they had white-on-red decals. All emergency vehicles had the red, white, blue, and gold city seal. This cruiser has red and blue rotators under clear lenses. The 351 Modified was only available in the LTD II and not in the LTD or Fairmont. This was the last year for the 351 Modified, a destroked version of the raised-block 400 Cleveland.

This 1979 Ford LTD II was with a Northern California police department. The four-door cruiser is white over blue with a red and blue Aerodynic. Note the roof-mounted spotlight. In its last year, the LTD II was available with the 302-ci small block, which had been introduced to police work in 1968. It was also available with the 351-ci Modified, a member of the 335-series Cleveland big-block family. This family included the 351 Cleveland, 400 Cleveland, and 351 Modified. All shared the same canted valvetrain, which gave superior breathing compared to the traditional wedge valvetrain. This was the last model year for any Cleveland-based V-8 in a Ford police car. The Cleveland engine represented one of Ford's better ideas.

In 1979, the California Highway Patrol began one of the most influential police car evaluations ever: the Special Purpose Vehicle Study. The results paved the way for wider police acceptance of the 108- to 112-inch-wheelbase police cars for patrol use. This study also resulted in the widespread use of short-wheelbase pony cars for pursuit use. One of the four test vehicles was this 1979 Ford Fairmont powered by the California-spec 133-horsepower, 302-ci two-barrel V-8. This 105.5-inch-wheelbase four-door sedan was also tested for other concepts. One was the use of strobe lights instead of rotating or flashing halogen lights. This unit is fitted with one red and one blue strobe. Another concept was to mount the siren speaker on the pusher bar. The engine compartment was becoming too crowded and insulated for the siren speaker. The more visible blue strobes and bumper-mounted siren caught on.

The U.S. Government assigned this 1979 Chevrolet Malibu to the Colorado School of Mines, founded in 1874. The light-blue, four-door sedan has a red and blue Twinsonic. It also has red passenger-side and white driver-side spotlights. These are in addition to the two lightbar-mounted alley lights. All the Malibu police cars came with fancy stamped-steel wheels and chrome center caps. The new-sized (downsized) Malibu had a four-wheel coil spring suspension.

An especially attractive graphics package marks this 1979 Chevrolet Malibu with the Orange (California) Police Department. The city of Orange is, of course, in Orange County, east of Los Angeles County. This four-door Malibu has a bold, orange stripe running from front bumper to taillight. The markings include the word "Police" in black, block letters and the seal of the city, which is in orange lettering with an orange in the center. While these graphics fit right in with the 1990s, this was very progressive for the late 1970s, especially set within the California fad for black-and-white or all-white cruisers.

The 1979 Chevrolet Malibu was selected as a part of the CHP's Special Purpose Vehicle Study. While the 165-horsepower, 350-ci four-barrel V-8 was available, the CHP picked the 125-horsepower, 305-ci four-barrel V-8 for its test cars. The CHP expected the 108.1-inch-wheelbase Malibu to be the "large sedan of 1985 and beyond." For the same reason, it picked the smaller of the two small-block V-8s. The test cars were fitted with dual A-pillar spotlights and standard pusher bumpers. The only change the CHP made to the Malibu was the use of thick-gauge steel wheels. After the 18-month study, the CHP concluded, "the basic sedan design, although smaller in size, is still acceptable for police work." This 305-ci, 108.1-inch Malibu prepared the CHP for a decade of the 318-ci, 112.7-inch Dodge Diplomat.

A very traditional-appearing 1979 Chevrolet Malibu police car is pictured here. This Rio Vista Police cruiser from south of Sacramento follows the Northern California theme for black-and-whites. The roof and just the front doors are white. In Southern California, the front and the rear doors are typically white. This four-door Malibu has a red and blue Aerodynic. The door shield is a black-and-silver seven-point star. *Car and Driver* magazine tested a 350-ci-powered Malibu with the 9C1 police package. They concluded, "The 9C1 happens to be one of the best American sedans, if not the best."

The 1979 Chevrolet Malibu could stay with nearly any traffic violator around a tight road course. Part of the reason is the top-notch training given by police-pursuit and EVOC instructors, like these two-stripe deputies with the Los Angeles County Sheriff's Department. Another factor is the Malibu's 9C1 police suspension, starting with the famous F41 sport suspension. To that, Chevrolet adds an even larger rear sway bar, stiffer suspension bushings and grommets, and stiffer body-on-frame mounts. Other upgrades included semi-metallic brake pads, a larger-capacity brake booster, and different front-to-rear brake proportioning. The F41 and 9C1 packages share the same springs, shocks, and steering gears. Both *Car and Driver* magazine and *Police Product News* magazine praised the LASD's choice of cruiser. *Police Product News* said, "The Malibu's handling is excellent, and the steering is lively and responsive."

The North Carolina Highway Patrol used the 1979 Chevrolet Impala, as did the state police in Maine, Washington, and Michigan. The NCHP also ran the Impala in 1978 but drove the Plymouth Fury in 1977. This NCHP cruiser has the paint scheme used since the 1940s. That scheme includes a silver roof over a black hood, trunk and top part of the fenders, and doors. The bottom part of the fenders and doors is silver, as are the wheels. In the mid-1980s, this color scheme was essentially reversed. The bottom of the fenders and doors became black while the entire upper part of the body was silver. The emergency light is a single four-bulb rotator with a blue lens. The NCHP was formed in 1929. The Tar Heel State dates back to 1775.

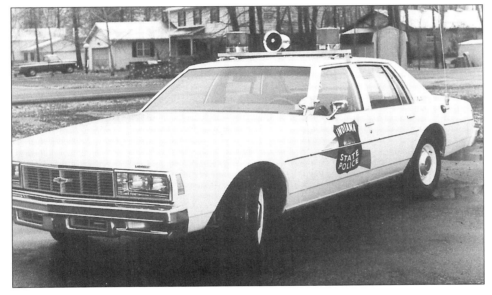

The Indiana State Police Department used the 1979 Chevrolet Impala powered by a 170-horsepower, 350-ci four-barrel V-8. This ISP cruiser is all-white with a silver and blue door shield and a gold, reflective "V" through the shield. The emergency lights are the Visibar with twin red lenses. Note the rear fender-mounted, low-band whip antenna. The ISP was organized in 1933. They used black patrol cars until the early 1960s. After a brief use of white-over-blue cruisers in the mid-1960s, in 1967 the ISP adopted all-white police cars. They used all-white cruisers until 1998, when they returned to all-black with the restyled Ford Crown Victoria.

By 1979, all of the big-block V-8s were gone. The police-car playing field was virtually level. Chevrolet, Ford, Dodge, and Chrysler all produced full-size police cars with a wheelbase between 114.4 and 118.5 inches. The maximum engine sizes were nearly the same: 350-ci Chevrolet, 351-ci Ford, and 360-ci Mopar. Plymouth and Dodge were no longer the obvious choices for state police and highway patrol cruisers. With equal footing, the small-block-powered Impala, tweaked since 1977, looked pretty good. Police agencies that had used Mopars for years, such as the Ohio State Highway Patrol, picked the Impala for good reason. This OSHP cruiser is all-white with an all-red lightbar. The door lettering and the famous winged tire symbol are in gold and black.

The county number 77 on the fender identifies this 1979 Chevrolet Impala as serving with the Summit County (Ohio) Sheriff's Department. Summit County includes Akron. This SCSD cruiser, like most Buckeye State sheriff's units at the time, has a white roof and doors over a black body with a red and blue Twinsonic. Some sheriff's cars had a white roof over a black body with black doors. This particular county used an auxiliary, clear-lens rotator on top of the lightbar. The fender, door, and trunk markings are brown-outlined gold. Like Indiana, the county is not identified on the sheriff's door star. This blue-and-gold five-point star simply reads "Sheriff, State of Ohio." Motorists speeding in Ohio had to keep a sharp lookout for the all-white highway patrol cars and the black-and-white sheriff's cruisers.

The Chardon Police Department in northeast Ohio used this black-and-white 1979 Chevrolet Impala. The four-door Bowtie has gold fender lettering and a gold, green, and black door shield. The lightbar has red and blue lenses. With the 170-horsepower, 350-ci four-barrel V-8, the 9C1 Impala reached 60 miles per hour in 11.1 seconds, and 100 miles per hour in 35.3 seconds. Its top speed with the 3.08 to 1 rear gear was 112.5 miles per hour according to the Michigan State Police vehicle testing. This put the 350-ci Impala ahead of the 351-ci Ford LTD and LTD II but behind the 360-ci Chrysler Newport and Dodge St. Regis. The Impala did, however, have the best brakes of any 1979 police cruiser and the best fuel economy rating. For many departments, average performance with excellent gas mileage served their needs precisely.

One of the most influential vehicles in the history of police cars is this 1979 Chevrolet Camaro Z28. This Camaro is one of the original twelve tested by the California Highway Patrol during its Special Purpose Vehicle Study. This was an 18-month study to help the CHP determine the future of police cars after the demise of the long-wheelbase, big-block four-door sedan. One of the solutions to the loss of the 440-ci, 122-inch-wheelbase sedans was a mixture of different vehicles within the same fleet. Some of the vehicles were the 108- to 112-inch, four-door sedans with small-block V-8s. Other vehicles were V-8-powered mid-size station wagons for very specific tasks. Still other vehicles were two-door sport coupes, such as this 350-ci Camaro, specifically for traffic enforcement.

Just three exceptions set this 1979 Chevrolet Camaro test vehicle apart from complete showroom stock. In an effort to increase top speeds, the CHP changed the rear axle ratio to 3.08 to 1 from the retail 3.42 or 3.73 rear gears. Upgraded brakes were the second exception. The Camaro was fitted with Nova police-package brakes, which in turn came from a full-size 1975 Bel Air. These brakes included front discs with semi-metallic pads and finned rear drums. The third exception was the tires. The retail Z28 came with steel-belted radials, which were not recommended for sustained high-speed driving. The OEM radials were replaced with Firestone fabric-belted radials designed for police use. Other than that, the CHP test Camaro was every bit a Z28 complete with front air dam, hood scoop, rear spoiler, bucket seats, and console shifter. The colorful Z28 decals were removed and the aluminum wheels were painted black.

This 1979 Dodge Aspen is with the Traffic Division of the Lisle Police in a southwest Chicago suburb. Lisle is the home of the best-judged car shows in the Chicagoland area. This four-door Aspen is all-blue with a gold, blue, white, and green door shield. The numbers and letters on the fenders and door are black. The Aerodynic has red and blue lenses. As a traffic-enforcement vehicle, this Aspen would be powered by the 195-horsepower, 360-ci four-barrel V-8. Believe it or nor, this cruiser was faster to 100 miles per hour than the legendary 1978 440-ci-powered Plymouth Fury! The Aspen was built on a 112.7-inch platform.

Pictured is an entire fleet of 1979 Plymouth Volares with the Sacramento, California, Police. These four-door sedans have a white roof and front door over black body. This is the California Highway Patrol-style of black-and-white. The Los Angeles Police Department and Los Angeles County Sheriff's Department's style of black-and-white has a white roof and all doors over a black body. This is the least of the differences between Northern and Southern California. These 112.7-inch-wheelbase Volares have red/amber and blue Twinsonics. Each police car has its unit number on the hood, C-pillar, and trunk. Each also has a dash-mounted shotgun, rear-seat partition, and chromed pusher bumpers. The black, gold, and blue door shield includes the city seal.

The Pleasanton Police outside the Bay area in Northern California used this 1979 Plymouth Volare. The all-white traffic unit has a white-on-gold seven-point star and red/amber and blue Twinsonic. Auxiliary lights, but no pusher bumper. In 1978, the Plymouth marque alone accounted for 80 percent of the police-car market. By 1979, Plymouth had lost nearly its entire market share. The reason is the loss of a long-wheelbase cruiser. This Volare is built on a 112.7-inch platform. While that was the standard in law enforcement in 1982, it was not in 1979. Many cops still wanted the biggest patrol car they could get. The 118.5-inch police cars from Chrysler Corporation were the Dodge St. Regis and Chrysler Newport. Plymouth did not make one of these R-body cruisers in 1979.

Shown is the rear-quarter view of a 1979 Plymouth Volare with the Pleasanton Police Department. This town of 50,000 people is in Alameda County but far from the hustle and bustle of San Francisco's East Bay. A few times a year, however, hordes of people from Fremont, Hayward, Oakland, and Berkeley descend upon tiny Pleasanton, the home of Alameda County Fairgrounds. That is when this canine unit comes in very handy. Police dogs often instill a respect and authority that people are not likely to question. The word "canine" is a police code word for, "You have the right to remain peaceful and law abiding."

In 1979, the California Highway Patrol tested four very different police cars, with the idea of fielding a mixed fleet. The need for the mixed fleet was the loss of the long-wheelbase, big-block-powered, four-door sedan. This 1979 Plymouth Volare station wagon was part of that Special Purpose Vehicle Study. The CHP put an average of 57,000 miles on each of twelve test vehicles sent to four very different patrol jurisdictions. Supervisors, shift sergeants, and K-9 officers have used wagons, but wagons were never well accepted by front-line cops. Patrol officers have always had full-size cars to carry cop gear and haul prisoners. After 1978, police cars with a wheelbase longer than 119 inches simply didn't exist. Although the station wagon did not provide the image of a Camaro, it did provide the storage space.

In 1979, Chrysler Corporation released its famous R-body, four-door sedans, such as this Dodge St. Regis used by the California Highway Patrol. Powered by the 190-horsepower, 360-ci four-barrel V-8 fitted with the California emission package, this 118.5-inch St. Regis hit 60 miles per hour in 11.3 seconds, and 100 miles per hour in 34.4 seconds. The top speed was 117.5 miles per hour. Although the acceleration and top speed were not what the CHP, or anyone else, was accustomed to, the performance was well-rounded and deemed acceptable. It became the standard against which the four patrol cars in the Special Purpose Vehicle Study were compared. Whatever the CHP traffic officers thought about the 1979 360-ci St. Regis, none of them were prepared for the 1980 St. Regis powered only by the 318-ci V-8.

The Manteca Police Department, near Stockton and Modesto in Northern California, used this 1979 Dodge St. Regis on the job. This white-over-blue, four-door sedan is labeled a canine unit. The tiny white lettering on the rear fenders was all the warning provided. This unit has the now-classic red/amber and blue Twinsonic. Three roof-mounted spotlights provide the illumination. The St. Regis was the new full-size car from Chrysler Corporation. Its 118.5-inch wheelbase was actually longer than the 117.4-inch 1978 Monaco. In fact, the 118.5-inch R-body platform was the largest chassis in all of Chrysler Corporation. Although short-lived as a retail car, the 1979 St. Regis was extremely popular among police officers.

The San Mateo (California) Police operated this bright-white 1979 Dodge St. Regis. The massive front pusher bumper identifies which state this cruiser serves. The gold-and-blue San Mateo door shield cuts right to the heart of the matter with the scales of justice. The lightbar is a red/amber and blue Twinsonic. The St. Regis was almost a totally new car. It was a blend of the 121.5-inch cars last used in 1977, and the 117.4-inch cars dropped after 1978. The 118.5-inch St. Regis was a total re-design. It did, however, retain the classic torsion-bar front suspension used since 1957. The St. Regis had more legroom and shoulder room than the 1978 Monaco. As recently as 1977, the full-size 1979 St. Regis would have been considered a mid-size cruiser.

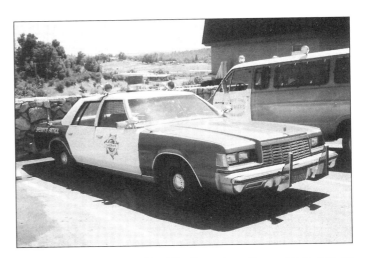

The 1979 Dodge St. Regis shown was assigned to the Police Division of the Sunnyvale (California) Department of Public Safety. The Sunnyvale DPS also provides fire and emergency medical services. This all-white St. Regis has a red/orange and blue Twinsonic. In 1979, the emphasis among automakers was weight reduction, even though the St. Regis was a full-size car. The A38 police package was becoming closer to a "towing" package. In fact, the exact police suspension, including a power steering oil cooler and firm-feel police power steering, was available on retail cars. It was called the Open Road Handling Package. As a reminder that big blocks were now gone, the 140-mile-per-hour certified and calibrated police speedometer only went to 120 miles per hour for 1979.

The El Dorado County Sheriff's Department's markings are on this 1979 Dodge St. Regis. Many Californians from the San Francisco Bay area and Sacramento travel through this beautiful county en route to Lake Tahoe. Most motorists are so focused on the lake, they don't even know they are in El Dorado County, unless, of course, they make a traffic infraction. If that happens, this white-over-brown St. Regis will become very memorable. With the contrasting color scheme, the sole purpose of this St. Regis is traffic enforcement. The emergency lights include a red rotator and twin three-lamp clusters of forward-facing continuous red, rear-facing flashing amber and side-facing alley lights.

A different emergency-light arrangement than other BPD Dodges marks this 1979 Dodge St. Regis with the Burlingame (California) Police. This St. Regis sports twin blue rotators along with the forward-facing continuous red and the rear-facing flashing amber. The wheelbase on these R-body cruisers was 118.5 inches. With the 195-horsepower Federal emissions version of the 360-ci four-barrel V-8, these Dodges accelerated to 60 miles per hour in 10.1 seconds according to Michigan State Police testing. The 190-horsepower California emissions version took 11.3 seconds, according to the California Highway Patrol.

Notice the rear view of the 1979 Dodge St. Regis with the Burlingame (California) Police. The roof bears two oversize blue rotators and two sets of rear-facing amber flashers and front-facing red lights. With the California-spec 190-horsepower, 360-ci four-barrel V-8, the St. Regis accelerates to 100 miles per hour in 34.4 seconds and has a top speed of 117.5 miles per hour. With the Federal-spec 195-horsepower, 360-ci four-barrel V-8, the St. Regis hits 100 miles per hour in 30.2 seconds and has a top speed of 122.9 miles per hour. This was the highest-performing four-door sedan in 1979.

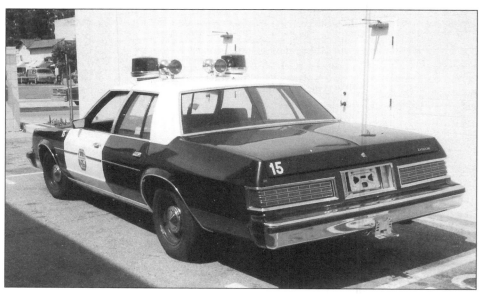

The Independence (Ohio) Police in the small, southeast suburb of Cleveland used this 1979 Chrysler Newport on the job. Along with the Dodge St. Regis, the Newport was available with a 318-ci V-8 or a 360-ci V-8. The 225-ci slant six used in the Dodge Aspen and Plymouth Volare was not available in the St. Regis and Newport. This all-blue Newport has a blue and gold door shield with a white liberty bell. The clear-lens lightbar has red and blue flashers, red and blue rotators, and a white center rotator for good measure. The Buckeye State police car has red and blue deck lights. This was one of the few times in history that a Chrysler-marque vehicle came with the police package.

The Macedonia Police in north central Ohio made use of this all-white 1979 Chrysler Newport. A red and blue Twin-sonic tops the roof and the door shield is gold, white, and blue. The front and rear fenders have blue lettering. With the 195-horsepower, 360-ci four-barrel V-8, the Newport hit 60 miles per hour in 10.2 seconds, 100 miles per hour in 31.5 seconds, and has a top speed of 121.3 miles per hour. For 1979, that was just about as much vehicle performance as any police car offered. Traveling around a 1.63-mile road-racing course with high-speed and low-speed corners and straightaway speeds of 90 miles per hour, the 360-ci Newport was 2 seconds faster than the 350-ci Chevrolet Impala and 4 seconds faster than the 351-ci Ford LTD.

The Tennessee Highway Patrol used this 1979 Chrysler Newport. The vehicle colors include a black hood, roof, and trunk over a cream/tan body. The police markings include the bold fender and front-door lettering and the seal of the state. A close inspection of the black background around the fender lettering shows that it is in the shape of the State of Tennessee. This cruiser is fitted with an all-blue strobe light-bar. Blue strobes work so much better than red ones that most of the Deep South uses them. This was the THP's first year for an enclosed lightbar and its first year for the use of strobe lights.

This is the 1979 Chrysler Newport on the job with the Philadelphia (Pennsylvania) Police. The white-over-blue cruiser has vented, dog-dish hubcaps. Lots of police Newports continued the upscale theme by using full-dress wheel covers. Blue wheels would have improved the looks of this cruiser. The Twinsonic has red and blue lenses and the siren speaker screen has a small, white-on-blue decal that reads, "Police." These large Chryslers were extremely popular among police officers from many city, county, and state agencies. This was the last year for a Newport police car.

The Virginia State Police Department is just one of the state police departments and highway patrols to use the 1979 Chrysler Newport. This Old Dominion State cruiser is deep blue over a gray body including gray wheels. This cruiser used a single red rotator. They transitioned to a single blue rotator in the 1980s. Given the choice of a 318-ci two-barrel V-8 and a 360-ci four-barrel V-8, the state agencies all went for the bigger engine. Even then, under the best conditions with slick-top squad cars and no spotlights, the top speed was still under 125 miles per hour. That was a culture shock from 1978.

The Texas Highway Patrol used this white-over-black Chrysler Newport. The big Chrysler has a red-and-blue Visibar and a single A-pillar spotlight. Genuine, Chrysler-marque, police-package vehicles were rare. The short list includes the 1961 to 1964 Newport, the 1976 Newport, this 1979 Newport, and the 1981 Le Baron. In every single case, a Chrysler-marque car was pushed into police service because of a shortcoming somewhere in the Dodge or Plymouth lineup. For 1979, a long-wheelbase Dodge was available (the St. Regis), but there was nothing comparable in the Plymouth fleet. This 360-ci four-barrel-powered Newport had a top speed of 121.3 miles per hour.

The Cuyahoga County (Ohio) Sheriff's Department operated this 1979 Chrysler Newport. The cruiser has a white roof over a black body with gold lettering and a gold and blue five-point star. This Greater Cleveland patrol car has an all-red Twinsonic fitted with two forward-facing spotlights used as takedown lights. The Newport and the Dodge St. Regis were similar in appearance, especially with the St. Regis' retractable headlight covers down. The Newport had twin signals under the headlights, while the St. Regis had turn signals that wrap around the fender. Of course, with the retractable covers over the headlamps, the St. Regis was easy to spot. The white roof over black body was the rule of Buckeye State county cars. However, some county cruisers also had white doors.

A Dodge promotional photo features a Scottsdale (Arizona) police officer, complete with riot helmet, along with his 1979 Dodge Aspen. The Aspen and the Plymouth Volare were built on a 112.7-inch chassis and used the soon-to-be controversial transverse torsion-bar front suspension. This was basically the same rolling chassis as the one used by the Dodge Diplomat and Plymouth Gran Fury through 1989. The A38 police-package Aspen and Volare were available with three powerplants: the 100-horsepower, 225-ci slant six; the 135-horsepower, 318-ci V-8; and the 195-horsepower, 360-ci four-barrel V-8. These 195-horsepower F-body cruisers were fast. The 0- to 100-mile-per-hour time was 2 full seconds faster than the 1978 440-ci-powered Fury. The 360-ci Aspen and Volare easily outran the 350-ci Chevrolet Malibu.

In 1979, the Missouri State Highway Patrol drove a mixed fleet of Chryslers and the Buick LeSabre such as the one pictured here. The police-package Buick was powered by a 155-horsepower, 350-ci V-8. This made the 115.9-inch-wheelbase Buick the slowest of all the "full-size" four-door sedans. It took a sluggish 46.4 seconds to reach 100 miles per hour and had a top speed of 110 miles per hour. In comparison, the 195-horsepower, 360-ci-powered Chrysler Newport, also used by the MSHP, hit 100 miles per hour in 31.5 seconds and had a top speed of 121 miles per hour. The Michigan State Police Department, in fact, disqualified the 1978 version of the LeSabre during its first year of testing. Note the new-style Aerodynic lightbar and the red unit numbers against a white background on the roof.

An Indiana State police trooper is shown ready to roll in his all-white 1979 Chevrolet Impala. This 116-inch four-door sedan sports a Visibar light rack with twin four-bulb rotators under red globes and an electronic siren. The door shield has white letters on a blue background over a gold "V." The 1977 and 1978 model years were rough on Chevrolet. Ford and Chrysler Corp. had big-block engines, but Chevrolet did not. Instead it tweaked its 350-ci "mouse" motor. The 170-horsepower V-8 outran the Fords in 1979, but was not enough for the 195-horsepower, 360-ci Mopar mill. That changed in 1982 when Chrysler dropped the 360-ci V-8. What Chevrolet learned in the late 1970s about small-block police engines paid off in the early 1980s. By the mid-1980s, Chevrolet was the car to beat, and it stayed that way until after 1996.

Chapter Nine
1980-1984

The 1980s were the single most turbulent and frustrating decade in the entire history of police cars. The 1980s hit absolute lows from sagging frames on many Dodge Diplomat models to 120-mile-per-hour top-speed ceilings from full-size police sedans. On the other hand, the 1980s also attained absolute highs, such as the 1982 special-service package Ford Mustang and the 1984 police-package, fuel-injected Ford (baby) LTD. The decade saw a changing of the guard among police car makes. Dodge was the police car sales leader in the early 1980s, thanks to the low-cost, but well-performing Diplomat. By 1986, Chevrolet took control of the market with the Caprice and held market dominance until the early 1990s.

When the 1980s drew to a close, Dodge and Plymouth, legends of performance and durability, exited the police market and abandoned their rear-wheel-drive sedan platform. From 1969 to 1978, Plymouth had ruled the police market, after which Dodge took over and dominated until 1985. Nevertheless, for all the success Mopar police cars enjoyed over the previous decade, it wasn't enough to propel them into the 1990s. The turbulent 1980s ended an era of police car.

The 1980s also started off with a huge controversy, and the 1980 model year will always be characterized as the "year of the dog." In 1980, the police package was available for the 118.5-inch-wheelbase, R-body Dodge St. Regis and Plymouth Gran Fury. The two engine options, the 318-ci V-8 and the 360-ci V-8, were available everywhere except California. The four-barrel version of the 318-ci V-8 was the only Chrysler Corporation

The 1980 model year was the "year of the dog" in California. The only Mopar V-8 certified by the California Air Resources Board (CARB) to power this Dodge St. Regis was the 155-horsepower, 318-ci V-8. CHP traffic officers soon complained they were being outrun by VW Beetles, the top speed on mountain grades was just 65 miles per hour, the cars were too slow to pace speeders, merge into traffic, or push stalled vehicles out of the traffic lane. "The car couldn't catch its own shadow, let alone a speeder on a mountain grade," according to officers suffering from "big-block withdrawal." The decision to fix the problem was three-fold. First, sell off as many cars as possible, prompting the *Los Angeles Times* headline, "CHP Unloading Its Dog Cars, 900 New Vehicles Too Slow to Catch Speeders." Second, put the cars in high-mileage patrols to hit the 70,000-mile retirement level as soon as possible. Third, replace the muffler, not the catalytic converter, with a straight pipe and install a B&M shift kit with a recalibrated valve body for higher and firmer shifts.

V-8 to be certified by the California Air Resources Board. The 318-ci-powered St. Regis, used by the California Highway Patrol, was indeed slow, although traffic officers were not slow to react to the cars' disappointing performance. In addition, the Los Angeles Times called the CHP cars "dogs" in a headline. The 1980 Chrysler Corporation police package was also available for the Dodge Aspen and Plymouth Volare. With the 360-ci engine, these were the fastest police cars on the road, but the car's shorter, 112.7-inch wheelbase was viewed as a drawback. Oddly enough, the Diplomat and the Gran Fury dominated the city, county, and state police departments during the 1980s and also had the same 112.7-inch wheelbase. Suddenly, there were no true "long"-wheelbase cars left. Because police agencies expressed so much interest in the 105.5- to 112.7-inch-wheelbase mid-size cars, the Michigan State Police Department established a separate test protocol for these vehicles. Of the mid-size cars, the 350-ci Malibu had the best overall performance, followed by the 360-ci Aspen, while the 318-ci Aspen and the 255-ci Fairmont were at the lower end of the spectrum. In 1981, Chrysler Corporation introduced its 112.7-inch M-body police cars—the Dodge Diplomat and Chrysler LeBaron. From 1982 to 1989, these M-body cruisers were the Dodge Diplomat and the Plymouth Gran Fury. These cars solved some performance problems, and caused other fleet-maintenance problems. These two models were America's police cars for the 1980s. The Diplomat led the police market from 1980 to 1985.

The 1981 Dodge Diplomat and Chrysler LeBaron were available with either 225-ci slant six or 318-ci V-8 engines. The Diplomat, the LeBaron, and later the M-bodied Gran Fury were never available with the 360-ci V-8. These M-bodies were never equipped with the four-speed automatic or fuel injection, even though police-fleet managers started the decade demanding fuel-injected engines.

Chrysler Corporation's lack of support makes the Diplomat one of the most remarkable police cars ever. The Diplomat, LeBaron, and Gran Fury (M) contained the 318-ci V-8 (the smallest V-8 in a full-size police car, fed by a carburetor, and bolted to a three-speed non-overdrive automatic), and it outperformed the fuel-injected, 350-ci and 351-ci engines and four-speed automatics from Chevrolet and Ford.

The 318-ci Diplomat was the performance leader for the first half of the decade, even against the highly developed and more advanced powertrains in the late 1980s. The Diplomat and Gran Fury out-accelerated or outbraked their competitors. The M-bodies would have the highest top speed or best ergonomics one year, then the next they would have the best road-racing course performance or fuel economy.

As long as the Diplomat and Gran Fury were around, a police-car manufacturer never swept all six of the Michigan State Police patrol vehicle test phases. The year after the Diplomat and Gran Fury were discontinued, the Chevrolet Caprice captured all six MSP tests.

The M-body saga began in 1981, and in an odd twist Chrysler Corporation elected to run its LeBaron as a police-package car instead of using a Plymouth nameplate for the 112.7-inch platform. The LeBaron was received as well as the Diplomat, and as well as the 1979 Chrysler Newport, but it was the last Chrysler-marque police-package sedan. The police package was available for the 118.5-inch, R-body Dodge St. Regis and R-bodied Plymouth Gran Fury fitted with 318-ci V-8 only. These were extremely comfortable and roomy urban patrol cars. For police duties where a 318-ci-powered long-wheelbase car worked, the St. Regis and Gran Fury (R) were very popular cars!

Chevrolet offered the 116-inch Impala and the 108.1-inch Malibu for 1981. Of the two Bowtie police cruisers, the Malibu 9C1 was much more competitive among the mid-size cars than

Unlike some traffic officers in California, the rest of the country loved the 1980 Dodge St. Regis. This all-white North Dakota State Patrol cruiser with an all-red Aerodynic lightbar is powered by the 185-horsepower, 360-ci four-barrel V-8. This potent mill pushed the 118.5-inch four-door sedan to 60 miles per hour in 11.5 seconds and a top speed of 123 miles per hour. By 1970 and 1990 standards, that was slow. But by 1980 standards, these R-body Mopars were the fastest full-size police cars on the road. The 360-ci St. Regis and Plymouth Gran Fury had the highest top speed of any American-built sedan in 1980. Only the L82 Chevrolet Corvette was faster. The Dodge St. Regis is easily identified by the clear, hide-away headlight covers, borrowed from the Dodge Magnum and last seen on the 1977 Dodge Royal Monaco.

Most city and county police officers liked the 1980 Dodge St. Regis, even those in California. This all-white Monterey County (California) Sheriff's Department unit has a brown body stripe, green-and-gold six-point star, and red/blue Twinsonic lightbar. The star also appears on the trunk. Older, solid-tan cruisers are in the background. The St. Regis was roomy, comfortable, and made a great office. The long-wheelbase R-body rode well, had excellent brakes, and, thanks to longitudinal torsion bars, had great high-speed stability. The 155-horsepower, 318-ci four-barrel V-8-powered St. Regis took 13.1 seconds to reach 60 miles per hour and had a top speed of 115 miles per hour. This was the only engine available in California versions of the St. Regis and Plymouth Gran Fury. Note the retracted headlamp covers.

Here's a 1980 Plymouth Gran Fury with the Miami (Florida) Police. Note the prisoner cage and the old-style red/blue Visibar lightbar. For 1980, the police package transferred from the Chrysler Newport to the Plymouth Gran Fury. A Chrysler-marque police car would return for 1981. This R-body Gran Fury shared the same 118.5-inch platform as the Dodge St. Regis. In spite of the whining from West Coast traffic officers, in a 1992 nationwide survey, the 1979 to 1981 Plymouth Gran Fury and Dodge St. Regis were voted "The Best Mopar Squad Cars Ever." In the other 49 States, the Gran Fury and St. Regis were available with the 120-horsepower, 318-ci two-barrel V-8; the 155-horsepower, 318-ci four-barrel V-8; and the 185-horsepower, 360-ci four-barrel V-8. The 318-ci engine made for an entirely successful urban patrol car. For pursuit-class police work, however, the 360-ci engine was needed.

This 1980 Ohio State Highway Patrol Plymouth Gran Fury is powered by the 185-horsepower, 360-ci four-barrel V-8. This all-white cruiser is marked with the famous winged tire, gold lettering, and a red/red lightbar. In 1980, four 360-ci V-8s existed: the 185-horsepower, federal emissions passenger-car version; the 180-horsepower, federal emissions van engine; the 170-horsepower, California emissions van engine; and the 190-horsepower, Canadian version. The 360-ci engine powering squad cars used by the Royal Canadian Mounted Police, the Ontario Provincial Police, and the Metro Toronto Police had higher compression than the U.S. version and was not required to use a catalytic converter. This was the last year a 360-ci engine was used in police cars. The largest Mopar police engine after 1980 was the 318-ci small-block V-8.

the Impala was among full-size cars. The Malibu won both the Los Angeles County Sheriff's Department's police-car tests and the Michigan State Police Department's tests of mid-size cars. The Malibu picked up where the Nova left off and continued that pace.

Ford fielded two police cars, the 114.4-inch full-size LTD and the 105.5-inch Fairmont. The big drivetrain news from Ford was the first four-speed automatic overdrive transmission to be used in a police-package car. The full-size LTD came standard with this four-speed transmission and lockup torque converter, which was two years ahead of Chevrolet.

The 1982 model year is famous for one car: the Mustang. Ford offered a "severe" service package for the pony car—a car that chased Porsches for a living.

Frustrated by two years of slow Enforcement-class vehicles, the CHP, armed with the results of its 1979 Special Purpose Vehicle Study, set out to find a good, old-fashioned pursuit car. They started by asking the question, "What is the fastest domestic-made car in America?" It was the 157-horsepower, 302-ci two-barrel Ford Mustang GL, which actually had a higher top speed than the Corvette. The CHP built its pursuit-class specs around the Mustang and Camaro Z28. The Mustang underbid the Camaro, and the rest is police pursuit–car history. The 1982 Mustang came to the rescue in law enforcement's darkest hour, and it became the darling of the police fleet for the rest of the decade!

For 1982, Chrysler offered the first-ever, front-drive police-type vehicles—the Dodge Aries K and Plymouth Reliant K. With a 99.9-inch wheelbase, these were the smallest and most fuel-efficient police cars ever built by Chrysler. These front-drive, four-cylinder "scout package" cars were not accepted by law-enforcement personnel. Law-enforcement agencies yearned for a fuel-injected, 360-ci V-8 118.5-inch, Dodge St. Regis. And what did they get? A front-drive, four-cylinder car that would fit in the trunk of the St. Regis. The real police cars from Chrysler Corporation were the 112.7-inch, M-body, Dodge Diplomat and Plymouth Gran Fury (M). These were the full-size police sedans to beat, and in 1982, Dodge was the number one make of police car.

Chrysler Corporation learned a very valuable lesson from 1982: that police-pursuit driving is extremely hard on front-wheel-drive cars. Chevrolet and Ford would have to learn the same lesson. To its credit, Ford simply backed away from the front-wheel-drive police business after its experience with the front-wheel-drive police-package Taurus. In 1983, Chrysler re-released its K-cars. They found out that even for the lightest-duty police work, the K-cars required a heavier-duty suspension, bigger brakes, better steering, more horsepower, and a change in final drive ratio. Meanwhile, Chrysler also offered the Dodge Diplomat and Plymouth Gran Fury with the 225-ci slant-six engine for maximum economy, the 318-ci two-barrel V-8 for economy and performance and the 318-ci four-barrel V-8 for the best performance. The M-bodies were equipped with the four-barrel carbs and outperformed all makes of police sedan. It was the last year for the 225-ci slant-six engine, and from 1984 on, the Diplomat and Gran Fury were powered by one of the two versions of the 318-ci V-8.

Chrysler Corporation established clear evidence that its focus was changing from V-8-powered, rear-drive cars to four-cylinder, front-drive cars. By the end of 1983, Chrysler dropped the fuel-injected 318-ci V-8 that had been developed for the M-body Imperial. Chrysler had the first fuel-injected V-8 suitable for a police car two years before Ford and four years before Chevrolet, but cops never saw it, even though the major police-fleet managers were in relentless pursuit of such an engine.

Despite these developments, Dodge was the king of the police-car market, selling more police-package cars than any other marque.

In 1983, Ford debuted its fuel-injected 302-ci V-8! Fuel injection increases the torque and flattens the horsepower and torque curves compared to a carbureted engine. It also means the engine is much more responsive throughout the rpm range.

The Ford police package was based on the full-size LTD and the compact Fairmont. The two police engines for the LTD were the newly injected 302-ci V-8 and the 351-ci Windsor HO V-8, and this powertrain combination remained essentially unchanged through 1991. This was the first year since 1950 that the full-size Ford police car was restricted to a four-door sedan.

The awesome 5.0-liter Mustang pursuit-car's performance reputation had spread across the country. Eleven states had adopted the special-service Mustang as a special traffic-enforcement vehicle. By 1991, The 5.0-liter Mustang pursuit car was used by at least 35 state police and highway patrols, and well over 100 major sheriffs' departments and county patrols. For 1983, the 302-ci V-8 got a four-barrel carb.

The big Chevrolet police-car news in 1983 was its first four-speed overdrive automatic, complete with lockup torque converter.

For 1980, the Chevrolet Impala, like this Madera (California) Police cruiser was restyled with a new grille, lower hood, and raised rear deck. The 1980 Impala was 100 pounds lighter, thanks to the increased use of aluminum and thinner sections of high-strength steel. New for 1980 was a 229-ci V-6 engine, which boasted an EPA city rating of 18 miles per gallon. In mid-year, a "special economy equipment package" for this new V-6 made the Impala the first full-size, gasoline-powered American sedan to reach an EPA city rating of 20 miles per gallon. With the new-for-1980 25-gallon gas tank, the Impala had a 500-mile cruising range. A busy sheriff's department will travel that many miles in just two shifts! This 115-horsepower, 3.8-liter engine was the first V-6 used in the full-size Chevrolet. However, the only Chevrolet police engine certified for California was the 155-horsepower, 305-ci V-8.

Here's a 1980 Lisle (Illinois) Police Dodge Aspen. In 1980, the A38 police package was available on the Aspen and on the Plymouth Volare. The two mid-size cars shared the same 112.7-inch wheelbase and all body panels. In fact, only the chrome bars on the front parking lights identify this as a Dodge instead of Plymouth. The mid-size Mopars were available with all four 225-ci, 318-ci, and 360-ci police engines, except in California where the Aspen and Volare came with either the 225-ci slant six or the 318-ci four-barrel V-8. The 360-ci-powered Aspen reached 60 miles per hour in 10.9 seconds making it the quickest accelerating police car of 1980. It had a top speed of 122 miles per hour.

In 1980, the Nevada Highway Patrol used the Chevrolet Impala powered by a 165-horsepower, 350-ci V-8. Oddly, this was the slowest of all the makes of full-size cruisers! Even with a slick top, the 350-ci Impala took a leisurely 12.9 seconds to hit 60 miles per hour and had a top speed of just 110 miles per hour. It was actually disqualified by the Michigan State Police Department for its slow acceleration! It was quite unlike the NHP to pick such a car. This Silver State 116-inch cruiser is silver over blue with silver wheels, a gold-and-blue seven-point star, gold fender and trunk lettering, and white diagonal door stripes. It is unlikely the NHP traffic officers gave the CHP traffic officers much sympathy about their slow Dodges. More likely were one-upmanship horror stories about how slow each other's patrol car was.

This 1980 Ford LTD "S" is with the City of Oakland (California) Police Services. The Bay-area cruiser is white over tan with a tan and brown door shield and a red/blue Aerodynic. The Ford police package was available on the fleet-oriented LTD "S" with single headlights per side and the baseline LTD with dual headlights per side. All models shared the same 114.4-inch wheelbase. The powerplants included the 130-horsepower, 302-ci V-8 and 140-horsepower and 172-horsepower versions of the 351-ci Windsor V-8. The only Ford engine certified for use in California was the 140-horsepower V-8. The 172-horsepower engine used in the other 49 states pushed the big Ford to 60 miles per hour in 11.5 seconds and produced a top speed of 121 miles per hour. The 1980 model year was the first for the High Output (HO) version of the 351 Windsor, which included a high-lift, long-duration cam and dual exhaust.

Here's a sharp-looking 1980 Chevrolet Malibu with the Brisbane (California) Police. While the Chevrolet Impala continued to struggle, the Malibu was extremely competitive. The 155-horsepower, 305-ci-powered Malibu captured the Los Angeles County Sheriff contract for the second year in a row. Against a different mix of cars, the Malibu came in second overall during Michigan State Police Department tests of mid-size cars and was clearly the fastest mid-size car around the road-racing course. The 9C1 Malibu was available with the 229c-i V-6, 305-ci V-8, and 350-ci V-8. The two V-8s pushed the 108.1-inch wheelbase Malibu to 60 miles per hour between 12.3 and 12.8 seconds with top speeds from 111 to 113 miles per hour. This Bay-area Brisbane cruiser is cream in color with a brown body stripe.

However, this package was restricted to the 350-ci-powered Impala. In 1984, the Chrysler Corporation AHB police package was available for the 112.7-inch-wheelbase Dodge Diplomat and Plymouth Gran Fury and also for the 100.3-inch Dodge Aries K and Plymouth Reliant K. The V-8-powered, rear-drive cars were the M-body Dodge Diplomat, Plymouth Gran Fury, and Chrysler Fifth Avenue. The police package was only available for the Dodge and Plymouth, and the full-size cars were powered by the 318-ci V-8, while the compact cars were available with a 2.2-liter or 2.6-liter four.

The Diplomat and Gran Fury four-barrel cars had used the 727 "big-block" TorqueFlite automatic from 1981 through 1983. For 1984, the four-barrel cars got a beefed-up version of the 904 "small-block" transmission called the 999. The 727 used close-ratio gear sets while the 999 used wide-ratio gear sets. The wide-ratio, three-speed transmission improved acceleration without any effect on fuel economy. The small-block trans could handle any torque produced by the small-block V-8 even with a four-barrel carb. It was no surprise that Dodge remained the number one brand of police car in 1984.

Chevrolet provided a front-wheel-drive car for 1984. The 1984 Celebrity replaced the 1983 Malibu as Chevrolet's

For 1980, the Ford Fairmont, like this Belmont, California, Police patroller, was available with the formal police package. This 105.5-inch-wheelbase sedan was powered by either the 200-ci six or the brand-new 255-ci V-8. The new V-8 was a de-bored version of the 302-ci small block. The goal was to provide the ever-elusive V-8 performance along with maximum fuel economy. The 119-horsepower, 255-ci V-8 had the slowest acceleration of any V-8-powered mid-size police car. It took 15.9 seconds to reach 60 miles per hour. The 90-horsepower, 225-ci slant-six-powered Aspen was faster. While the V-8 Fairmont ran the quarter mile in the mid-20 second range, it was able to stumble and wheeze up to a top speed of 112 miles per hour.

mid-size car, and the 104.9-inch Celebrity was powered by a 2.8-liter V-6.

In 1984, Ford released a new mid-size car, the 105.5-inch LTD, not to be confused with the full-size, 114.4-inch LTD Crown Victoria. California cops gave the smaller Ford the name "Baby LTD," and the name stuck. The Baby LTD was built on the same platform as the Fairmont, but the two cars could not have been more different. The LTD, essentially a stretched Mustang with four doors, performed like a slightly longer Mustang. With the same fuel-injected, 302-ci HO V-8 used in the Mustang, the Baby LTD was the nation's hottest mid-size sedan. The injected LTD exactly split the differences in overall performance between the Mustang pursuit car and all of the full-size police sedans. The LTD had four doors, and most of the space of a full-size sedan, yet ran almost like a pursuit pony car.

The Mustang was available with either a fuel-injected 302-ci V-8 or a four-barrel version of the same High Output engine. The injected engine came only with the four-speed automatic, while the four-barrel engine came with the five-speed stick only. For the next two years, the 302-ci V-8 was available in both versions, and each year the four-barrel engine was much more powerful. It was eventually replaced by "sequential" fuel injection.

The Indiana State Police Department was among the first to adopt the 1981 Dodge Diplomat in its first year with the A38 police package. For 1981, with the 360-ci V-8 no longer available, the 165-horsepower, 318-ci four-barrel V-8 became Dodge's most powerful police engine. The four-barrel version used the heads from the 360-ci V-8 with its larger valves and passages. It also used the 360-ci intake manifold and carburetor. These, along with a larger-diameter single exhaust, account for the 35 horsepower difference between the 318-ci two-barrel engine and the 318-ci four-barrel engine. The 165-horsepower V-8 pushed the Diplomat to 60 miles per hour in 12.8 seconds and a top speed of 116 miles per hour. This all-white ISP Diplomat has a twin red-globe Visibar. The door emblem has white letters against a blue shield with a gold "V" and gold state seal.

Long known as having the hottest Dodges in the country, and having taken a bunch of criticism from the press, from politicians, and from its own patrolmen over its 1980 cars, the CHP resolved that its 1981 cars were going to be faster. This Dodge Diplomat had won the bid, but the CHP insisted on confirming the performance. In February 1981, all three of the CARB-approved California police cars eligible to compete met at the Mather Air Force Base for some high-stakes drag racing. It was the 318-ci Dodge Diplomat versus the 350-ci Chevrolet Malibu versus the 351-ci Ford LTD. The winner was sure to influence CHP purchases for years to come. The Malibu was fastest to 60 miles per hour and to 100 miles per hour and the LTD had the highest top speed. All three cars met the CHP standard of performance. The Diplomat had vindicated the good name of Dodge in its very first year as a police package.

In 1981, the Dodge police package was available on the 118.5-inch St. Regis and on the 112.7-inch Diplomat. Both cars were available with the 90-horsepower, 225-ci slant six and the 165-horsepower, 318-ci four-barrel V-8. Cars outside California were also powered by the 130-horsepower, 318-ci two-barrel V-8. The 318-ci-powered St. Regis, like this San Carlos (California) Police patroller actually made a good urban police car for the times. The four-barrel version pushed the St. Regis to 60 miles per hour in 13.1 seconds and to a top speed of 115 miles per hour. This was almost as fast as the Diplomat with the same engine, yet the St. Regis was much roomier and rode much better. This all-white San Carlos unit is sporting a red/blue Aerodynic. Note the chromed pusher bars and roof-mounted spotlight.

This 1981 Dodge St. Regis is a traffic-enforcement unit with the Campbell (California) Police. The California Vehicle Code required the color of the roof and doors on traffic cars to contrast with the body color. Campbell used a cream-colored roof and doors with a tan body. Pretty, but not much of a contrast! This Orchard City patroller has a tan seven-point star with the city seal and brown car numbers. This unit sports a red/blue Aerodynic lightbar. Note the older Plymouth Volare in the background with a red/blue Twinsonic. This Campbell cruiser was powered by the 165-horsepower, 318-ci four-barrel V-8. Small-block V-8s in long-wheelbase police cars had served thousands of urban police departments well for decades.

A number of state police and highway patrols across the country continued to use the long-wheelbase 1981 Plymouth Gran Fury even though the potent 360-ci V-8 was no longer available. This is a Louisiana State Police cruiser. The Arizona Highway Patrol also used the full-size, 318-ci-powered Gran Fury, as did the Virginia State Police and the Michigan State Police. Not even an underpowered police car will keep a good trooper down. The fender markings on this LSP cruiser are notable. The lightning bolt through the state outline means this trooper recovered a stolen car and caught the thief. The lightning bolt by itself means the trooper got either the car or the thief. The small-block engine just made this decorated trooper try harder! The LSP Gran Fury is all-white with red lettering, a red lightbar, and a blue state shield.

In 1981, Plymouth was back with a full-size police car, the R-body Gran Fury. The 118.5-inch R-body had been a Chrysler and Dodge police car in 1979 and a Dodge and Plymouth police car in 1980. This was the last year for the R-body platform. After 1981, the largest Mopar squad car would be the 112.7-inch M-body Dodge Diplomat and Plymouth Gran Fury. Be careful! A great deal of difference exists between the 1981 Gran Fury (R) and the 1982 Gran Fury (M). This all-white Gran Fury is a patroller with the Reno (Nevada) Police. It has a red/blue Aerodynic, dash-mounted shotgun and twin, A-pillar spotlights. For 1981, all Mopar police cars had lock-up torque converters, which improved the gas mileage under urban conditions by 4 percent and during rural and interstate driving by 6 percent.

New for 1981 was a Chrysler-marque police car, the M-body LeBaron. The LeBaron and Dodge Diplomat shared the same powertrains and 112.7-inch chassis. This cruiser is with the Mesquite Police, just east of Dallas. The unit has a unique paint scheme: a tan hood, roof, and trunk over a white car with brown lettering and a brown door seal. This Mesquite cop car sports a red/blue Aerodynic. The first Chrysler-marque police car was the 1961 Newport Enforcer. The most recent one was the 1979 R-body Newport. The 1981 LeBaron was the last of the Chrysler-marque police-package cars.

In 1981, the Nevada Highway Patrol ran the Chrysler LeBaron. This sharp-looking Silver State cruiser has a silver roof with an all-red Aerodynic over a deep-blue body with gold lettering, a gold star, and white stripes. The slot-ventilated heavy-duty steel wheels are clear in this shot. Note the dash-mounted shotgun. A white cloth is frequently placed over the dash-mounted radar antenna in the summer to prevent the sun from getting the unit too hot. Powered by the 165-horsepower, 318-ci four-barrel V-8, the LeBaron hit 60 miles per hour in 12.9 seconds and had a top speed of 115 miles per hour. Note the chromed front pusher bars. The tiny decal under the door shield reads "Department of Motor Vehicles." It used to read "For Official Use Only."

Here's an extra-sharp-looking 1981 Chrysler LeBaron with the New York City Police Department. What NYPD cop ever dreamed he would patrol the mean streets of the Big Apple in a genuine Chrysler? Note the red deck lights. This white-over-blue Radio Motor Patrol was powered by the 85-horsepower, 225-ci slant six. Contrary to popular belief, many big-city police departments use the smallest and most fuel-efficient engines. In densely populated cities the police cars are used like taxis, not pursuit cars. In New York City, only the Highway Patrol Bureau cars got the big engines and the four-barrel carbs. From 1974 to 1980, Chrysler Corporation warned police departments to disconnect the rear anti-sway bar if bias-ply tires were used. For 1981, Chrysler changed its approach: "The use of bias or bias-belted tires is NOT recommended."

In 1981, the Wisconsin State Patrol was privileged enough to get the Chrysler LeBaron as a general-issue patrol car. This WSP unit is white and blue with a red, white, and deep-blue door shield. The Visibar has twin red globes. The 318-ci, four-barrel-powered LeBaron ran extremely well during the annual Michigan State Police Department patrol vehicle tests. The LeBaron equaled or beat all the other makes of police car, including the larger Dodge and Plymouth cruisers. The Wisconsin State Patrol would drive the 112.7-inch LeBaron, Diplomat, and Gran Fury every year until the demise of the platform after the 1989 model year.

Here's a 1981 Ford LTD "S" with the Lee County (Florida) Sheriff's Department. Lee County includes Fort Myers and Cape Coral on the Gulf side. The police package was available for the dual headlight LTD "S" and the quad headlight LTD. The 1981 LTD "S" is easily identified as one of only two years with a solid front bumper, that is, grille slots, and the lack of a blue oval in the grille. The blue oval appeared in 1982. This sheriff's cruiser is all-white with a green body stripe, green lettering, and a gold five-point star. The lightbar has twin BLUE globes. The 114.4-inch police LTD was powered by the 130-horsepower, 302-ci V-8; the 145-horsepower, 351 Windsor; the 165-horsepower, 351 Windsor HO; and new for full-size cars in 1981, the 120-horsepower, 255-ci V-8.

The Chicago Police used the Ford LTD "S" in 1981. This all-white patroller has a blue body stripe, red lettering and numbering, and a MARS-brand lightbar with twin blue rotators and twin blue/red can lights. The 9000-series car number identifies this cruiser as being with the Patrol Division. As such, it probably was powered by the 130-horsepower, 302-ci V-8. The big driveline news for 1981 was the use of a four-speed automatic overdrive transmission (AOT) in all LTD police cars. Ford was two years ahead of Chevrolet with such a transmission. The Dodge, Plymouth, and Chrysler police cars never had a four-speed automatic, even though one that would fit was developed for light trucks. This four-speed AOT was a major drivetrain advancement for Ford.

In 1981, the Orlando, Florida, Police Department patrolled in the Ford Fairmont. This 105.5-inch-wheelbase police-package compact has a brown roof over a cream-colored body with a gold and brown door shield. The lightbar has blue and red lenses and an auxiliary takedown light mounted on top of the siren speaker. The Fairmont was available with an 88-horsepower, 140-ci SOHC four; an 88-horsepower, 200-ci six, and a 115-horsepower, 255-ci V-8. The new-for-1981 four-cylinder engine had the same horsepower as the six but much less torque. The V-8-powered Fairmont took 13.6 seconds to hit 60 miles per hour, while the six took an embarrassing 18.8 seconds. No one even wanted to test the four-cylinder version.

Here's a department-restored 1981 Haysville (Kansas) Police Chevrolet Impala. The four-door cruiser is all-white with a blue body stripe and door shield and an all-red Twinsonic. The 9C1 police-package Impala was available with the 110-horsepower, 229-ci V-6; the 155-horsepower, 305-ci V-8; and the 165-horsepower, 350-ci V-8. With the same horsepower as the previous year, the 350-ci Impala now did remarkably well at the Michigan State Police Department tests. It was the fastest full-size sedan to 100 miles per hour, had the most powerful brakes, highest ergonomic rating, and was the quickest around the road course. The Impala was the only full-size police car to get into the 18-second quarter-mile bracket. The Impala was starting to show the performance that would lead it to the top in just a few years.

The 1981 Chevrolet Malibu, such as this 9C1 police-package Palo Alto (California) Police unit, had to be considered the police car of the year. Powered by the 165-horsepower, 350-ci V-8, the Malibu won the Michigan State Police Department contract for mid-size police cars. Powered by the 155-horsepower, 305-ci V-8, the Malibu won the Los Angeles County Sheriff's Department contract. Two of the most important police departments in the country when it comes to police cars both pointed to the Malibu 9C1 as the best police car of 1981. While the 350-ci Malibu had a top speed of just 112 miles per hour, it ran the quarter mile in the low-18-second bracket. The Malibu was the fastest police car around the road-racing course at Michigan International Speedway and the flat track at the Los Angeles County Pomona Fairgrounds.

Red. Lots and lots of red. In fact, this 1981 Chrysler LeBaron has so much red it is difficult to associate it with law enforcement. Fire, yes. Police, no. The facts are, however, the color scheme for upstate New York sheriffs' departments are red over white. Red hoods, red trunks, red front doors, red rear doors, red and white lettering, twin red gumballs, and red and white clear-globe rotators. This LeBaron is with the Putnam County (New York) Sheriff's Department. The word from Big Apple cops is that these deputies are given a lot of grief about its color scheme when they drive to the city on official business.

"This Ford Chases Porsches for a Living." The most influential Ford police car of the 1980s, and one of the most influential of the century, is this 1982 California Highway Patrol Mustang. The performance of the Mustang forced cops to rethink the entire concept of a pursuit car. It was once thought that pursuit cars had to have an 122-inch wheelbase, weigh at least 3,800 pounds, and have at least a 380-ci multiple-carbureted big-block V-8 engine. The car that reversed all of this thinking had a 100.5-inch wheelbase, a weight of 2,970 pounds, and was powered by a two-barrel small-block V-8. Stung by low-performance Enforcement-class cars, the CHP wanted as fast a car as America made, period. The 157-horsepower, 302-ci two-barrel HO V-8 hit 60 miles per hour in 6.9 seconds and had a top speed of 128 miles per hour, which was 3 miles per hour faster than the Chevrolet Corvette! At $6,868.67, the Mustang GL outbid the Camaro Z28, and the rest is police car history.

This 1982 Gladstone (Missouri) Public Safety cruiser is based on the upscale LTD. The Ford police package was available on the fleet-oriented LTD "S" with dual headlights and on this mid-trim level LTD, identified by quad headlights. This cruiser is white with a wide yellow body stripe, black lettering, and red numbers. The full-size Ford was available in three power plants: the 122-horsepower, 255-ci V-8; the 132-horsepower, 302-ci V-8; and the 165-horsepower, 351 Windsor HO. For 1982, the standard-output 351-ci engine was discontinued for police and retail cars alike. The only remaining large-displacement engine was the High Output 351 Windsor. The 351 HO would last through 1991 when it and the 302-ci V-8 were both replaced by the 4.6-liter SOHC V-8.

Here's a 1982 Ford LTD "S" with the Oklahoma Highway Patrol. This cruiser is black and white with a red passenger-side spotlight and a red/white roof rotator. Note the OHP trademark extension of the white body trim under the C-pillar. The 1982 LTD "S" can be identified from the 1981 version by the blue oval on the driver's side of the grille. The 114.4-inch Ford with the 351-ci Windsor HO engine reached 60 miles per hour in 12.6 seconds and had a top speed of 116 miles per hour. The only transmission used in these full-size Fords was its excellent four-speed Automatic Overdrive. Note the front pusher bars.

Here's a well-equipped 1982 Ford LTD "S" with the Cross Plains (Wisconsin) Police. Cross Plains is near Madison. This cream-colored cruiser has a red/blue Aerodynic, twin red grille lights, and a red "Kojack" light on the dash. The proper name of the dash light is a Federal Signal "Fire Ball" introduced in 1955. This was the last year of the dual-headlight, low-cost, fleet-oriented LTD "S" model. After 1982, the full-size Ford had quad headlights. The emblem on the lower front quarter panel reads "Overdrive." The use of a four-speed transmission made it more likely than a three-speed that the engine would be inside its peak power band at any given time. As a result, the big Ford was the quickest full-size sedan around the road course during the Michigan State Police Department testing.

In 1982, the Los Angeles County Sheriff's Department briefly released its ban on cars with transverse torsion bar front suspensions. This 1982 Plymouth Gran Fury broke a long string of Chevrolet Malibu and Chevrolet Nova police cars dating back to 1975. This was the first year for the police-package M-body Gran Fury but the last year for the LASD to drive a Chrysler Corporation police sedan. The 1982 M-body Gran Fury replaced the 1981 M-body Chrysler LeBaron. The only V-8-powered, rear-drive car in the entire Plymouth Division was the Gran Fury. This same year, the Dodge Division had only the Diplomat and Mirada. In 1982, just 10 percent of Dodge and Plymouth passenger-car sales were rear-wheel drive. Less than 10 percent were V-8 powered. How long could this platform last? Until 1989.

In 1982, the Chrysler Corporation A38 police package was available on the two M-bodies, the Dodge Diplomat, and this new-for-1982 Plymouth Gran Fury used by the Idaho State Police. The ISP Gran Fury is white over black with a gold state-profile door shield and twin diagonal stripes running from the rear tires to the hood ornament. The wedge-shaped lightbar has all-blue lamps. The 112.7-inch M-body was the largest passenger car produced by Chrysler Corporation. Its wheelbase was quite short compared to the 114.3-inch Ford LTD and 116-inch Chevrolet Impala. Even still, the Gran Fury and Dodge Diplomat were rapidly adopted by the nation's state police and highway patrols. Everyone else followed the California Highway Patrol lead. The Plymouth Gran Fury and Dodge Diplomat became the city, county, and state police car of choice almost overnight.

This 1982 Dodge Diplomat has the square-jawed, all-business look for which the Mopar M-body police cars were legendary. This white-over-black Diplomat was used by the New Mexico State Police. The door markings include a gold shield in the exact shape of the troopers' badge and twin diagonal stripes used since the 1950s. This slick-top Dodge has twin red lights mounted on the pusher bars, a prisoner cage, and twin deck-mounted red flashers. The 165-horsepower, 318-ci four-barrel V-8 pushed the Diplomat to 60 miles per hour in 12.2 seconds, the fastest of any full-size cruiser. These cars had a top speed of 115 miles per hour. They ran the quarter mile in the low-19-second bracket, which was the fastest of any police-package sedan. Only the "severe service" Mustang 5.0-liter HO was faster. And it was a *lot* faster!

This 1982 Dodge Diplomat is with the Tulare (California) Police. Tulare is in central California in the San Joaquin Valley. This cruiser is black and white with an older-style red/blue Twinsonic. The newer Aerodynic is on cars in the background. The Tulare door shield is a gold eagle on a blue city seal. The big news for 1982 California cop cars was a change in California law that exempted emergency vehicles from state smog-control standards. This was due in part to the 1980 fiasco with the 318-ci-powered CHP St. Regis. The 1982 emergency vehicles were only required to meet federal emissions standards. Three engines were available for the 1982 Diplomat and Plymouth Gran Fury: the 90-horsepower, 225-ci slant six; the 130-horsepower, 318-ci two-barrel V-8; and the 165-horsepower, 318-ci four-barrel V-8.

The big news from Chrysler Corporation in 1982 was a light-duty "scout car" package for the Dodge Aries K and this Plymouth Reliant K. The K-car literally saved Chrysler Corporation from bankruptcy. The K-car, like this tan Federal Protective Service unit with an all-red lightbar, was the first attempt at a front-drive car for police work. With the K-car, Chrysler Corporation made a "no-looking-back" shift from rear-drive cars to front-drive cars. Not a single police or special service package front-drive sedan has been successful in the American police market. Chrysler's 1982 Kwaint Kop Kars were powered by either an 84-horsepower, 2.2-liter four or a 92-horsepower, 2.6-liter four. These 99.9-inch-wheelbase cars took 17 seconds to reach 60 miles per hour. Chrysler advertised the K-car as a six-passenger car with more legroom than the Ford LTD and more hip room than the Diplomat. Yeah, right.

This 1982 Ford Fairmont is with the Boca Raton (Florida) Police. Boca is north of Fort Lauderdale. The 105.5-inch compact cruiser is black and white with a blue and brown door shield, an all-blue lightbar, and white lettering. As in 1981, the Fairmont was available with a 140-ci four, 200-ci six, and 255-ci V-8. The V-8 Fairmont hit 60 miles per hour in 13.8 seconds and had a top speed of 107 miles per hour. New for 1982, the six and V-8 got lockup torque converters but still used the three-speed Select-Shift transmission. For the first time, the Michigan State Police Department tested the Fairmont with all three engines. Compared to the 200-ci six, the spunky, overhead-cam 140-ci four had much faster acceleration and a higher top speed! Note the padded rollbar and prisoner screen in this unit.

In 1982, for only the third time since 1956, a police car other than a Chrysler product was used by the California Highway Patrol, the 1982 Chevrolet Impala. The 9C1 police-package Impala would turn out to be a much tougher competitor to the police Diplomat in the 1980s than the Biscayne was to the Polara in the 1960s, or the Bel Air was to the Monaco in the 1970s. The powerplants for the 116-inch-wheelbase Impala were either the 110-horsepower, 229-ci V-6 or the 150-horsepower, 350-ci V-8. The 350-ci-powered Impala proved to be faster around a pursuit-oriented road-racing course than the best from Dodge, Plymouth, and Ford. Oddly enough, however, the 350-ci Impala had the lowest top speed of any full-size cruiser at just 108 miles per hour. It also had the slowest acceleration of the big four-door sedans. Not a peep from CHP traffic officers—they now had the 5.0-liter Mustang!

This 1982 Chevrolet Impala is on the job with the Tallahassee (Florida) Police. The full-size Chevrolet is all-white with a silver-over-blue body stripe, an all-blue lightbar, and a gold door shield. No, the 9C1 police package did not come from the factory with whitewall tires! By 1982, the unrest and changes among police-package cars had settled down. For the rest of the 1980s, the changes to all of the full-size police cars would be minor. For its part, the Impala would continue to be powered by the 350-ci V-8, get a four-speed overdrive transmission in 1983, and fuel-injection in 1989. In spite of this stability, the Impala would steadily improve while the other makes stood still. Chevrolet would capture the police market, fair and square, by the mid-1980s, and keep it for a decade.

New for 1982, the Chevrolet Malibu Classic, such as this North Platte (Nebraska) Police unit, was restyled with quad headlights. The new mid-size Malibu grille was so similar to the full-size Impala that speculation was again fueled that the Impala would be dropped. The Malibu Classic was available with either the 229-ci V-6 or the 305-ci V-8. The 108.1-inch Malibu Classic with the 305-ci V-8 was quicker to 60 miles per hour and faster around the Los Angeles County fairgrounds flat track than either the 105.5-inch, 255-ci-powered Ford Fairmont or the 112.7-inch, 318-ci-powered Plymouth Gran Fury. The Gran Fury, however, turned in a lower bid. During Michigan State Police Department testing, the 305-ci Malibu Classic hit 60 miles per hour in 13.3 seconds and had a top speed of 110 miles per hour.

In 1983, the Texas Highway Patrol used these slick-top Dodge Diplomats. The Lone Star State cruisers have a white hood, roof, and trunk over black doors and fenders with a gold outline of Texas as the door shield. On the dash is a traffic radar unit and antenna. These Texas DPS Diplomats were powered by the 165-horsepower, 318-ci four-barrel V-8. The 0- to 60-mile-per-hour time was 12.8 seconds while the top speed had climbed slightly to 119 miles per hour. The 318-ci four-barrel cars came with the close-ratio, big-block 727 TorqueFlite. The 225-ci slant six and 318-ci two-barrel cars used the wide-ratio, small-block 904 TorqueFlite. All of the V-8 powertrains included a lockup torque converter for the best fuel economy. The California Highway Patrol returned to the Diplomat for 1983. This was also the first year for the CHP to add a blue light to the package tray in addition to the red and amber lights. This happened first to the slick-top Diplomat and then to the Mustang.

West Virginia State Police trooper Mark Smith stands next to his 1983 Dodge Diplomat. This gold-over-blue cruiser sports a rare Whelen strobe lightbar with red, white, and blue lenses. From 1980 to 1983, the Dodge Diplomat and Plymouth Gran Fury were assembled in Windsor, Ontario, Canada. In 1983, production of these M-body Mopars moved to Fenton, Missouri, outside St. Louis. The rear-wheel-drive Diplomat and Gran Fury remained at Fenton until mid-1987 when production shifted to the former AMC plant in Kenosha, Wisconsin. The Diplomat and Gran Fury remained with a 112.7-inch wheelbase throughout the decade of their production. At the Michigan State Police Department patrol vehicle tests, the 318-ci four-barrel Mopars achieved the highest top speeds, up to 120 miles per hour, had the strongest brakes, and the best 0- to 100-mile-per-hour acceleration.

This 1983 Plymouth Gran Fury was used by the North Olmsted (Ohio) Police. The Gran Fury used by urban departments was often powered by the 225-ci slant six or the 318-ci two-barrel V-8. This was the last year for the slant six, introduced in 1960. If the 318-ci two-barrel-powered cars seemed a bit slow, the reason is the 2.24 to 1 rear axle ratio that came with these cars. The four-barrel cars had the 2.94 to 1 axle. The 2.24 ratio was the lowest ever used on a police car. The purpose was an ill-fated attempt to improve fuel economy. The facts are that cops actually got worse mileage with an axle such as this because they gave the car so much gas to get up to speed they negated any savings from the low axle ratio. In 1983, the Missouri State Highway Patrol, Michigan State Police, Oklahoma Highway Patrol, and the Highway Patrol Bureau with the New York City Police used the four-barrel-powered 1983 Gran Fury.

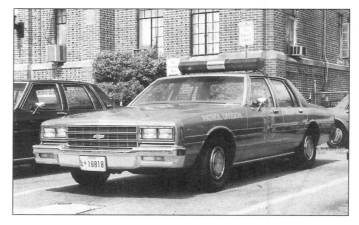

Here's a sharp-looking 1983 Chevrolet Impala with the Morgan Hills (Maryland) Police. The big news for 1983 full-size Bowtie cop cars was the "700R4" four-speed overdrive automatic with a lockup torque converter. This gave the 350-ci Impala the best EPA city and highway fuel ratings of any full-size police car with a pursuit-class engine. This was a major achievement for Chevrolet, given the way things were in the early 1980s. For example, in 1983, the Michigan State Police gave the fuel-economy rating as much weight in overall scoring as the lap times around the road-racing course. These two phases made up half the total score! The 155-horsepower, 350-ci Impala ran the quarter mile in 18.6 seconds. This was the quickest of any full-size cruiser.

For 1983, the Dodge Aries K and the Plymouth Reliant K, such as this Quebec Provincial Police unit, were greatly improved. The suspension was upgraded with stiffer front and rear sway bars and larger diameter shocks. The front disc and rear drum brakes had 32 percent more swept area. The "firm feel" rack-and-pinion steering was given a much quicker steering ratio. Horsepower on the 2.2-liter four-cylinder engine was boosted by 12 percent to 94 horsepower. The final drive ratio on the 2.6-liter four-cylinder cars was increased to 3.02 to 1, giving it better acceleration and throttle response. Powered by the 93-horsepower, 2.6-liter four, the 100.3-inch patroller reached 60 miles per hour in 15.5 seconds and had a top speed of 103 miles per hour. Don't laugh. It would outrun a 225-ci slant-six-powered Diplomat. The Contrôle Routier (truck enforcement) used twin reds as opposed to red and blue used by other branches. The door shield reads "Sûreté du Québec Police."

This 1983 Chevrolet Impala was used by the San Clemente (California) Police. This 116-inch cruiser is white with a broad blue body stripe and black fender letters and numbers. While the 350-ci V-8-powered Impala got the four-speed automatic, the Impala with the 229-ci V-6 used the three-speed Turbo Hydra-Matic. The full-size Impala had been available with a 250-ci six or a 229-ci V-6 since the downsizing for 1977. Many officers thought this 110-horsepower, V-6 engine was too small for the 3,713-pound Impala. The 1983 Michigan State Police tests confirmed this: 0 to 60 miles per hour in 17.4 seconds! The quarter mile in 21.5 seconds! The four-cylinder K-car was a dragster in comparison. The police Impala would be available with an urban-oriented police engine of 265 ci or less every year from 1977 to 1996 except 1991 to 1993.

This 1983 Chevrolet Malibu was used by the Fort Worth (Texas) Police. The four-door, 108.1-inch patroller is all-white with shadow-style, blue lettering. The light rack is a haphazard collection of cop gear randomly bolted in place! The rack has a red, four-bulb rotator in the center and twin blue lollipop lights. The siren speaker and the auxiliary takedown lights clearly look like afterthoughts. Ugh. In 1983, the Malibu was powered by either a 305-ci V-8 with the Turbo Hydra-Matic 350 trans or a 229-ci V-6 with the THM 250 trans. This was the final year for the mid-size Malibu. The 145-horsepower, 305-ci Malibu was quicker to 60 miles per hour than any other police- or special-service-package vehicle except the 350-ci Impala and the 5.0-liter Mustang. Its top speed of 116 miles per hour was one mile per hour faster than the 350-ci Impala.

This gold-over-dark-green 1983 Plymouth Gran Fury is a canine unit with the Vermont State Police. The VSP was formed in 1947. An oversize blue rotator serves as the only emergency light. These M-body Pursuits were available in three power-plants: the 90-horsepower, 225-ci slant six; the 130-horsepower, 318-ci two-barrel V-8; and the 165-horsepower, 318-ci four-barrel V-8. In 1983, Chrysler Corporation produced 13,106 Diplomat police cars and 8,400 Gran Furys with the A38 police package. The 318-ci, four-barrel Gran Fury had the highest top speed of any police car at 120 miles per hour. It took 12.4 seconds to reach 60 miles per hour. In comparison, the 305-ci, four-barrel Camaro Z28 hit 60 miles per hour in 7.4 seconds and topped out at 134 miles per hour.

For 1983, Ford changed the name of its full-size, 114.4-inch police car from "LTD" to "LTD Crown Victoria," a name that first appeared in 1955. This 1983 Chandler (Arizona) Police unit has simple but attractive markings. A blue body stripe over a red one on an all-white car complement the red and blue lightbar and the word "Police" in red letters. In 1983, the LTD Crown Victoria was powered by either the 130-horsepower, 302-ci V-8 or the 165-horsepower, 351 Windsor V-8. For the first time since its introduction of the formal police package, Ford did not offer the full-size police car as a two-door sedan. The package would only be available on four-door sedans. Ford kept the two-door police car longer than any other make.

Here's a 1983 Ford LTD Crown Victoria with the Burlingame (California) Police parked along with a Benicia Police Diplomat and a Menlo Park Police cruiser. The big news from Ford for urban police departments such as these was a fuel-injected 302-ci V-8! The Chevrolet Impala would not get an injected engine until 1985. While Chrysler Corporation had had an injected 318-ci V-8 in 1981, police-package cars were never allowed to use it. The injected 302-ci engine produced 130 horsepower, which was comparable to the two-barrel version. However, the peak power occurred at a lower rpm and the peak torque occurred at a higher rpm. The basic effect of fuel injection was to "flatten" the torque curve and make the engine more responsive throughout the rpm range. Fuel injection is one of the most significant driveline advances ever.

The Georgia State Patrol caught on to the use of the special-service-package 5.0-liter Ford Mustang right away! By 1983, eleven states had joined California in using the Mustang as a special traffic-enforcement pursuit car. This 1983 GSP Mustang is silver over blue with silver fender and door lettering. The big news for the special-service Mustang was the upgrade from a two-barrel carb to a four-barrel carb, resulting in 175 horsepower. Full-size police sedans ran the quarter mile in between 18.6 and 19.3 seconds. With two troopers on board, the 5.0-liter Mustang reached the traps in 16.7 seconds. It had a top speed of 132 miles per hour. The last time any police vehicle broke the 130-mile-per-hour barrier was 1978 with the 440-ci-powered Plymouth Fury! In fact, the 5.0-liter Mustang grew to have the same reputation among traffic officers as the old 440-ci big-block Mopars.

In 1984, the Montana Highway Patrol used the Dodge Diplomat. This all-white unit has a blue-and-gold door shield and a blue lightning bolt similar to the Washington State Patrol. For 1984, all full-size Dodge and Plymouth police cars were powered by the 318-ci V-8. The two-barrel engines produced 130 horsepower and were teamed with the wide-ratio A998 TorqueFlite and sluggish 2.24 to 1 rear gears. This MHP unit used the four-barrel version. This engine produced 165 horsepower and was bolted to the brand-new close-ratio A999 TorqueFlite and 2.94 to 1 gears. Prior to 1984, the 318-ci four-barrel engine had been bolted to the close-ratio A727 "big-block" TorqueFlite. The newer wide-ratio transmission improved acceleration without hurting fuel economy.

Check out the roof gear on this 1984 Colorado State Patrol Plymouth Gran Fury! The scissors-gear platform raised the entire lightbar off the roof of the car for maximum visibility. The elevated amber and blue rotators on the lightbar and the amber arrow flashers could be seen at much greater distances than a roof-level warning signal. The use of a McDermott-style light rack was very rare outside the New York City area. This is too bad. Every state has congested urban areas where these warning lights would greatly benefit motorists. This CSP Gran Fury is powered by a four-barrel version of the 318-ci V-8. This cruiser is all-white with an orange and blue door shield, orange car numbers, and blue trunk lettering.

This traditional-looking, black-and-white 1984 Plymouth Gran Fury is with the Reno (Nevada) Police. The 1984 model year is remembered as the best of the 1981-to-1989 M-body police cars. This was the last year for the Carter Thermo Quad four-barrel carb. After 1984, Chrysler's police cars were fed by General Motor's Rochester QuadraJet four-barrel carb. A GM carb on a Mopar cop car rubbed people the wrong way! This was the first year for the A999 wide-ratio TorqueFlite, which produced quicker acceleration than the older transmissions, all else being equal. This was one of the last years of the 8.4 to 1 compression. For 1986, the compression would be lowered to 8.0 to 1. Of all the years of M-body cop cars produced, the 1984 Gran Fury had the quickest quarter-mile time (18.2 sec), the highest quarter mile speed (77.5 miles per hour), the second-best fuel economy (14.6 miles per gallon), and the highest top speed (121.4 miles per hour).

This 1984 Plymouth Gran Fury was used by the New Orleans Police. The Mopar patroller is white over light blue with white fender and door markings. This Gran Fury is equipped with a red and blue Twinsonic. The 1984 Gran Fury and Dodge Diplomat were the only M-bodies to use a Carter ThermoQuad, 8.4 to 1 compression ratio, and wide-ratio TorqueFlite transmission. The 1984 M-bodies were the first Dodge and Plymouth squads to be faster around a road-racing course than the highly respected 1980 Dodge St. Regis and Gran Fury powered by the 185-horsepower, 360-ci V-8. The 318-ci four-barrel V-8 in the 1984 Diplomat and Gran Fury produced 165 horsepower. The bleak police-car performance years from 1980 to 1983 ended in 1984. From 1984 on, police-car performance would slowly improve every year.

This 1984 Dodge Aries K was used with the Traffic Division of the Annapolis Police. The home of the U.S. Naval Academy, Annapolis is also Maryland's capitol. In 1984, Chrysler Corporation changed the police-package code from A38 to AHB. The AHB police package was available for both the Aires K and the Plymouth Reliant K. For 1984, the 2.6-liter four-cylinder got a boost in compression and a change in carburetion and ignition timing to be rated at 101 horsepower. Both the 2.2-liter cars and the 2.6-liter cars got snappier final gear ratios. As a result, the 101-horsepower, 2.6-liter four-cylinder Aries K had the same 0- to 60-mile-per-hour time (13 seconds), the same top speed (105 miles per hour), and the same quarter-mile performance as the 130-horsepower, 318-ci two-barrel V-8-powered Dodge Diplomat!

In 1984, the California Highway Patrol adopted the Ford Crown Victoria as its Enforcement-class vehicle. This was the first Ford-marque CHP E-class cruiser in 30 years! The Crown Vic was mostly a carryover from 1983 with the exception of a much stronger 351-ci Windsor HO V-8 now rated at 180 horsepower. This compared to the Chevrolet 350-ci at 155 horsepower, and the Mopar 318-ci at 165 horsepower. Horsepower, however, did not tell the whole performance story. The 114.3-inch Crown Vic was heavier (4,084 pounds) than the other full-size sedans. As a result, top speed and acceleration honors went to the Mopars while the Chevrolet Impala had the best brakes. In 1984, the CHP was among six state police departments to install air bags in five of its Crown Victorias as a test.

This 1984 Ford Crown Victoria is on the job with the Louisville (Kentucky) Police. The all-white cruiser has twin blue stripes and a red, white, and blue door shield, which matched the officers' shoulder patch. The Louisville Police Department has been a pioneer in using the correct police engine for the task dating back to the 1950s. This 1984 Crown Vic is powered by the 302-ci fuel-injected V-8. This was the ideal kind of powerplant for urban patrol. This was one of the most fuel-efficient small-block V-8s. The 302-ci Crown Vic took 14.4 seconds to reach 60 miles per hour and had a top speed of 101 miles per hour. The 140-horsepower, 302-ci V-8 was very different from the 165-horsepower, 302-ci HO V-8 used in the mid-size Baby LTD.

This 1984 Ford Crown Victoria, used by the Suffolk County (New York) Police, is with the Highway Patrol Bureau and as such is equipped with the awesome McDermott light rack. At a traffic accident or other scene of congestion, the SCPD Highway officer would simply raise the arms of the light rack, making the warning signal visible from greater distances, even in heavy traffic. Patrolling the west end of Long Island, this cruiser is all-white with twin blue stripes, blue wheels, blue fender and trunk lettering, and a blue-on-white door shield. Note the term "Highway Patrol" in blue letters on the McDermott rack. Also note the heavy-duty rear anti-sway bar under the axle. As a Highway Patrol unit, this big Ford certainly had the High Output 351 Windsor engine.

The big news for 1984 was a police package based on the 105.5-inch-wheelbase Ford LTD. The so-called Baby LTD used the same platform as the Granada and Fairmont. It came with one of two powerplants: the 88-horsepower, 140-ci one-barrel four or the 165-horsepower, 302-ci fuel-injected HO V-8. This V-8 was exactly the same engine as used in the Mustang and 25 horsepower more powerful than the one used in the full-size LTD Crown Victoria. Of the 11 four-door sedans tested in 1984 by the Michigan State Police, the 302-ci HO Baby LTD had the quickest 0- to 60-mile-per-hour time, the quickest 0- to 100-mile-per-hour time, the fastest quarter-mile time, the highest top speed at 123 miles per hour, and the fastest road-racing-course lap times. The Baby LTD ran the quarter mile in 17.8 seconds! That was less than a second behind the Mustang! The performance of the Baby LTDs made them popular with county sheriffs and state police alike. This all-white cruiser with a green body stripe and green-and-gold seven-point star is with the Monterey County (California) Sheriff's Department on the central coast.

The 1984 mid-size LTD was an instant success. It had almost enough room but plenty of performance. In fact, think of the 165-horsepower, 302-ci HO-powered Baby LTD as a four-door Mustang. The Kansas City (Missouri) Police used this tan LTD fitted with a light rack using twin speakers, twin red globes, and alley lights. The Florida Highway Patrol also used the year's highest-performing four-door police sedan. The mid-size 302-ci LTD hit 100 miles per hour a full 10 seconds faster than the full-size 351-ci Crown Vic. The Cook County (Chicago) Illinois Sheriff's Police Department used the four-door rocket sled. In 1984, cops had suffered with low-performance sedans for three years. The hot Mustang could not be used for a wide variety of enforcement tasks, but the hot LTD sure could. History has proven most cops want their cruisers to perform. The Baby LTD did.

This 1984 Chevrolet Impala was used by the Medina (Ohio) Police in a rural area south of Cleveland. This cruiser is all-white with a wraparound green stripe that comes to a "V" on the hood. This was very innovative for the Medina cops. Oftentimes a city police department will mark its cars in a way similar to the state police department, showing no creativity or autonomy at all. Or the city will adopt very generic markings. The green V-stripe and the green door lettering instead of a door shield are quite progressive! The use of the latest-generation Jetsonic lightbar, with red and blue lenses, also speaks well for these Buckeye State crime fighters. The 1984 Impala itself was powered by the 110-horsepower, 229-ci two-barrel V-6 teamed with the three-speed 250C Turbo Hydra-Matic or the 155-horsepower, 350-ci four-barrel V-8 bolted to the four-speed 700R4 auto.

This 1984 Ford LTD was used by the Hayward (California) Police on the east side of the San Francisco Bay as a canine unit. This 105.5-inch LTD is all-white with a 1968-era Twinsonic. The 1978 to 1983 Ford Fairmont never did live up to the expectations in the CHP Special Purpose Vehicle Study. This was due, in part, to the fact the 302-ci engine was only available during the year of the CHP test. The 1984 Baby LTD, however, was the kind of car the CHP had envisioned in 1979: a powerful, mid-size sedan that could be a very effective police vehicle. The hot LTD shared one shortcoming with the hot Mustang: brakes that were too small for the incredible performance. In this regard, the LTD was a better car for state police, rural sheriffs, and special-purpose (K-9) city police vehicles where brake-critical pursuits are less common.

In 1984, the Ford Mustang returned as the hottest police car on the road, period. This all-white, 5.0-liter HO-powered special-service-package Mustang was used by the Milpitas (California) Police Department in San Francisco's South Bay-area. It has been fitted with the latest aerodynamic lightbar, the Federal Jet-Sonic introduced in 1982. Compare this low-profile bar to the Aerodynic on the Bronco in the background. New for 1984, the Mustang was available with one of two 302-ci HO engines. This was the first year for central fuel injection on the Mustang's V-8. The CFI engine produced 165 horsepower. The other choice was the Holley four-barrel engine, which had been bumped from 175 horsepower to 205 horsepower. The injected engine came with a four-speed automatic, while the carbureted engine came with a five-speed stick. The four-barrel car was 5 seconds faster to 100 miles per hour and had a top speed of 129.6 miles per hour, compared to 118 miles per hour for the CFI Mustang.

In 1984, the Phoenix (Arizona) Police used the Chevrolet Impala. The 155-horsepower, 350-ci Impala was closing the performance gap between itself and the 165-horsepower Mopars and the 180-horsepower Ford. At the same time, it was opening the gap in areas where it already had an advantage. For the first time since the 1978 start of the Michigan State Police Department patrol vehicle testing, the 350-ci Impala turned in the fastest time on the heavily weighted road-racing course. It was the only full-size police sedan to run the quarter mile in the 17-second bracket. The other makes ran in the 18- and 19-second brackets. The Impala also proved to have the strongest brakes of any police- or special-service-package vehicle. The Impala would continue to improve and to cut into the market controlled by the Dodge Diplomat.

The big news for 1984 was Chevrolet's first entry into the front-drive police-car market, the 104.9-inch-wheelbase Celebrity. The V-6-powered, front-drive Celebrity, such as this Prince George's County (Maryland) Sheriff's Department unit, replaced the V-8-powered, rear-drive Malibu. The Celebrity was considered to be a special-service vehicle, not a heavy-duty police-package vehicle. The Celebrity 9C1 was powered by a 2.8-liter two-barrel V-6 teamed with a three-speed 125C Turbo Hydra-Matic transaxle. The Celebrity 9C1 was pretty spunky at the bottom end. It hit 60 miles per hour in 12.3 seconds, which was actually faster than the 351-ci Ford Crown Victoria! However, the Celebrity took over 60 seconds to reach 100 miles per hour and had a top speed of just 110 miles per hour.

Chapter Ten
1985-1989

In 1985, Dodge remained the top-selling make of police-package car. The full-size Mopar police-car engines were revised, with the 318-ci two-barrel V-8 receiving higher compression and a roller cam, while the 318-ci four-barrel V-8 got a Rochester QuadraJet in place of the Carter ThermoQuad. A General Motors carburetor was used on a Chrysler Corporation police car! And why not? Chevrolet would not be needing the QuadraJet in the future, since all its police cars would have fuel injection!

Chevrolet released its first fuel-injected police engines since the 1957–1959 283-ci V-8. The Celebrity used a 130-horsepower, 2.8-liter V-6 from the Eurosport, and the Impala used a fuel-injected 262 ci, which, oddly, produced 130 horsepower. The 2.8-liter V-6 used the more advanced multiport fuel injection while the 4.3-liter V-6 had the more conventional throttle body injection. The 350-ci V-8 offered for the Impala continued to use a four-barrel carb through 1988.

In 1985, the Ford police package was available on the 114.4-inch, full-size LTD Crown Victoria and the 105.5-inch mid-size (baby) LTD. The special-service package was also available for the "darling" Mustang. The 302-ci EFI HO-powered LTD was the fastest and most powerful police sedan available, and the 351-ci HO-powered Crown Victoria was the nation's most powerful full-size police sedan.

The 1985 Plymouth Gran Fury was used by the Portsmouth (Rhode Island) Police. In a stark departure from traditional color schemes, this M-body cruiser is white over deep red and accented by gold lettering and a gold city seal on the door. The car is made even more striking by the all-blue Twinsonic light-bar. In 1985, for the first time since 1975, Dodge and Plymouth police cars came with steel-belted radials. For an entire decade, police-pursuit radials had been fabric belted because steel belts had a tendency to separate at higher speeds. The Goodyear Eagle GT was the first of the modern speed-rated, steel-belted radials on police cars. These H-rated radials were good for 130 miles per hour. With every police and special service package car in 1985, the H-rating was plenty!

The awesome police Mustang kept getting more power every year. For 1985, the Mustang's High Output engine got roller tappets and a much higher-performance cam, and it was still available in both fuel-injected and four-barrel versions. It was the last year for the hot 302-ci HO LTD. Mid-size police cars have not been the same ever since. The 302-ci LTD was to the mid-1980s what the 350-ci Nova was to the mid-1970s. These were both truly powerful, well-balanced, economical mid-size police cars. Even though the front-drive Taurus would replace the Baby LTD in the retail market, and itself become a police car in 1990, the Taurus

Here's a 1985 Chevrolet Impala with the Marietta (Ohio) Police. They celebrated Ohio's 200th year in 1988. To commemorate their 200th year, they re-marked all their police vehicles with white door markings, including this jet-black four-door sedan that had already been in service for three years. In 1985, both the Impala and the Celebrity were available with fuel-injected engines. These were the first Chevrolet fuel-injected police engines since the 283-ci V-8 in 1959. The Impala was available in two engines: the 155-horsepower, 350-ci four-barrel V-8 and the 130-horsepower, 262-ci throttle body fuel-injected V-6. With a bore of 4.00 inches and a stroke of 3.48 inches, the new V-6 was frequently called "a 350-ci V-8 with the back two cylinders chopped off." Chevrolet more properly called its new 4.3-liter engine "a standard V-6 that acts like a V-8."

In 1985, the Indianapolis Police used the Chevrolet Impala powered by the 155-horsepower, 350-ci V-8. This was the last year for the Impala nameplate, which had first appeared on 1958 retail cars. The Impala was the primary Chevrolet police car from 1976 through 1985. The 1976 Impala replaced the Bel Air nameplate. This Circle City cruiser is solid blue with an all-red Aerodynic and a white and gold door shield. The 350-ci Impala was a contender at the Michigan State Police vehicle tests by finishing first in some tests, in the middle in others, and last out of four in still other phases. It seemed to have lost the edge it had in 1984. The top speed was just 114 miles per hour.

would never measure up to the mid-size LTD. Not even close.

For 1986, two of Chrysler Corporation's police cars got fuel-injected engines, the 2.2-liter four and 2.5-liter four, and of course, the engines were used on the K-cars. After all, it was the front-drive K-car that saved Chrysler Corporation from bankruptcy, not the V-8-powered, rear-drive Diplomat and Gran Fury. Actually, the Diplomat and Gran Fury got Chrysler into a "heap of trouble" in 1986.

In 1957, Chrysler Corporation had shocked the motoring public by unveiling its torsion bar front suspension, which were straight bars developed from uncoiled coil springs. The design had worked quite well, giving the Mopars a subjectively better road feel at high speed. The last Mopar police cars to use these straight torsion bars were the R-body 1979 to 1981 R-body Newport, Gran Fury, and St. Regis. In 1976, Chrysler reinvented the torsion bar suspension, utilizing L-shaped bars instead of straight bars on the transverse torsion-bar front suspension for the 1976 F-body Aspen and Volare. This same exact suspension was used on the 1981 M-body Diplomat and LeBaron, and later Gran Fury carried the suspension.

By 1980, Car & Driver magazine called the suspension, "tried-but-not-so-true." In 1980, the Los Angeles County Sheriff's Department declared, "torsion bars designed in a transverse configuration are not acceptable." Two problems developed with cars using this design. It had a more rapidly sagging suspension, causing a negative camber and tire wear. The resulting toe-out alignment also caused severe brake pull, often from side-to-side. Chrysler Fleet recommended checking the ride height with every oil change, and if the ride height was okay, the camber and toe-out would be okay. Unfortunately, the problem was not so easily solved, because, first, aggressive driving could cause the springs to sag, sometimes within a week, and, second, the K-member itself, the structure the whole front suspension was bolted to, would actually bend. This meant the ride height could not be adjusted by adjusting the torsion bars. This problem appeared to be limited to police cars and taxi cabs, the two cars that are driven the hardest. The K-frame was simply not strong enough. This problem was most prevalent on the 1985 and 1986 Diplomat and Gran Fury, while all M-bodies up to mid-1987 are suspect.

Chrysler Corporation issued Technical Service Bulletin P-4482 to assist the proper alignment and/or reworking of the K-member. The February 1986 announcement, and the fact that Chrysler swapped out up to 400 K-members on new and in-service CHP Diplomats, probably signaled the beginning of the end of the Diplomat and Gran Fury for police use.

The top-selling police-car title migrated from Dodge to Chevrolet. The 350-ci V-8-powered Impala improved slowly and steadily despite the trend of downsizing that began in 1977. By 1986, it overtook all of the competition, even though both the prestigious California Highway Patrol and the influential Michigan State Police used the Dodge Diplomat in 1986! The 1986 Ford police cars were based on the full-size LTD Crown Victoria and the pursuit-oriented Mustang. The Crown Vic had a fuel-injected 302 ci or the variable-venturi 351-ci versions. The 5.0-liter Mustang was upgraded to sequential fuel injection, replacing the central fuel injection on one engine and the four-barrel carb on the other engine.

For 1987, the Chevrolet police package was available for the four-door Caprice only, but it was available with either the economy-oriented 4.3-liter EFI V-6 or the performance-oriented 350-ci four-barrel V-8. And perform it did. In 1987, the 350-ci Caprice won five of the six test phases conducted by the Michigan State Police: road racing course, acceleration, top speed, ergonomics, and fuel economy.

This began a string of MSP "most bang for the buck" wins for the Caprice that would run for 10 years in a row. The Diplomat and Gran Fury had earned top honors at the MSP run-offs in the early and mid-1980s with middle-of-the-pack performance and the lowest prices. For the next 10 years, Chevrolet won under the influential MSP protocol by having the highest vehicle performance and middle-of-the-pack prices.

The MSP testing and bidding procedure produced the best-performing police car for the money. The 318-ci Plymouth Gran Fury (M) followed by the 318-ci Dodge Diplomat had been the best police cars of the early 1980s. By the exact same performance-based bid-adjustment procedure, the best police car of the late 1980s was the Chevrolet Caprice.

In 1988, the Chevrolet Caprice was the nation's number one police car, and it was the only Chevrolet to have a police package that year. However, the U.S. Border Patrol used retail 1988 Camaro Z28s and retail Pontiac Trans Ams as pursuit cars in an illegal-alien drug-interdiction program called "Project Roadrunner." These musclecars were actually faster than the special-service-package Mustang! For 1988, the Caprice 9C1 came with either the 262-ci/4.3-liter V-6 or the 350-ci/5.7-liter V-8. This was the last year the 350-ci V-8 would use a carburetor. In 1988, the fleet of Chrysler Corporation police cars that had numbered as high as seven different vehicles was down to just two: the venerable Dodge Diplomat and Plymouth Gran Fury. Chrysler was a front-wheel-drive company, and law enforcement did not like front-wheel-drive cars. As a result, Chrysler hasn't fielded another police sedan up until the year 2000, but the early-1990s Dodge Dynasty and the late-1990s Dodge Intrepid looked like suitable police-pursuit-package cars.

The 1988 model year also marked the last time the California Highway Patrol used a Chrysler product as an Enforcement-class vehicle. In this case it was the 1988 Diplomat. In the 33 years between the 1956 release of the Dodge police package and the 1988 model year, the CHP had used Mopar E-class cruisers 28 times! This was truly the end of an era.

In 1989, the Dodge Diplomat and Plymouth Gran Fury were powered by a 360-ci fuel-injected V-8, teamed with the four-speed A500 automatic overdrive from the light-truck line. The M-body chassis was upgraded with four-wheel disc brakes and controlled by an Antilock Braking System. The two Mopar cruisers promptly set a track record for four-door sedans at the Michigan International Speedway road course during the annual Michigan State Police patrol vehicle tests. The four-door Mopars had the same lap time as the 5.0-liter Mustang, and reached 141 miles per hour during the top-speed tests.

Unfortunately, all of the above is "what might have been" if a generation of Mopar-loving cops and fleet managers had had their way. After all, Mopar sedans never posted this kind of performance.

This 1985 Dodge Diplomat was used by the Jefferson City (Missouri) Police. In 1985, the Dodge Diplomat and Plymouth Gran Fury were available with either the 140-horsepower, 318-ci two-barrel V-8 or the 175-horsepower, 318-ci four-barrel V-8. Big changes took place on both engines for 1985. The two-barrel engine used for urban patrol got higher compression, roller tappets, a change from a Carter carb to a Holley carb, and combustion chambers revised with "fast-burn" technology developed for the four-cylinder engines. The result was a 10-horsepower boost to 140 horsepower. Chrysler Corporation had hoped to also boost the fuel economy but it was actually a half-mile per gallon worse! The 1985 upgraded two-barrel V-8 pushed the Diplomat to 100 miles per hour a full 7 seconds quicker than in 1984. The tweaked engine also produced a 7-mile-per-hour higher top end at 116 miles per hour. That was almost as fast as the larger-engined and four-barrel cars.

This 1985 Dodge Diplomat was used by the Peoria County Sheriff's Police in central Illinois. This county police car has markings almost identical to the Illinois State Police. The twin gold stripes on an all-white car, the gold six-point star, and the lettering "Sheriff's Police" on either side of the star are as close as possible to the state markings at the time. How about a little creativity? This county cruiser is powered by a four-barrel version of the 318-ci V-8. For 1985, the Carter ThermoQuad was dropped in favor of the Rochester QuadraJet. The 1985 four-barrel cars had 10 more horsepower and 10 more pounds of torque than the 1984 four-barrel cars and fleet engineering was positive the increase in horsepower came strictly from the better flow of the Rochester QuadraJet. From 1985 through 1989, the four-barrel-powered Diplomat and Gran Fury would carry the 175-horsepower rating.

This 1985 Plymouth Gran Fury was with the Carson City County (Nevada) Sheriff's Department. This county cruiser is all-white with a green body stripe. Even though the Dodge and Plymouth police cars used a General Motors four-barrel carburetor, the Mopars did reasonably well at the Michigan State Police tests. The Diplomat and Gran Fury shared top honors in braking power and top speed. Both the CHP and the MSP selected the Dodge Diplomat in 1985. This was the first Dodge selected by the MSP process. New for 1985, Chrysler Corporation released just the thing for Nevada police cars, and all the other patrol scenarios where vapor lock was a problem. The "Anti-Vapor Lock Package" was simply a gas-tank-mounted electric fuel pump used in conjunction with the engine-mounted mechanical fuel pump.

This 1985 Ford Crown Victoria was used to patrol the Windy City. Shown on the shores of Lake Michigan with the Chicago skyline in the background, this 114.4-inch Crown Vic has a wide blue stripe and red door letters. The MARS warning lights are a combination of blue rotators and blue/red can lights. The Chicago Police Department is the second-largest metro police department in the nation. They are the only police department in Illinois authorized to run all-blue lights. Settled in 1779, Chicago could boast the first steel-frame skyscraper in 1885 and the first McDonald's restaurant in 1955, the same year the O'Hare Airport began operation. Patrol cars like this Crown Victoria helped the Chicago cops to respond to 1.7 million dispatched calls per year.

With the decision by Chrysler to focus exclusively on front-drive cars, the V-8-powered rear-drive Diplomat and Gran Fury simply did not fit its core business. In mid-1989, Chrysler halted production of the Diplomat and Gran Fury, and thus the company exited the police-car business, which they helped define and develop. Over the years, Chrysler police cars unquestionably set the standard for both performance and durability.

For 1989 the Chevrolet Caprice was the number-one-selling police car, and the Chevrolet fuel-injection 350-ci V-8 was offered for police service. Other Caprice police engines included the fuel-injected 305-ci V-8 and the fuel-injected 262-ci V-6. All three were teamed with the four-speed automatic overdrive. Fuel-injection allowed Chevrolet to increase the rear gear ratio from 3.08 to 3.42 to 1 and produce a responsive, high-performance four-door sedan. The Caprice was clearly the best police-package car of the year.

For 1989, the Ford law-enforcement vehicles were the 55A police-package Crown Victoria and the special-service-package Mustang. The Mustang was clearly in its glory days, and it didn't have any competition from Chevrolet, Dodge, Plymouth, or anyone else. Every traffic cop in the nation wanted one, and almost nothing on the road could outrun one.

The Dodge Aries K and this Plymouth Reliant K were restyled for 1985 with sleeker sheet metal. This pale-green K-car with a red and blue lens Aerodynic was used by the 716th Military Police Battalion at the U.S. Army base at Fort Riley, Kansas. The "Patrol" package K-car was powered by one of two four-cylinder, two-barrel engines. One was the Chrysler-made 2.2-liter in-line four with 96 horsepower. The other was the Mitsubishi-made 2.6-liter in-line four with 101 horsepower. The 100.3-inch-wheelbase K-car was rated as a six-passenger car. Do you suppose six MPs would fit in this Plymouth? Perhaps that's why MPs are always in such a foul mood! With the 2.6-liter four, the K-car hit 60 miles per hour in 14.4 seconds, ran the quarter mile in 20 seconds, and had a top speed of 100 miles per hour. The 0- to 60-mile-per-hour acceleration with six MPs on-board was slower yet.

Here's a 1985 Ford Crown Victoria with the New Hampshire State Police sporting an all-blue lightbar. The cruisers have a very distinctive copper-over-dark-green paint scheme with a gold "V" through the state seal as a door shield and gold fender lettering. The white-on-gold decal below the door shield reads "Department of Safety." The NHSP was founded in 1937. The 1985 Ford was mostly a carryover from 1984, except for the use of nitrogen-charged shocks. Once again, the big Ford was available with the 140-horsepower, 302-ci EFI V-8 and the 180-horsepower, 351-ci Windsor HO V-8. In 1985, Ford made five different 302-ci engines. The 140-horsepower non-HO version was restricted to the police Crown Vic, while a 155-horsepower version of the 302-ci HO was restricted to the retail Crown Vic. A 165-horsepower version of the HO powered all of the LTDs. The Mustang got either a 180-horsepower, EFI version of the HO engine or a 210-horsepower, four-barrel version of the 302-ci HO.

This 1985 Ford Crown Victoria is with the Virginia State Police. The single roof rotator is the Federal PA-Light with a blue globe. This is basically a combination of a four-bulb Power Light on the top with the siren mounted in the base. The chrome base is heavily perforated to let the sound out. These lights were used from the early 1970s to the early 1990s. These were especially popular among eastern and southern states. This VSP Ford is dark-blue-over-silver with blue and white door markings. The Virginia State Police Department was formed in 1942. They have used the blue-over-silver color scheme since the early 1970s and are still using it in the late 1990s. The 180-horsepower, 351-ci Windsor HO V-8-powered Crown Vic was the nation's most powerful police sedan. Among full-size cars, the Crown Victoria had the fastest road-course time, the quickest 0- to 100-mile-per-hour time, and the best quarter-mile performance.

Here's a 1985 Reno (Nevada) Police Ford LTD. The Baby LTD had a 5-inch-longer wheelbase than the Mustang, and, in fact, ran like a four-door Mustang. The door shield is the seal of the city. Notice that the word "Police" does not appear on the door! In fact, the only place "Police" appears anywhere on the vehicle is in tiny letters on the rear-fender 911 decal. With twin spotlights lighting in your mirror, an Aerodynic blinding you with 360 flashes per minute and high-beam headlights in wig-wag mode, the side of the car really doesn't need to say "Police," does it? At 16.1 miles per gallon, this 302-ci LTD got the best gas mileage of any police sedan that could run the quarter mile in the 17-second bracket. The 302-ci LTD was the ONLY police sedan that could run the quarter that fast!

Here's a 1985 Ford LTD with the Carrollton (Texas) Police just north of Dallas. The mid-size cruiser is all-white with blue and green body stripes, blue door and fender lettering, and a blue and green "C" on the door. The 105.5-inch Ford LTD was only available with a police package for two years: 1984 and 1985. Too bad. This was a time of low performance from the full-size cruisers and extremely poor performance from the mid-size patrollers. In contrast, the 302-ci LTD was a true high-performance, mid-size sedan. The Baby LTD was well on its way to being another Chevrolet Nova in the eyes of city and county cops. Even the state police departments and highway patrols were using the mid-size LTD. Ford dropped the LTD for 1986 in favor of the retail Taurus.

The 1986 Dodge Diplomat was the last Chrysler product to be selected by the Michigan State Police "most-bang-for-the-buck" testing and bid procedure. Since 1978, the MSP has tested all areas of vehicle performance from acceleration and top speed to ergonomics and fuel economy. The performance in each test gets factored into the bid process. The MSP does *not* buy the lowest-bid police cars. Instead, they purchase whatever police car has the best combination of high performance and low cost. This is, by far, the smartest use of tax dollars to purchase a police fleet. In 1986, for the eighth time in nine years, a Chrysler product was the calculated winner of the MSP run-offs. This would be the last time. For the next 10 years straight, the Chevrolet Caprice would be the top gun.

The Washington State Patrol joined the Florida Highway Patrol, the Oregon State Patrol, and the Cook County (Chicago, Illinois) Sheriff's Police in using the 1985 Ford LTD. Brake fade was a common complaint with these hard-running police cars. It could be that the brakes, sized for the 400-pound-lighter Mustang, were a little small for the LTD. However, it could "also" be that the cops were not used to a car with this much power and simply over-drove the brakes! During 1984 and 1985 testing by the Michigan State Police, the hot LTD turned in a braking performance that was the exact average for all police and special-service vehicles. At the same time, the 302-ci LTD turned in the fastest road-racing-course times of any police sedan, period. The Baby LTD also had the highest top speed of any sedan at 121 miles per hour. The 165-horsepower mid-size Ford reached 100 miles per hour 9 seconds sooner than any other police sedan. It would be missed.

In 1985, the Washington State Patrol used this 5.0-liter Mustang. In 1985, the Idaho State Police, Texas Highway Patrol, Georgia State Patrol, Nevada Highway Patrol, and, of course, California Highway Patrol were among the 15 other states that used the Mustang as a special traffic-enforcement vehicle. This 1985 WSP Mustang has a blue spotlight. For 1985, the Mustangs still used four-bolt steel wheels with chrome centers. The 1985 5.0-liter HO engine got a higher lift and longer-duration cam while the five-speed stick got a stronger-pulling first gear and a closer-ratio fifth gear. Again, the 180-horsepower, central-fuel-injected engine was only available with the four-speed auto while the 210-horsepower, four-barrel engine was only available with the five-speed stick. While the fuel-injected Mustangs used 70-series, 14-inch radials, the four-barrel cars got 60-series, 15-inch, V-rated Goodyear "Gatorbacks," the first unidirectional tire used on a police car. The four-barrel Mustang ran the quarter mile in 16.1 seconds at 87 miles per hour and had a top speed of 136 miles per hour.

Check out this 1986 Kansas Highway Patrol Dodge Diplomat. It's an award-winning show car now; however, it was once one of 148 Diplomats purchased by the KHP in 1986. As delivered to Gladstone Dodge, the Diplomat was solid Nightwatch Blue. Some remained all-blue. The hood and trunk on this unit were painted the more traditional KHP Gray. This light-gray-over-deep-blue paint scheme was used from 1937 through 1992! This Diplomat was used for the first 3 years by Trooper R.D. Duffey and for the next 5 years by Sgt. L. Connors. Upon its retirement, this Diplomat was the oldest marked car in the KHP fleet. The car was scheduled to be used as a "target" vehicle by the Kansas Law Enforcement Training Center but was somehow spared. It now leads a pampered life of police-car cruises and car shows with as many car washes and hand-rubbed wax jobs as any Ferrari.

This 1986 Dodge Diplomat was used by the Marin County (California) Sheriff's Department. When you get off the Golden Gate Bridge north of San Francisco, you are in Marin County. This is the Bay-area's richest and most beautiful county. Marin County is where parklands and rolling dairy farms preserve half the county from the Bay-area's urban sprawl. One wonders what a sheriff's deputy does in an area filled with quaint towns and an old-world charm. Perhaps deputies stand guard on the bridge to keep Marin County urbane and suave. This slick-top Dodge is white over sea green with white trunk lettering. Importantly, this rear shot shows the deck light scheme adopted by California cop cars in 1983. Amber and blue flashers are on the driver's side and a red flasher is on the passenger's side. This MCSD Diplomat is also fitted with a roll cage and rear-seat partition. Apparently, sometimes the tourists object when being taken back across the bridge.

Here's a sharp-looking 1986 Dodge Diplomat with the San Mateo County (California) Sheriff's Department. This attractive squad car is all-white with a wide blue body stripe and gold door, fender, and trunk lettering. This is a slick-top patroller with a red spotlight, tri-color deck lights, and front pusher bars. The powertrain in the 112.7-inch M-bodies was either the 140-horse-power, 318-ci two-barrel V-8 or the 175-horsepower, 318-ci four-barrel V-8. The two-barrel cars were now optimistically called Pursuits while the four-barrel cars were labeled Interceptors. In fairness, the two-barrel cars did have the more aggressive 2.94 to 1 rear axle ratio this year, instead of the sluggish 2.24 to 1 ratio. This alone got them to 60 miles per hour in 12.1 seconds, 2 seconds faster than previous years. They hit 100 miles per hour a full 10 seconds faster.

Here's a 1986 Plymouth Gran Fury with the Wisconsin State Patrol. The cruiser is dark-blue with a white body stripe. By 1986, the red and blue twin globes of the Federal Visibar had become quite dated, but yes, they still got the job done! In 1986, the Dodge Diplomat and Plymouth Gran Fury with the 175-horse-power, 318-ci four-barrel V-8 had the highest top speeds, at between 119 and 122 miles per hour. They also had the best brakes and the fastest 0- to 100-mile-per-hour times. In 1986, both the Dodge Aires K and Plymouth Reliant K got fuel-injected four-cylinder engines replacing the two-barrel carbs. These became Chrysler Corporation's first fuel-injected police cars at a time when most cops wanted the 318-ci V-8 to be fuel-injected.

For 1986, the name of Chevrolet's full-size police car changed from Impala to Caprice. The Caprice, like this Virginia State Police unit, would be the basis for the police package from 1986 through 1996. This would be Chevrolet's glory years! The name Caprice first appeared on top-of-the-line retail cars in 1965. For 1986, the Caprice got a greatly restyled grille but kept the old-style headlights. This would be the only year of this look. This VSP unit also had a carryover in color scheme. The Caprice was dark-blue over silver with white on blue decals on the hood, doors, and trunk. The emergency light is a blue-globe Federal PA-Light with the siren speaker in the base of the rotator.

This 1986 Chevrolet Caprice is on the job with the New Jersey State Police. The all-white 116-inch cruiser has an all-red Aerodynic. The door markings include a wide gold stripe in front of a wide blue stripe. Yes, that is a gold stripe on the trooper's blue uniform pants. The door shield has gold lettering on a blue background. The 1986 model year is the only year the Caprice had a solid amber front turn-signal lens. In the later years it had a clear lens on top of the amber lens. The drivetrains for 1986 were very similar to 1985. The full-size Caprice came with either a 140-horsepower, 4.3-liter/262-ci EFI V-6 or a 15-horsepower, 5.7-liter/350-ci four-barrel V-8. The 140-horsepower V-6 was okay for urban use. With a 19.5-second quarter mile and a 108-mile-per-hour top end, it was only slightly faster than the Chrysler K-cars.

This slick-top Idaho State Police unit is a 1986 Chevrolet Caprice. This was the only year the grille used from 1986 to 1990 was teamed with the individual-lens quad headlights used from 1977 to 1986. This cruiser has a white roof over a black body with white diagonal stripes that form a point on the hood. The door shield is a gold outline of the Gem State. The only forward-facing emergency light is a blue globe "Fire Ball." During the annual Michigan State Police vehicle tests, the 155-horsepower, 350-ci Caprice turned in only average performance. The 0- to 60-mile-per-hour time was a potent 10.92 seconds but all the other full-size cruisers outran it through the quarter mile. The Caprice turned in a 117-mile-per-hour top end, besting only the 351-ci Crown Victoria.

This 1986 Chevrolet Celebrity with a red and blue Aerodynic was used by the Long Beach (California) Police. While the 104.9-inch wheelbase was a little small, the Celebrity had much better performance than either of the K-cars. New for 1986, the Celebrity was restyled for the first time since its 1982 retail debut. The Celebrity got a new grille, but like the Caprice, kept its individual-bezel, quad headlights. This was also the last year for the special-service-package Celebrity, introduced in 1984. During this time, less than 1,000 units per year were sold. The Celebrity went out with a bang. The Celebrity came with either a 112-horsepower, two-barrel or 125-horsepower, EFI version of the 2.8-liter V-6. In a showdown against other front-drive police cars, the Celebrity had the fastest acceleration, highest top speed, strongest brakes, and quickest road course times.

In 1986, the police in beautiful Flagstaff (Arizona) drove the Ford Crown Victoria. This all-white, 114.3-inch Ford has blue and gold body stripes and the city seal as a door shield. Snow tires on this Arizona cruiser remind us that Flagstaff is in the Kaibab National Forest, with nearly the highest elevation in the Grand Canyon State. The big news for 1986 was an upgrade from central fuel injection to sequential electronic multiport fuel injection on the 302-ci used in the Crown Vic. More compression, roller tappets, and redesigned combustion chambers resulted in a 150-horsepower engine. Even compared to a CFI engine, SEFI flattened the horsepower and torque curves, produced the peak horsepower at a lower rpm, and increased the torque at roughly the same rpm. Every single one of these made for a better police engine.

This 1986 Ford Crown Victoria was used by the Highway Patrol Bureau of the Nassau County (New York) Police. This was the year of the new markings. Blue letters and numbers adorn the hood, fenders, door, and trunk. A blue stripe runs from the headlight, down through the blue, gold, and orange door shield, then on to the taillight. An orange stripe starts at the door shield and runs, along with the blue stripe, back to the taillight. As a Highway Patrol car, this Ford has three features not always found on the other NCPD patrollers. One is the awesome McDermott light rack with three amber flashers attached to each of the extendible arms. Another is the very-heavy-duty pusher bumper with auxiliary red light. Finally, this Crown Vic was powered by the largest police engine, the 180-horsepower, 351-ci HO V-8. This big, bad Ford was the fastest full-size sedan around the Michigan State Police road course.

This 1986 Ford Crown Victoria is with the Rhode Island State Police. The cruiser is silver with blue lettering and an all-red Federal JetSonic. The front fenders say "State Police." The doors say "State Police." The rear fenders say "State Police." The trunk lid says "State Police." The funny part is that motorists have approached the fully marked squad car and have asked the uniformed driver, "Are you with the State Police?" True story! The 1986 Crown Vic was available with one of two engines, the 150-horsepower, 302-ci SEFI V-8 and the 180-horsepower, 351-ci Windsor HO V-8 using the variable venturi carburetor. The upgrade to sequential fuel injection on the 302-ci-powered Crown Vic cut the 0- to 100-mile-per-hour time by more than 12 seconds. The 0- to 60-mile-per-hour time of 12.1 seconds was close to the 11.7 seconds required by the 351-ci Crown Vic.

Ford had some exciting news for pilots of the 1986 Mustang such as this Utah state trooper. The news was sequential fuel injection, which made obsolete both the four-barrel carburetor and central fuel injection. While the 200 horsepower from the SEFI 5.0-liter V-8 engine was down slightly from the four-barrel version, the peak occurred at a lower rpm and the amount of torque was way up. The 200-horsepower SEFI 5.0-liter engine gave the special-service Mustang the kind of performance known to most enthusiasts: 0 to 60 miles per hour in 7 seconds, 0 to 100 miles per hour in 19 seconds, a 15-second quarter mile at 90 miles per hour, and top speeds from 135 to 137 miles per hour. This 1986 Utah Highway Patrol Mustang shows the last year of the deeply recessed, quad headlights.

In 1987, the most-bang-for-the buck process used by the Michigan State Police since 1978 resulted in its adoption of the Chevrolet Caprice. The 180-horsepower, 350-ci four-barrel Caprice won five of the six categories (road course, top speed, acceleration, fuel economy, and ergonomics) to capture the influential MSP contract. The Caprice would go on to win under the MSP test method for the next 10 years straight. A boost in compression and the use of roller lifters pushed the horsepower of the 350-ci V-8 from 155 horsepower to 180 horsepower. The 180-horsepower Caprice finally broke into the 17-second quarter-mile bracket but the top speed was still only 118 miles per hour.

The 1987 Chevrolet Caprice was used by the New York City Police. This white and blue Highway Patrol Bureau cruiser has a red and clear lens Aerodynic light gear. More important, this unit is fitted with the McDermott "Multi-Level" light rack, shown in the elevated position. Each arm of the McDermott has two red/amber flashers and one spotlight. One of the NYPD HWY 3 units in the background has a McDermott with five spotlights and one red/amber flasher per arm. On the topic of spotlights, this Queens-based Highway car has a rack of auxiliary spotlights designed to sit on the hood. These extra lights are portable and not permanently mounted on the hood. Likewise, the McDermott arms are lowered when the car is in motion. The NYPD Highway Patrol units were all powered by the 180-horsepower, 350-ci four-barrel V-8. This was the first model year for the one-piece composite headlight lens.

This all-white with blue stripes 1987 Plymouth Gran Fury was used by the Mt. Vernon Police in downstate Illinois. New for 1987, Chrysler Corporation renamed its police-package engines. The K-car engines, regardless of size, were called "Patrol" engines. The 140-horsepower, 318-ci two-barrel V-8 was referred to as a "Pursuit" engine. With a 0- to 60-mile-per-hour time of 14.7 seconds, this description proved Chrysler Corporation at least had a sense of humor. The 175-horsepower, 318-ci four-barrel V-8 was labeled the "Interceptor" engine. The top speed of 117.5 miles per hour from this engine did not make for much of an interceptor. The 125-miles-per-hour-certified speedometer that came on these AHB police-package cars was about right.

Here's a 1987 Plymouth Caravelle with the Metropolitan Toronto (Ontario) Police. Caravelle was the Canadian name for the Gran Fury. It's easy to tell a Gran Fury or Caravelle from a Dodge Diplomat. From 1981 to 1989, the Dodge used a black-accented grille, while the Plymouth used a bright argent/silver grille. This MTP cruiser is chrome yellow with a red/clear rotator and a variety of red, takedown, and alley lights also mounted on the busy light rack. In 1987, Chrysler Corporation purchased American Motors. Late in the model year, production of the Plymouth Caravelle and Gran Fury and the Dodge Diplomat was transferred from Fenton (St. Louis), Missouri, to the former AMC assembly plant in Kenosha, Wisconsin. M-body output remained in Wisconsin until the Diplomat and Gran Fury were discontinued in mid-1989.

This 1987 Dodge Diplomat was used by the University of Western Ontario Police in London, Ontario. London is the home of the Ford Crown Victoria assembly plant. Of course, what makes this police car significant is the use of a black-outlined red lens "pull-over" light. When illuminated, the light reads "Police Stop." By the 1980s, about the only other police agency using a pull-over light was the Michigan State Police. Pull-over lights were extremely popular in the 1950s. The only change for the Dodge Diplomat and Plymouth Gran Fury was the use of a stainless-steel exhaust. The oversize diameter of the single exhaust remained the same. Stainless steel dramatically extended the life of the exhaust.

Here's a slick-top 1987 Dodge Diplomat with the Illinois State Police. The cruiser is all-white with a single, brown-outlined, gold stripe. Prior to 1976, the ISP cars were black over white with a door shield and no body stripes. In 1976, the ISP went to twin body stripes. From 1977 to 1986, the ISP continued to use two gold stripes. From 1987 to 1990 they used one gold stripe along the top of the body. In 1991, the gold stripe was used in the center, running through the door shield. For 1995, the single gold stripe was changed to a wedge-shaped stripe and the door shield was replaced with a separate six-point gold star and the gold lettering, "Illinois State Police." ISP cars from the 1980s with a door shield but no stripe were assigned to the Toll Authority in Chicagoland.

This 1987 Dodge Diplomat was used by the special-response team with the Benton County (Indiana) Sheriff's Department. In Benton County, the patrol cars are two-tone brown over tan, following Indiana Sheriffs' Association guidelines. However, special-purpose units, such as this Diplomat and the Cherokee used for K-9 duties, are white with a gold and brown five-point star. This door shield reads "Benton County Police Indiana." The door shield on most Hoosier sheriffs' department vehicles simply read "Sheriff Indiana." This 1987 Diplomat has a red and blue Visibar and red/blue lights on the dash, deck, and grille. The author, shown, is both an active traffic officer and a rifleman with the BCSD special-response team. The Diplomat is powered by a 175-horsepower, 318-ci four-barrel V-8 and has seen its top speed of 117 many times. This unit was originally used by the Oxford (Indiana) Police where the town marshal, turned county sheriff, liked Dodge police cars so much he personally waxed the car.

This 1987 Plymouth Reliant K was used by the U.S. Air Force Security Police. The little K-car driven by this USAF Staff Sergeant is all-white with twin blue stripes and a red/blue strobe bar. The U.S. government was a major customer of the Plymouth and Dodge K-cars. The K-cars were powered by the fuel-injected 97-horsepower, 2.2-liter four or the fuel-injected 100-horsepower 2.5-liter four. The 100-horsepower Reliant K took 15 seconds to hit 60 miles per hour and had a top speed of 100 miles per hour. However, it was quicker in the quarter mile than the M-body Gran Fury powered by the two-barrel version of the 318-ci V-8. The 1987 model year was the last year for the AHB police package on the Reliant K and Aries K. Regardless of rumors about the Dynasty and Intrepid police packages, the K-cars remain the only front-drive police cars ever produced by Chrysler Corp.

In 1987, the Cleveland (Ohio) Police used the Ford Crown Victoria. These black-and-white four-door sedans were a welcome color scheme compared to the awful "Safety Green" used from late 1960s to late 1970s. Of course, cops in San Francisco are not proud of the white-and-powder-blue cruisers used in the mid-1970s either! The gold-on-blue scroll below the blue-on-gold shield reads "Proud To Serve." For 1987, Ford engineers tweaked an additional 10 horsepower out of their fuel-injected 302-ci V-8. Now rated at 160 horsepower, the engine would remain basically unchanged until replaced by the 4.6-liter SOHC V-8 in late 1992. The injected 302-ci mill was ideal for patrol in heavily urbanized Cleveland. It got almost 5 miles per gallon better mileage than the 351-ci Windsor. It also got to 60 miles per hour in 11.9 seconds, compared to 12.0 seconds for the 351-ci-powered Crown Vic.

The Ontario Provincial Police used the 1987 Ford Crown Victoria with a California Highway Patrol-style black-and-white color scheme. The fender and door lettering is gold. This 351-ci-powered Ford is a serious traffic-enforcement car. That's a Decatur Electronics traffic radar antenna and display on the dash. The roof gear includes a red rotator and individual red flashers along with a siren and public address system speakers. The 180-horsepower, 351-ci Windsor engine in this OPP cruiser was unchanged for 1987. This same year, Ford announced it had plans for the V-8-powered, rear-drive Crown Vic only through the 1989 model year. While Chevrolet concentrated on improving the Caprice, Ford shifted its focus to front-drive cars and halted all development on the Crown Vic. Ford later extended the life of the Crown Vic to 1997, then to 2001, and most recently to 2006, much to the delight of V-8-powered, rear-drive, full-size car enthusiasts.

This beautiful blue 1987 Ford Crown Vic with white doors was used by the Royal Canadian Mounted Police. The multiple-colored crest on the door includes the blue initials RCMP and GRC. The F-series Dominion emergency lights quickly identify that this particular cruiser served at the Toronto International Airport. The two outboard rotators have a red globe. The center rotator has an amber globe. The amber light is used while the patrol car is on the runways, taxiways, ramp, and flight deck. Not quite as fast as a Lear Jet, the 180-horsepower, 351-ci-powered Crown Vic had a top speed of just 115 miles per hour. In 1987, the Crown Vic was also used by the Indiana State Police, New Jersey State Police, and Wyoming Highway Patrol.

The Hall County (Georgia) Sheriff's Department used this 1987 Ford Mustang as a DUI Task Force and Traffic Enforcement vehicle. The all-white pony car with all-blue strobe lights is shown on an autocross course. HCSD deputies who were issued the 100.4-inch-wheelbase, 5.0-liter HO Mustang also had to take high-speed training at the nearby Road Atlanta road-racing course. New for 1987, the horsepower of the 5.0-liter Mustang engine was boosted from 200 horsepower to 225 horsepower. With both the four-speed auto and five-speed stick, the special-service-package Mustang set an all-time Ford police car top-speed record at 139 miles per hour. No Ford police car before or since has been faster than the 1987 Mustang. This was also the first year for the flush-bezel dual headlights, replacing the deeply recessed, quad headlights. From 1987 to 1989, black-painted aluminum wheels would be standard on the special-service-package Mustang, while brushed-aluminum wheels were indeed optional.

In 1988, the Iowa State Patrol used this solid-brown Chevrolet Caprice with a black-on-yellow door shield. In 1988, law-enforcement fleet managers demanded that the automakers pull their police cars out of the performance slump just as they had done for many retail cars. The Camaros, Mustangs, and Firebirds in 1988 ran the quarter mile in the 15-second bracket and had top speeds over 140 miles per hour. No police sedan was a match for these common sporty cars. They ran the same 19-second quarter miles and had the same 118-mile-per-hour top ends as police sedans in the early 1980s. None of the large-engine, full-size police cars had antilock brakes, fuel injection, or four-wheel discs. The police car had been the fastest car on the road in the 1970s. The fleet managers wanted that edge back. Of the major automakers, only Chevrolet responded. This was the last carbureted Caprice.

This 1988 Dodge Diplomat was used by the California State University at Long Beach. The 112.7-inch all-white sedan has gold fender lettering and a red/blue Street Hawk lightbar. CSULB Cpl. John Bellah is such a Mopar enthusiast he drove the Diplomat squad car long after it was semi-retired in favor of a new fleet of Caprices. In 1988, Chrysler Corporation fielded just two police-package cars, the Dodge Diplomat and the Plymouth Gran Fury, available in just the 318-ci two-barrel and 318-ci four-barrel V-8. This was the smallest fleet with the least combinations since the Mopar police package was introduced in 1956! These were the only rear-wheel-drive cars in the entire corporation, the only V-8-powered cars, and the only carbureted cars. By 1988, it was obvious Chrysler was clearly planning to exit the rear-wheel-drive police-car and passenger-car market. They would last just through the first half of the 1989 model year.

This 1988 Chevrolet Caprice was used by the Delaware State Police. At the state police and highway patrol level, the Caprice was rapidly replacing the Diplomat and Gran Fury. This DSP Caprice is medium-blue with a gold-outlined black body stripe, gold lettering, and a gold-and-blue-on-tan door shield. The light-bar is the Federal Street Hawk with red and blue lenses. The DSP Caprice was powered by the 180-horsepower, 350-ci four-barrel V-8 in the last year for the Rochester QuadraJet carburetor. For the second year in a row, the Caprice won the annual Michigan State Police patrol vehicle tests with a 10.6-second 0- to 60-mile-per-hour time, 18.0-second quarter-mile run, but a top speed of just 116 miles per hour. A 140-horsepower, 4.3-liter V-6 was also available on the 116-inch Caprice.

This 1988 Dodge Diplomat was used by the Honolulu (Hawaii) Police. The four-door sedan is all-white with white-on-blue fender markings, blue on gold door shield, and an all-blue Aerodynic lightbar. Other departments to use the 1988 Diplomat and Plymouth Gran Fury included the Dallas (Texas) Police; the Philadelphia (Pennsylvania) Police; the Portland (Oregon) Police; the Prince George's County (Maryland) Sheriff; and the Winston-Salem (North Carolina) Police. By 1988, Dodge and Plymouth combined produced just 10,593 AHB-package police cars, compared to a market for 60,000 cruisers. Late in the 1988 model year, Chrysler Corporation confirmed the rumors that Diplomat and Gran Fury production would halt in mid-1989. The Diplomat and Gran Fury, however, kept up the pace at the annual Michigan State Police tests. The Mopar cruisers were tied for the top speed at 117 miles per hour. The 175-horsepower, 318-ci four-barrel-powered Diplomat got to 60 miles per hour in 11.6 seconds.

This 1988 Dodge Diplomat served with the New York-New Jersey Port Authority Police. The cruiser is all-white with a blue band running along the fender sides and tops. The slotted steel wheels were also blue. The door shield was two-tone blue. This Dodge has some special equipment to handle Port Authority details. One is the massive, tow truck–style pusher bumper and grille guard. Take that, California cops! The other, of course, is the roof-mounted "Hi-Lo Lifesaver" high-rise warning device made by Acme Precision Products. This unit raises a directional arrow lightboard 42 inches above the roof, along with the light-bar, which happens to be a red/blue Aerodynic. This Diplomat was assigned to the George Washington Bridge connecting northern Manhattan to Ft. Lee, New Jersey. The New York City–area Dodges were powered by the gas-miserly 140-horsepower, 318-ci two-barrel V-8, which took 14 seconds to hit 60 miles per hour, but got 14.6 miles per gallon.

This 1988 Plymouth Gran Fury was used by the Ohio State Highway Patrol and has been restored to show-car status. The silver OSHP cruiser has gold door and trunk lettering, the famous gold-and-black winged tire door shield, and a red/blue JetSonic. Note the MHP Industries traffic radar antenna on the dash. Other state agencies to use the Gran Fury and Diplomat included the Kansas Highway Patrol, Minnesota State Patrol, Montana Highway Patrol, Nebraska State Patrol, New York State Police, North Dakota Highway Patrol, Oklahoma Highway Patrol, Tennessee Highway Patrol, Vermont State Police, and Wisconsin State Police. Most significantly, the California Highway Patrol used the Dodge Diplomat for the last time. In the 33-year span from 1956 to 1988, the CHP used Chrysler Corporation police cars 28 times. This was truly the end of an exciting era.

Here's an attractively marked 1988 Dodge Diplomat used by the McHenry County Sheriff's Department in north central Illinois. This all-white Mopar has twin, gold-outlined blue body stripes and a clear lens Aerodynic with red and white rotators. Beginning in May 1988, the Diplomat and Plymouth Gran Fury became the first full-size police-package cars to come from the factory with a driver-side air bag. The Chevrolet Caprice did not get an air bag until 1991, while it was mid-1992 before the Ford Crown Vic came so equipped. These advances were too little and too late for the Diplomat and Gran Fury. The only surprise is that the Mopars kept up with the fuel-injected, four-speed automatic, sleek sheet metal police cars from Ford and Chevrolet as well as they did.

In 1988, the California Highway Patrol covered its bet by getting some Ford Crown Victorias. The Diplomat was on the way out and the Crown Vic had not been a CHP Enforcement-class vehicle since 1984. The CHP may have been surprised to find the 1988 Crown Vic to be unchanged since the 1984 model! The 351-ci Windsor HO V-8 still used a "variable venturi" carburetor, still produced 180 horsepower and still had a 117-mile-per-hour top speed. The Crown Vic was restyled for 1988 with slightly sleeker sheet metal, including an aerodynamically blended front bumper and wraparound taillights. The 1988 model year would be nearly identical to the 1990 and 1991 models. A wide chrome stripe was at the bottom of the fenders and doors only in 1988. For 1990 and 1991, this would be a very thin strip and not attached to the doors.

This black 1988 Ford Mustang was with the New York State Police and assigned to the New York State Thruway. The NYSP police cars that were not Thruway units were dark blue with basically the same markings except for the Thruway decal. This 225-horsepower, 5.0-liter V-8-powered Mustang has a gold body stripe; gold hood, trunk, and fender lettering; gold door shield; and an all-red strobe lightbar. All-red strobes were extremely rare. The color temperature of red strobe lights was so close to sunlight that the emergency lights "washed out" during the day, meaning they were hard to see. The 5.0-liter HO Mustang had a top speed of 134 miles per hour, got to 60 miles per hour in just 6.9 seconds, and to 100 miles per hour in 19 seconds. It ran the quarter mile in 15.5 seconds at 91 miles per hour.

This 1989 Chevrolet Caprice with the Georgia State Patrol is silver over bright blue. The fender, trunk, and door lettering is silver while the strobe bar is all-blue. The big news for 1989 was the use of throttle body fuel injection on the 350-ci V-8. This bumped the power from 180 horsepower to 190 horsepower. More important, fuel-injection flattened the torque curve and gave the V-8 outstanding bottom end punch. In a year of transition from Dodge and Plymouth to something else, fuel-injection on the 350-ci V-8 was a huge advantage for Chevrolet. The 1989 Caprice was selected by the California Highway Patrol, and by the vast majority of city, county, and state police departments across the country. In 1989, the 350-ci-powered Impala got to 60 miles per hour in 9.8 seconds. This was the best a full-size police sedan had run since 1978 and the big-block era!

This 1989 Chevrolet Caprice is on the job with the Maryland State Police. The cruiser is tan with the agency's trademark olive drab/brown body stripe, gold fender and trunk lettering, and the gold, brown, and red door shield. New for 1989, Chevrolet re-introduced the 170-horsepower, 305-ci fuel-injected V-8 to join the 4.3-liter V-6 as an urban patrol engine. The 350-ci fuel-injected V-8 in this MSP unit produced 190 horsepower. New for 1989 were 3.42 to 1 rear gears with the 350-ci engine. Higher compression increased the horsepower, fuel injection flattened the torque curve, and more aggressive rear gears resulted in the fastest acceleration and highest top speed in 10 years. For the third year in a row, the 350-ci Caprice won the Michigan State Police patrol vehicle competition by capturing four of the six test phases.

The Tennessee Highway Patrol used the 1989 Dodge Diplomat in its last year as a police car. This black-over-cream-cruiser has white-on-black fender and door lettering, the state seal as a door shield, and an all-blue Jetsonic. From the mid-1980s on, Chrysler Corporation didn't touch the police-package engine, transmission, brakes, suspension, or sheet metal. Once the ultimate police cars, Dodge and Plymouth were simply passed by Ford and especially Chevrolet in all areas of performance, economy, comfort, safety, and styling. The competition had four-speed automatics, fuel-injected engines, sleek sheet metal and on the drawing boards had four-wheel discs and antilock brakes. Dodge and Plymouth did not get beat by others in the police market. They simply quit trying themselves.

The New York State Police selected the 1989 Dodge Diplomat in its last year as a police-package car. This deep-blue cruiser with a gold body stripe, gold door shield, and all-red lightbar was powered by the 175-horsepower, 318-ci four-barrel V-8. The last of the famous Dodge police cars got to 60 miles per hour in 11.8 seconds, ran the quarter mile in 18.8 seconds, and had a top speed of 119 miles per hour. Chrysler Corporation simply stopped developing its V-8-powered, rear-drive vehicles by 1983. In 1989, Chrysler Corporation produced 17 variations of 12 basic engines for its 7 different car platforms. Of the 17 engines, the 15 front-drive engines were all fuel-injected. Five were turbocharged. Most had a single overhead cam. The rear-drive, V-8-powered sedan was as foreign to Chrysler engineers in 1989 as the front-drive, four-cylinder Omni/Horizon was to Chrysler engineers in 1975.

The Oklahoma Highway Patrol used the 1989 Plymouth Gran Fury. So did the New York City Police, the Wisconsin State Patrol (M-bodies were built in Kenosha), and the Vermont State Police. The Kansas Highway Patrol, the Portland (Oregon) Police, and the Philadelphia (Pennsylvania) Police all knew that 1989 was the last year for the Gran Fury and Dodge Diplomat. Rather than changing their specs to something else, they remained loyal to the cars that dominated at least the first half of the 1980s. The 175-horsepower, 318-ci four-barrel engine produced a top speed of 120 miles per hour in the Gran Fury. The problem was that in 1989 the retail Ford Taurus SHO hit 141 miles per hour, the Corvette L98 reached 153 miles per hour, the 20th Anniversary Pontiac Trans Am reached 162 miles per hour, and the Corvette ZR-1 hit 181 miles per hour. If Chrysler did not want to improve the Diplomat and Gran Fury, exiting the market was the best thing.

This 1989 Plymouth Gran Fury is parked in front of the Ohio State Highway Patrol Academy in Columbus. The silver cruiser has gold lettering, a rear seat partition, and a red/blue JetSonic. This square-jawed vehicle just LOOKED like a police car. However, on the 75th anniversary of the Dodge Brothers business, Dodge and Plymouth pulled out of the police market and ceased all rear-drive-sedan production. "Chrysler is a front wheel drive company. Rear wheel drive involves a totally different set of technologies, like driveshafts and differentials and our engineers are concentrating on other things" according to the press release. Chrysler found itself in a Catch-22. Cops did not like front-wheel-drive cars, and all Chrysler made was front-wheel-drive cars.

This 1989 Ford Crown Victoria is on the job with the Keene (New Hampshire) Police. The all-white cruiser has a gold-outlined blue body band and an all-blue Whelen strobe bar. The 114.3-inch cruiser with the 55A police package came with either the 160-horsepower, 302-ci EFI V-8 or the 180-horsepower, 351 Windsor HO variable-venturi V-8. With the 302-ci EFI engine, the big Ford was the full equal to the Chevrolet Caprice with its 305-ci EFI V-8. In the areas of acceleration, top speed, road course times, braking power, and fuel economy, these two cars were door-handle to door-handle. In all these areas, both vehicles were superior to the 318-ci two-barrel versions of the Dodge Diplomat and Plymouth Gran Fury. The Ford and Chevrolet ran 3.08 to 1 rear gears. The Mopars with the two-barrel engine used 2.24 to 1 gears which hurt BOTH performance and economy! For urban police use, both Ford and Chevrolet passed the Mopars in the mid-1980s.

In 1989, the Royal Canadian Mounted Police used the Ford Crown Victoria. This bright-blue Ford has white front doors and twin, oversize red rotators. For 1988, the 114.3-inch wheelbase was restyled with sleeker sheet metal and wraparound taillights. The only change for this year was a much smaller chrome strip below the fenders. With the 180-horsepower, 351 Windsor HO engine, the big Ford was just slightly faster around a road course than the four-barrel Diplomat and Gran Fury. While the Ford had the same 119-mile-per-hour top speeds as the Mopars, it got to 100 miles per hour much quicker. Regardless, the 351-ci Ford was no match for the 350-ci Caprice. This performance gap would continue to widen for the next seven years!

This 1989 special-service-package Mustang was a morale-builder with the Kleberg County (Texas) Sheriff's Department. This 225-horsepower, 5.0-liter HO-powered pursuit pony is all-white with a gold-outlined blue body stripe and blue lettering. The lightbar is a low-profile Whelen strobe unit with red and blue lenses. By 1989, two-thirds of the state police departments and highway patrols had a fleet of special-service-package Mustangs. So did literally hundreds of county sheriffs' departments, both urban and rural. Available once again with either a four-speed auto or, more frequently, a five-speed stick, the hot pony car hit 100 miles per hour 10 seconds faster than the 350-ci fuel-injected Caprice, was 4 full seconds faster around an 86-second road course than the Caprice, and had a top speed of 138 miles per hour, 16 miles per hour faster than the Caprice. The Caprice would close that gap by 1994 and the Camaro would power away from the Mustang in 1991, but for the time being, the Mustang was the cock of the walk.

Chapter Eleven

1990-1994

In 1990, the law-enforcement community from fleet managers to traffic officers were in a state of shock and disbelief. Dodge and Plymouth had pulled out of the police-car market—a market owned by Dodge and Plymouth from the late 1960s to the mid-1980s.

In 1990, the choice of a V-8-powered police sedan became even more limited than it had been in the 1980s. Chevrolet offered its 116-inch Caprice, and Ford offered its 114.4-inch Crown Victoria. That was it! Ford offered a front-drive police car for the first time—the 106-inch Taurus. Unlike the Chrysler K-cars and the Chevrolet Celebrity before it, the Taurus came with the heavy-duty, unlimited-use, genuine "police" package. Previous front-drive cars had been labeled as light-duty "special service" package cars, but time has shown that the Taurus wasn't a legitimate heavy-duty police car. It had the acceleration, braking, and cornering to be a police car, but in spite of Ford's best efforts, the car's lack of durability meant that it only merited a special-service label. However, it was a giant step forward for a front-drive, V-6-powered, mid-size sedan. It was the first car of its kind to actually be able to keep up with the traditional V-8-powered, rear-drive police sedans.

In 1991, Chevrolet dramatically restyled its Caprice, and the result was its best-ever police car. The new aero-appearance was also the inspiration for countless jokes from cops all across America.

This attractive 1990 Chevrolet Caprice is with the North Providence (Rhode Island) Police. The cruiser has a light-blue roof over an all-white body with deep-blue and red body stripes and red lettering and numbering. The 1990 model year was the last for the boxy-style Caprice. For 1990, the 350 ci used in nearly every Caprice got a little more compression, which increased the torque, but the horsepower remained the same at 190 horsepower. The 170-horsepower, 305-ci V-8 and the 140-horsepower, 262-ci V-6 were also available. The V-6-powered Caprice had a top speed of 110 miles per hour, while the smaller V-8 reached 113 miles per hour. All Caprice police cars used the four-speed automatic overdrive transmission.

It was called everything: bathtub, jellybean, Hudson, turtle, Nash, whale, Shamu — all because of the integral rear fender skirts. It got so bad that some traffic officers and road deputies got a little defensive about the cars they were issued.

The 1991 Caprice, for as different as it looked, was almost unchanged in terms of powertrain. While the car's stunning acceleration remained the same, something was very different: a 130-mile-per-hour top speed! Police sedans had not seen 130 miles per hour since 1978. Ford introduced its new Crown Victoria in 1992, but the new car would not run 130 miles per hour! In addition, Chevrolet introduced the Camaro RS with a special-service package and upped the stakes in the pursuit-car class. During the 1979 CHP Special Purpose Vehicle Study, the Camaro Z28's performance had opened the door for pony cars as pursuit vehicles. Despite the brilliant performance, the Mustang underbid the Camaro and got all the fame!

However, for 1991, the Camaro RS was available with a 5.0-liter V-8 teamed with a five-speed stick or a 5.7-liter V-8 bolted to a four-speed automatic. While the 5.0-liter Mustang had indeed been the fastest car on the road in 1982, the Camaro was faster during the mid-1980s. The Camaro was now among the fastest cars with unparalleled top speed of 150 miles per hour. While the Camaro was much faster on paper than the 5.0-liter Mustang, in practical terms the Mustang and the Camaro were plenty fast for pursuit and traffic-enforcement duties. The special-service package for the Mustang would be dropped after 1993; however, the Camaro would remain in police service through 2000.

At Ford, the Taurus' 3.8-liter V-6 engine received a boost from 140 horsepower to 155 horsepower. This upgrade allow the Taurus to clearly out-accelerate the 5.8-liter Crown Vic and outrun the 5.7-liter Caprice around the Michigan International Speedway road course. The 1991 model year gave cops a lot to think about. Would the front-drive, V-6-powered, mid-size sedan be the police car of the future? It sure looked like it.

For 1992, Chevrolet retained the title of top-selling police-car manufacturer in spite of the aero-look of the fender-skirted Caprice. The reason was simple. At the beginning of the model year, when most police cars are ordered, the only available full-size police sedan was the Caprice. The newly remodeled, wedge-style Ford Crown Victoria wasn't available until mid-year. Although some police departments thought the new Ford was worth the wait, most departments could not wait.

Chevrolet made its second and ill-fated attempt at producing a front-wheel-drive police car in the form of the 3.1-liter V-6-powered, mid-size Lumina. Technically, the Lumina was a light-duty, special-service-package vehicle and not a heavy-duty, police-package car like the Taurus. Life on the mean streets has proven that even heavy-duty police-package, front-drive cars should be restricted to light duty.

For the 1992 model year, the newly styled and re-engineered Ford Crown Victoria stole the show. It was literally the talk of the entire automotive industry, mainly due to the 4.6-liter SOHC V-8 engine. This powerplant was the first of Ford's new family of "modular" V-8 engines that could be built on the same assembly line and could use many of the same components but could have different displacement and head configurations. The 4.6-liter SOHC, the 4.6-liter dual overhead cam (DOHC), and the 5.4-liter SOHC engines are all part of the same family.

All else being equal, the 1992 Ford SOHC engine produces around 40 percent more horsepower than the 1991 Ford overhead-valve engines. The new Ford had its own version of aero-styling, which was considerably more attractive than Chevrolet. The Ford used four-wheel disc brakes for the first time since 1978, the first ABS used on a full-size Ford, the first air bag on a full-size Ford, and a new electronic four-speed automatic overdrive transmission. However, it was the revolutionary SOHC engine that made the headlines.

Here's a 1990 Chevrolet Caprice with the Mason County (Washington) Sheriff's Department. This cruiser has a peanut-butter-yellow over pickle-green color scheme with an all-blue lightbar. And sheriffs' deputies in New York get grief over their red and white cruisers! New for 1990, Chevrolet moved the shoulder-harness attachment point from the B-pillar to the front doors. The door-mounted, "passive front seat belt systems" were new to the Caprice. The three-point system was supposed to both hold the driver in the seat and keep the front door from opening in the event of an accident. The problem was if the door opened during a crash, the driver would lose the effectiveness of the seat belt. Chevrolet moved the shoulder harness anchor back to the B-pillar for 1991 and it remained there through 1996.

Here is a solid-red 1990 Chevrolet Caprice with the Kansas City (Missouri) Police. The driver is Sgt. Jim Post, on the day of his retirement. Post promptly started the "Police Car Owners Of America," the nation's oldest and largest police-car club. The PCOOA holds national conventions every year and even has its own, fully stocked police museum in Eureka Springs, Arkansas. Membership to the PCOOA is open to all enthusiasts, both police officers and civilians. In 1990, the 190-horsepower, 350-ci Caprice squared off against only the 180-horsepower, 351-ci Ford Crown Victoria at the annual Michigan State Police vehicle tests. For the first time since the MSP conducted patrol vehicle testing, one car won outright all six of the test phases, the 350-ci Caprice. The Caprice would win all six phases two more times, once in 1991 and again in 1996, its final year.

This 1990 Ford Crown Victoria was used by a Sector Sergeant with the Des Moines (Iowa) Police. This is Des Moines, the capital city, located in the center of the state, not Des Moines County, located on the southeast corner of the state on the Mississippi River. The 114.3-inch Crown Vic is white with a black hood and black trunk. The all-red lightbar includes integral front takedown and side alley lights. The unusually shaped door shield is gold and tan. Note the dog-dish hubcaps, as opposed to full-dress wheel covers. In 1990, the 55A police package was available for the low trim LTD Crown Victoria "S" and the upscale "LX" version. New for 1990 was a driver's air bag, a year behind Dodge and Plymouth but a year before Chevrolet.

This 1990 Ford Crown Victoria is with the Ontario Provincial Police. The OPP is comparable to the state police or highway patrol in America, except Ontario stretches from Minnesota to New York! This Crown Vic is all-white with gold-over-blue stripes, gold fender lettering, and black-outlined gold door lettering. Note the twin siren and public address system speakers. This OPP cruiser is powered by a 180-horsepower, 5.8-liter V-8. It was photographed at a rest stop halfway between Windsor and London. This was the cruiser that was used to escort 50 vintage police cars from the Police Car Owners Of America National Convention in Detroit to the Ford Assembly Plant in London. The 351-ci Windsor engine in this OPP cruiser, and the assembly of the Crown Vic itself, all took place in Ontario. All Crown Vics are assembled in London.

The 4.6-liter SOHC V-8 wasn't a threat to the Chevy small-block V-8, but it was a vast improvement over Ford's own two police V-8s in terms of both power and economy.

For 1992, Chrysler Corporation was back in the police market with the Jeep Cherokee. Powered by a High Output 4.0-liter six, the Cherokee was available as a rear-wheel drive with a Hotchkiss live rear axle or as an all-wheel drive, and it completely filled a wide-open hole in the market. In the early 1990s, sport/utes were just starting to catch on, and they outperformed cars on sand, mud, snow, and ice. Although it made sense to offer the vehicle, the Cherokees were not widely used by law enforcement or the general public until the early 1990s. By the late 1990s, half of the vehicles submitted to the Michigan State Police for its annual testing were sport/utility vehicles. Most significantly, the Cherokee did not handle like a typical high-centered, 4x4 sport/ute. It handled like a Chrysler police car.

In 1993, Chevrolet continued to dominate the police market with the tweaked-out aero-Caprice and changed the styling by opening the rear wheelwells. For 1993, the front-wheel-drive Chevrolet Lumina was available with either a 9C3 "police" package or a B4C "special purpose" package. Both were powered by the 3.1-liter V-6. In 1993, the fourth-generation Chevrolet Camaro was released. It now was powered by its own version of the Corvette LT-1 350-ci V-8. The LT-1 V-8 was only one of the significant upgrades in the new Camaro. The Short/Long Arm front suspension replacing the MacPherson struts was a significant development. A newly restyled 1993 Camaro received larger brakes and ABS for the first time. In addition, the Camaro was available with either a four-speed auto or a six-speed stick, which replaced the five-speed stick.

This 1990 Ford Crown Victoria is with the Prince William County (Virginia) Police. Prince William County is south of the Washington, D.C., area and includes a long section of Interstate 95, the only southbound interstate out of the D.C. Metro area. I-95 is infamous for trouble! This attractive Crown Vic is blue with a white hood, roof, and trunk. The cruiser has an all-blue Federal Street Hawk, one of the best, if not THE best, high-profile lightbars ever made. The Old Line State cruiser also has white door letters and a broad white body stripe that makes the 114.3-inch cruiser look even longer. This county police car has a 351-ci or 5.8-liter V-8 producing 180 horsepower. The 4,152-pound cruiser had a top speed of 121 miles per hour.

Ford released four different kinds of police- and special-service-package vehicles for 1993. The first was the full-size, 114.4-inch, Crown Victoria powered by the 4.6-liter SOHC V-8. A chrome grille replacing the "grille-less" front end was the only change from its mid-1992 debut. The mid-size, 106-inch Taurus powered by the 3.8-liter V-6 was the second police car, and it remains the best-selling mid-size police sedan. Third, the 100.5-inch-wheelbase, 5.0-liter HO V-8-powered Mustang pursuit car was available with a special-service package for the last time.

The Ford that chased Porsches for a living had served its purpose, and it had bridged the performance gap from the 1980s. The full-size, four-door sedans' performance standards were high enough, so that the Mustang was no longer needed for traffic enforcement. Full-size cars didn't have the compromises of a pony car. The 1980 318-ci Dodge St. Regis, which had forced the adoption of a pursuit pony car, had only been able to run the quarter mile in the high 19-second range with a top speed of 115 miles per hour. The full-size police sedans now ran the quarter mile in the 16-second bracket with top speeds averaging 130 miles per hour.

The special-service-package Explorer was the fourth police-package vehicle from Ford, and it was available in 4x2 or 4x4 configuration. Powered by a 4.0-liter six, it was rushed into police service as a competitor to the Jeep Cherokee. Big mistake. While the 111.9-inch Explorer was roomier than the Cherokee, the Explorer underperformed when compared to the Cherokee.

The Jeep Cherokee was back for 1993 with hard-edged performance. The Jeep's police package clearly outperformed the less-developed Explorer, which was essentially a retail sport/ute pressed into police service.

This 1990 Ford Mustang is a special-service-package vehicle with the Everett (Washington) Police. The all-white 5.0-liter Mustang has a blue stripe, blue lettering, and a blue door shield. The low-profile JetSonic has red and blue lenses. From 1987 to 1989, the Mustang came equipped with powder-coat black-painted wheels as standard equipment, while brushed aluminum was optional. From 1990 to 1993, brushed-aluminum wheels were the only ones available on the special-service-package cars. The 5.0-liter V-8 produced 225 horsepower and could be teamed with either a four-speed auto or five-speed stick. The five-speed car was quicker to 100 miles per hour; however, the road-course times and top speeds were nearly the same. The Mustang remained the only true high-performance car from 1982 to 1990.

A no-nonsense-looking 1990 Ford Crown Victoria with the Ohio State Highway Patrol, this 114.3-inch Ford is all-silver right down to the silver wheels. The door markings include gold lettering and the famous black and gold winged tire. The most important marking on this OSHP cruiser is the license plate. The ACE license plate means the state trooper driving this Ford has recovered five or more stolen cars. Every truly active traffic officer has something for motivation, whether it is drunk driving, drug trafficking, stolen vehicles, or wanted persons. This hard-working trooper has a nose for stolen cars, and a rear seat complete with cage for his next catch.

In 1990, Ford entered the harsh and hostile front-wheel-drive police-car market with its 140-horsepower, 3.8-liter, 106-inch-wheelbase Taurus. This sergeant with the Wayne County (Michigan) Sheriff's Department is shown with one of the very first police-package cars. Early evaluations of the front-drive Taurus were also performed by the San Diego, California, Police and the Utah Highway Patrol. Unlike the 1982 Dodge Aries K and the 1984 Chevrolet Celebrity that came with the light-duty, special-service package, the 1990 Taurus was introduced with the full-blown, heavy-duty, police package. These police-package cars are easy to recognize by their unique cooling slots in the grille. The Taurus ran the Michigan State Police road course more than a second quicker than the 351-ci Crown Vic, got to 100 miles per hour just as fast, had better brakes, and much better gas mileage.

For 1991, the Chevrolet Caprice was dramatically restyled. The aerodynamically sleek styling inspired many jokes and derogatory nicknames. However, the new Caprice, like this Benton County (Indiana) Sheriff's unit, reached a top speed of 130 miles per hour. That was the highest top end in well over 20 years! The jump from 122 miles per hour in 1990 to 130 miles per hour in 1991 was due strictly to the aero-styling. The 350-ci V-8 had been bumped up 5 horsepower to 195 horsepower; however, the 1991 Caprice was also 240 pounds heavier. This BCSD Caprice is two-tone county brown: a brown hood, roof, and trunk over tan fenders and doors. This cruiser is equipped with the Federal JetSonic lightbar sporting red and blue lenses. The door shield is a brown and gold five-point star. Note the plastic wheel covers, called frisbees in 1991, due to their tendency to fly off the wheels.

This sharp-looking 1991 Chevrolet Caprice is with the Grand Traverse County (Michigan) Sheriff's Department. The sleek cruiser is white with a gold-outlined, dark-brown stripe containing gold lettering. The door shield is a brown and gold six-point star along with the outline of the state of Michigan. This county patroller has the police officer's most popular way to meet new people, a dash-mounted traffic radar antenna. The black B- and C-pillars on this Caprice identify it as a 1991 model. For 1992, the B- and C-pillars were painted body colors. This cruiser also has the optional stainless-steel wheel covers. The plastic wheel covers came off the wheels with such ease and frequency that Chevrolet Fleet replaced the plastic "frisbees" with these stainless wheel covers upon request and at no charge.

This 1991 Chevrolet Caprice was used by the Tennessee Highway Patrol. The cruiser has an all-blue JetSonic lightbar, A-pillar spotlight, and dash-mounted traffic radar antenna. The Volunteer State cruisers are brown over tan with brown and gold stripes, door shield, and lettering. Powered by the 195-horsepower, 350-ci V-8, the 115.9-inch Caprice got to 60 miles per hour in 9.4 seconds and ran the quarter mile in 17.3 seconds at 81 miles per hour. Compared to the 1990 Caprice, the greatly restyled 1991 Caprice was longer, wider, and taller with more shoulder and hip room. The Caprice was judged by the Michigan State Police to be a more comfortable "office" based on a 27-point checklist. Lots of cops and citizens made jokes about the styling, but the 1991 Caprice was the best police car for highway patrol use since the 1978 Dodges and Plymouths.

In 1994, Chevrolet installed the hot LT-1 350-ci V-8 in its full-size Caprice to produce its best police car ever. With this one change, the 116-inch police Caprice went from running a high 16-second quarter mile with 130 miles per hour top speeds to running a low 16-second quarter mile at 140 miles per hour. This one change made obsolete the need for the Mustang and Camaro. The police Camaro would continue to be offered through the turn of the century, but the performance void no longer existed.

Chevrolet produced three LT-1 engines: a 260-horsepower version for the police Caprice and Impala SS, a 275-horsepower version for the special service and retail Camaro, and a 300-horsepower version restricted to the retail-only Corvette. The new Caprice had dual air bags, four-wheel disc brakes, a 3.42 rear gear, and a four-speed "electronic" automatic overdrive, all for the first time. The new Caprice came with bolt-on center hubs from the Chevy truck line. Neither city potholes, nor county washboard roads, nor the median between state roads can dislodge these wheel covers. Chevrolet Fleet, thank you for these! For 1994, Chevrolet continued to be the number-one-selling brand of police car.

A 265-ci V-8 engine, which used LT-1 pushrod technology and generated 30 horsepower more than the 305-ci V-8, was available. The Chevrolet police package had started out powered by a 265-ci V-8 in 1955, and Chevy ended its police-car involvement with a 265-ci V-8 offered from 1994 to 1996. That makes these 265-ci-powered 9C1 Caprices very nostalgic! In 1994, Ford fielded three police-type vehicles. These included the full-size Crown Victoria, the mid-size Taurus, and the Explorer sport/utility.

In 1994, Chrysler Fleet continued to make life tough for anyone thinking about competing in the 4x4 police market. The 4.0-liter High Output Jeep Cherokee continued to out-accelerate, out-brake, outcorner, and otherwise outrun the Ford Explorer.

The black B- and C-pillars on this white Pennsylvania State Police Chevrolet Caprice identify it as a 1991 model. In 1991, the PSP changed its color scheme from the blue and white used since 1974, to white with a gold-outlined black stripe. They also changed to a new door shield, which matched the officers' new shoulder patch. This 1991 PSP Caprice is equipped with the novel, seven-pod, V-shaped Federal Vision lightbar introduced in 1991. New for 1991 was a driver-side air bag and an Anti-Lock Braking System. ABS brakes became controversial when an Indiana police lieutenant died after he lost control of his new Caprice. The ABS brakes were the immediate suspect. In reality, lack of training in how to use and what not to do with ABS was the culprit. Chevrolet spearheaded a nationwide effort to raise awareness and training on the topic of ABS.

Here's a 1991 Chevrolet Caprice with the New York City Police. This was the first year for this kind of marking. The NYPD cruisers had been blue with a white stripe from 1973 up to 1991. In fact, some 1991 NYPD patrollers still had the old-style markings, which used the shoulder patch as a door shield but used small fender lettering. New for 1991, the NYPD made the door shield smaller, added a second white stripe, and the bold and oversize letters "NYC Police." The lightbar is a new-for-1991 Federal Vision, with two white pods and five red pods. The precinct number, which was prominently marked on the rear doors, was moved back to the rear fenders in much smaller numbers. What is the most surprising part of this photo? That's right, the cruiser has its hubcaps. Surprising enough in New York, anyhow, it is shocking that this RMP was able to keep the plastic frisbees in place. They flew off with the first pothole, first washboard road, or first crossed median.

This white-over-black 1991 Chevrolet Caprice was used by the Wyoming Highway Patrol. For 1991, the 195-horsepower, 350-ci-powered Caprice repeated the performance set by the 1990 Caprice during Michigan State Police testing. For the second year in a row, the Caprice won all six test phases (acceleration, top speed, braking, road course, fuel economy, and ergonomics) to be judged the most police car for the money. This was the fifth straight year the Caprice took on all comers and won under the test method where performance is adjusted into the bid price. The Caprice would go on to win this most-bang-for-the-buck evaluation for another five years in a row. The 1991 to 1996 Chevrolet Caprices were probably the best police cars ever built.

This 1991 Ford Crown Victoria was used by the San Francisco Police. The Northern California cruiser uses the white-over-black color scheme with four white doors like the Southern California departments. Many northern police cars use the CHP color scheme of white front doors but black rear doors. The police markings are the same used for five decades: S.F.P.D. in gold letters inside a gold-outlined, blue seven-point star. The script lettering under the star reads "Serving Our City." Note the rear-seat partition and the bar across the rear windows. The emergency lights are a Whelen Edge strobe bar with red and blue lenses. In 1991, the big Ford was powered by either the 160-horsepower, 5.0-liter V-8 or the 180-horsepower, 5.8-liter-HO V-8. These Fords were comfortable patrol cars.

Here's a 1991 Ford Crown Victoria used by the Glynn County (Georgia) Police. This Georgia Sheriff's Department cruiser has a tan hood, roof, and trunk over a brown body. The door shield is the same as the uniform patch and reads "Police, Glynn County, Golden Isles." The lightbar is the Whelen Edge, the most famous of the strobe lightbars, and it is fitted with both red and blue lights. That's a little unusual. Most Georgia Sheriffs' cars and the Georgia State Patrol ran all-blue emergency lights. Glynn County is famous among cops as the home of the Federal Law Enforcement Training Center. FLETC trains Border Patrol agents and U.S. Marshals; however, courses from firearms to pursuit driving are also open to officers from city, county, and state police departments across the nation.

The Utah Highway Patrol was one of the first police departments to test the Ford Taurus and the first state police department to adopt the Taurus for patrol use. Here's an all-white UHP Taurus with the brown on gold "beehive" and a red, driver-side spotlight. The Taurus was greatly improved for 1991. Ford bumped the horsepower of the 3.8-liter V-6 from 140 horsepower to 155 horsepower. That was what it needed! The Taurus stole the show at the Michigan State Police tests. It had the fastest road-course lap time of any four-door sedan, including the 350-ci-powered aero-Caprice. A V-6-powered, front-drive, mid-size car outrunning the best V-8-powered, rear drive, full-size car gave cops a lot to think about! The Taurus bested the Crown Vic in four of the six MSP test phases! Could this be the future number one police car for America?

In the 1990's, all-white police cars were as common as all-black ones were in the 1950s. This 1991 Ford Crown Victoria is with the Herndon (Virginia) Police outside Washington, D.C. It has a blue stripe, blue fender markings and a blue and gold police shield on the door. The cruiser is fitted with a red and blue lens Federal Street Hawk. This was the last year for this square body style, introduced in 1988. The 1991 Crown Vic was powered by either the 180-horsepower, 351-ci/5.8-liter HO Windsor V-8 or the 160-horsepower, 302-ci/5.0-liter V-8. This was the last year for these drivetrains in a police sedan. The 351-ci and 302-ci powerplants had top speeds of 121 and 108 miles per hour, respectively.

This 1991 California Highway Patrol Ford Mustang sports the new-for-1991 Federal Vision lightbar. So does the 1991 Ford Crown Victoria parked next to it. The special-service Mustang was a carryover from 1990 and 1986. It really had not changed since then. The Mustang had been the only true high-performance police car for nearly a decade. However, the Mustang did not continue to improve in the late 1980s, opening the door to the Chevrolet Camaro Z28. In 1991, retail Mustangs received new five-spoke aluminum wheels. Ford Fleet, however, decided to retain the 10-spoke bushed-aluminum wheels for the police version. From 1991 to 1993, the special-service-package Mustang was the only Mustang to come with these wheels. By 1991, the special-service Mustang was used extensively throughout the United States and Canada. The top speed from the Ford pony car this year was 136 miles per hour.

In 1991, Chevrolet had a very nasty surprise for Ford: a special-service package for the Camaro RS. The traffic-enforcement-oriented Camaro B4C, like this 1991 silver-over-blue Nevada Highway Patrol unit, came with either a 230-horsepower, 305-ci V-8 and a five-speed stick or a 245-horsepower, 350-ci V-8 and a four-speed auto. Both engines produced top speeds of 150 miles per hour. Both Camaro B4C pursuit cars ran the quarter mile in the 15-second bracket. The 5.7-liter Camaro B4C set a new Michigan State Police road-racing track record in its first year out. The Camaro outperformed the Mustang in every category but fuel economy and ergonomics. The Camaro had some of the best braking performance seen during the MSP testing, while the Mustang picked this year, of all years, to fail to meet the MSP's minimum requirement for braking!

This imposing black and white 1992 Chevrolet Caprice is with the Los Angeles County Sheriff's Department. By 1992, Chevrolet had discontinued the plastic "frisbee" wheel covers. The 9C1 police package now included dress, stainless-steel wheel covers that were optional in 1991. The 1991 and 1992 wheel covers were unique. They had a black circle with the word Caprice in the center. The 1993 versions had a gold bowtie in the center. The smaller 305-ci V-8 engine maintained its 170-horsepower rating and was now available with 2.56 to 1 "economy" rear gears. The larger 350-ci V-8 was bumped up 10 horsepower to 205 horsepower, thanks to a less-restrictive exhaust, larger-exhaust pipe diameters, and a lower back-pressure catalytic converter. The 1992 Caprice now ran the quarter mile in the same 16-second bracket as the 5.0-liter automatic trans Mustang.

Here's a 1992 Chevrolet Caprice used by the Sandwich (Illinois) Police. Yes, Sandwich. It is a town of 5,600 people located well outside of Chicago. This all-white Caprice is very typical of the small-town police cars found from coast to coast in 1992: All-white with a custom door shield and a Federal Street Hawk red/blue lightbar. In 1992, Ford delayed the introduction of its restyled car until mid-year. This gave an estimated 70 percent of the police market to Chevrolet, almost by default. But what if you didn't like the styling of the fender-skirted rear wheelwells of the 1991 and 1992? (And most cops did not.) Too bad! Can we interest you in a nice front-drive Taurus? While the 1992 Caprice was an excellent car, people were still not accustomed to the look. Many cops drove the Caprice simply because there was no other full-size police car available!

This all-white 1992 Chevrolet Caprice is with the Del Rey Oaks (California) Police. The Del Rey Oaks patroller has attractive blue and aqua body stripes, which is fitting for its Monterey Bay-area patrol jurisdiction. With the 205-horsepower, 350-ci V-8, the 1992 Caprice was 3 seconds faster to 100 miles per hour than the 1991 version and 1.5 seconds quicker around a road course during MSP testing. Since the 5.7-liter Caprice now reached top speeds of 133 miles per hour, it required the use of V-rated pursuit tires. The H-rated tires from 1991 were good only to 130 miles per hour. Police departments could still order the less expensive H-rated tires, but Chevrolet installed a speed limiter on those cars! This 1992 Caprice is easy to spot from a 1991 version. The B- and C-pillars are body color instead of black.

In 1992, Chevrolet introduced a special-service package for its front-wheel-drive Lumina. The North Dakota State Patrol gave the 140-horsepower, 3.1-liter V-6-powered, 107.5-inch-wheel-base sedan a try. On the dash is a traffic radar unit. This was a genuine traffic-enforcement vehicle. Chevrolet borrowed from the Euro's F41 sport suspension to develop its re-entry into the front-drive market. In fact, the special-service Lumina is basically a Euro 3.1 with the addition of extra oil coolers and with steel wheels instead of the alloy wheels. Cops urged Chevrolet to use the 200-horsepower, 3.4-liter DOHC V-6 from the Z34 but Chevrolet was reluctant to put a high-performance engine in a special-service police-package car intended for light-duty police.

The 1992 Chevrolet Caprice was clearly the car of choice for many of the state police departments and highway patrols. Here's a silver-over-black North Carolina Highway Patrol unit sporting an all-blue JetSonic. The 205-horsepower, 350-ci V-8 Caprice faced off against a 210-horsepower, 281-ci SOHC V-8 Ford Crown Victoria at the Michigan State Police vehicle tests. It was the most anticipated match race since the California Highway Patrol tested cars to replace the St. Regis in 1981. The Chevrolet-versus-Ford race was basically overhead valves and bottom-end torque versus overhead cams and high-end horse-power. The new Ford was a little lighter, a little sleeker, and had four-wheel disc brakes with ABS. The 5.7-liter Caprice captured the top speed, acceleration, road course and ergonomics phases, and did well enough in the braking and fuel economy phases to win the overall showdown. That made it six years in a row for the 5.7-liter Caprice.

In 1992, the 100.5-inch-wheelbase Ford Mustang was again available with the special-service package. The pony car was powered by the 225-horsepower, 5.0-liter HO V-8 teamed with either a four-speed auto or five-speed stick. This brand-new Missouri State Highway Patrol pursuit car still has the window sticker! The unit is jet-black with gold and blue markings and all-red emergency lights. In 1992, the 5.0-liter Mustang ran about as hard as it ever did. Once again, the five-speed stick car was slightly faster than the four-speed automatic car. The Mustangs ran the quarter mile in the mid-15-second to low-16-second range and had a top speed of 136 miles per hour. The Mustang was a good, solid pursuit car. However, by 1992, the higher-performing Chevrolet Camaro had captured much of the Mustang's police market.

For 1992, the Ford Taurus, such as this Delaware State Police cruiser, got new and sleeker sheet metal. This was the first redesign since the retail introduction in 1986. The front end of the police-package Taurus no longer had cooling slots in the grille. The rear end now sported a tiny ducktail spoiler. In 1992, a passenger-side air bag became an option. In the battle of the front-drive cars, the T3.8-liter Taurus won five of the six test phases against the 3.1-liter Lumina. Once again, the 3.8-liter Taurus had a higher top speed, at 128 miles per hour, than the Crown Victoria. The Taurus was still quicker around the road course while the big Ford now had quicker acceleration and better brakes. In the early 1990s, the front-drive cars, especially the Taurus, were treated much more seriously than in the past. And the future of the V-8-powered, rear-drive sedans was not at all certain.

The big news from Ford in mid-1992 was the totally restyled and re-engineered Crown Victoria. New for 1992 were a sleek, aerodynamic styling, four-wheel disc brakes, and speed-sensitive power steering. Options included antilock brakes, which included an ABS-based Traction Assist feature. Ford had been first with four-wheel discs on its 1976 to 1978 police sedans. They were once again first to return to them. The Dodge Diplomat and Plymouth Gran Fury never had four-wheel discs. The Chevrolet Caprice would not get four-wheel discs until the LT-1-powered cars in 1994. Chevrolet got ABS in 1991 followed closely by Ford in mid-1992. Given the fiasco caused by ABS, it was Ford's good luck that Chevrolet was the first out with ABS! The big Ford easily outbraked the Caprice at the Michigan State Police tests. This Fremont (California) Police cruiser clearly shows the unique grille used in 1992. The FPD patroller is all-white with a blue body stripe, blue and gold door shield, and red and blue, ALL-light Federal JetStream.

Here's a 1992 Ford Crown Victoria with the Merced County (California) Sheriff's Department. This all-white Ford has gold and green body stripes with a gold and brown six-point star. The big news for mid-1992 was the 4.6-liter/281-ci Single Overhead Cam (SOHC) V-8 used in the police cars. At 210 horsepower, the 4.6-liter V-8 had 30 horsepower more than the 5.8-liter overhead-valve V-8 used in 1991. This was the first SOHC engine used in a full-size police sedan. This was the first time Ford's primary police engine was fuel-injected. The 5.8-liter V-8 used the variable-venture carburetor through 1991. The 4.6-liter SOHC engine was teamed with an electronic four-speed automatic. The 4.6-liter V-8 was the first "modular" V-8 built at Ford's Romeo, Michigan, Engine Plant. The 4.6-liter engine would later be bumped to 5.4 liters for use in trucks and upgraded to Double Overhead Cams for the Lincoln and Mustang.

Here's a very traditionally marked 1992 Ford Crown Victoria used by the Hastings (Nebraska) Police. The cruiser is black and white with black door lettering and the seal of the city. The red and blue Code 3 MX-7000 lightbar and a single A-pillar spotlight complete the cop gear. The 4.6-liter SOHC pushed the new Crown Vic to a disappointing top speed of 123 miles per hour. The 4.6-liter V-8 Crown Vic would improve every year but never match the 5.7-liter V-8 Caprice. However, it was a much better police car than the older Crown Vics with the same top speed, but faster acceleration and better fuel economy. The SOHC "modular" V-8 was a great replacement for the proven 302-ci and 351-ci engines, introduced to police cars in 1968 and 1970, respectively. The 302-ci and 351-ci overhead-valve engines produce around 32 horsepower per liter of displacement, while the new overhead cam engines produced around 44 horsepower per liter. The four-speed electronic overdrive trans with electronic torque converter lockup were also new for mid-1992.

New for 1992, Chrysler Corporation was back in the police-car business with a special-service package for the Jeep Cherokee, such as this Spokane (Washington) Police unit. The all-white Jeep with a red and blue lightbar and black-on-white door shield was powered by a 190-horsepower, 4.0-liter in-line six. With 190 horsepower, this overhead-valve in-line six was indeed a High Output engine producing as much horsepower per liter as Ford's new SOHC V-8. The Cherokee was based on a 101.4-inch wheelbase, 3 inches shorter than the Grand Cherokee. While sport-utility vehicles had been available since the 1967 Ford Bronco, they had never been taken seriously as a general-purpose patrol vehicle until the Jeep Cherokee. The Jeep wowed the fleet managers with straightline performance like a quarter-mile run in 17.9 seconds at 76 miles per hour. The big surprise was during the road-course phase. Many skeptics expected the high-ground clearance, "too tall" Jeep to simply roll over on its back as it braked from 80 miles per hour in preparation for a tight, uphill turn. Instead, the Cherokee powered around the course raising the inside front tire just like a Porsche. The hot Cherokee ended up out-running the 305-ci Caprice and 3.1-liter Lumina and was just 0.2 second behind the brand-new 4.6-liter Crown Vic.

Here's a 1992 Chevrolet Camaro RS with the B4C special-service package. This Centennial State pony car sports twin A-pillar spotlights with the passenger-side spot having a red lens. The low-riding, all-white cruiser has the CSP gold and blue winged tire as a door shield and blue fender and trunk lettering. This B4C Camaro is packing a 245-horsepower, 350-ci V-8 teamed with a four-speed automatic overdrive and 3.23 rear gears. This cop car runs the quarter mile in 15.1 seconds at 93 miles per hour. That's like the big-block police interceptors of the late 1960s. It also has a top speed of 152 miles per hour! New for 1992, the B4C Camaro used 1LE four-piston, twin caliber disc brakes developed for the Corvette. At the Michigan State Police vehicle tests, the Camaro re-set top speed, acceleration, and road-racing course records. Even the 230-horsepower, 305-ci V-8 version, which came only with the five-speed stick, had a 150-mile-per-hour top end. Otherwise, the 5.0-liter Camaro and the 5.0-liter Mustang had a very similar overall performance.

When New York City cops call for the cavalry, in 1993, they arrived in either a Ford one-ton pickup truck or this Chevrolet Caprice. This cruiser is with the legendary NYPD Emergency Services Unit. No other police department in the nation is structured quite like Emergency Services. They are a combination SWAT team and Rescue unit. They are the guys to call for anything from a barricaded gunman or emotionally disturbed person to a train wreck. The World Trade Center bombing rescue was handled by Emergency Services and they sent teams to assist in the Oklahoma City federal building bombing. Emergency Services is made up of the finest of New York's Finest. This particular Caprice is white over blue with an all-red Federal Vision and a McDermott "Multi-Level" light rack loaded with enough spotlights to illuminate mid-town Manhattan.

Here's a 1993 Chevrolet Caprice clearly marked as being with the 3rd District of the New York City Transit Police. At the time, NYC Transit handled enforcement duties in the city's subways and NYC Housing handled enforcement duties in the city's housing developments. These were separate departments from the New York City Police. By the mid-1990s, Transit and Housing were combined into the NYPD. The nation's largest police department just became larger, with a total of 38,000 sworn police officers. This 1993 Caprice has a dark-blue hood and trunk and dark-blue lettering on an otherwise white cruiser. The lightbar is an all-red Whelen Edge strobe unit. This cruiser also has red grille lights. Note the beautiful New York City skyline. There is no place quite like the Big Apple.

This 1993 Chevrolet Caprice is with the Bergenfield (New Jersey) Police. Bergenfield is just across the Hudson River from Yonkers, New York, in northern New Jersey. For 1993, the Caprice was powered by either the 170-horsepower, 350-ci V-8 or the 205-horsepower, 305-ci V-8. Many heavily urbanized police departments opted for the 305-ci engine. In fact, one-third of the 9C1 police-package Caprices came with the smaller engine. With this 170-horsepower engine, the 115.9-inch-wheelbase Caprice ran the quarter mile in the mid-18-second bracket just like a decade of 165-horsepower to 175-horse-power Dodge Diplomats. The top speed of 121 miles per hour was also typical of the 1980s. In some jurisdictions, this was all the performance that was needed.

For ages, the U.S. Border Patrol drove pale-green vehicles marked only with its gold and blue door shield. In the early 1990s, the Immigration and Naturalization Service changed to all-white cruisers with a wide green body stripe. This 1993 Chevrolet Caprice bears the new markings complete with the famous door shield and pale-yellow fender lettering. This particular cruiser sports a red and blue Federal JetSonic. The Caprice was mercifully restyled for 1993. The fender-skirt-style wheel-wells from 1991 and 1992 were opened up for 1993. That subtle change made all the difference! The jokes about the 1991 Caprice looking like a turtle stopped when it became known that the cars ran 130 miles per hour. The jokes about the Caprice looking like a Nash lingered until 1993. The restyle made for an attractive full-size sedan.

The Seattle (Washington) Police did an especially good job of marking their 1993 cruisers. This Chevrolet Caprice has an especially-striking blue and white paint scheme. Many departments struggled putting straight stripes on the decidedly rounded Caprice. The cruiser has both a formal door shield and blue door and fender lettering at a time when some departments used either a door shield or lettering but not both. New for 1993 were full-dress stainless-steel wheel covers with a gold bowtie in the center. These would be optional through 1996 on the 9C1 police package. For the seventh year in a row, the 350-ci Caprice won the Michigan State Police vehicle tests by capturing five of the six test phases, including most braking power.

In 1993, Chevrolet offered two kinds of Luminas for police work. One was the B4C special-service-package Lumina, introduced in 1992. The other was the 9C3 Police-package Lumina, such as this Whitewater (Wisconsin) Police unit. This is no meter maid car. The Decatur Electronics traffic radar antenna on the dash confirms the role of this Lumina. Both the police and the special-service Lumina used the 140-horsepower, 3.1-liter V-6 teamed to a four-speed automatic. Both used aluminum alloy wheels and the F41 sport suspension. The 9C3 Lumina came standard with 65-series Goodyear Eagle GT+4 radials and Recaro front seats. The 107.5-inch Lumina had the dubious honor of being the slowest police or special-service car around the Michigan International Speedway. It would remain one of the lowest-performing police cars even when it was upgraded to the 3800 V-6 in the late 1990s.

This 1993 Ford Crown Victoria was used by the Manteca (California) Police. Manteca is in Northern California, over the Altamont Pass from the San Francisco Bay area. This Ford sports all the stuff you expect from a California cruiser, including twin pusher bars, red spotlight, and a dash-mounted shotgun. It also has the latest-generation Federal Vision lightbar in red and blue, rearview-mirror-mounted red lights, and rear seat partition. The all-white Ford that patrols the beautiful Manteca area has a broad blue body stripe. New for 1993, the Crown Vic was changed from a "grille-less" front end to a chrome grille with twin chrome cross-bars. This grille was used in 1993 and 1994. The 1995 to 1997 models shared the single cross-bar grille.

For 1993, the Maui County (Hawaii) Police used the Crown Victoria. Hawaii has no state police nor highway patrol. This Crown Vic, with cheap-looking dog-dish hubcaps, is all-white with blue stripes, blue fender markings, blue strobe lights, and a gold and blue door shield. For 1993, the 4.6-liter SOHC modular V-8 produced 210 horsepower and was identified from the retail engine by the use of dual exhausts. This was a good police car for urban patrol. With 16.7 miles per gallon, the 4.6-liter V-8 Crown Vic got almost as good a gas mileage as the 5.0-liter V-8 Caprice. Yet the 210-horsepower Crown Vic was much faster than the 170-horsepower Caprice. The 1993 Crown Vic ran the quarter mile in the mid-17-second range. That was faster than any full-size police sedan from the entire decade of the 1980s.

Quick! What is wrong with this 1993 San Francisco Police Ford Taurus? That's right, no dents. The SFPD has the same reputation for dinged and dented police cars on the West Coast as the NYPD has on the East Coast and the Chicago Police has in the midwest. Of course, these agencies all claim the dents as badges of honor, proof they actually hit the streets and do something. For 1993, the horsepower on the 3.8-liter V-6 was bumped from 155 horsepower to 160 horsepower; however, the vehicle performance was still the same. The 106-inch-wheelbase Taurus was clearly the best-performing mid-size sedan. The front-drive Taurus ran the quarter mile as fast as the 4.6-liter Crown Vic, had the same 123-mile-per-hour top end, and was a bit quicker around a road-racing course. By 1993, however, transaxle durability problems started to show up. The Taurus quickly became a lightning rod for all problems with all front-drive cars, and an outlet for frustrated cops who did not like the small car nor front-wheel drive. The police package would be dropped after the 1995 model year due largely to these issues.

Check out the attractive graphics on this 1993 Ford Crown Victoria used by the Cassia County (Idaho) Sheriff's Department. The all-white cruiser has brown and tan stripes and lettering that quickly and professionally identify this as a county patrol car. The CCSD patroller has a red and blue lightbar, A-pillar spotlight, and a dash-mounted traffic radar unit. The high-revving 4.6-liter SOHC V-8 produced acceptable performance, using horsepower at high rpms to make up for lack of torque at low rpms. Even so, cops still asked for more bottom-end punch. Ford Fleet discussed a "city" police package, which would have used 3.73 rear gears and a "highway" package using the standard 3.27 rear gears. The 3.73 rear gears would have gotten the SOHC V-8 into its powerband quicker. While it would have limited the top speed, the 3.73 rear gears would have given the 281-ci-powered Crown Vic much better throttle response. No action was ever taken.

This 1993 Ford Mustang sports the new graphics of the Oregon State Police. They changed the graphics from a small door decal with plain lettering to the bold and instantly clear block letters and five-point star. This was a great improvement! This would be the last year for the brushed-aluminum, 10-hole wheels, used only on the special-service package from 1991 to 1993. The retail 5.0-liter Mustangs used five-spoke aluminum wheels. The 1993 Mustang was unchanged from 1992 because Ford was working on the next-generation Mustang. This new car would not be available with a special-service package. The horsepower on the 1993 Mustang was lowered from 225 horsepower to 205 horsepower due strictly to the way horsepower was measured. Even so, the 1993 Mustang turned in the best performance ever for the special-service-package pursuit car. It ran the quarter mile in 15.2 seconds at 92 miles per hour.

Here's a 1993 Jeep Cherokee with the King County (Washington) Police. The all-white cruiser has a gold-outlined green body stripe, a gold-outlined green and gold door shield, and a red and blue Federal StreetHawk. Note the roof-mounted spotlight and the bumper-mounted winch. Serious cops! For 1993, the 190-horsepower, 4.0-liter six-powered Cherokee continued to provide outstanding service in a niche of law enforcement. The 101.4-inch-wheelbase Cherokee was available as a rear-wheel drive and as an all-wheel drive. It was also available in both two-door and four-door versions. The four-door 4x4 Cherokee reached 60 miles per hour in 9.8 seconds, ran the quarter mile in 17.5 seconds, and had a 115 miles per hour top speed. It was faster around a road course than some conventional police sedans.

Here's the 1993 special-service-package Mustang, used by the cops who re-invented pursuit cars, the California Highway Patrol. This was also the last year for the special-service-package Mustang. In 1979, the CHP conducted a test of special-purpose patrol vehicles. Those tests proved the small-block V-8-powered, short-wheelbase "pony" car could be very effective in a narrow range of police duties, specifically traffic enforcement. The contract went to the 1982 Mustang GL. The 5.0-liter Mustang was the fastest police car on the road from 1982 through 1990, during a time when cops desperately needed a good, old-fashioned pursuit car. In 1991, Camaro joined the fray and in 1993, Ford elected to drop the special-service package. The 5.0-liter CHP Mustang will always be remembered as the car that changed the way cops thought about pursuit cars. It will always be remembered as "the Ford that chased Porsches for a living."

The biggest news from Chevrolet is 1993 was a totally re-engineered, fourth-generation Camaro, such as this South Carolina Highway Patrol unit. This SCHP cruiser is silver with blue stripes, and blue on gold fender and door markings. The new Camaro came with a 275-horsepower, 350-ci LT-1 V-8 bolted to either a four-speed automatic overdrive or a six-speed (not five-speed) stick. The 305-ci V-8 was no longer available in a special-service-package Camaro. Also new for the Camaro was a Short-Long Arm A-arm front suspension replacing the awful MacPherson struts. The Saginaw rack-and-pinion steering was new. So were dual-side air bags. ABS was standard for 1993. While the Camaro no longer used dual-piston disc brakes, the single-piston discs had more swept area than the older brakes. Once again, the LT-1 Camaro set road-course, acceleration, and top-speed records for police and special-service-package cars. The Camaro reached speeds of 154 miles per hour, something no police-type vehicle had ever done before.

In 1993, as a mid-year release, the Ford Explorer 4x4 was available with a special-service package. This Explorer is a DUI Enforcement vehicle with the Center (Colorado) Police. Ford had the first police 4x4 with the 1967 Bronco. This was dropped by 1987 but re-introduced as a smaller 111.9-inch sport/ute in 1993. The Explorer was powered by a 160-horsepower, 4.0-liter V-6. With 800 pounds more weight and 30 horsepower less, the Explorer was NO match for the Jeep Cherokee. The Explorer took 12.5 seconds to reach 60 miles per hour, ran the quarter mile in 18.7 seconds, and had a top speed of just 104 miles per hour. The Explorer was slow enough around the MSP road-racing course to make the Lumina look good. In fact, the Explorer would cause a controversy in 1998 such that for 1999, the Michigan State Police stopped testing special-service-package vehicles on the road course.

Let's say you were a town marshal in a small town in southeast Missouri. Let's say you had driven the same police car since 1972. Let's say it came time to replace that police car, since, after all, it had accumulated an entire 25,600 miles on it. What police car could possibly replace that kind of car, a car that had literally become a landmark? Well, if the old police car was a Chevrolet, darn tootin' the new police car would be, too. That is exactly what happened in Frohna, Missouri, population 245. They sold their 1972 402-ci big-block V-8-powered Chevrolet Bel Air to a police-car collector and purchased this 1994 LT-1-powered Caprice, retired from the Missouri State Highway Patrol. The old cruiser was Sequoia Green and the townsfolk expected the new one to be the same color, you know, for old time's sake. Instead, this 350-ci-powered cruiser is white with a red-outlined blue body stripe and a red and blue lightbar. The word is the same police-car collector will buy this cruiser, once it too, has been in service for 25 years!

Here's a 1994 Chevrolet Caprice used by the Benton County (Indiana) Sheriff's Department, sitting in the median on U.S. Highway 41. Benton County is midway between Chicago and Indianapolis. This BCSD cruiser is brown over tan with a gold five-point star and gold-outlined door, fender, and trunk lettering. This was the new markings used by all Hoosier sheriffs' departments in 1994. This cruiser is topped by a red and blue JetSonic. The low profile of this lightbar allows this county mountie to hit the highest top speeds but still have the 360-degree coverage only available from a roof-mounted lightbar. New for 1994 were bolt-on hubcaps from the Chevy truck line. As one who lost many hubcaps crossing this exact median, and one who has spent hours searching for hubcaps before reporting the loss, the bolt-on hubcaps were the best thing to happen to this traffic officer since fuel injection. Really.

Here's a 1994 Chevrolet Caprice with the Woodridge (Illinois) Police. This black and white cruiser has a very traditional color scheme but unique door markings. The gold and black five-point star is cleverly incorporated into the word "Police." The best police-car markings have both a star or shield and easy-to-read lettering. This marking format is one of the best. New for 1994, Chevrolet introduced bolt-on center hubs, the easiest way to identify a 1994 to 1996 cruiser. However, the full-dress wheel covers with the gold bowtie were options from 1993 to 1996. The easiest way to identify a 1994 model is the outside rearview mirror mounted on the door, instead of the window, and the sharply angled D-pillar. For 1995 and 1996, the D-pillar was rounded. In 1994, cops had their choice of a 265-ci V-8 or a 350-ci V-8. Both used Gen III LT-1 technology.

This silver-over-deep-blue 1994 Chevrolet Camaro with gold markings and white stripes was used by the Nevada Highway Patrol. The Silver State pursuit car has a full-width, red and blue JetSonic, as opposed to the mini-bars used earlier. In 1994, the awesome B4C-package Camaro was upgraded from tuned port injection to sequential port injection. The six-speed cars now came with Computer Aided Gear Selection which blocks second and third gear at low throttle positions to improve fuel economy. The four-speed cars now came with the new electronic 4L60-E transmission, standard on all of the 9C1 Caprices. In 1994, the 275-horsepower, 350-ci-powered Camaro hit 153 miles per hour. These LT-1-powered pony cars ran the quarter mile in the low-15-second bracket and, once again, set a new MSP road racing track record.

This 1994 Chevrolet Caprice was used by the Joliet Police in northern Illinois. This cruiser has a great new twist on the old black and white theme. This cruiser has both lettering and a seven-point star to identify the cruiser, although the rear door is a very unusual place for the door shield! In 1994, Chevrolet introduced the awesome 350-ci LT-1 V-8 engine. With 260 horsepower, it was the best thing to happen to Chevrolet police cars since 1976! The LT-1 V-8 pushed the Caprice to a top speed of 141 miles per hour, faster than any 5.0-liter Mustang. The LT-1 Caprice ran the quarter mile in the same low-16-second range as the 5.0-liter Mustang with an automatic. Most important, the LT-1 police Caprice ran the road racing course just as fast as the 5.0-liter special-service-package Mustang. Starting in 1994, the full-size Caprice did everything the Mustang could do, but did it with more room and comfort.

Here's the 1994 Chevrolet Caprice used by the St. Louis Metro Police. New for 1994, these cars got fresh new markings. The all-white cruisers have twin gold over a blue body stripe, blue lettering, a silver and black door shield, and a silver arch. New for 1994, the Caprice came with rear disc brakes. Also new was a new version of the small-block displacing 265 ci. That's right. The latest small-block V-8 has the same size, bore, and stroke as Chevrolet's first small-block V-8! The 200-horsepower, 265-ci L99 V-8 was very popular among police departments such as the Los Angeles Police, Houston Police, and New York City Police. The 265-ci V-8 was actually 30 horsepower stronger than the 305-ci V-8 it replaced. As for the 350-ci-powered Caprice, for the eighth year in a row, yes, the eighth straight time, the Caprice captured the "most bang for the buck" Michigan State Police patrol vehicle tests. The 1994 to 1996 LT-1 Caprices were the best police cars ever built.

This 1994 Ford Crown Victoria was used by the Vancouver, British Columbia, Police. The all-white Ford has gold, blue, and green stripes, blue lettering, and an ornate door shield. The department's selection of emergency lights is quite odd. In the mid-1990s, these cruisers used the twin gumballs, which date back to 1964! The cruisers have red and blue rotators, red and blue flashers, and bar-mounted auxiliary lights. Note the dog-dish hubcaps. For 1994, Ford fielded three police- and special-service-package cars: the 114.4-inch Crown Victoria, the 106-inch Taurus, and the 111.9-inch Explorer in both 4x4 and 4x2. New for the Crown Vic were heavier brake rotors with internal vents, both bucket seats, and dual air bags as standard equipment.

In 1994, the Nassau County (New York) Police used this Ford Crown Victoria in its Highway Patrol Bureau. This all-white cruiser has an orange upper stripe, blue lower stripe, and an extremely impressive orange, gold, and blue door shield. The blue fender lettering identifies this as a Highway unit. So does the novel McDermott "Multi-Level" light rack mounted behind the all-red Whelen Edge strobe bar. In 1994 the Highway Bureau cops had to be wondering why they were issued the 210-horsepower, 4.6-liter Crown Vic instead of the 260-horsepower, 5.7-liter Caprice for their traffic-enforcement duties. The Crown Vic took 5 seconds longer to reach 100 miles per hour and was more than a second slower in the quarter mile. The top speed of 128 miles per hour was plenty for most enforcement duties. However, a faster 0- to 100-mile-per-hour "catch" time really was needed.

The Lafayette (Indiana) Police Department was among many agencies to use the 1994 Jeep Cherokee. Indiana has more than its fair share of blowing and drifting snow. Sitting at the Tippecanoe County jail, this 4x4 is black with white doors and a black door shield, designed after the Indiana State Police shield. This Jeep uses a red and blue Federal Street Hawk and twin amber grille flashers. All of the police Jeeps were powered by the 190-horsepower, 4.0-liter six. The perky, 101.4-inch-wheelbase Cherokee continued to wow police-fleet managers with its incredible acceleration, braking, and cornering. Locked in 4x4 mode, the Cherokee ran the quarter mile in the 17-second bracket, had shorter stopping distances than nearly all police cars, and got around the MSP road course as fast as the 265-ci V-8 Caprice.

In 1994, the Ford Taurus was all alone in the front-drive, mid-size police market. Chevrolet did not field a police Lumina this year. This 1994 Taurus was used by the U.S. Navy Police at the Pearl Harbor Naval Base. It has blue-over-gold stripes, a blue and gold door shield, and an all-blue Whelen Edge strobe bar. The police-package Taurus used a 160-horsepower, 3.8-liter V-6. Dual air bags were now standard. For 1994, the Taurus got larger brake rotors and bigger brake pads. To accommodate the larger brakes, the police Taurus now came with 15-inch wheels. The 160-horsepower Taurus was as quick around the MSP road-racing course as the 200-horsepower Caprice and had a top speed of 129 miles per hour. The nimble Taurus had excellent brakes and, perhaps its biggest advantage, got nearly 19 miles per gallon.

Chapter Twelve

1995-1999

In 1995, Chevrolet continued its dominance of the police market, both in terms of police-car sales and police-car performance. For 1995, the 116-inch Caprice was restyled ever-so-slightly, using the styling cues from the 1994 Impala SS. The top cop cruiser continued to be powered by either the 265-ci V-8 or the 350-ci LT-1 V-8. A full one-third of the full-size cruisers were powered by the smaller V-8.

From the New York City Police to the Los Angeles Police, the 265-ci V-8 was a very popular and economical engine. The 9C1 Caprice with the 265-ci V-8 didn't perform as well as the 4.6-liter/281-ci SOHC V-8 Crown Vic, but the performance was acceptable for heavily urbanized police work. The 350-ci LT-1 V-8's performance was, of course, legendary.

Chevrolet's re-introduced Lumina received a much more powerful 3.1-liter V-6 engine, new MacPherson strut rear suspension,

These are two professional-looking troopers with the West Virginia State Police, along with their 1995 Chevrolet Caprice. The WVSP used this circular state seal as its door shield for years, up to the mid-1980s. Then they used a triangular shield with simple lettering. In the mid-1990s they changed back to the orange door shield and added twin orange stripes. The cruiser itself has a gold roof over a deep-blue body. The 1995 Caprice with its 260-horsepower, 350-ci LT-1 V-8 was the police car to beat at the annual Michigan State Police vehicle tests. The Caprice hit 60 miles per hour in 7.5 seconds, ran a low-16-second quarter mile, and had a top speed of 135 miles per hour. It won five of the six test phases against the 4.6-liter Ford Crown Vic and tied for the sixth phase. That made it nine wins in a row for the 350-ci Caprice.

rear disc brakes, new styling, and heavier-duty steel wheels. Chevrolet was making slow and cautious improvements to its police-package Lumina, and performance increased without reducing reliability and durability. The Lumina continued to improve every year and closed out its police career in 1999 with a clean record: no mistakes, no controversies, just solid, low-profile performance.

By 1995, asymmetric-tread police radials like the Goodyear Eagle RS-A were used on nearly all police cars. Indeed, it provided better performance and longer wear, and it was the first significant change in police-spec radial tires since the return to steel-belted radials in 1984.

A special-service package was available as a very late 1995 release for the new, totally re-engineered Explorer, but the Explorer was introduced too late in the model year to be tested by either the Michigan State Police or the Los Angeles County Sheriff. In missing these two profoundly influential tests, the new Explorer wasn't recognized as a police-type vehicle until 1996. However, all of the special-service-package Explorers were 4x4s.

Technically a 1995 model, the Explorer had vastly different sheet metal and an entirely new suspension. Ford's famous Twin I-Beam (4x2) and Twin Traction Beam (4x4) coil spring front suspensions were wisely replaced with an independent short/long arm suspension with front torsion bars. The change in suspension and springs allowed the engine to sit lower in the chassis for better handling.

In February 1995, Chevrolet Fleet made a fateful announcement: the Arlington, Texas, assembly plant would cease production of the rear-wheel-drive Caprice and would be converted to produce full-size trucks and sport/utes. In May 1995, General Motors made the final decision. The 1996 model year was the last year for the V-8-powered, full-size, rear-drive GM300 platform, and the four-door police sedan it perfected.

The clear consensus among police-fleet managers was that the Caprice should outlive the Crown Victoria. But Chevrolet had a different approach. Jon Moss and Lewis Cole Jr. breathed new life into the sagging sales of the Caprice by designing the incredible Impala SS. Chevy could not keep up with the demand for this thinly veiled, LT-1-powered cop car, and the upscale and high-margin Impala SS generated badly needed profits back into the product line.

General Motors' withdrawal from the law-enforcement market was a surprise, but Chevrolet Fleet agreed to honor already existing orders for 1996 9C1 Caprices. The build date even extended well into the 1997 model year, but in the end, the best police car ever built—the 9C1 LT-1-powered Caprice—was discontinued.

For 1996, Chevrolet also fielded the 107.5-inch, mid-size, 3.1-liter V-6 Lumina and the 101-inch pursuit Camaro. The Camaro's LT-1 received a 10 horsepower boost that wasn't readily apparent or necessary. The Lumina was the ideal candidate for the LT-1, and the Lumina really needed to be in the 210- to 225-horsepower range. (That would happen in the year 2000.)

Chevrolet announced a police package for the two-wheel drive, 4-Tahoe sport/utility vehicle in an effort to dampen the loss of the Caprice. According to Chevy, the Tahoe would be Caprice-like, and the lowered and beefed-up Tahoe was a sort of

Arkansas State Police Trooper Shelby Bodenhamer stands proudly with his 1995 Chevrolet Caprice after winning the In-Service class at a national police-car collectors show. The Natural State cruiser is all-white with a blue "V" stripe, a red and blue six-point star, and an all-blue Whelen Edge strobe bar. New for 1995, Chevrolet made the outside rearview mirrors much larger and moved them from the doors to the window frames. The other subtle styling change involved rounding the D-pillar to make all Caprices look like the Impala SS in this area. Bolt-on center hubs were standard equipment, while these gold bowtie, full-dress stainless-steel wheel covers were optional. The LT-1-powered Caprice was as quick around a road-racing course as the old 5.0-liter Mustang. Even through the hills and hollers of Arkansas, the police-package Caprice was the King of the Road.

The twin stripe "V" on this 1995 Chevrolet Caprice with the Idaho State Police adds an aggressive appearance. This ISP unit has a white roof over a black body with white stripes and lettering. The image of the state is in gold. Of course, this unit has traffic radar. The bolt-on chrome center caps give the Caprice that absolute no-nonsense look. The 1995–1996 Caprices are easily distinguished from the 1993-1994 models by the rounded D-pillar and the outside rearview mirror located in the front door window patch. The Caprice 9C1 powertrains included the 200-horsepower, 265-ci V-8 and the 260-horsepower, 350-ci V-8. One-third of the police Caprices used the 200-horsepower engine! This state unit, of course, has the 260-horsepower LT-1 V-8.

This 1995 Chevrolet Caprice was used by the Arizona Department of Public Safety (DPS). The all-white Caprice has a wide blue body stripe, a blue and red seven-point star, and a red and blue lightbar. This big, bad Bowtie was used by Trooper Tony Bruhn in the Nogales area on the U.S.-Mexico border. Note the chrome beauty rings added to the wheels. While not a factory option, cops all across the nation dressed up their take-home cruisers with these rings. In 1993, the Arizona DPS added blue stripes to its previously all-white cars, along with the name State Patrol-DPS with State Patrol on the trunk. In 1996, the side markings changed to "Arizona-DPS" with the trunk reading "Highway Patrol," which is what it used to read prior to 1993. The 9C1 Caprice was just a thinly veiled Impala SS.

For 1995, the Chevrolet Camaro came just one way: fast. Whether the gearing was controlled by a four-speed automatic overdrive or six-speed manual, the 275-horsepower, 5.7-liter LT-1 V-8-powered police Camaro was blisteringly fast, faster than any police vehicle in 30 years. And no police vehicle had ever before reached the 152- to 155-mile-per-hour top speeds of these Camaros. This particular 1995 pony car was used as a Freeway unit by the Royal Canadian Mounted Police. Note the mounted rider on the rear fender. In tests conducted by both the Michigan State Police and the Los Angeles County Sheriff's Department, the four-speed Camaro ran the quarter mile in 14.95 seconds. The 409-horsepower, 409-ci dual four-barrel V-8-powered 1962 Biscayne with a four-speed stick ran the quarter in 14.90 seconds.

hot rod. It ran the Michigan State Police road course faster than the Crown Vic and accelerated faster. It was a commendable performance, but it wasn't a Caprice.

When Chevy announced its withdrawal of the Caprice from the police market, Ford, the only remaining full-size rear-wheel-drive police-pursuit-package manufacturer, became the sales leader in the police-car market.

Although General Motors made the announcement in mid-1995, Ford could not ramp up production of the Crown Victoria fast enough to handle the increased demand. Ford's London, Ontario, plant attempted to meet the increased demand, but it could not increase production capacity by 30,000 to 40,000 police cars all at once.

In an effort to increase production, Ford restricted the variety of paint schemes on its police cars. Ford put orders for all-white cars at the top of the list, and other standard colors such as two-tone colors and all special colors were all given a very low priority. That's right. Cops could have any color of Ford police car they wanted as long as it was white.

The re-engineered Explorer had a special service package, and it was a better overall vehicle. The new front suspension slightly helped its road-course time and the brakes were minutely better. But engine performance took a dive; the new 4.0-liter Explorer had slower acceleration and a lower top speed than the older Explorer. Ford tried really hard not to be directly compared to the Jeep Cherokee. Unfortunately, the comparison was both obvious and valid. To add insult to injury, the top-performing Cherokee even got better gas mileage than the Explorer. The Explorer remained the more comfortable and roomy of the available sport/utes.

In 1997, the Ford Crown Victoria had the full-size, rear-drive, V-8-powered police market all to itself. This situation has remained unchanged through the turn of the century, and Ford Fleet has further indicated a full-size, rear-drive police sedan will be available through the year 2006.

Traffic officers and road deputies accustomed to the powerful, road-holding Caprice were not pleased with the Crown Vic. The big Ford lacked bottom-end punch, and it felt unsteady at speeds over 100 miles per hour, and no one was able to identify the exact cause. Some blamed the Ford speed-sensitive steering, that was indeed lighter (more assist) than the Caprice. Some blamed the Crown Victoria's shorter wheelbase and lighter weight. And some simply chalked it up to a difference in feel between the Ford and Chevy. The Crown Vic didn't provide a confidence-inspiring ride for some officers, and the seat-of-the-pants feedback was uneasy enough that many refused to drive it over 100 miles per hour.

In addition, the 1997 Crown Vic failed to meet the minimum acceleration standards set by the Michigan State Police and agreed upon by the automakers. Police-fleet managers had flashbacks to the 318-ci-powered 1980 Dodge St. Regis being outrun by Volkswagen and top speeds of 85 miles per hour on a mountain pass.

In 1997, like the mid-1980s, cops simply had to bite the bullet and drive what was available. After all, the 4.6-liter Crown Vic was a better choice than the front-wheel-drive 3.1-liter Lumina. The 5.7-liter Tahoe was not yet available, and the 4.0-liter

Cherokee and 4.0-liter Explorer were not good choices for an entire fleet of general-patrol vehicles. Ford heightened optimism when it tested its two-wheel-drive Expedition powered by the 5.4-liter SOHC V-8. Every cop yearning for more power, and suffering Chevy LT-1 withdrawal, hoped Ford would keep the Expedition but put the 5.4-liter engine in the Crown Vic!

For 1997, Chevrolet fielded the 3.1-liter Lumina and the 5.7-liter Camaro, offering the most awkward mix of police cars since the 1955 introduction of a Chevy police package. The 5.7-liter Tahoe was officially available, but the powerful sport/utility suffered production delays. Even when it was available, it cost substantially more than the Crown Vic.

In 1997, the Jeep Cherokee was restyled for the first time since appearing in uniform, and once again it was offered as a special-service police-package vehicle.

In retrospect, the 1997 model year was a bleak one for law enforcement. The Crown Victoria didn't offer the acceleration, top speed, or handling that cops demanded, and there was no other comparable vehicle on the market. With a price tag twice that of a Crown Vic, the Volvo 850 Turbo's attempt to enter the American police market wasn't humorous enough to snap law enforcement out of its despair.

The 1998 model year was as good as the 1997 model year was bad. The Ford Crown Victoria received a much-needed redesign. Ford didn't drop the oft-requested 5.4-liter SOHC V-8 in the Crown Vic, but the proven 4.6-liter SOHC V-8 horsepower output slightly increased. In addition, much larger front brakes significantly enhanced braking power. The rotors and calipers of the Crown Vic were so big the car needed 16-inch wheels to clear the brakes. The 16-inch tires mounted on 7-inch wide wheels provided greatly improved steering response. Traction Assist (which operates at speeds under 35 miles per hour) was upgraded to Traction Control, which operates at all speeds.

Most important, for 1998, Ford discovered the culprit of the high-speed instability problem that had plagued the Crown Vic. Ford upgraded from a four-link rear suspension to a full Watts Link rear suspension. The four-link suspension had been shifting side-to-side, ever so slightly, during cornering, acceleration, and high-speed driving, that caused the uneasy driving-control sensation at speeds over 100 miles per hour. To make the Crown Vic as stable and responsive as possible, a wider rear track, the Watts Link suspension, and a tweaked speed-sensitive steering were employed. At 130 miles per hour, the 1998 Crown Vic feels as stable and as controllable lane-to-lane, as the 1996 Caprice did at 130 miles per hour.

In 1998, Chevrolet built a much more powerful 3.8-liter V-6 engine for the Lumina, which had much more torque than the older 3.1-liter V-6. This engine upgrade was badly needed in Lumina since its 1992 introduction as a special-service vehicle. The Lumina was now a very real police-package car.

For 1998, the B4C-package Camaro was restyled with composite headlights and a bluntnose grille. The addition of an all-aluminum "LS-1" 350-ci V-8, designed for the fifth generation Corvette was exciting news. The LS-1 was a significant improvement over the now-legendary LT-1. To control the 305 horsepower, the special-service-package Camaro was given much bigger front and rear disc brakes, the next-generation ABS system, and a

The big news from Chevrolet in 1995 was the restyled Lumina, such as this Algonquin (Illinois) Police cruiser. This particular front-drive patroller is all-white with a red-outlined blue "V" stripe and a red, white, blue, and gold five-point star. The Federal Street Hawk with red and blue lights seems almost too big for this 107.5-inch mid-size car. New for 1995, the Lumina's Gen III 3.1-liter V-6 was rated at 160 horsepower thanks to a roller cam, sequential fuel injection, higher compression, and large-volume exhaust. MacPherson struts replaced the transverse leaf-spring rear suspension. The police package now sported rear disc brakes, which it needed. In 1995, a heavy-duty steel wheel was designed specifically for police use. The car ran the quarter mile in 18.2 seconds with a top speed of 118 miles per hour.

Here's a 1995 Ford Crown Victoria with the Santa Cruz County (California) Sheriff's Department. Santa Cruz County is south of the San Francisco Bay area and includes a lot of oceanfront near the Monterey Bay. The SCCSD car is green with white doors, a black and gold seven-point star, and gold door lettering. This cruiser has a star (or shield) and the word "Sheriff." That's how law-enforcement vehicles should be marked! This 1995 Crown Vic sports the new grille with a single crossbar holding the blue oval. The 1995 to 1997 models would share the same chrome grille. The 1995 Crown Vic was powered by the same 210-horsepower, 4.6-liter SOHC V-8 as in previous years. The big news was the EEC-V engine-control computer. This was long overdue. The EEC-IV computer dates back to at least 1984.

Here's an attractively marked California cruiser. This A95 Ford Crown Victoria with the Selma Police is all-white with red over blue hockey-stick stripes, blue lettering, and a red and blue pod Federal Vision. Of course, the car has twin spots and front pusher bars. By 1995, Ford engineers had started to get the most from the 4.6-liter SOHC V-8. The Crown Vic ran the same 17.3-second quarter mile as it always had and always would from 1992 to 1997. However, for the first time since the 1970 428-ci Cobra Jet–powered Custom, the big Ford broke the 130-mile-per-hour top speed barrier. Its 132-mile-per-hour blast was just 3 miles per hour behind the 5.7-liter V-8-powered Caprice. The decision to remain with the 4.6-liter SOHC V-8, instead of using the 5.4-liter SOHC V-8 wanted by traffic cops, seemed justified. (Just wait to see what happens in 1997!)

In 1995, the Arlington Heights (Illinois) Police, on the northwest side of Chicago, used the Ford Crown Victoria. This cruiser is all-white with a red-outlined black body stripe with the word POLICE in red. Ford called its package the Interceptor Police Package. The tweaked 4.6-liter SOHC V-8 teamed with a four-speed AOD and 3.27 rear gears helped the big Ford to keep up with the more powerful 5.7-liter Chevrolet Caprice. The biggest differences between these two full-size sedans was the vastly superior 0- to 100-mile-per-hour time for the Caprice. In literally every other area, the Crown Vic was right behind the Caprice. Except for the 0- to 100-mile-per-hour "catch" time, the 4.6-liter Crown Vic really was closing the gap with the 5.7-liter Caprice. The 4.6-liter Crown Vic, of course, was vastly superior in nearly all regards over the 4.3-liter Caprice.

next-generation traction control system. The Chevrolet Tahoe was available with the police package and was now available in large quantities. The 5.7-liter "Vortec" V-8-powered Tahoe was only available as a two-wheel drive with the police package.

For 1998, the special-service-package sport/ute market got crowded. The full-size Ford Expedition joined the fray as a 4x2 or 4x4, powered by either a 4.6-liter SOHC V-8 or a 5.4-liter SOHC V-8. The mid-size Ford Explorer was also available as either a 4x2 or 4x4, powered by either a 4.0-liter SOHC V-6 or a 5.0-liter overhead-valve V-8.

In late 1997, Ford issued a bulletin explaining that neither the Explorer nor Expedition were designed for nor intended to be used as pursuit vehicles. Ford, who invented the police package, was now the first to sharply define the difference between a police vehicle and a special-service vehicle. This distinction would be further clarified for 1999.

For 1999, under the direction and urging of the Michigan State Police, all law-enforcement automakers redefined what constitutes a police package as opposed to a special service package. Historically, the term police package has meant heavy-duty wheels, brakes, tires, electrical systems, cooling systems, shocks, springs, sway bars, and even interior seat fabric, and floor covering. The term special-service package has meant special features but generally less durability than the police package. The term police package has always meant more durable components or features that enhanced reliability in a wide range of police use, from around-the-clock squad car-style calls in an urban setting to high-speed traffic enforcement on an interstate.

Over time, a separate class of police-type vehicle emerged, the special-service vehicles. The pursuit-oriented Camaro and Mustang were special-service vehicles, so were the front-drive Chrysler K-cars and Chevrolet Celebrity from the 1980s as well as the 4x4 Expedition and Explorer. Some police departments have unwisely used straight retail cars, such as the 1990s Pontiac Bonneville and 1990s Dodge Intrepid for patrol use—a practice done in the 1930s and 1940s! In all cases, the manufacturer did not design nor intend its vehicles to be used that way. This goes for all retail cars and many special-service cars.

In 1999, the package definitions formally changed from an "equipment" standard to a "performance" standard. The police-package vehicle was defined as any vehicle designed by the manufacturer and intended to be used in the full spectrum of law-enforcement patrol service, including high-speed pursuits. A special-service-package vehicle was defined as any vehicle designed for specialized use such as off-road, inclement weather or canine use, but was not designed nor intended for pursuit situations. It is the manufacturers, not the police departments, that defined the intended end use.

In 1999, Ford fielded just one police-package car, the 4.6-liter Crown Victoria, now renamed Police Interceptor. Ford also offered a special-service package for the 111.6-inch Explorer and the 119.1-inch Expedition. The 4.0-liter SOHC V-6 Explorer was available in a 4x4 and, new for 1999, a special-service-package two-wheel-drive version. The 4x4 or 4x2 Expedition was powered by a 4.6-liter SOHC V-8 or a 5.4-liter SOHC V-8.

New for 1999, the 4.6-liter SOHC V-8-powered Police Interceptor was improved again, and featured improved acceleration.

Ford used old drag-racing tricks and reduced the diameter of the torque converter and bumped up the rear axle ratio from 3.27 to 3.55. Ford had two goals for its Interceptor, a 0- to 60-mile-per-hour time of 8 seconds and a 130-mile-per-hour top speed. The Interceptor met the top-speed goal and was only a half second off that 0-to-60 time.

In 1999, Ford removed two computer-controlled features that were a source of complaints on police cars. Speed-sensitive steering was dropped in favor of a constant-rate power-steering boost, and Traction Control robbed so much power under aggressive, enforcement-style driving that cops wanted it eliminated or at least defaulted to the "off" position. In its place was ABS along with the good, old-fashioned limited-slip differential.

In 1999, Chevrolet fielded a 5.7-liter Tahoe, 5.7-liter "LS-1" Camaro, and 3.8-liter Lumina, which were carried over from the dynamic 1998 model year. One new vehicle was added, a four-wheel-drive version of the four-door Tahoe. Chevrolet announced the 2000 model-year release of the Impala. There had been a definite void in the Chevy police-pursuit line of cars since the departure of the Caprice in 1996. The Tahoe and Lumina were no Caprice, and the Impala might be a worthy successor to the legendary Caprice. Technically, the 2000 Impala is a replacement for the Lumina, and in terms of size, it is situated midway between the Lumina and the Pontiac Bonneville. The Impala is powered by the world-class, 3800 V-6 and indeed shares the front-drive layout.

The Lumina's shortcomings had been the overall size and brakes. The 2000 Impala has a 3-inch-longer wheelbase and brakes from the Camaro! All of this makes for a very promising police car to start the next millennium.

This charcoal-black 1995 Jeep Cherokee is quite obviously with the Ohio State Highway Patrol. It has the traditional winged tire as a door shield. It also has two pairs of gold pin stripes, which do a good job of accenting the gold door lettering. For 1995, the 190-horsepower, 4.0-liter Cherokee was available as a 4x4 and as a 4x2. For 1995, the Cherokee was all alone as a four-wheel-drive police-type vehicle. Ford did not field a special-service-package Explorer this year. It's just as well. All the Explorer did was make the Cherokee look good. Really. The 4.0-liter Cherokee screamed around the MSP road course faster than the 3.1-liter Lumina, 3.8-liter Taurus, and 4.3-liter Caprice and was right on the tail of the 4.6-liter Crown Vic! And the MSP always ran the Cherokee in four-wheel drive, which robs power!

Here's a 1995 Ford Taurus used by the Grand Traverse County (Michigan) Sheriff's Department. The all-white Taurus has a gold-outlined brown body stripe and an especially attractive combination six-point star and Michigan state outline in gold and brown. The 55A police-package Taurus was powered by a 160-horsepower, 3.8-liter V-6. This was the same rating as the 3.1-liter V-6 Lumina, except the larger Taurus engine produced much more torque and torque wins drag races. The Taurus easily out-accelerated, out-stopped, and otherwise out-performed the Lumina. In fact, for the first time since front-wheel-drive showdowns which started in 1992, the Taurus won all six MSP test phases. Ironically, this was the last year for the police package in a Taurus.

Here's Tom Yates' famous photo of the 1996 Chevrolet Caprice making its final lap around the road-racing course during MSP testing. This LT-1-powered Caprice won the 1996 most-bang-for-the-buck, heads-up police-car competition, making it 10 years straight for the Caprice. Thanks to the objective MSP method of combining performance with the bid price, the best police cars ever built can be factually determined: the 1994 to 1996 LT-1-powered Caprice! These cars had the 140-mile-per-hour top speeds like the big-block V-8 pursuit cars of old. The 116-inch, 4,249-pound, four-door sedans ran a road-racing course as fast as a 5.0-liter Mustang and had better brakes than any police sedan before or since. From 1994 to 1996, Ford's competition in the police market was really a re-badged Impala SS!

This 1996 Chevrolet Caprice was used by the Honolulu (Hawaii) Police. This big, bad Bowtie is sporting the new Honolulu markings, which feature both police lettering and a police shield. That's the right way to do it! This all-white cruiser has a blue body stripe, gold and blue door shield, and an all-blue Whelen Edge strobe bar. The 1996 model year was the 30th Anniversary of the Caprice as a separate series. The powertrain for the Caprice, in its last year, was the 200-horsepower, 4.3-liter V-8 and the 260-horsepower, 350-ci LT-1 V-8. This HPD cruiser is powered by the 200-horsepower, 4.3-liter V-8, which ran the quarter mile in 18 seconds and got 18 miles per gallon. This was a good engine for urban use. After all, where on the small Oahu island would HPD cops be able to reach the 139 miles per hour possible from the LT-1 version?

In 1996, the Chevrolet Lumina, such as this Seattle (Washington) Police traffic unit, was the only front-drive, mid-size police car. The high-performance but durability-plagued Taurus was no longer available with a police package. This slick-top Seattle cruiser is silver-blue with a white body stripe, blue door shield, and red and blue emergency lights on the dash and on the pusher bar. The passenger-side spotlight is blue. The 160-horsepower, 3.1-liter V-6-powered, 107.5-inch Lumina had a quicker quarter-mile time than the 4.3-liter V-8 Caprice. The Lumina was within a second of the Caprice on the MSP road course and it turned in the best braking performance to date. It was important for the Lumina to perform well in 1996, because cops everywhere were trying to figure out what to drive after the 1996 Caprice was discontinued.

Here's the 1996 Chevrolet Caprice with the Menlo Park (California) Police. This all-white cruiser has a gold-outlined green body stripe. Production of the 9C1 police Caprice, Impala SS, Caprice Classic, Buick Roadmaster, and Cadillac Fleetwood was halted on December 13, 1996. The GM300 platform, originally called the GM B-body, dating back to 1959, was history. Chevrolet wanted the capacity at the Arlington, Texas, assembly plant to build the more profitable full-size trucks and sport/utes including the Tahoe. In the history of Michigan State Police vehicle testing, a single full-size police car has won all six test phases just three times. The 1990 Caprice. The 1991 Caprice. And in its last year, the 1996 Caprice. No other police car has done it even once!

Here's a 1996 Chevrolet Caprice used by the Lisle (Illinois) Police on Chicago's west side. This all-white cruiser has attractive gold fading to black markings and is topped by a red and blue Federal StreetHawk. The question of whether this Caprice has a 4.3-liter V-8 or a 5.7-liter V-8 is answered by the traffic radar unit mounted on the dash! In its last year as a police package, the big Chevrolet faced a challenge at the MSP vehicle tests from an old adversary, the Volvo sedan. The mid-size, front-drive Volvo was much more of a competitor to the Lumina; however, Volvo Fleet bragged they came to the MSP runoffs specifically to knock off the outgoing LT-1 Caprice. This was a grudge that dates back to 1975 when the Volvo 164E police sedan produced slightly better performance than the 350-ci Nova, but the LASD selected the Nova. Volvo tried again unsuccessfully in the mid-1980s with its 240 Turbo. They came back in 1996 to square off against the best police sedan ever built. What a joke. The Volvo 850 Turbo could not even keep up with the 4.6-liter Crown Vic, let alone the awesome 5.7-liter Caprice.

This 1996 Chevrolet Camaro B4C was used by the Wyoming Highway Patrol. This red-hot pony car has a white roof over a black body with a gold door shield. The seven-pod Federal Vision has a combination of three red lights, two blue lights, and two white lights. For 1996, the Camaro's LT-1 V-8 got a better cam profile and a less restrictive intake and exhaust system to now be rated at 285 horsepower. Acceleration Slip Regulation traction control announced in 1995 was available on the 1996 Camaros to allow them to be an all-season enforcement vehicle. For the first time during MSP testing, the Camaro with both the four-speed AOD and the six-speed CAGS ran the quarter mile in the 14-second bracket. The top speeds were 159 miles per hour and 157 miles per hour, respectively. A pursuit, anyone?

Here's a great shot of the 1996 Ford Crown Victoria with the Chicago skyline in the background. The Sears Tower is as much a symbol of Chicago as the arch is of St. Louis, the Statue of Liberty is of New York City, and the Trans-America Building is of San Francisco. This all-white cruiser with an all-blue Federal Jetstrobe has a blue body stripe, red door lettering, and red fender numbers. The term "CAPS" in the blue scroll across the silver five-point star stands for Chicago's Alternative Policing Strategy. This is Chicago's version of community-oriented policing, which began in 1993 and reached all 25 police districts by 1995. Under CAPS, beat officers work the same beat on the same watch for at least a year. This gives the cops more of a chance to get to know and work with the citizens in their beat.

Here's a 1996 Ford Crown Victoria with the Illinois State Police. This all-white cruiser sports the brown-outlined, wedge-shaped, gold stripe and lettering introduced in 1995. The gold six-point star on the front fender reads, "Illinois State Police Trooper." This Crown Vic is also fitted with front pusher bars, indicating it is assigned to one of the Chicagoland tollways or expressways. The Code 3 MX-7000 "all-light" lightbar on this cruiser has clear lenses and red and blue rotators. This ISP Crown Vic is powered by the 210-horsepower, 4.6-liter SOHC V-8 teamed with the 4R70W four-speed automatic overdrive and 3.27 to 1 rear gears. In 1996, due to the announcement of Chevrolet's intent to withdraw from the police business, many departments adopted the Crown Vic.

This 1996 Ford Crown Victoria is used by the Cook County (Chicago, Illinois) Sheriff's Department. This cruiser is noteworthy for its bright and clear, but professional and progressive markings. The all-white cruiser has a blue-outlined gold body stripe, blue-outlined door lettering, and a blue and gold six-point star. This car is instantly recognizable as an emergency vehicle and then as a sheriff's car. These are outstanding markings. For 1996, Ford offered just two police-type vehicles. One was this 114.4-inch Crown Vic. The other was the 4x4 4.0-liter V-6 Explorer, available only with a special-service package. The police package was no longer available for the front-drive Taurus.

This restyled 1996 Jeep Cherokee is a Tactical Unit with the Belleville (Michigan) Police on the southwest side of Detroit. The jet-black Jeep 4x4 has a red and blue Federal Vision. The door markings include the word "Police" in blue against a maroon and silver graphic. In 1996, the Dodge-fast, Plymouth-tough, police-package Cherokee faced off against the feeble 4.0-liter Ford Explorer and the silly 1.6-liter Geo Tracker. This no-contest match-up simply served as a humorous distraction from the high-stakes, Caprice-Crown Vic-Volvo shootout. Once again, on both the Michigan International Speedway road-racing course and at the 4.1-mile oval at Chrysler's Chelsea Proving Ground, the 190-horsepower, 4.0-liter Cherokee proved it is more of a police car than many police cars.

In late 1995, the Ford Explorer was restyled and re-engineered. Since it was released too late for the two major police car tests, the first time most cops saw the 112-inch Explorer, such as this 1996 Amtrak Railroad Police unit, was the next model year. The special-service package was available only for the four-door, four-wheel-drive version. The new Explorer got a better-handling Short/Long Arm torsion-bar front suspension, replacing the old Twin Traction Beam front suspension. The 160-horsepower, 4.0-liter V-6 could be teamed with either a five-speed stick or a four-speed auto. While the Explorer was very comfortable, it was not much of a performance vehicle. The 4.0-liter V-6 Explorer replaced the 3.1-liter Lumina as America's slowest police or special-service vehicle. It ran the quarter mile in the mid-18-second range.

Chevrolet's worst-kept police secret was a police package for its two-wheel-drive Tahoe, such as this Texas Highway Patrol unit. The two-wheel-drive Tahoe was highly modified for police work. It was lowered by an inch, and given lower-profile tires from the Caprice mounted on wheels from the 454 SS pickup truck. The police Tahoe includes specially valved shocks, heavy-duty springs, and larger front and rear sway bars. The Tahoe was powered by the 255-horsepower, 5.7-liter Vortec V-8. This is the truck version of the LT-1 V-8. The Tahoe was built on a 117.5-inch wheelbase compared to a 115.9-inch wheelbase for the Caprice. The police Tahoe came only in two-wheel drive and only as a four-door. The Tahoe hit 60 miles per hour in 9.4 seconds and reached speeds of 121 miles per hour. The Tahoe had the fastest straightline acceleration of any sport/ute and, in fact, ran the quarter mile faster than the 4.6-liter Crown Vic!

Check out this 1996 Ford Crown Victoria used by the Kimberly Police in southern Idaho near Twin Falls. The all-white cruiser has a purple-to-light-blue series of body stripes, the word "Police" in blue, and "Kimberly" and "To Protect & Serve" in silver. Eyecatching, however, are the large but truncated, gold five-point stars on the hood and rear fenders. Don't be fooled by unusual markings. This is a serious patrol car, as evidenced by the MPH Industries traffic radar antenna on the dash. This cruiser is powered by the 210-horsepower, 4.6-liter V-8. However, new for 1996 was a dedicated Natural Gas Vehicle (NGV) based on the 4.6-liter Crown Vic. In 1996, Ford became the first to offer a police car exclusively powered by natural gas. With nearly a 19-second quarter mile, one word describes the NGV Crown Vic: slow.

This 1996 Ford Crown Victoria was used by the Pierce County (Washington) Sheriff's Department. This green-gray Crown Vic has attractive gold body stripes, gold lettering, and a gold seven-point star. A red and blue lightbar and front pusher bars all add to the cop gear. The annual Michigan State Police vehicle tests were important for Ford in 1996. The closer the 4.6-liter Crown Vic ran to the 5.7-liter Caprice, the easier the transition from Chevrolet to Ford in 1997. Against the 9-year winning streak of the Caprice and the smug arrogance of the Volvo team, the Crown Vic turned in the best performance since its 1992 introduction. For the first time, it ran the quarter mile in the 16-second bracket. For the first time, it equaled the top speed of the 5.0-liter HO Mustang by hitting 135 miles per hour. The Crown Vic looked very good. Perhaps cops didn't need the 5.4-liter V-8 after all.

With the Caprice gone, the 1997 Chevrolet Lumina was heavily scrutinized by city, county, and state cops everywhere. The Vermont State Police tested the Lumina for patrol work, as did just about everyone else. This 107.5-inch, V-6-powered mid-size is deep green with a gold body stripe and lettering and an all-blue strobe bar. The 160-horsepower, 3.1-liter Lumina was what it was. It was not a 5.7-liter Caprice. Nor was it a 4.6-liter Crown Vic. It was good for light-duty, urban police work involving low speeds, no pursuits, and no prisoner transports. Its front-wheel drive was useful in snowy climates such as Vermont's. The Lumina got to 60 miles per hour in 11 seconds and had a top speed of 121 miles per hour. As long as the rear-drive, V-8-powered, full-size Crown Vic was available, the Lumina would never be a truly popular police car.

This sharp-looking 1997 Chevrolet Camaro is with the Contra Costa County (California) Sheriff's Department. CoCoCo includes the northeast part of the San Francisco Bay including the San Pablo Bay and Suisun Bay areas. This Camaro is assigned to the Diablo Police Services. Many small towns contract with the county sheriff for police support. The small town of Diablo, at the foothills of Mount Diablo, is one such community. This all-white Camaro has gold and brown stripes, a gold and brown seven-point star, and brown door and trunk lettering. The 285-horsepower, 5.7-liter LT-1-powered Camaro was a carryover from 1996. That is a good thing. With a 15-second quarter mile, a top speed of 157 miles per hour, and road handling like a Corvette, no one is likely to outrun one of these Camaros!

In 1997, the New York City Police drove the Ford Crown Victoria. The BIG news from the Big Apple was a totally new color scheme. The NYPD had used blue cars with white stripes since 1973. They added bold white NYPD lettering to the car doors in 1991; however, the cars remained blue. For 1997, the NYPD changed to white cars with blue stripes and blue lettering. The door shield was moved to the front fender, and the CPR (Courtesy, Professionalism, Respect) program was emphasized. But why white? NYPD cars had never been white. With the exit of the Caprice, Ford was swamped with more orders than its London, Ontario, assembly plant could handle. In all assembly plants, the paint booth is the bottleneck. To increase output through the paint area, Ford restricted the number of changeovers between paint colors. In a very odd twist on the old Ford expression, police departments could have any color they wanted, as long as it was white.

This 1997 Ford Crown Victoria was used by the Ontario Provincial Police. The cruiser has gold and blue body stripes with blue-outlined fender and door lettering. This particular unit is parked in front of its home, literally. It's at the Ford Assembly Plant in St. Thomas, Ontario. The plant opened in 1967 producing the Ford Falcon. Since then St. Thomas has assembled the Maverick, Pinto, Fairmont, and Escort. In 1983, St. Thomas became the home of the Crown Victoria and Mercury Grand Marquis. The 4.6-liter SOHC V-8 engine is made in Windsor, Ontario, while the four-speed electronic overdrive transmission is made in Livonia, Michigan. It takes about 22 hours to assemble 1,695 components down a 12-mile-long assembly line to produce a Crown Victoria. The 2,700 employees at St. Thomas assemble 60 Crown Victorias per hour.

The 1997 Ford Crown Victoria was the first Ford used by the Michigan State Police in roughly 30 years. With Dodge, Plymouth, Buick, and Chevrolet no longer making full-size police cars, the MSP runoffs should have been easy. The Crown Vic literally had no competition. Not quite. Since 1978, the MSP has had minimum acceleration requirements. For each new year these are 10-percent tougher than the average performance from the previous year's qualifying cars. All the 1997 Ford had to do was beat the average time of the 1996 Caprice and 1996 Crown Vic. The 1997 Crown Vic could not do it! Running against only itself, it disqualified itself! The 210-horsepower, 4.6-liter SOHC Ford took 10.5 seconds to reach 60 miles per hour versus a standard of 10 seconds flat. The same thing happened at 80 miles per hour and 100 miles per hour. Since the beginning of the MSP testing, this has happened to every single make of police car at one time or another except Plymouth. What awful timing for Ford! So what did the MSP do? What else could they do? They bought the Crown Vic anyhow!

Here's an attractively marked 1997 Ford Crown Victoria with the Benton County (Washington) Sheriff's Department. Benton County is where the Snake River and Columbia River join in southern Washington. This cruiser has a clever black-on-silver stripe scheme including black door lettering and a tiny, gold five-point star. This 210-horsepower, 4.6-liter Ford sports a red and blue, seven-pod Federal Vision lightbar. The black front pusher bars accent the color scheme of the car, but we wonder where in the land of Rattlesnake Hills these would be used. This Crown Vic is also packing a dash-mounted traffic radar unit, which would give the 210 horsepower something to do. In 1997, the Crown Vic ran the quarter mile in the mid-17-second range. It had a top speed of 129 miles per hour.

Here's a 1997 Ford Crown Victoria with the San Jose (California) Police. The San Jose police cars are white over a unique blue-grey with an ornate seven-point door shield. This SJPD cruiser has an all-light Federal JetStream with red and blue lenses. Yes, by golly, this California cruiser also has front pusher bars and twin A-pillar spotlights. The rear fender decal tells readers to call 911 for fire, police, and medical emergencies. The 1992 to 1997 Crown Vics made good urban police cars. The 114.4-inch-wheelbase cruisers had a tighter turning radius than the Caprice, and the speed-sensitive steering on the Crown Vic made urban patrolling easy. For a full-size car, it had nimble handling at low and moderate speeds. At high speeds, the big Ford did not feel as steady, and Ford had plans to correct that for 1998.

This 1997 Ford Crown Victoria was used by the Franklin County (Ohio) Sheriff's Department. Franklin County includes Columbus, the Buckeye State capitol city. The rear fender lettering indicates this particular unit is assigned to the Norwich Township. This cruiser has extremely high-profile markings, which is the way that police cars should be! The FCSD car is jet-black with gold fender stripes, a huge, gold five-point star, and large, gold black letters that clearly show who has just arrived at the scene: "Sheriff." This cruiser sports the Federal Street Hawk, one of the highest-profile lightbars ever designed. The lightbar provides 360 degrees of coverage with red, blue, and white lights. Many police departments around the country should take note of the Franklin County cruisers, and mark their cars accordingly!

In 1997, the Jeep Cherokee was available as a two-wheel drive and as a four-wheel drive. Powered by a 190-horsepower, 4.0-liter HO six and teamed with a four-speed electronic overdrive trans, these 101.4-inch Cherokees continued to act more like police cars than sport/utes. The Cherokee ran the quarter mile in the mid-17-second range and had a top speed limited to 111 miles per hour. Both the two-wheel-drive and four-wheel-drive Cherokee got around the Michigan State Police road-racing course faster than the 4.6-liter Crown Victoria and faster than the 5.7-liter Chevrolet Tahoe. There was simply no purpose in even trying to compare the Cherokees to the 5.0-liter and 4.0-liter Ford Explorers, affectionately called Slow and Slower. The only complaints ever heard about the Cherokees was somewhat tight interior room. These were valid enough to make Cherokee driving cops yearn for a police package on the slightly larger Dodge Durango.

The big news for the restyled 1998 Ford Crown Victoria, such as this Fowler (Indiana) Police unit, involved the back half of the cruiser. New for 1998, the four-bar link suspension was dramatically upgraded to a Watts Link rear suspension. The 1992 to 1997 Crown Vics felt unsteady enough at high speeds that some officers refused to drive these cars over 100 miles per hour. The speed-sensitive steering was blamed for the uneasy driving sensation at high speeds, but the real problem was the rear suspension. The Watts Link fixed the problem. The Watts Link prevents the axle from swaying during turns or when the driver accelerates, a motion that would make the car feel loose. In addition, the front track was widened by 0.6-inch and the rear track was widened by a full 2 inches. This, too, improves high-speed stability. This Fowler patroller has black-over-blue body stripes, black lettering, and the ultra-bright Code 3 MX7000 lightbar, which has red and blue lights and white corner sweepers.

For 1998, the Indiana State Police selected the re-engineered Crown Victoria as its battle cruiser. Trooper Rich Kelly stands at ease next to his commission, which sports a back-to-the-future paint scheme. ISP cars had been black with a gold body stripe and a gold "V" on the hood in the 1930s. They kept the black with gold side stripe theme through 1959. In 1960, the ISP adopted white-over-blue cars, then all-white cruisers in 1967. ISP cruisers remained white until the re-styled 1998 Crown Vics. The 1998 cars are black with twin gold side stripes. The hood has a gold "V" stripe all of its own. The fenders used to say either "Trooper" or "Corporal" to designate the rank of the driver. The 1998 cars read "State Trooper" because regardless of rank, they are all state troopers. The trunk lid continues to read "State Police," as it has since 1960.

This slick-top, black-and-white 1998 Ford Crown Victoria is with the Millbrae (California) Police. Millbrae is just south of San Francisco with the Bay on one side and the Montara mountains on the other side. This cruiser has red and blue lights mounted near the inside rearview mirror. It also has strobes built into the headlight and outside rearview mirrors as well. Look closely. The black A-pillar spotlights are harder to see than the chromed ones, making slick-top cruisers even harder to spot in traffic. Same for the black pusher bars. From the front, this would be nearly impossible to spot until way too late. From the side, the black and white color scheme and the large, blue and gold seven-point star make it obvious this is the POLICE!

A major change in sheet metal is just the excuse many departments need to update their graphics. It happened when the Ford went from rounded to wedge in 1992. It happened again in 1998 when the wedge-shaped Ford took on a rounded, upscale look. The Menlo Park (California) Police took this opportunity to change from green stripes and a gold star to blue stripes and silver, black, and blue lettering. New for 1998, the Crown Vic received much larger disc brakes, race-inspired dual piston calipers and, for the first time in recent history, 16-inch wheels. Required by the larger brakes, the 16-inch by 7-inch-wide wheels are the biggest, widest wheel ever put on a Ford police sedan. The 70-series radial used since the early 1980s has been upgraded to 60-series for both better traction and faster steering response.

This 1998 Ford Crown Victoria is just one of the cars being prepared for duty by the Missouri State Highway Patrol fleet maintenance section near Jefferson City. MSHP cruisers continue to come in all colors but bear the same gold-on-aqua blue markings. This Crown Vic has also been fitted with a Code 3 MX7000 with red and blue lamps. New for 1998, the computer-controlled, speed-sensitive steering was revised to give more assist at low speeds but less assist at higher speeds to resolve the unsteady sensation at speeds over 100 miles per hour. New for 1998, the 4.6-liter SOHC V-8 was tweaked by 5 horsepower to now be 215 horsepower. Torque was also improved. Also new for 1998, Traction Assist that worked at speeds up to 35 miles per hour was upgraded to Traction Control, which worked at all speeds.

Look closely. This was what the 1998 Ford Crown Victoria first looked like! At the very last minute, Ford moved its blue oval to the center of the grille and added seven vertical bars to the lower air intake. Which version do you like? For 1998, the police-package Crown Victoria remained based on the 114.4-inch wheelbase, but the additional width and the revised sheet metal added 200 pounds. This was offset by the slight horsepower increase. The average 1992 to 1997 Crown Vic ran the quarter mile in 17.3 seconds. The newly styled 1998 Crown Vic ran the quarter in 16.9 seconds. The 0- to 100-mile-per-hour times improved by 1.4 seconds while the top speed remained the same at 130 miles per hour. The greater stability of the Crown Vic was noted by MSP test drivers, and the Watts Link-equipped cruiser was almost 2 seconds faster around the road course. The more powerful, better-handling, and stronger-braking 1998 Crown Vic was still behind the lap times of the 1996 Caprice. Where is the 5.4-liter SOHC V-8 when you need it?

For 1998, the Chevrolet Tahoe, such as this Michigan State Police unit, hit the streets in force. Available only as a two-wheel drive four-door, the Tahoe is a real hot rod. It is powered by the 255-horsepower, 5.7-liter Vortec V-8 bolted to a four-speed automatic overdrive. The 4.11 rear gears that gave the 1997 models incredible acceleration and throttle response were backed off to 3.08 rear gears for better economy. The Tahoe is based on a 117.5-inch C/K truck chassis. It has front discs and rear drums even though some of the very early prototypes had rear discs. Actually, the Tahoe could use more braking power! During the 1998 testing, the Tahoe took the longest distance to stop of all thirteen vehicles tested. The C/K truck line has bigger brakes available. Also during MSP testing, the 5.7-liter Tahoe hit 60 miles per hour in 9.4 seconds and achieved a top speed of 123 miles per hour.

For 1998, the incredible special-service-package Chevrolet Camaro received a restyled hood, front fenders, and composite headlights and fascia, giving it a much blunter nose and a more prominent grille. Compact, lower-profile windshield wipers were also new. These greatly improved forward visibility. Also new for 1998 were much bigger front and rear disc brakes. Acceleration Slip Regulation was toned down a bit, allowing more wheelspin on hard acceleration. ASR is operational at all speeds and can be turned off by pushing a button on the dash. This 1998 Camaro was used by the Pittsburg (California) Police in the San Francisco Bay area, more specifically the well-inland Honker Bay area. The traffic enforcer is white over black with a red and blue Federal Vision and a gold and blue door shield. Hard to imagine anyone outrunning one of these B4C Camaros.

Check out the new graphics on this 1998 Chevrolet Camaro used by Trooper Jeff Leathley with the Nevada Highway Patrol. The deep-blue color remains, but the twin white diagonal stripes gave way to a gold-outlined white swirl. The gold fender lettering and gold seven-point star clearly indicate who is making the vehicle stop. The big news for 1998 Camaros was the change from the 285-horsepower LT-1 engine to the 305-horsepower LS-1 engine. The Chevy 350-ci small block was totally redesigned for use in the fifth-generation Corvette. The LS-1 uses an aluminum block and heads, which are 60 pounds lighter than the cast-iron block in the LT-1. Both the four-speed auto and six-speed stick versions got to 60 miles per hour in 6 seconds, ran the quarter mile in 14.4 seconds, and had top speeds of 159 miles per hour. Every MSP police vehicle performance record was broken by the 1998 LS-1 Camaro.

Here's the 1998 Chevrolet Lumina used by the Des Plaines (Illinois) Police in suburban Chicago. The 107.5-inch, front-drive patroller is white with blue and gold stripes and blue lettering. The big news for the 1998 Lumina was the 200-horsepower, 3800 V-6, which finally replaced the 160-horsepower, 3.1-liter V-6. The 3800 is General Motors' most proven and most durable V-6 engine. To handle the more powerful engine, the transaxle was upgraded to the beefier 4T65-E four-speed. The 200-horsepower Lumina hit 60 miles per hour in 9.6 seconds, ran the quarter mile in 17.3 seconds, and now reached 123 miles per hour instead of merely 113 miles per hour. With the new 3800 V-6 engine, it was now as fast around the road course as the 5.7-liter Tahoe and closing the gap on the 4.6-liter Crown Vic. The 3.8-liter V-6 Lumina hit 100 miles per hour 5 seconds faster than the old 3.8-liter V-6 Taurus.

Here's the 1998 Jeep Cherokee with the Santa Cruz County (California) Sheriff's Department. The 4.0-liter six-powered 4x4 is deep green with a white roof and front doors. A gold seven-point star, gold door lettering, and red and blue Federal Street Hawk provide a law-enforcement identity. In 1998, half of the 15 patrol vehicles tested by the Michigan State Police and by the Los Angeles County Sheriff were 4x4 or 4x2 sport/utes. These include the Tahoe, Cherokee, Explorer, and Expedition in a variety of powertrain layouts. Of these, the 190-horsepower, 101.4-inch Cherokee and the 25-horsepower, 117.5-inch Tahoe were the only 4x4s that met the definition of a "police" vehicle. The definition of police vehicle and special-service vehicle would be further clarified for the 1999 model year.

Here's the award-winning, "red, white and blue" 1998 Ford Expedition with the Folsom (California) Police outside Sacramento. Check out the thermal imaging gear on the roof behind the red and blue lightbar. The 119-inch Expedition was available with a special-service package for 1998. The biggest sport/ute to date came as a 4x4 or a 4x2 and was powered by either the 215-horsepower, 4.6-liter SOHC V-8 or the high-torque, 230-horsepower, 5.4-liter SOHC V-8. The Expedition, even the police version, was speed-limited to 106 miles per hour. At the beginning of the 1998 model year, Ford took the lead to clarify the role of its Expedition and Explorer. Ford made it clear these vehicles had certain special purposes for which they were suitable; however, these two sport/utes were not to be used for high-speed operations, emergency response, and pursuit scenarios.

Here is the 1999 Ford Police Interceptor. Ford elected to give the Police Interceptor a look of its own with a black grille, black side and fascia trim, and black rearview mirrors. New for 1999, Ford has eliminated the speed-sensitive steering in response to officer requests for a more predictable, constant rate of assist. The road-course times of the Crown Victoria have not change much since the 1992 introduction of the 4.6-liter SOHC V-8. However, the quarter-mile times for the 1999 Police Interceptor are about a half-second quicker than the average 1992 to 1997 police Crown Vic, even though the newer model is 200 pounds heavier. The 215-horsepower 1999 Police Interceptor runs the quarter mile in 16.6 seconds at 84 miles per hour. The 1996 LT-1 Caprice ran it in 16.1 seconds at 88 miles per hour. Ford could equal the legendary LT-1 Caprice simply by using its 230-horsepower, 5.4-liter SOHC V-8 in the Police Interceptor.

For 1999, Ford renamed the police-package car from the name "Crown Victoria" to the name "Police Interceptor." This 1999 cruiser, from the Michigan State Police tests, has the name "Police Interceptor" as a chrome die-cast emblem on the trunk instead of the name "Crown Victoria." The big drivetrain news also took place at this end of the car. The rear gear ratio was increased from 3.27 to 3.55, an idea from 1993. This increased the throttle response and acceleration by getting the high-revving but low-torque SOHC V-8 into its power band faster. For 1999, all-speed Traction Control was dropped. Too many officers complained that during aggressive emergency driving, the Traction Control was activated, which reduced engine torque at just the time the officers wanted it. In its place, a good, old-fashioned limited slip axle was available.

New for 1999, Chevrolet released a special service package for the four-wheel-drive version of the four-door Tahoe. This particular Tahoe is with the Los Angeles County Sheriff's Department but is assigned to La Habra Heights. This black-and-white has the gold lettering "Sheriff" on the door and "Los Angeles County Sheriff" on the rear doors, but the Tahoe has a La Habra Heights city seal on the door. The four-wheel-drive special-service-package version is very easy to tell from a two-wheel-drive police-package version. The four-wheel drive has four headlights while the two-wheel drive has two headlights. The four-wheel-drive Tahoe has the same 255-horsepower, 5.7-liter Vortec V-8 powertrain and the same 117.5-inch wheelbase as the two-wheel-drive police Tahoe. However, it has the retail-type heavy-duty suspension geared for 4x4 work, taller 75-series tires, and a ground clearance almost 2 inches higher than the two-wheel-drive police-package Tahoe. The four-wheel-drive version hits 60 miles per hour in 11.1 seconds and has an electronically limited top speed of 97 miles per hour.

This 1999 Ford Police Interceptor is used by the Oxford (Indiana) Police. This 1999 Crown sports a Federal Jetstream all-light lightbar with red and blue lights. This matches the red and blue body stripes and lettering. Ford's goal for its Police Interceptor is a 0- to 60-mile-per-hour time of 8 seconds and a top speed of 130 miles per hour. The 1999 Police Interceptor hits 60 miles per hour in 8.5 seconds and it has a top speed of 129 miles per hour. The 5.4-liter V-8, with more torque, would give cops and Ford Fleet alike the acceleration expected of a police interceptor. The Ford Police Interceptor is the only full-size, rear-drive, V-8-powered police car available. Ford was the choice of cops starting in 1932. Ford had the first police package in 1950. Ford outlasted at least a dozen other makes of police sedan. The Police Interceptor is truly the last of a breed. We have now come full circle back to where we were in 1932: Ford, with no real competition.

Here's the 1999 Chevrolet Tahoe that was used during the annual Michigan State Police testing. The lowered and suspension-tweaked police Tahoe comes only as a two-wheel-drive four-door. In 1999, the MSP forced the automakers themselves to decide what kind of vehicles they were marketing to police. Their vehicles either *were* engineered and intended for high speed and pursuit driving or their vehicles *were not*. The 1999 model year was a turning point in the definition of a "police" car versus a "special service" vehicle, a definition that had been blurred since the first police package was introduced in 1950. The two-wheel-drive Tahoe is intended for pursuits, while the four-wheel-drive version is not. Since its 1997 debut, the New York State Police has gathered the largest fleet of Tahoes. The two-wheel-drive version is used for patrol while the four-wheel-drive version is used by K-9 officers and other support services.

What is red with black stripes and is the fastest-accelerating, hardest-braking, highest-top speed police car ever made, period? The answer is this 1999 Chevrolet Camaro. The 305-horsepower, 5.7-liter LS-1 V-8-powered Camaro can bury a 155-mile-per-hour speedometer! It reaches 100 miles per hour in the quarter mile! It hits 60 miles per hour in just 6.1 seconds! Around a 1.63-mile road course, the LS-1 Camaro finishes 33 car lengths ahead of the nation's only full-size, V-8-powered police car. When it comes to police cars, and especially traffic-enforcement cars, the title "pursuit capable" may be the understatement of the 1990s. The only real question with the police-package Camaro is how long General Motors will continue making the F-body Camaro and Pontiac Firebird. As of 1999, the Camaro is scheduled to be dropped after the 2001 model year, if it makes it that long.

Here's the 1999 Chevrolet Lumina at the Chrysler Chelsea Proving Ground undergoing a series of brake tests during the Michigan State Police evaluation. In its last year, the mid-size, front-drive, 107.5-inch Lumina is once again powered by the 200-horsepower, 3800 V-6. Unlike the durability issues that forced the Ford Taurus out of the police market, the Lumina seems to have served well since its 1992 debut. The fact is, in the police market, all front-drive vehicles face a tough patrol environment and a skeptical bunch of cops. No, the Lumina is no longer slow. It reaches 60 miles per hour in 9.3 seconds, runs the quarter mile in 17.1 seconds, and has a top speed of 124 miles per hour. That is faster than a whole decade of 1980s police sedans. However, it is still front-wheel drive. The real question is how well the Lumina's model year 2000 replacement will be accepted.

2000 Impala Police Package

This is the future of Chevrolet police cars, the model year 2000 Impala. Shown with the car fit to wear the Impala symbol are the police-car movers and shakers at Chevrolet (left to right): Eric Jorgenson, Senior Project Engineer; Brian Tolan, Senior Development Engineer; Jamie Boerkoel, Manager Specialty Vehicles; Bruce Wiley, Manager Police and Taxi Vehicles; and Don Parkinson, Brand Manager High-Mid Program. The police-package Impala is a front-drive, four-door sedan based on a 110.5-inch wheelbase and powered by a 210-horsepower, 3.8-liter V-6. The new Impala is longer, wider, and slightly taller than the Lumina it replaces. The Impala has been beefed up for police work with the heaviest engine cradle ever designed for a front-drive car of this size. Some aluminum front suspension parts have been replaced by cast-iron components. The police-spec Impala reaches 60 miles per hour in 8.6 seconds, exactly like the Ford Police Interceptor, and has the same 16.6-second quarter-mile time as the big Ford. The top speed of the 2000 Impala is the same 124 miles per hour achieved by the 1999 Lumina. The new Impala uses four-wheel disc brakes from the Camaro, along with 16-inch wheels to clear the big rotors. In prototype testing, the Impala stopped from 60 miles per hour in 120 feet, which is an unheard of 1-g of deceleration. That's the best braking performance ever from a police-package vehicle.

Common Sense Police Car Restoration

Every 25-year-old police sedan, like this 1972 Chevrolet Bel Air, needs paint and body work. Few of these cars are worth an exotic restoration. The chain paint shops like MAACO also do economical body work, including wire-welded patch panels.

Every 10- to 30-year-old police sedan will be in need of some kind of body work. This varies widely by the car and by the patrol jurisdiction. Police cruisers that served with large-city departments are certain to have seriously dented fenders, hoods, and doors. These simply must be replaced.

The problems with most 20-year-old police cars, however, are simply rusted quarter panels and faded paint. Cars from the Northern states and both coasts will be much more likely to have surface rust and rust holes than cars from the South. In addition to the road salt used during the winter, the Northern cars get exposed to corrosive industrial atmospheres, the same thing that causes acid rain. The salt water from the coastal states can also attack the body and paint.

Simply put, the used police car will need a little body work. This may vary from a few pin holes in the quarter panels and a fender repainted, to fender replacements and new coat of paint. While some enthusiasts can rebuild engines, recover seats, weld patch panels, and paint the entire car, most owners can only do one of those tasks.

The most logical place to get body work done, for those who cannot do it, is a body shop. We contacted a number of body shops about a 1972 Bel Air project car. It had pin holes in one rear

quarter panel and large amounts of rust around the back glass. The second layer of paint was starting to peel.

Many body shop owners put on their "classic car restorer" hat when talking about older cars. Their repair estimates of up to $5,400 reflected it. It is time for a reality check.

The *Old Cars Weekly* Price Guide is the definitive publication for enthusiasts, collectors, and old car dealers. The Price Guide bases the worth of the car depending upon which of six conditions it is in. Excellent (Condition 1) is a restoration to maximum professional standards, a work of art that is trailered, not driven, and a guaranteed national show-class winner that is stored in a climate-controlled facility. Parts Car (Condition 6) is the class for rusty, stripped and/or wrecked cars that may or may not run.

The old Bel Air started off somewhere between Good and Restorable. The only value-adder for the mid-trim level car was for the 402-ci big block, which added a hefty 30 percent to the car. Even still, the total value of the car in Good (Condition 4)

The police car engine compartment simply must be detailed. It is easy to do and does not require the engine to be removed. Simply disconnect all the accessories, clean, and paint. Spray can products are widely available to make aluminum, cast iron, and cad-plated brackets look new.

was objectively just $910. Meticulously restored to Fine (Condition 2), which is the highest reasonable expectation, the car is still only worth $3,100.

The harsh reality is, most used police cars are worth about the same. Exceptions exist, of course, for police cars based on the classics from the 1950s and the musclecar platforms from the 1960s. However, these ARE the exceptions. The rule is used police cars only have value from their police-car heritage.

See the problem when talking with most body shops about a restoration? They treated the car as if it were a 1970 Chevelle 454 SS worth $24,000. No, it's an old, high-mileage taxi with a big engine and a sway bar. It just needs a little putty and some paint. It is not a museum piece. To add insult to the injury of the outrageous repair estimates, it was going to take them *one year* to finish the job!

Police cars do not fit many of the existing concepts that car collectors have. They wonder why anyone would want to fix up an old four-door sedan. However, the opposite should also be true. Why would we want to spend more for patch panels and paint than the whole car is worth?

Perhaps 10 police cars in the whole country are so valuable that they should be towed in an enclosed trailer from a temperature- and humidity-controlled garage to the car show, hand-pushed under a tent, and roped-off from the public until their

return trip. These cars need to go to a body shop and sit for a year while they undergo an expensive restoration. The rest of the 60,000 police cars produced each year do not necessarily need such treatment. Yet, it can be next to impossible to convince a body-shop owner of the difference!

One of the best possible solutions for nearly every police-car owner is one of the "chain" body and paint shops. We chose MAACO Auto Painting and Bodyworks. This concept may be a culture shock for some automotive purists. We are not restoring the first Hemi Road Runner ever built. It's a police car! We went to the MAACO in Lafayette, Indiana, owned by Jack Williams. He wanted to be sure that we knew his shop did not do "restorations." Great! We didn't want one!

What MAACO did do was what the car needed and what we could afford. This is also what 99 percent of used police cars need: Very good body work and paint in 5 to 7 days for about $1,200. If we had done the patch panel work on the quarter panel and put putty on the sail panel, the job would have been done in 3 to 5 days for about $400. THAT is what makes sense (cents) for most police cars.

The work at MAACO starts off with a menu. The owner has a choice of pre-paint body preparation, choice of several quality levels of paint, and choice of several paint additives. The key to a good finish is a good start. Having a car painted involves more than just applying paint. New paint will not hide existing scratches, chips, cracks, or rust. Unlike the reputation of some fast-food chain paint shops that mask the car "as is" and paint it, MAACO fully prepares the car for paint. This includes a chemical cleaning, machine-sanding, and hand-sanding. This is followed by a spot prime and block sanding for a seamless repair. When the sanding is done, a coat of two-component polyurethane primer undercoat is applied.

After the sanding, the body shop has a very good idea of how much extra-cost body work has to be done before the paint. Since most MAACO paint shops are also collision repair shops, they can repair big dents and seriously rusted body panels. This includes everything from wire-welding patch panels to replacing fenders to filling in rough spots with fiberglass-based body putty. For bigger dents and dings, MAACO uses the traditional dent-pulling techniques involving stud welding.

The Bel Air project car had one bad spot by the back glass typical of this era of Chevrolet. The area was cleaned down to bare steel and smoothed out with fiberglass body filler. Same for the pinholes in the rear quarter panel. This body repair plus smoothing out some rough spots on the roof and quarter panels added about $600 to the cost of the basic paint job.

After the body was repaired and sanded, it was ready to be masked and primed. The body men remove the die-cast emblems that can be easily removed. Headlight and taillight chrome is either masked or removed. Windows, windshield, chrome, and difficult-to-remove emblems are masked. Since most police cars are low trim levels, they don't have much chrome. After masking, the car gets a spray coat of sealant. While this is not a true primer coat, it serves a similar purpose. It does not need to be wet-sanded after the sealer is applied. After sealing, the car is ready for the coat of fresh paint.

MAACO has a number of grades of paint. These include the baseline enamel paint, the workhorse of the industry for 50 years. They also have a high-build, high-solids enamel for more durability and gloss. Another option is the two-component polyurethane enamel, which has the most resistance to UV light, chemical pollutants, and tough road conditions. This is still a single coat typical of the cars up through the 1970s. The top-of-the-line is the two-step application of a base coat and a clear top coat. This is an exact duplication of the OEM finishes on cars from the 1980s and 1990s. Before that time, cars all had just one coat of paint without a clear top coat. By custom-blending, all of the factory colors and some custom colors are available, including the Sequoia Green used on the 1972 project car.

A wide variety of paint additives are available. The ultraviolet sunscreen is recommended for cars that see a lot of sunlight. UV additives are strongly recommended for any red paint. Remember, fire departments frequently use police-package cars and fire cars are an important part of the emergency-vehicle "family." MAACO also has an integrated clear coat with hardeners. It is recommended for car that will see a lot of wear from washing and waxing or cars that are not normally garaged.

Paint is applied in a number of thin coats while each layer of paint below it is still tacky. It takes about three to four medium coats to paint the car. After the paint is applied, the car is moved from the paint booth into a 145-degree Fahrenheit oven for 45 to 60 minutes. This is done to "bump" or initially cure the paint. The paint cures enough to wash in 3 to 4 hours and can be waxed in 6 to 8 weeks. All of the paint used by MAACO is enamel, which is the original-equipment paint for most cars. MAACO does not wet-sand the car. They leave that labor of love up to the car owner. And that's how it should be!

Most police cars will need to have the interiors replaced and the engines detailed. Carpet, seat coverings, headliners, and dashes are readily available through local upholstery and mail-order outfits alike. Most of the interior parts for the Bel Air came from Impala Bob's in Mesa, Arizona. Police-car enthusiasts can thank musclecar enthusiasts for the wide availability of restoration parts. A dash for an Impala SS can be used on a Biscayne. Carpet for a Road Runner can be used on a Belvedere.

The engine compartment on all used police cars will need to be detailed. Don't wait until the engine is pulled for a rebuild to do the engine compartment detailing. And don't leave the filthy, oily, and rusty engine compartment as is! Especially if the engine is one of the legendary big blocks, it MUST be detailed.

The good news is the engine compartment can be upgraded to class-winning condition with the engine still in the car. The process is as simple as unbolting as many accessories as possible, cleaning the parts, and painting them. The engine and inner fenders can be alternatively masked and painted. Thanks to a wide variety of spray-can products from Eastwood, for a fraction of the cost and very little effort, the job will look like a pro did it. Enthusiasts who cannot rebuild engines or paint cars certainly can replace interiors and detail the engine compartment!

Appendix Two

History of Police Vehicle Warning Equipment

By Ned E. Schwartz

Modern law enforcement relies heavily upon the use of emergency vehicle warning equipment. This was not always so. The "natural" association between police vehicles and special-warning equipment had not yet arisen when the first police began patrolling American streets in the mid-1800s.

Before the turn of the century, some horse-drawn patrol wagons were furnished with the first form of specialized police-vehicle warning gear. This was an audible device, rather than a visual one, namely, a gong-style bell. The bell was powered mechanically and mounted on the front floorboard or on a sideboard.

The vintage gong served the same purpose as today's sirens and they reflected the first technological solution to the problem of securing an emergency right-of-way. Gongs continued to be affixed to some of the new "horseless" patrol wagons of the early 1900s. By about 1930, however, most departments had phased out the gong in favor of the siren.

The earliest sirens, believed to have been made shortly before World War I, were of the hand-crank variety. These sirens were mounted within arm's reach of the occupants and were operated simply by hand-turning a crank. Not surprisingly, the sound produced by the siren varied with the speed that the rotor was turned past the stationary air intake slots (stator).

The first electro-mechanical, or "electric," sirens were powered by the car's 6-volt electric system. These were frequently externally mounted, either in front of the grill or atop a front fender. Others were concealed under the hood, where the siren was better protected from the weather, the expense of chrome-plating could be avoided, and passenger compartment noise was lessened. With the advent of steel-roofed police cars in the late 1930s, the roof-mounting of electro-mechanical sirens grew somewhat more common. The earliest electro-mechanical sirens often had large megaphone-style projector bells (front openings).

In 1929, the State of California enacted a safety provision under its Vehicle Code requiring emergency vehicles to display a forward-facing, nonflashing, steady-burning red lamp visible a distance of 500 feet. Later, another provision required emergency vehicles parked near the road to display a flashing amber light to the rear. This front-red-lamp requirement was a progressive step in an era when most U.S. police cars had no warning lights at all.

By the 1930s, warning lights began to catch on. These warning lights, always colored red and in some instances flashing, were forward-facing only. These were mounted in a variety of locations, including around the windshield frame, in front of the grill, or above the front bumper. Sometimes called pursuit lights, they were basically fixed spotlights with a red lens. The main purpose of the red lights of the time was to clear a path by projecting a forward visual signal.

The first warning device to be used on an emergency vehicle was a mechanical siren. The pitch produced by the siren varied by the hand-cranking speed. This vintage unit is probably a Sireno brand, circa 1920.

With the new emphasis on traffic-safety law enforcement, another piece of equipment began to appear on some 1930s cars: the "Pull-over" or "Stop" light. Produced in various shapes and sizes, this was a red lamp that usually had the lettering "Police" or "Stop" across the lens. It was mounted on the passenger-side front fender, and positioned sideways to be seen by the traffic violator when the patrol car pulled abreast.

The pull-over light marked totally new and different purposes for warning equipment. It signaled a motorist not to merely yield the right-of-way, but rather to pull over and stop. Further, by adding the word "Police," these lights also served an identification function. This was particularly valuable at a time when most police cars had minimal markings and were generally painted a single, dark color. With the notable exception of the Michigan State Police, by 1965, the pull-over light had vanished from most U.S. police car hoods or fenders.

During the late 1930s, the combination electro-mechanical siren and warning light was introduced. This was typically a roof-mounted, streamlined unit incorporating a red, usually flashing, light in the front portion of the siren housing. These combination units reached the zenith of their popularity during the 1950s and remained in use by a few agencies into the mid-1960s.

A major development occurred after World War II. In 1948, Federal Sign and Signal Company introduced the Model 17 "Beacon Ray." The Beacon Ray was the first device to provide a full 360-degree, light-house-style signal and became the most common revolving light in use during the 1950s and 1960s. The Beacon Ray used two automotive spotlights, mounted back to back, which rotated at 40 rpm producing 80 flashes per minute. Interestingly, this light was designed as an outgrowth of efforts to produce a weatherproof siren!

During the early 1950s, some police agencies were still not using any warning lights at all. Many other departments saw a need for only frontal protection. A small number of departments chose dual-facing oscillating lights. In California, double-facing stationary flashers called "soup can lights" or "tin can lights" were introduced by some departments, notably the Los Angeles Police. The Nassau County (New York) Police Department, outside New York City, used a nonrotating, four-lamped, four-way, flashing light. Installation of roof-mounted, moveable spotlights began in the 1950s.

Throughout the 1950s, a wide range of electro-mechanical sirens was available, including coaster versions with and without quick-stop brakes, and high- and low-pitch models. Other warning equipment developments included Federal Signal's introduction of the small, teardrop-shaped "Fire Ball" revolving light for unmarked cars in 1955. The compact size and magnetic base of this and other "dash lights" offered the ability to instantly switch between dashboard and roof mounting.

Clear-domed revolving lights having mixed red and clear lamps began to appear in the early 1960s and continued into the 1970s. However, in some areas of the country, the familiar red dome was replaced by blue. Although the red lights remained dominant nationally, as the decade wore on blue lights could be found in more and more locations, such as Chicago, Boston, Baltimore, Honolulu, and much of the South. A 1968 study reported that 16 states allowed or required blue lights for police vehicles.

Around 1967 it became increasingly common for departments to add more "punch" by supplementing the revolving light with stationary flashing lights astride it. Perhaps the most common arrangement was a pair of 7-inch "lollipop" or "mouse ear" bi-directional lights wired to flash alternately.

Starting in the early 1960s, a new generation of siren, the solid-state electronic siren, began to hit the streets. This siren consisted of a control box with a sound generator and an external speaker. It had no moving parts and provided multiple functions, including that of public address loudspeaker and a variety of siren sounds. By the late 1960s, the electronic siren had nearly replaced its mechanical older cousin. Accordingly, some aficionados view this era as the end of "real" sirens.

Circa 1964, Federal Signal introduced its Model 11 "Twin Beacon Ray" system, consisting of an open "Visibar" lightbar and a pair of Model 14 revolving lights. The rotation of the lamps was synchronized by a chain connecting the two lights for maximum visual impact. The Twin Beacon Ray Visibar permitted a full 360-degree coverage by the lights with no blockage by the speaker.

Federal Signal engineers noticed that some of the light from the rotating lights at the end of their Visibar light rack randomly reflected from the chromium-plated speaker mounted at the center of the bar. In 1967, they devised a set of mirrors, arranged along a parabolic curve, to reflect the wasted light toward the front or rear of the vehicle and increase the conspicuousness of the emergency lights. In order to protect the mirrors from weather and dirt, a plastic housing was designed to enclose the entire light system.

In 1968, Federal introduced its "TwinSonic," a fully enclosed lightbar incorporating two synchronized rotating light units,

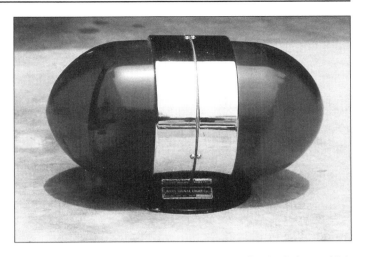

The MARS Signal Company was famous for its lights, which oscillated back and forth rather than rotated. This MARS DX-40 is a bi-directional oscillating light with red lenses in both the front and rear. Used in the 1950s and 1960s, this was advertised as producing a 360-degree signal. The front and rear lights acted independently.

amplifying parabolic mirrors, and a siren speaker behind a grill. The Visibar, TwinSonic, AeroDynic, JetSonic, and later products, introduced both a new look to police vehicles' roofs as well as the practice of employing multiple rotating lights.

Another development in the 1960s was the idea of lifting flashing lights into the air for greater visibility at scenes of accidents or road hazards. The earliest example is the Julian A. McDermott company's Multi-Level light unit. This was first installed on some New York City Police cars in 1966. In updated versions, McDermott lights are in heavy use today, but are seldom seen outside the greater New York City metropolitan area.

In the mid-1970s, but with a fair number of geographic exceptions, the single revolving roof light was rapidly replaced by the Visibar-style light racks often used in combination with supplemental bi-directional flashers and a siren speaker, or it was replaced by the totally enclosed lightbar. In both cases, this marked a major shift from using separate warning components, all individually wired, to a warning "system," which was typically installed, and later reused, as a single unit.

During the mid-1970s energy crisis, aerodynamic tests revealed that boxy lightbars caused wind drag and thus increased fuel consumption. This concern led to the 1977 introduction of the second generation of enclosed lightbars. The most notable of these was the Federal Model 24 AeroDynic, the first streamlined lightbar. The oval-cross-section design resulted in a substantial reduction in aerodynamic drag compared to the previous square and boxy shapes. The use of halogen bulbs in lieu of incandescent bulbs was introduced, circa 1977, setting the stage for a gradual changeover in coming years.

Another high-tech development, the strobe light, was introduced to the U.S. automotive market in 1965 by Whelen Engineering. Strobes began to appear on the street in the early 1970s. Unlike the rotating sealed beams and incandescent flashing bulb systems of the time, the strobe light had no moving parts. The lights used Xenon tubes and a high-voltage power supply to create extremely

The light rack concept might be traced back to the "trio platter" made specifically for the Los Angeles County Sheriff's Department. An electro-mechanical siren, twin red lights, and a rear-facing amber light were bolted to a triangular aluminum platform, which was then bolted to the roof. The LASD used this kind of system from 1948 to 1971.

brilliant but brief flashes of light. Some departments were attracted by the intense light, which is particularly striking at night, while others were disappointed by the short dwell time, which yielded both a poorer point of visual reference and some daylight washout. The "dwell" or "on" perception of strobe lighting was subsequently lengthened with the invention of the double or secondary flash.

Red-and-blue dome combinations caught on further during the 1980s. Halogen bulbs with reflectors began to supplant rotating sealed beams in some lightbars. Built-in alley lights and "take-down" lights were commonly ordered options, as were wide assortments of lighting configurations.

In 1982, what might be viewed as the third generation of enclosed lightbars was introduced: the low-profile, Federal Jet-Sonic. During the second half of the 1980s, enclosed strobe light-bars also became noticeably popular, including Whelen's 8100 series and its low-profile Edge 9000 series bar, introduced in 1983.

The strobe-versus-halogen debate was in full swing during the 1980s. The California Highway Patrol studied strobe lights in 1980 and determined them to be unsuitable. They found strobe light caused temporary blindness to the officer and motorist when in close proximity to the light. Nonetheless, strobe lights continue to be widely used in many locales, especially agencies such as Chicago and in the Deep South where all-blue lights are used.

In 1993, Tomar Electronics took strobe lights one step further by introducing Neobe technology. With this system, each strobe head produces six flashes per burst, creating a 50% on-time of nearly constant appearance. The six flashes of equal intensity produce a neon-like flickering burst.

Another trend of the late 1980s was the "slick-top" police car. This is a marked unit having no roof-top warning equipment whatsoever. It is also known as a "clean top," or in LAPD lingo, a "hybrid unit." Although having such units was a longstanding practice in the CHP and other western states, it was a practice that had not been seen widespread use since the 1950s. This "back-to-the-future" idea, reminiscent of decades long past, was motivated by several reasons, namely, improved fuel economy, increased top speed, lower equipment costs, and stealth for traffic-enforcement duties. In place of the usual lightbar would typically be some combination of rear deck lights, dash and visor lights, flashing headlights, and grille and colored spotlights.

The slick-top approach, although typically involving a variety of powerful warning lights, did not provide the same level of absolute, unobscured, long-range, intersection-clearing, 360-degree coverage as roof-mounted rotating beacons or omni-directional strobe units. Indeed, the National Bureau of Standards recommended that primary warning lights be roof-mounted for visibility (NBS Special Publication #480-37). Thus, the 1990s popularity of slick-tops heralds an era in which some agencies have seemingly stepped back from achieving maximum visibility and side coverage, in favor of other priorities.

In the late 1990s, manufacturers are offering ever more elaborate bars, providing far more than basic 360-degree protection. Among these are double-decker lightbars, like the Federal StreetHawk, providing additional lights within the same footprint, traffic-merge/arrow lights, and the addition of oscillating lights at the front corners or center of lightbars. This trend coincides with the latest trends emphasizing increased "corner" or intersection side protection and "all-light" lightbars. With all-lightbars, the siren speaker is no longer installed inside the lightbar, but rather is mounted under the hood or on the front bumper, leaving room for extra lighting. A sizable siren-noise reduction inside the passenger compartment results from removing the siren speaker from atop the car. The placement of the siren under the hood, or on the front bumper, of course, is not a new idea, but rather represents another trend returning to practices of long ago. In less than a decade, the all-light bar seems to have already come close to retiring the older speaker-light bars.

The basic assumption that lightbars were linear in shape changed with the 1991 introduction of Federal Signal's Model V7 Vision and Vector series V-shaped bars. These consist of seven individual light pods. These quickly began appearing in fleets across the country. In 1997, Federal took the next logical step and fully enclosed the same basic V-pattern in a lightbar called the Vista.

Finishing out the 1990s is the third aspect of the return-to-the-past. First, underhood sirens. Second, slick-top patrol cars. Now the latest vehicle graphics trend is the badge, patch, seal, or other symbolic door emblem of authority being deleted in favor of large door lettering alone. These door symbols have been a nearly universal feature on police cars for the last 40 years. Thus, we find that some of the trendiest 1990s police cars resemble those of the 1930s. Neither have warning equipment on the roof and both have wording instead of an emblem on their doors! What will the new millennium bring? Perhaps electronic gongs!

Index